Self-Disclosure

Theory, Research, and Therapy

PERSPECTIVES IN SOCIAL PSYCHOLOGY

A Series of Texts and Monographs • Edited by Elliot Aronson

THE DILEMMA OF DIFFERENCE: A Multidisciplinary View of Stigma
Edited by Stephen C. Ainlay, Gaylene Becker, and Lerita M. Coleman

ELIMINATING RACISM: Profiles in Controversy
Edited by Phyllis A. Katz and Dalmas A. Taylor

HUMAN AGGRESSION
Robert A. Baron

INTRINSIC MOTIVATION
Edward L. Deci

INTRINSIC MOTIVATION AND SELF-DETERMINATION IN HUMAN BEHAVIOR
Edward L. Deci and Richard M. Ryan

NONVERBAL BEHAVIOR AND SOCIAL PSYCHOLOGY
Richard Heslin and Miles Patterson

THE PHYSICAL ATTRACTIVENESS PHENOMENA
Gordon L. Patzer

REDEFINING SOCIAL PROBLEMS
Edited by Edward Seidman and Julian Rappaport

SELF-DISCLOSURE: Theory, Research, and Therapy
Edited by Valerian J. Derlega and John H. Berg

SCHOOL DESEGREGATION
Harold B. Gerard and Norman Miller

SCHOOL DESEGREGATION: Past, Present, and Future
Edited by Walter G. Stephan and Joe R. Feagin

UNIQUENESS: The Human Pursuit of Difference
C. R. Snyder and Howard L. Fromkin

A Continuation Order Plan is available for this series. A continuation order will bring delivery of each new volume immediately upon publication. Volumes are billed only upon actual shipment. For further information please contact the publisher.

Self-Disclosure

Theory, Research, and Therapy

Edited by
VALERIAN J. DERLEGA
Old Dominion University
Norfolk, Virginia
and
JOHN H. BERG
University of Mississippi
University, Mississippi

Springer Science+Business Media, LLC

Library of Congress Cataloging in Publication Data

Self-disclosure: theory, research, and therapy.

(Perspectives in social psychology)
Includes bibliographies and index.
1. Self-disclosure. 2. Interpersonal relations. 3. Psychotherapy. I. Derlega, Valerian J. II. Berg, John H. III. Series. [DNLM: 1. Counseling. 2. Interpersonal Relations. 3. Psychotherapy. 4. Self-Disclosure. BF 697 S465]
BF697.5.S427S35 1987 155.2 87-18654
ISBN 978-1-4899-3525-0 ISBN 978-1-4899-3523-6 (eBook)
DOI 10.1007/978-1-4899-3523-6

Originally published by Plenum Press, New York in 1987
Softcover reprint of the hardcover 1st edition 1987

Dedicated to the memory of Alan L. Chaikin

Contributors

Richard L. Archer Department of Psychology, Southwest Texas State University, San Marcos, Texas

Leslie A. Baxter Communications Department, Lewis and Clark College, Portland, Oregon

John H. Berg Department of Psychology, University of Mississippi, University, Mississippi

Bruce N. Carpenter Department of Psychology, University of Tulsa, Tulsa, Oklahoma

Gordon J. Chelune Department of Psychiatry, Cleveland Clinic Foundation, Cleveland, Ohio

Dan Coates Department of Psychology, University of Missouri-St. Louis, St. Louis, Missouri

Mark H. Davis Department of Psychology, Eckerd College, St. Petersburg, Florida

Valerian J. Derlega Department of Psychology, Old Dominion University, Norfolk, Virginia

Mary Anne Fitzpatrick Department of Communication Arts, University of Wisconsin, Madison, Wisconsin

Stephen L. Franzoi Department of Psychology, Marquette University, Milwaukee, Wisconsin

Susan S. Hendrick Department of Psychology, Texas Tech University, Lubbock, Texas

Charles T. Hill Department of Psychology, Whittier College, Whittier, California

Lynn Carol Miller Department of Psychology, Scripps College, Claremont, California

Stephen J. Read Department of Psychology, University of Southern California, University Park, Los Angeles, California

William B. Stiles Department of Psychology, Miami University, Oxford, Ohio

Joseph P. Stokes Department of Psychology, University of Illinois at Chicago, Chicago, Illinois

Donald E. Stull Department of Sociology, University of Akron, Akron, Ohio

Edward M. Waring Department of Psychiatry, University Hospital, London, Ontario, Canada

Tina Winston Department of Psychology, University of Wisconsin, Madison, Wisconsin

Preface

Decisions about self-disclosure—whether to reveal one's thoughts, feelings, or past experiences to another person, or the level of intimacy of such disclosure—are part of the everyday life of most persons. The nature of the decisions that a person makes will have an impact on his or her life. They will determine the kinds of relationships the person has with others; how others perceive him or her; and the degree of self-knowledge and awareness that the person possesses.

The study of self-disclosure has interested specialists from many disciplines, including personality and social psychologists, clinical and counseling psychologists, and communications researchers. Our book brings together the work of experts from these various disciplines with the hope that knowledge about work being done on self-disclosure in related disciplines will be increased.

A strong emphasis in each of the chapters is theory development and the integration of ideas about self-disclosure. The book's chapters explore three major areas, including the interrelationship of self-disclosure and personality as well as the role of self-disclosure in the development, maintenance, and deterioration of personal relationships, and the contribution of self-disclosure to psychotherapy, marital therapy, and counseling.

The first chapter, by John H. Berg and Valerian J. Derlega, presents an overview of the historical role of self-disclosure in psychological and communications research as well as a description of the contributions of self-disclosure theory and research in the fields of personality, personal relationships, and counseling/psychotherapy. The second chapter, by Gordon J. Chelune, examines self-disclosing behavior in the light of current neuropsychological research on hemispheric specialization and functional asymmetry in the brain. Chapter 3, by Lynn Carol Miller and Stephen J. Read, presents a goal-based model of personality, which is used to predict when self-disclosure will occur. The fourth chapter, by Mark H. Davis and Stephen L. Franzoi, examines the relation between individual differences in level of private self-consciousness and self-disclosure. The fifth chapter, by Charles T. Hill and Donald E. Stull, reviews the relationship between gender and self-disclosure and evaluates research strategies for examining this issue.

Chapter 6, by John H. Berg, considers the applicability of responsiveness as a concept in understanding disclosure reciprocity, the disclosure-liking effect, and the contribution of self-disclosure in counseling. Chapter 7, by Mary Anne Fitzpatrick, introduces a typological approach to marital interaction and indicates how couples in different types of marriages prefer and use different communication (and self-disclosure) styles with one another. Chapter 8, by Leslie A. Baxter, based on the rhetorical/strategic perspective that communication is a goal-directed strategic activity, examines the role of self-disclosure in the disengagement of personal relationships.

Chapter 9, by Joseph P. Stokes, presents a model of the relation between self-disclosure and loneliness, emphasizing that appropriate, intimate self-disclosure may lead to decreased loneliness provided the disclosure is followed by acceptance and understanding by the target person. Chapter 10, by Bruce N. Carpenter, explores how self-disclosure is related to psychopathology, including how pathology changes disclosure behavior and the role of disclosure deficits in the development of pathology.

Chapter 11, by Dan Coates and Tina Winston, considers the benefits and costs of "distress disclosure," which involves the open expression of unpleasant feelings: the authors also consider how the personality variable of self-monitoring may distinguish between individuals who are more or less skilled at distress disclosure. Chapter 12, by William B. Stiles, presents a "fever model" of disclosure indicating how (similar to a fever's relation to physical infection) self-disclosure is both a sign of psychological disturbance and part of the process of restoration: implications for patient disclosure in psychotherapy are considered. Chapter 13, by Edward M. Waring, explores the therapeutic use of self-disclosure in marital therapy, especially cognitive self-disclosure that involves sharing attitudes, beliefs, and ideas about one's own marriage—as well as one's parents' marriage—with the partner. Chapter 14, by Susan S. Hendrick, focuses on theory and research about self-disclosure counseling, examining the contributions of self-disclosure to the counselor–client relationship and to counseling outcomes. Finally, Chapter 15, by Richard L. Archer, provides a commentary on the preceding chapters, indicating how a functional analysis of the uses of self-disclosure represents a common theme throughout the volume.

The editors wish to express thanks to the individuals who contributed to the completion of this book. We gratefully appreciate the contributions made by the authors of the chapters and the patience they showed through the evolution of the project. Thanks are extended to the editorial staff at Plenum Press and particularly to Eliot Werner and Elliot Aronson for their support. Personal thanks are extended by Val Derlega for the social support and advice provided by Barbara A. Winstead and Stephen T. Margulis.

VALERIAN J. DERLEGA
JOHN H. BERG

Contents

CHAPTER 3

Why Am I Telling You This? Self-Disclosure in a Goal-Based Model of Personality 35

Lynn Carol Miller and Stephen J. Read

CHAPTER 4

CHAPTER 5

1

Themes in the Study of Self-Disclosure

JOHN H. BERG AND VALERIAN J. DERLEGA

Few areas of psychological investigation have attracted people from as many different disciplines as the study of self-disclosure. Social psychologists, clinical and counseling psychologists, specialists in interpersonal communication, and others have all been drawn to some extent to this topic. What types of information and feelings do people disclose about themselves? How do people disclose? When do people disclose? What types of people disclose? What are the effects of disclosure on the individual disclosing and on the relationship he or she has with the person disclosed to? How is disclosure related to psychological problems, and what role does it play in therapy? These are only some of the questions that have concerned those interested in self-disclosure and, as is apparent, the questions cut across a large number of specialty areas.

Although people from different and diverse areas may all be interested in self-disclosure, they are often unaware of one another's work, especially about new theoretical approaches. Self-disclosure researchers typically publish in different journals, have different professional affiliations, and attend different scientific meetings. Therefore, a major goal of this book is to include the work of individuals in various disciplines.

JOHN N. BERG • Department of Psychology, University of Mississippi, University, Mississippi 38677. VALERIAN J. DERLEGA • Department of Psychology, Old Dominion University, Norfolk, Virginia 23508.

We hope that this approach will increase researchers' knowledge of work being done on self-disclosure in related disciplines.

It was not our intention, however, to accumulate reviews of past work. Such reviews already exist, most notably perhaps in a volume edited by Chelune (1979) that contains a collection of reviews of self-disclosure studies. Although numerous studies are referenced in the chapters of this volume, the emphasis throughout has been on theory development. This emphasis on theory stands in contrast to many past reviews and studies of self-disclosure, which have tended to be extremely *atheoretical.* The emphasis on theory stems from several factors. First and foremost, the theoretical work contained in this volume can serve as an impetus and guide for future investigations and applications. Second, an understanding of theoretical approaches of self-disclosure researchers from diverse disciplines can ultimately result in a greater appreciation of the rich body of work in those areas and a greater understanding of self-disclosure itself. Finally, in our view, theory is simply more interesting.

It may be beneficial at the outset to briefly discuss three different themes that have run through the field of self-disclosure research from its beginnings and that are represented in various chapters of this book. These three themes deal with (a) self-disclosure as a personality factor and the role of individual differences in self-disclosure, (b) the role of self-disclosure in the development, maintenance, and dissolution of relationships, and (c) the role of self-disclosure in the etiology and treatment of psychological distress. Although a few earlier instances of work may be found, credit for the seminal work on each of these issues clearly belongs to Jourard (see Jourard, 1971a, for a collection of much of this pioneering work). In this introduction, we would like to briefly trace the conceptual developments regarding each of these issues from the early work to those chapters in the present book that offer new conceptual directions.

SELF-DISCLOSURE AND PERSONALITY

Jourard viewed self-disclosure as both a sign and a cause of a healthy personality. Disclosure was viewed as a relatively stable personalty characteristic that was related to other positive personality characteristics. Numerous studies attempted to relate scores on the Jourard Self-Disclosure Questionnaire (JSDQ; Jourard, 1958) to almost every other aspect of personality that could be measured (for reviews, see Archer, 1979; Cozby, 1973; and Goodstein & Reinecker, 1974). Unfortunately, relatively few consistent relationships between JSDQ scores and other variables emerged from these studies. Moreover, the ability of the JSDQ to predict respondents' self-disclosing behavior was found to be quite weak. This state of affairs led Goodstein and Reinecker (1974) to call for the abandonment of the JSDQ and the development of more valid self-disclosure measures. Although other measures assessing individual differences have been subsequently developed, the picture of who is a high-disclosing individual has remained unclear. Cautioning that the picture was incomplete and often based on mixed evidence, Archer (1979) described the high discloser as

> likely to be women or at least persons who possess feminine psychological characteristics . . . usually not first-born children . . . from the white majority . . . not introverts . . . may have the socially outgoing and gregarious nature of the field dependent person . . . not likely to be neurotic or overconcerned with obtaining approval. (Archer, 1979, pp. 37–38)

The search for better individual difference measures of self-disclosure continues and includes the Self-Disclosure Situations Survey (SDSS) developed by Chelune (1976). It attempts to take situational variations into consideration in measuring individual differences in self-disclosure. However, this approach also has had problems (see Chapter 3). In Chapter 3, Miller and Read reconceptualize personality differences in self-disclosure as representing differences in the goals, strategies, resources, and beliefs of individuals rather than conceiving of a single trait as has been done in the past. The Miller Topic Survey (MTI) and the Opener Scale (OS) developed by Miller, Berg, and Archer (1983) are two individual difference measures that are based on this new approach and promise to be useful measures of self-disclosure (see Chapter 6, by Berg, and Chapter 14, by Hendrick, in this volume). It is worth noting that the Opener Scale, instead of identifying individuals who are more likely to disclose, attempts to identify those people who are more likely to *receive* disclosure from others. This emphasis on the disclosure recipient represents a rather marked contrast from previous work that emphasized only the discloser.

A deemphasis on disclosure as a trait in itself is seen in other chapters that are concerned with individual differences. Davis and Franzoi (Chapter 4) discuss possible reasons that differences in the personality trait of private self-consciousness (which involves the extent people are aware of inner thoughts and feelings) might lead to differences in self-disclosing behavior. Hill and Stull (Chapter 5) suggest how gender and sex-role considerations may influence self-disclosure. And in an innovative chapter, Chelune (Chapter 2) discusses the role of neuropsychological factors in self-disclosure.

All of these chapters present novel theoretical approaches to conceptualizing individual differences in self-disclosure. These theoretical approaches and their supporting studies that are described point rather explicitly to future directions for research.

SELF-DISCLOSURE AND RELATIONSHIPS

The most consistent and frequently cited finding regarding the interpersonal effects of self-disclosure is disclosure reciprocity. This concerns the increased likelihood that recipients of a self-disclosure input will respond by disclosing about themselves at a comparable level of intimacy (e.g., Cozby, 1973; Derlega, Harris, & Chaikin, 1973; Ehrlich & Graeven, 1971; Jourard, 1959; Jourard & Resnick, 1970; Rubin, 1975; Worthy, Gary, & Kahn, 1969). In brief, three different explanations have been proposed to explain this finding.

The first explanation is based on a trust–liking approach and holds that receiving intimate disclosure increases trust in and liking for the discloser. The recipient is then expected to return intimate disclosure in order to demonstrate these feelings. The second explanation emphasizes the influence of social norms. It holds that social norms similar to those of equity (e.g., Adams, 1965; Walster, Berscheid, & Walster, 1973) theory govern exchanges of disclosure and obligate the recipient of disclosure input from another to reveal in turn information that is of comparable intimacy. The third explanation holds that much of disclosure reciprocity is simply the result of modeling with the recipient of disclosure imitating the initial speaker.

Although experiments that have attempted to compare the relative efficacy of these various explanations (e.g., Davis & Skinner, 1974; Derlega, Chaikin, & Herndon, 1975; Derlega, *et al.*, 1973; Lynn, 1978) tend to lend greater support to the normative explanation than to the others; only the trust–liking hypothesis can be ruled out as specifying the necessary condition for reciprocity to occur. None can be ruled out as specifying contributing factors.

A second interpersonal consequence of self-disclosure, although it is not nearly as consistent as the reciprocity effect, is for self-disclosure to result in increased liking for the discloser (e.g., Archer, Berg, & Runge, 1980; Worthy *et al.*, 1969). A number of studies have failed to find this effect, even though reciprocity still occurs (e.g., Derlega *et al.*, 1973; Ehrlich & Graeven, 1969). In response to these inconsistent findings, researchers began to search for additional variables that could explain when the disclosure-liking effect would and would not occur. Perhaps the most promising of these explanations involved the attribution made by the disclosure recipient to explain the disclosure. The basic idea was that if the disclosure was perceived as personalistic (i.e., intended only for the disclosure recipient), it would lead to increased liking. Several studies have found support for this idea (e.g., Archer & Burleson, 1980; Taylor, Gould, & Brounstein, 1981; Wortman, Adesman, Herman, & Greenberg, 1976; for an exception, see Derlega, Winstead, Wong, & Hunter, 1985).

Altman and Taylor (1973) in their theory of social penetration processes have done the most ambitious work dealing with the interpersonal consequences of disclosure. Social penetration theory describes the formation, maintenance, and dissolution of close relationships. A central role is given to self-disclosure that is viewed as the sine qua non for the development of closeness. Consequently, it should not be surprising to find that numerous other theorists (e.g., Chelune, Sultan, & Williams, 1980; Cutrona, 1982; Jourard, 1968; Rogers, 1970) have hypothesized that the lack of ability and/or opportunities to exchange intimate disclosure with others is a primary cause of loneliness.

These interpersonal issues are also addressed and developed in this book. Berg (Chapter 6) proposes an alternative explanation that is hypothesized to underlie both the reciprocity and the disclosure-liking effects and also has implications for the use of disclosure in counseling situations. Fitzpatrick (Chapter 7) and Baxter (Chapter 8) propose general models of the maintenance and the dissolution of relationships, respectively, and discuss the role played by self-disclosure in these processes. It is noteworthy that, as with the chapters dealing with disclosure and individuals' personalities, the emphasis in the chapters that explore these interpersonal correlates (Berg's, Fitzpatrick's, and Baxter's chapters) is not on self-disclosure per se. Instead, self-disclosure is seen and discussed as one component of a general framework that, in keeping with work dealing with close relationships (e.g., Kelley *et al.*, 1983), emphasizes interdependence or mutual influence between the relationship partners. Finally, Stokes (Chapter 9) proposes a theoretical model describing the relationship between self-disclosure and loneliness.

SELF-DISCLOSURE IN COUNSELING AND PSYCHOTHERAPY

Clinical and counseling psychologists as a group have consistently expressed the greatest interest in self-disclosure. Virtually all forms of counseling and psychotherapy emphasize the importance of self-disclosure on the part of clients. This may be either because such disclosure is viewed as central to the self-exploration required for successful counseling or because the primary source of *some* client problems is seen as stemming from problems in disclosure.

Considerable attention has thus been given to questions involving the role of self-disclosure in the development and treatment of psychological distress and how the counselor or psychotherapist might facilitate client disclosure and self-exploration. The belief that self-disclosure will be important in psychological health and in successful counseling is highlighted by the fact that virtually every chapter in this book comments on the potential applications of self-disclosure for clinical and counseling issues. (In particular, see the chapters by Stiles [Chapter 12], Coates and Winston [Chapter 11], Waring [Chapter 13], and Hendrick [Chapter 14].) The ways in which social and clinical/counseling psychology can establish linkages with one another in studying self-disclosure is an important contribution of Hendrick's chapter. She points out ways in which the theories, methodologies, and findings of social psychologists might be relevent to questions of greatest interest to counselors. Hendrick reviews evidence concerning the effects of counselor disclosure and concludes that the question of whether or not a counselor should disclose to a client (which has been a hotly debated issue for counselors and psychotherapists) needs to be rephrased. The appropriate question according to Hendrick is not if, but when, a counselor should disclose, and she proposes a general plan for investigating when counselor disclosure is helpful and not helpful.

The effect that psychological distress has on disclosure as well as the influence of disclosure on distress is the focus of attention for Stiles (Chapter 12) and Coates and Winston (Chapter 11). Both propose models of the distress-disclosure relationship, note work supporting these models, and point to future directions. Stiles applies the biological analogy of a fever in presenting a theoretical model of the distress-disclosure relationship. Just as an infection leads the body to mobilize its defensive capabilities, psychological distress is seen as leading to the activation of one's psychological defenses. In the case of physical infection, the mobilization of resources is accompanied by fever. According to Stiles, activation of one's psychological defenses occurs through and is accompanied by self-disclosure.

Coates and Winston develop the relation between distress and disclosure in a different way. Although they note that disclosing distress may sometimes lead to receiving support from others, they also note that such disclosures can also serve to alienate members of a support network. If this latter event happens, it is unlikely that the disclosure will result in distress reduction. Their model then is concerned with the manner in which distressed persons attempt to resolve the conflict between wanting to disclose to others but not wanting to alienate them.

Rather than disclosing distress, Waring (Chapter 13) proposes that marital couples who are experiencing difficulties will benefit from cognitive self-disclosure (i.e., disclosing what they think and why they think in a certain way). In other words, couples are advised to engage in what might be called *explicit metacommunication* (Chelune, Robison, & Kommer, 1984). The result of this is hypothesized to be increased intimacy and marital satisfaction. Waring also describes and illustrates the use of a therapeutic technique for facilitating such cognitive self-disclosure.

Carpenter (Chapter 10) takes a rather different approach to the role of disclosure in clinical settings. His chapter is concerned with severe types of psychological problems. In contrast to other views (e.g., Jourard, 1971b), he believes that disturbances in self-disclosure are more often the results rather than the causes of severe emotional problems. Carpenter proposes a theoretical model to describe the different ways in which severe forms of pathology may affect disclosure.

In the concluding chapter to this book, Archer (Chapter 15) provides a conceptual overview in which the common threads running through the various contributions are collected and discussed, especially, in terms of their implications for theory, research, and therapeutic applications of self-disclosure. It is our sincere hope that readers will find the book useful and rewarding as they consider the relevence of the various chapters for their own work on self-disclosure.

REFERENCES

Adams, J. S. (1965). Inequity in social exchange. In L. Berkowitz (Ed.), *Advances in experimental social psychology*: New York: Academic Press.

Altman, I., & Taylor, D. A. (1973). *Social penetration: The development of interpersonal relationships*. New York: Holt, Rinehart & Winston.

Archer, R. L. (1979). The role of personality and the social situation. In G. J. Chelune (Ed.), *Self-disclosure*. San Francisco: Jossey-Bass.

Archer, R. L., & Burleson, J. A. (1980). The effects of timing and responsibility of self-disclosure on attraction. *Journal of Personality and Social Psychology, 38,* 120–130.

Archer, R. L., Berg, J. H., & Runge, T. E. (1980). Active and passive observers' attraction to a self-disclosing other. *Journal of Experimental Social Psychology, 16,* 130–145.

Chelune, G. J. (1976). The self-disclosure situation survey: A new approach to measuring self-disclosure. *JSAS Catalog of Selected Documents in Psychology, 6,* 111–112.

Chelune, G. (1979). *Self-disclosure*. San Francisco: Jossey-Bass.

Chelune, G. J., Sultan, F. E., & Williams, C. L. (1980). Loneliness, self-disclosure, and interpersonal effectiveness. *Journal of Counseling Psychology, 27,* 462–468.

Chelune, G. J., Robison, J. T., & Kommer, M. J. (1984). A cognitive interactional model of intimate relationships. In V. J. Derlega (Ed.), *Communication, intimacy, and close relationships*. New York: Academic Press.

Cozby, P. C. (1972). Self-disclosure, reciprocity and liking. *Sociometry, 35,* 151–160.

Cozby, P. C. (1973). Self-disclosure: A literature review. *Psychological Bulletin, 79,* 73–91.

Cutrona, C. (1982). Transition to college: Loneliness and the process of social adjustment. In L. A. Peplau & D. Perlman (Eds.), *Loneliness: A sourcebook of current theory, research and therapy* (pp. 291–301). New York: Wiley.

Davis, J. D., & Skinner, A. E. (1974). Reciprocity of self-disclosure in interviews: Modeling or social exchange? *Journal of Personality and Social Psychology, 39,* 779–784.

Derlega, V. J., Harris, M. J., & Chaikin, A. L. (1973). Self-disclosure and reciprocity, liking, and the deviant. *Journal of Experimental Social Psychology, 9,* 227–284.

Derlega, V. J., Chaiken, A., & Herndon, J. (1975). Demand characteristics and disclosure reciprocity. *Journal of Social Psychology,* 301–302.

Derlega, V. J., Winstead, B. A., Wong, P. T. P., & Hunter, S. (1985). Gender effects in an initial encounter: A case when men exceed women in disclosure. *Journal of Social and Personal Relationships, 2,* 25–44.

Ehrlich, J. H., & Graeven, D. B. (1971). Reciprocal self-disclosure in a dyad. *Journal of Experimental Social Psychology, 7,* 389–400.

Goodstein, L. D., & Reinecker, V. M. (1974). Factors affecting self-disclosure: A review of the literature. In *Progress in experimental psychology and research.* New York: Academic Press.

Jourard, S. M. (1958). Some factors in self-disclosure. *Journal of Abnormal and Social Psychology, 56,* 95–99.

Jourard, S. M. (1959). Self-disclosure and other cathexis. *Journal of Abnormal and Social Psychology, 59,* 428–431.

Jourard, S. M. (1968). *Disclosing man to himself.* Princeton, NJ: D. Van Nostrand.

Jourard, S. M. (1971a). *Self-disclosure: An experimental analysis of the transparent self.* New York: Wiley-Interscience.

Jourard, S. M. (1971b). *The transparent self.* New York: D. Van Nostrand.

Jourard, S. M., & Resnick, J. L. (1970). The effect of high-revealing subjects on the self-disclosure of low-revealing subjects. *Journal of Humanistic Psychology, 10,* 84–93.

Kelley, H. H., Berscheid, E., Christensen, A., Harvey, H. H., Huston, T. L., Levinger, G., McClintock, E., Peplau, L. A., & Peterson, D. R. (1983). *Close relationships.* New York: Freeman.

Lynn, S. J. (1978). Three theories of self-disclosure exchange. *Journal of Experimental Social Psychology, 14,* 466–479.

Miller, L. C., Berg, J. H., & Archer, R. L. (1983). Openers: Individuals who elicit intimate self-disclosure. *Journal of Personality and Social Psychology, 44,* 1234–1244.

Rogers, C. R. (1970). *Carl Rogers on encounter groups.* New York: Harper & Row.

Rubin, Z. (1975). Disclosing to a stranger: Reciprocity and its limits. *Journal of Experimental Social Psychology, 11,* 233–260.

Taylor, D. A., Gould, R. J., & Brounstein, P. J. (1981). Effects of personalistic self-disclosure. *Personality and Social Psychology Bulletin, 7,* 487–492.

Walster, E., Berscheid, E., & Walster, G. M. (1973). New directions in equity research. *Journal of Personality and Social Psychology, 25,* 151–176.

Worthy, M., Gary, A. L., & Kahn, G. M. (1969). Self-disclosure as an exchange process. *Journal of Personality and Social Psychology, 13,* 59–63.

Wortman, C. G., Adesman, P., Hermon, E., & Greenberg, R. (1976). Self-disclosure: An attributional perspective. *Journal of Personality and Social Psychology, 33,* 184–191.

2

A Neuropsychological Perspective of Interpersonal Communication

GORDON J. CHELUNE

Self-disclosure, the process of revealing personal information about oneself to another, has been extensively studied by social and clinical psychologists interested in interpersonal communication and close relationships. Although questions concerning how and why people engage in self-disclosure have led to considerable research and theory generation over the years (e.g., Altman & Taylor, 1973; Berscheid & Walster, 1978; Chelune, 1979; Derlega, 1984; Derlega & Chaikin, 1975; Jourard, 1971a,b; Phillips & Metzger, 1976), little attention has been given to the potential biological underpinnings of this complex behavior. To some degree, this paucity of interest reflects the prevailing social psychological view that social behavior is largely a function of situational contingencies and constraints (Mischel, 1968).

Although situational factors exert considerable influence on communication patterns in close relationships, individual differences still can be observed, even in the face of powerful social-situational stimuli. For this reason, even the most ardent critics of trait psychology acknowledge that individuals bring into relationships their own unique sets of cognitive and behavioral competencies (e.g., Mischel, 1973, 1977), which mediate the impact of stimuli on the individual and form the basis of

---

GORDON J. CHELUNE • Department of Psychiatry, Cleveland Clinic Foundation, Cleveland, Ohio 44106.

individual differences These cognitive/behavioral competencies influence how individuals encode and decode linguistic and paralinguistic communication cues, compare and contrast current messages with those from previous interactions, and formulate expectations for future interactions. Recent advances in clinical and experimental neuropsychology suggest that these individual differences may, in part, be biologically rooted in the functional organization of the brain.

This chapter examines interpersonal communication in close relationships within the context of current neuropsychological theory and knowledge. By virtue of space limitations, this discussion represents only an introduction to the very complex but potentially rich interface between neuropsychology and the social phenomenon of interpersonal communication. A general model of interpersonal communication within close relationships is first presented wherein communication is viewed as a complex representational system in which information is conveyed and interpreted via both linguistic and affective channels. The neurological substrates for these communication modalities are described and illustrated by examples from the clinical neuropsychological literature. Evidence of variations in hemispheric specialization and functional asymmetry is then presented as a potential physiological basis for individual differences in communicational styles.

A MODEL OF COMMUNICATION IN CLOSE RELATIONSHIPS

Although our focus here will be on the biological basis of individual differences among interactants, it is important to first examine the nature of close relationships and the role communication plays within these relationships. Certainly one of the key elements of a close relationship is a sense of intimacy (Hinde, 1978, 1981). Elsewhere, my colleagues and I (Chelune, Robison, & Kommor, 1984) have presented a cognitive interactional model of intimacy in which we define an intimate relationship as *"a relational process in which we come to know the innermost, subjective aspects of another, and are known in a like manner"* (p. 14). As in all relationships, intimate relationships are extended in time and involve a series of interactions. However, if we focus on a single *intimate experience* (Schaefer & Olson, 1981) or interaction, the central features of the model can be depicted as in Figure 1. This model borrows heavily from the work of Waring and his colleagues (Waring, Tillman, Frelick, Russell, & Weisz, 1980) who examined the basic concepts people in the general population use to characterize their intimate relationships.

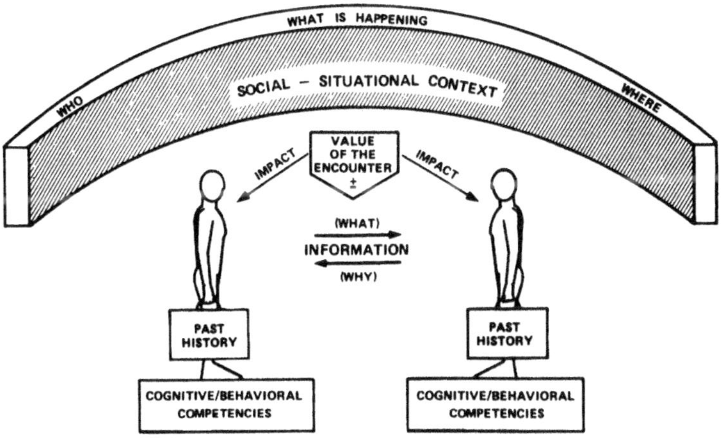

FIGURE 1. Schematic diagram of the major elements involved in intimate encounters between interactants.

Exchange of Information

First, communication in an intimate relationship involves the mutual exchange of information, and the depth and breadth of this information distinguishes it from other forms of relationships (Hinde, 1978). The subjective appraisal of intimacy is based, in part, on the sharing of private thoughts, beliefs, and fantasies as well as goals, backgrounds, and interests. However, something more is involved than merely the exchange of self-relevant information. For interactants to come to know the subjective, innermost aspects of one another, they must be able to encode and decode both *what* is said and *why* the message was sent (Satir, 1967). To do so involves the simultaneous synthesis of multiple messages. As Jackson and Weakland (1961) observe:

> In actual human communication a single and simple message never occurs, but that communication always and necessarily involves a multiplicity of messages, on different levels, at once. These may be conveyed via various channels such as words, tone, and facial expression, or by the variety of meanings and references of any verbal message in relation to its possible contexts. (p. 32)

Thus information is conveyed and interpreted by both linguistic (phonemes, semantics, and syntax) and paralinguistic (tone, rhythm, gestures) cues. Although these communication modalities may express a single, congruent message, difference and incongruity are the general rule. Their synthesis provides for both the richness and range of nuances observed in human communication and forms the basis for the "why" or metamessage beneath the literal (what) message (Bandler, Grindler, & Satir, 1976). As we will see, the human brain plays an integral role in the simultaneous synthesis and expression of these messages.

The Process of Sharing

If intimacy merely involved the exchange of personal information, it would be synonymous with what we generally think of as self-disclosure. Although self-disclosure has been associated with the development of intimacy (Altman & Taylor, 1973; Derlega & Chaikin, 1975; Jourard, 1971b), the two are not identical (Waring & Chelune, 1983). As can be seen in Figure 1, intimacy is a transactional process; that is, the *process* of sharing is "valued" as much as *what* is shared (Waring *et al.*, 1980). Furthermore, consistent with Hinde's (1981) dynamic view that "relationships influence the nature of individuals, and individuals influence the nature of the relationship they enter" (p. 5), Waring and his associates (1980) also found that the process of sharing personal information "impacts" on both the nature of the relationship and the individuals in the relationship. Through the process of sharing, interactants believe that they develop a sense of mutuality or weness that is unique to their relationship (see Walster, Walster, & Berscheid, 1978) and experience a greater degree of self-differentiation and clarification of their personal identities as individuals (see Derlega & Grzelak, 1979).

Past History

Consistent with the behavioral truism that past behavior is the best predictor of future behavior, Waring *et al.* (1980) found that early experiences and observations of intimate relationships were important determinants of current perceptions of intimacy. These past experiences may have been with parents, friends, or even the significant other in the current relationship, and they represent a kind of emotional luggage that individuals carry with them into all of their relationships. These interpersonal memories of intimate exchanges not only shape and modify the manner in which individuals exchange personal information, but they also affect the value placed on such exchanges and influence expectations regarding future interactions (see Altman & Taylor, 1973). For Mischel (1973), an individual's past experiences and observational learning constitute an important individual difference variable "that each person brings to the situation" (p. 269). From a neuropsychological perspective, the capacity to draw upon one's past to compare and guide current behavior as well as to formulate expectations for the future involves both learning and memory, processes with complex neural substrates (Square & Butters, 1984). Although biologically mediated, one's past history is acquired and can be contrasted with other important neurologic substrates that are constitutional in nature (see the section, The Individual).

The Social-Situational Context

To those fundamental aspects identified by Waring and his colleagues (1980) as influencing perceptions of intimacy, one must consider the potential impact of the social-situational contexts in which intimate encounters occur (Chelune, 1976; Chelune *et al.*, 1984). Situations, like personality variables, show considerable variation in the degree of constraint they place on behavior via social rules (Price, 1974; Price & Bouffard, 1974). *Who* is in the situation, *where* the interaction is taking place, and *what* is happening all affect the perceived meanings and topography of interactions between individuals (Pervin, 1976). Between intimates, even slight deviations from the social norms for appropriate discourse in a given social-situational context can take on special meaning (see Jackson & Weakland, 1961).

The Individual

The final element of our model of intimate relationships, and the one of primary concern to our present discussion, is the individual interactant. The individual members of a relationship are the repositories of the information they exchange, and they bring to the relationship their own unique histories of past intimate experiences. They are the ones who engage in the process of sharing and modify this transactional process according to their perceptions of the social-situational context. They are, in essence, the focal points of the relationship.

Although social contingencies and situational constraints are important determinants of interpersonal communication, their relative impact is mediated by the individual's unique cognitive/behavioral competencies or "discriminative facility" (Mischel, 1973); that is, the individual's capacity to discern differences between social-situational cues and modulate his or her disclosures accordingly (cf. disclosure flexibility, Chelune, 1977). It is the thesis of this chapter that this individual difference variable is, in part, constitutionally determined. Greater appreciation of the potential biological bases of individual differences underlying complex social behaviors may aid the social scientist in "predicting more of the people more of the time" (Bem & Funder, 1978, p. 485). To illustrate this point, we will focus on the neurological underpinnings of one aspect of our model; namely the exchange of information between intimates. However, it should be noted that this focus is merely an exemplar and that the basis premise could be expanded to other aspects of the model.

THE NEUROPSYCHOLOGY OF INTERPERSONAL COMMUNICATION

To develop our neuropsychological model of interpersonal communication, let us begin with a brief overview of general principles. As noted earlier, the experience of intimacy involves the mutual sharing of the innermost aspects of self through the process of communication. Interactants in this process are concurrently senders and receivers engaged in complex behaviors at a number of levels within a social-situational context (Satir, 1967). Although messages are conveyed via numerous cues (e.g., auditory, visual, tactile), they can be grouped into two general modalities: linguistic and paralinguistic. Meaning in the linguistic modality is conveyed by the words, syntax, and sentence structure of the message, whereas information in the paralinguistic modality is communicated by *prosody,* the melodic line of speech produced by pitch, rhythm, and intonation (Monrad-Krohn, 1957), and by nonverbal behaviors such as eye contact, body posture, and facial expressions (Key, 1965). These modalities may communicate a single congruent message or, more frequently, may be at variance with one another. Especially in the latter circumstance, it is the juxtaposition of the messages in the two modalities that carries the actual meaning or pragmatic value of the message.

From a neuropsychological perspective, the functional organization of the human brain is uniquely equipped to encode and decode the multiple levels of meaning inherent in communication. It is generally well known that the brain consists of two halves or cerebral hemispheres. Popularization of the recent experimental work on hemispheric specialization (see review by Bryden, 1982) and clinical studies of patients who have had the major connections between the two hemispheres surgically severed (i.e., commissurotomy) for medical reasons (see review by Nebes, 1974) has led to the overly simplified view that the brain is composed of two separate processing units: one for language-related activities and the other for visual-spatial material. In reality, both hemispheres have relatively equal access to incoming sensory stimuli, especially those of a visual or auditory nature. However, as these stimuli are analyzed and grouped into functional units with distinct cognitive meaning (i.e., percepts), hemispheric differences begin to emerge. In neuropsychology this is referred to as the *law of progressive lateralization of functions* (Luria, 1973, p. 77). However, this fundamental principle does not necessarily imply that at higher levels of perception and cognition the two hemispheres differ in the *types* of tasks they perform. Rather, the lateralization of functions refers to the progressive differentiation in information processing *styles* the two hemispheres have for handling sensory stimuli (Springer & Deutsch, 1981). The left hemisphere is particularly adept at sequentially analyzing temporally ordered stimuli and abstracting out relevant details. Thus, its information-processing style is well suited to linguistic tasks, which require the phonemic analysis of speech sounds and the ordering of these sounds into temporal sequences that have semantic and syntaxical meanings. On the other hand, the right hemisphere tends to "organize and treat data in terms of complex wholes, being in effect a synthesizer with a predisposition for viewing the total rather than the parts" (Nebes, 1974, p. 13). Thus, the right hemisphere is adept at generating holistic percepts based on fragmentary information such as complex visual or auditory arrays that are not easily subject to linguistic analysis.

Although the two cerebral hemispheres can be characterized as having different information-processing styles, it is important to keep in mind that they operate concurrently rather than alternatively, each processing the same information but in a different manner. The physical compartmentalization of these processing styles into separate hemispheres is believed to have adaptive value. Kinsbourne (1982) suggests that the progressive lateralization of higher cognitive functions

> provides neural distance, not between alternative mutually exclusive acts, but between complementary component processes that combine to program a unitary pattern of behavior. (p. 413)

The greater the "functional cerebral space" between the neural loci mediating dissimilar but complementary activities, the greater is our capacity to process these activities simultaneously. Thus we are able to concurrently read a book and listen to music because these activities are mediated by functionally distant neural centers, whereas it is difficult to simultaneously read a book and listen to the dialogue of a TV program because these activities rely on neurologically related areas.

With the preceding general principles in mind, we can now turn our attention to how the brain enables us to encode and decode the complexities of interpersonal communication. First, the relative contributions of each of the cerebral hemispheres to the communication process will be examined as well as their neurologic substrates. From an analysis of these substrates and the types of difficulties that arise when they become dysfunctional, a model for describing individual differences in communication styles will be described.

THE ROLE OF THE LEFT HEMISPHERE

In 1861, the young anatomist Paul Broca published a paper describing the observed relationship between a disturbance of expressive speech and brain lesions in the lower posterior region of the left frontal lobe. A decade later, the German psychiatrist Carl Wernike described a series of patients with lesions in the posterior portion of the left superior temporal gyrus who were unable to comprehend audible speech (Luria, 1973). Since these early clinicopathological observations, researchers have firmly established the relative superiority of the left cerebral hemisphere for speech and language-related activities. For most right-handed people and the majority of left-handed individuals, disturbances in various regions of the left hemisphere result in language disorders involving the perception of verbal sensory stimuli, the integration of these stimuli with prior knowledge, and the activation of verbal response mechanisms (Benson & Geschwind, 1972).

A simplified diagram of the major language centers of the left hemisphere is presented in Figure 2. Auditory stimuli are projected to an area on the superior surface of the temporal lobe known as Heschl's gyrus. Here sensory information is stabilized and temporally ordered before being passed on to the secondary zones of the auditory cortex, known as Wernike's area, for analysis and organization into a phonemic structure. Although lesions affecting Heschl's gyrus do not result in disturbances of language *per se*, disorders affecting Wernike's area can result in varying degrees of impairment of speech-sounds perception; that is, speech may be perceived as unarticulated noise in extreme cases

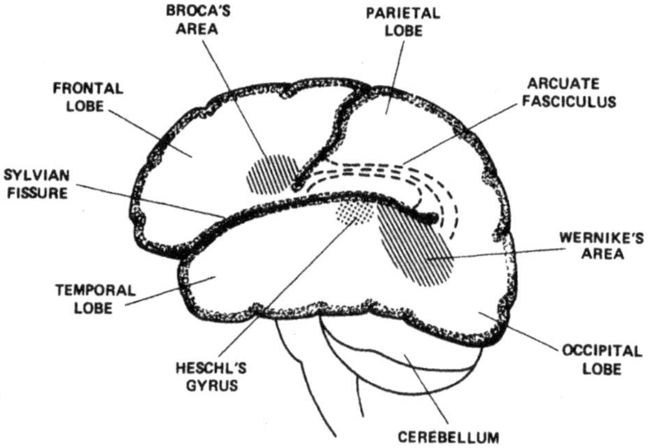

FIGURE 2. Diagram of the primary language centers in the left hemisphere.

or simple misperceptions (e.g., *vine* for *wine*) in mild cases. Without adequate appreciation of the phonemic structure of language, individuals not only have difficulty comprehending oral communications, but they also have problems using the differentiated phonemic system of language to speak clearly, cue from memory the correct names for objects, and spell and write using the acoustic content of words. As one moves further back in Wernike's area to where the temporal lobe merges with the occipital and parietal lobes, more complex forms of comprehension deficits are observed with local brain lesions. Although individuals may be able to understand the meaning of specific words, they may have difficulty comprehending grammatical constructions as a whole, especially those involving relationships (e.g., "spring before summer" or "my uncle is mother's brother"). The integration of visual input with linguistic information may also become dysfunctional, resulting in impaired reading comprehension (Luria, 1973).

Brain lesions in Broca's area of the left frontal lobe affect the motor association cortex representing the face, tongue, lips, and pharynx, interfering with the formation of motor speech patterns (verbal encoding). The person's speech is sparse, poorly articulated, and produced with effort due to increased difficulty in switching between articulemes (palatoglossal positions). Expression in the form of writing is also affected, typically manifested by "poorly formed scribbling" and "complicated by misspelling and omission of letters" (Benson and Geschwind, 1972, p. 6).

The anterior expressive language centers in Broca's area and the more posterior language comprehension centers in Wernike's region are connected by U-shaped nerve fibers called the *arcuate fasciculus*. Disorders affecting this nerve tract disconnect the areas of language comprehension and expression, resulting in a condition known as *conduction aphasia*. Persons with conduction aphasia show good comprehension and relatively fluent spontaneous speech. However, they are unable to accurately repeat what they hear or read aloud because they cannot send the precise information they perceive in Wernike's area to the motor output centers in Broca's area. Instead, they show many word-finding problems and frequently use incorrect words (i.e., paraphasic errors).

Although some caution must be exercised in drawing inferences about how healthy brains process information on the basis of observations derived from patients with neurological illnesses, the careful clinical study of patients with various language disorders has greatly advanced our knowledge of how the intact brain processes linguistic information. Many of the same findings derived from clinical studies have been demonstrated among normal, healthy individuals in the experimental literature.

The typical experimental paradigm used to assess functional asymmetries in the brain is to place the two cerebral hemispheres in competition by controlling the sensory input each receives through such procedures as visual tachistoscopic or dichotic listening presentations. Because each hemisphere receives predominately different information, it is assumed that the hemisphere that is able to perform the task with fewer errors or more quickly has a functional superiority for that type of task. Although there are numerous methodological issues and nuances in this type of research, Bryden's (1982) volume on functional asymmetries in the intact brain provides an excellent and comprehensive review of this literature and clearly reveals that the left hemisphere is superior to the right for the processing of linguistic information among most individuals. This superiority is true whether the linguistic stimuli are visually or auditorily presented. The one possible exception is the visual recognition of emotional versus nonemotional words, in which case the right hemisphere appears to play a more salient role than the left (Graves, Landis, & Goodglass, 1981).

Given our discussion of the role that the left hemisphere plays in the production and comprehension of language, the relative importance of this neural substrate for interpersonal communication should be apparent. The danger is in overascribing importance to the left hemisphere. Many patients with severe language disorders are still capable of expressing their basic needs and desires and can understand and follow the gist of what others are saying to them, especially in interactions with spouses and family members. To some degree, the preservation of elemental communication skills among these patients may be attributable to the intact functioning of the right hemisphere. It is to these functions that we will now turn our attention.

The Role of the Right Hemisphere

As noted earlier, both cerebral hemispheres have relatively equal access to incoming sensory data, and the functional differences between them lie not so much in the types of tasks they perform but in how they perform the tasks. Although the left hemisphere is more analytic and temporally oriented in its manner of processing information, the right is more synthetic and holistic in its processing style. Although the right hemisphere does process linguistic cues, it does so in a holistic manner and lacks the capacity to make the fine phonemic distinctions and temporal discriminations necessary for speech and language. However, the right hemisphere does play a major role in interpersonal communication. Recall from our initial model of intimacy that the communication process involves the exchange of messages in both the linguistic and paralinguistic modalities. Whereas messages conveyed in the linguistic channel are language oriented (i.e., involve words with logical grammatical relationships), those in the paralinguistic modality are more affectively oriented (emotional) and are conveyed by nonverbal cues (Ross, 1983). Because of its predisposition to synthesize fragmentary cues into holistic percepts, the right hemisphere is ideally suited to process information from the nonverbal expressions and prosodic qualities that simultaneously accompany messages in the linguistic modality.

Although Hughlings Jackson (1878) was probably the first to note that the right hemisphere may have a role in affective communications, it has only been in the last 15 years that neuropsychologists have begun to fully appreciate the relative importance of this role. Based on clinical studies of patients with lesions in the posterior temporal and parietal regions of the right hemisphere, Heilman, Scholes, and Watson (1975) described a syndrome called *auditory affective agnosia.* These patients had considerably more difficulty identifying the emotional tone of verbally presented sentences with semantically neutral content when they were read with different emotional intonations than patients with aphasia (i.e., language disorders) from left-hemisphere lesions. In a subsequent study by Tucker, Watson, and Heilman (1977), it was demonstrated that patients with right-hemisphere disease involving the temporal and parietal areas were unable to repeat sentences with affective intonation. In 1979, Ross and Mesulam reported on two patients with brain lesions in the right frontal and anterior parietal regions who had a striking inability to impart emotions in their language or gestures but retained their ability to comprehend and appreciate affective communications. Based on these clinical studies, Ross (1981, 1983) has proposed that right-hemisphere lesions may disturb affective speech processes (expressions, comprehension, and repetition) in a manner parallel to language disorders from left-hemisphere lesions. These affective language disorders are called *aprosodias,* and may result in Broca-, Wernike-, or conduction-type disorders involving the perception of affective, nonverbal sensory stimuli, the integration of these stimuli with prior emotional knowledge, and the activaton of paralinguistic response mechanisms (e.g., gestures, facial expressions, prosody). In short, it is believed that the right hemisphere has neural centers, parallel to those in the left hemisphere, that process the affective components of speech.

Although the clinical documentation of the aprosodias is still meager, there is considerable experimental data from normal subjects indicating that the right hemisphere is, indeed, a major substrate for the expression and perception of emotion. Tachistoscopic presentation of emotional faces to the right and left hemispheres reveals a right-hemisphere advantage in terms of perceptual accuracy (e.g., Ley & Bryden, 1979; Safer, 1981; Strauss & Moscovitch, 1981). As noted earlier, the right hemisphere also appears to be superior to the left in perceiving emotional versus nonemotional words in a lexical decision task (Graves *et al.*, 1981). Similar results have been obtained with auditory stimuli using dichotic listening procedures. Left-ear (right hemisphere) advantages have been reported for identifying the emotional tone of sentences that have been paired with speech babble (Haggard & Parkinson, 1971), nonverbal emotional stimuli (e.g., cries, laughter), and even musical passages differing in emotional tone (Bryden, Ley, & Sugarman, 1982). In a double dissociation-type of paradigm, Ley and Bryden (1982) were able to demonstrate a right-hemisphere advantage for identifying emotional quality and a left-hemisphere advantage for identifying semantic content among the same subjects. This latter study is particularly impressive because it demonstrated the functional asymmetries of the two hemispheres for the perception of emotional and semantic content, with the subjects serving as their own controls. Finally, several studies have shown that the expression of emotion is asymmetrically associated with the right hemisphere. Whether in the laboratory or in field settings, the left side of the body and face (controlled by the right hemisphere) tends to be more expressively intense than the right side (Borod & Caron, 1980; Moscovitch & Olds, 1982; Sackheim, Gur, & Saucy, 1978).

Taken together, the data from clinical and experimental studies of right-hemispheric functioning suggest that the right hemisphere also plays an important role in the process of interpersonal communication, albeit in a subtle manner to the untrained observer. Consider the clinical situation in which two men have suffered strokes affecting the anterior (frontal) regions of their brains: one on the left side and the other on the right. The patient with the left-hemisphere stroke turns to his wife, touches her hand, and says "I . . . uh . . . la . . . lab . . . ewe" with a smile. Despite the dysfluent and effortful production (Broca's aphasia) of this statement, the wife is likely to understand what her husband is attempting to say; her right hemisphere enables her to synthesize the fragmentary linguistic cues into a semantic whole as well as discern its affective components. Although she may have more difficulty understanding the specific semantic content of longer and more complex utterances, she will generally be able to get the gist of what her husband is trying to communicate through an integration of his paralinguistic and dysfluent semantic cues. The situation is apt to be quite different for our patient with the right-hemisphere stroke. He may turn to his wife and say "I love you" very clearly but does so in a monotone voice with little or no change in facial expression or body posture. Although the wife has no difficulty comprehending the semantic content of his statement, the absence of supporting affective cues in the paralinguistic modality seems to negate or distort the semantic meaning. She could well doubt the sincerity of her husband or even feel that he is mocking her and could react in a manner that makes her husband feel misunderstood. Such attribution errors have not been uncommon in our clinical work with neurology patients and their spouses.

We have also noted marital communication difficulties between spouses where one partner has had posterior right-hemisphere dysfunction affecting the comprehension of affective components of language. Here the affected individual understands *what is said* but seems to miss *what is meant,* often to the consternation and frustration of the unaffected spouse. Careful observation of the couple's communications typically reveals that the intended message is being communicated through qualification of the semantic content by subtle variations in paralinguistic cues. For example, a wife, feeling momentarily frustrated and overwhelmed by the burden of having to dress and bathe her husband who has recently suffered a right-hemisphere stroke, might say to him in an exaggerated and sarcastic tone of voice, "I just *love* having to take care of you like this!" Not appreciating the inconsistency of the prosodic aspects of this statement and only hearing that his wife "loves" taking care of him, the husband might simply smile, totally missing the wife's intended message, and negating her feeling state. Unaware that her husband's response is the result of a subtle neurological deficit, the wife is apt to incorrectly attribute her husband's behavior to insensitivity or some perverted sense of enjoyment over her frustration. Although perhaps exaggerated, this type of communication problem is not that dissimilar from what is often encountered in couples with marital difficulties (Chelune, Rosenfeld, & Waring, 1985), where, compared to healthy functioning couples, there is little correspondence between what is disclosed and how it is disclosed (affective manner of presentation).

It is clear from the preceding discussion that the human brain is intimately involved in the process of interpersonal communication. Both the left and the right cerebral hemispheres simultaneously serve as neural substrates for different components of this complex interactional process, and impairment of the normal functioning of these substrates can result in disturbed communication patterns. This is not to imply that all individual differences in the ability to encode and decode the linguistic and affective components of language are necessarily the direct result of brain dysfunction. In the next section we will examine how variations in the functional lateralization of linguistic and paralinguistic skills among normal individuals may influence their cognitive/affective competencies in interpersonal communication.

THE BIOLOGICAL BASES OF INDIVIDUAL DIFFERENCES

Since the pioneering work of Broca and Wernike in the latter part of the nineteenth century, language functions have generally been associated with the left hemisphere. This, however, is only a general rule, one that holds for the majority of people. The clinical research literature documents that linguistic disorders of language can arise from the right-hemisphere dysfunction in a certain percentage of the general population (Benson & Geschwind, 1972). Similarly, either no functional asymmetry or a slight right-hemisphere advantage for language functions has been demonstrated for some normal individuals in the experimental literature (Bryden, 1982). Although less than perfect, these exceptions to the general rule tend to be associated with preferred handedness. Approximately 90% of the population cross-culturally prefers to use the right hand for most fine motor tasks, and among these right-handed individuals, 95% to 99% will show a clear left-hemisphere superiority for linguistic language functions (Benson & Geschwind, 1972; Rasmussen & Milner, 1977). In contrast, only 70% of the left-handed individuals have speech and language functions mediated primarily by the left hemisphere (Luria, 1973); approximately 15% have a reversed (right hemisphere) pattern of hemispheric specialization for language, and the other 15% show bilateral or diffuse representation of language (Rasmussen & Milner, 1977).

Such deviations from the "general rule" have fascinated neuropsychologists who have sought to identify the underlying neuroanatomical mechanism for these variations in hemispheric dominance. Although direct evidence is still lacking, Geschwind and Levitsky (1968) have demonstrated the presence of an important anatomical asymmetry between the two hemispheres that may explain, in part, why the linguistic aspects of language are primarily mediated by the left hemisphere in most, but not all, individuals.

FIGURE 3. (A) The left hemisphere and Sylvian fissure. (B) Representation of the sectioning technique employed by Geschwind and Levitsky (1968). (C) Drawing of the superior surface of the temporal lobes revealing the anatomical asymmetries involving the temporal plane. From "The Anatomical Basis of Hemispheric Differentiation" (p. 14) by N. Geschwind, in S. J. Dimond and J. Beaumont (Eds.), *Hemisphere Function in the Human Brain*, 1974, New York: Halstead Press. Copyright 1974 by Halstead Press. Adapted by permission.

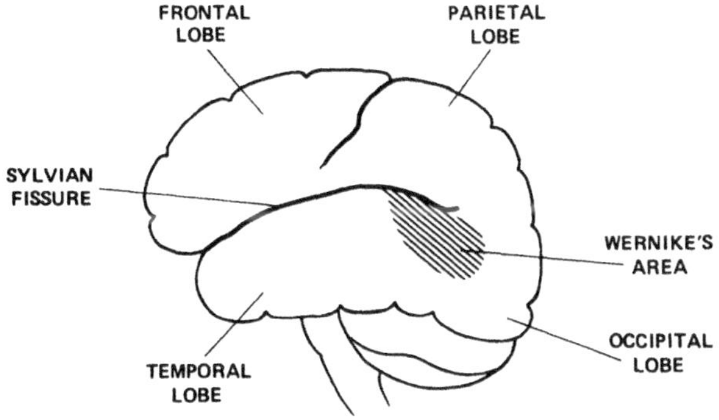
FRONTAL LOBE
PARIETAL LOBE
SYLVIAN FISSURE
WERNIKE'S AREA
OCCIPITAL LOBE
TEMPORAL LOBE

(A)

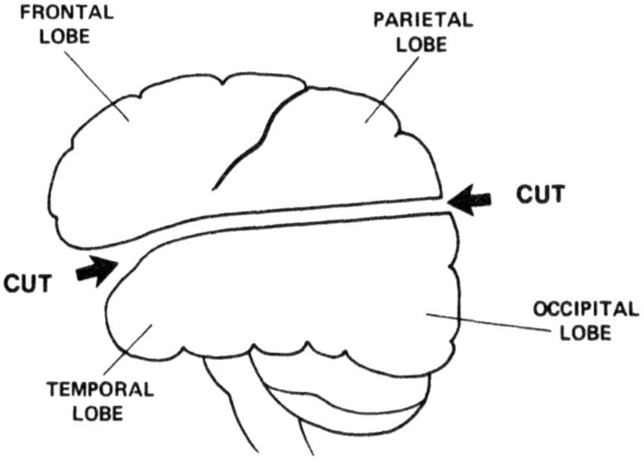
FRONTAL LOBE
PARIETAL LOBE
CUT
CUT
OCCIPITAL LOBE
TEMPORAL LOBE

(B)

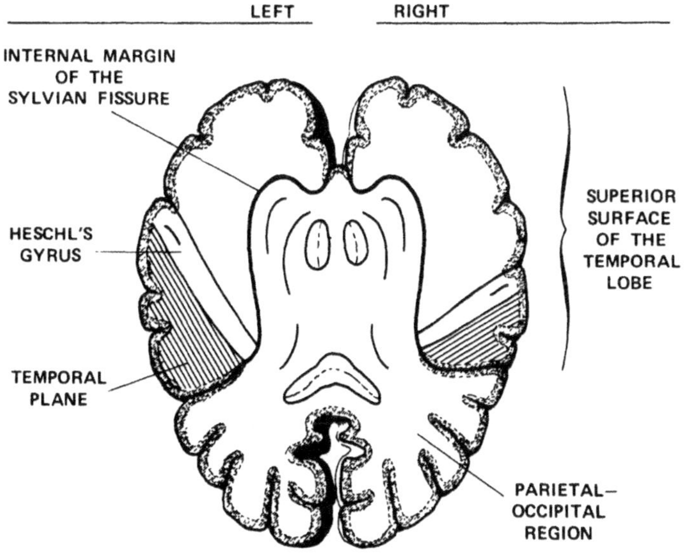
LEFT
RIGHT
INTERNAL MARGIN OF THE SYLVIAN FISSURE
HESCHL'S GYRUS
TEMPORAL PLANE
SUPERIOR SURFACE OF THE TEMPORAL LOBE
PARIETAL–OCCIPITAL REGION

(C)

On gross inspection, the human brain appears to be composed of two halves or hemispheres that are mirror images of one another. Although global analyses of the two hemispheres have revealed slight differences in weight, surface area, and length, they have not been related to functional asymmetries (von Bonin, 1962). However, localized asymmetries, especially along the Sylivian fissure that separates the temporal lobe from the superior regions of the brain (see Figure 3a), have been noted. Connolly (1950) pointed out that the Sylvian fissure tends to be longer on the left than the right, and Pfeifer (cited in Geschwind, 1974) observed that Heschl's gyrus on the superior surface of the temporal lobe was angled forward more sharply on the left than the right.

Intrigued by these and other reports, Geschwind and Levitsky (1968) decided to explore these differences along the Sylvian fissure by passing a broad-bladed knife along the line of this fissure, thereby exposing the entire upper surface of the temporal lobe, which is normally hidden from view (see Figure 3b). Of the 100 brains of normal adults studied at autopsy, they found that the posterior internal margin of the Sylvian fissure was angled backward more sharply on the left than the right, accounting for its greater length along the lateral surface. Similarly, Heschl's gyrus was observed to angle forward more sharply on the left than the right in the majority of cases as suggested by Pfeifer. As seen in Figure 3c, the net result of these findings was that the surface area, known as the *temporal plane,* bounded by these two anatomical landmarks was generally larger in the left hemisphere than in the right in 65% of the cases, with 24% being approximately equal, and 11% being larger in the right hemisphere.

The significance of this anatomical asymmetry is threefold. First, the temporal plane corresponds to what is clinically refered to as Wernike's area—the classic center of receptive language. The fact that this area tends to be larger in the left hemisphere than in the right may account for the relative "superior linguistic talent of the left hemisphere" (Geschwind, 1979, p. 196). Second, the statistical distribution and direction of this asymmetry corresponds relatively well with clinical observations that about 30% of patients who initially develop language disorders after left-hemisphere injuries show significant or total recoveries (Luria, 1970), approximately the same number that have equal or larger temporal planes in the right hemisphere. The distribution also conforms to the relative breakdown of language functions in the left hemisphere among right- and left-handers. Finally, because the two hemispheres are roughly the same size, a larger temporal plane in one hemisphere must mean that an adjacent area in that hemisphere must be smaller. In the case where the temporal plane is larger on the left than on the right, the area posterior to it is smaller on the left than on the right (see Figure 3c). This area corresponds to the junction or tertiary zones of the temporal, parietal, and occipital lobes—a region that plays "a basic role in the organization of *complex simultaneous* (*spatial*) *synthesis*" (Luria, 1973, p. 147). Because this area tends to be larger in the right hemisphere in the same distribution that the temporal plane is larger in the left, this may account for the right hemisphere's relative superiority for processing visual-spatial and paralinguistic cues observed among most individuals.

A MODEL OF INDIVIDUAL VARIATION IN COMMUNICATION SKILLS

The work of Geschwind and Levitsky (1968) is especially relevant for our discussion of differences in interpersonal communication styles. First, it provides a possible, albeit presumptive, anatomical basis for explaining why the two hemispheres are differentially "dominant" for dealing with linguistic and paralinguistic/affective information. What is more important is that their work demonstrates that these anatomical asymmetries are a matter of degree and vary among the general population.

Recall our discussion (see The Neuropsychology of Interpersonal Communication) of the adaptive value of having functional cerebral space between the neural loci of dissimilar but complementary activities (Kinsbourne, 1982). If the anatomical asymmetries along the Sylvian fissure and its adjacent areas are the neural loci for processing the linguistic and paralinguistic/affective components of language, then variations in their degree of anatomical lateralization could well give rise to functional differences in communication style. For example, individuals who have clear-cut anatomical asymmetries in the language-related areas of the brain would have maximal functional cerebral space to simultaneously process both linguistic and paralinguistic information. They would be biologically predisposed to develop through learning and experience a heightened degree of "discriminative facility" (Mischel, 1973) or "disclosure flexibility" (Chelune, 1977) in their interactions with others. That is, those individuals with clearly lateralized linguistic and paralinguistic processing centers are maximally equipped to simultaneously encode and decode the complementary component processes of language in a unified manner. As such, they would have a biological advantage for discerning and using subtle juxtapositions of linguistic and paralinguistic cues to meet a broad range of social-situational demands. In contrast, those with a lesser degree of relevant anatomical asymmetry may experience less efficiency in the simultaneous processing of linguistic and paralinguistic cues due to a crowding effect or competition in functional cerebral space (Kinsbourne, 1982; Levy, 1974). These individuals might be expected to show a discrepancy or bias in their ability to process linguistic and paralinguistic information (Dean, Swartz, & Smith, 1981; Kail & Siegel, 1978; Miller, 1971). That is, individuals who have more diffusely organized language functions may be prone to encode and decode communication in a more restricted manner, resulting in less flexible communication styles. These inferences, derived from the neuropsychological literature and applied to the study of communication patterns, provided the basis for an innovative dissertation project by Christiane O'Hara, which attempted to relate variations in cerebral lateralization to differences in the ability to perceive discrepancies in the linguistic and paralinguistic modalities of communication (O'Hara, 1982; O'Hara & Chelune, 1982). The results of this study are described later.

A Study of Handedness and the Perception of Incongruent Communication

Common experience suggests that not all individuals are equally adept in their ability to decode interpersonal communications. Consistent with the view presented in this chapter, one potential factor that may account, in part, for these individual differences is variation in the degree to which linguistic and paralinguistic/affective processes are differentially lateralized in the brain. Because permission to directly observe the brains of student volunteers is not likely to pass most university human subjects review boards, alternative methods of determining hemispheric specialization are required. The least intrusive and most readily available source of this information is handedness. Although studies examining the relationship between handedness and hemispheric specialization are not entirely consistent, it is generally concluded that many left-handers and most ambidexterous individuals demonstrate less clearcut functional asymmetries than do right-handers (Bryden, 1982). Furthermore, it has been argued that writing posture (Levy & Reid, 1976) and familial history of left-handedness (Dee, 1971; McKeever & Van-Deventer, 1977) moderate strength of handedness and the degree of cerebral specialization. Thus, O'Hara and I postulated that handedness, as a rough index of the degree to which paralinguistic and linguistic processes are differentially lateralized, may be a useful variable in explaining individual differences in the perception of communication cues. More specifically, it was hypothesized that strongly lateralized hand preference (and presumably hemispheric specialization) would be associated with a greater ability to encode incongruencies in both the linguistic and paralinguistic modalities of self-disclosing communications.

From a larger pool of research participants, 60 male college students were selected on the basis of their scores on a handedness questionnaire that sampled manual preferences on 14 fine motor tasks. Twenty subjects were strongly right-handed and had no familial history of sinistrality (i.e., left-handedness) or showed an inverted handwriting posture[1]; 20 subjects were strongly left-handed; 55% had a history of familial sinistrality, and 75% showed inverted hand postures when writing; and 20 subjects were ambidexterous or mixed-handed, with 30% having a familial history of left-handedness and 20% a "hooked" (inverted) writing style. All of the subjects were neurologically intact and performing well in their classes.

To assess their encoding skills, the subjects were shown a videotape, the Incongruency Discrimination Assessment (Tyroler, 1980), which consists of a short introductory segment of an actress talking about her life, followed by 12 vignettes of 20 to 30 seconds in which she engages in personal disclosures. Each stimulus scene was carefully constructed and systematically manipulated in terms of its linguistic and paralinguistic cues to create a specific type and level of incongruency in that scene. That is, in some scenes the linguistic cues were all congruent, but the paralinguistic cues were at variance with one another, whereas in others the paralinguistic cues were all consistent, but the linguistic cues were inconsistent with one another. For example, in a scene with paralinguistic incongruency, the actress might make several statements about feeling depressed and being under much stress (congruent linguistic cues) in a slow, tired voice, sitting in a slumped position in her chair but with a smile on her face. By varying the percentage of discrepant cues in each scene, three levels of incongruency were created for each modality. Thus, the stimuli represent a 2×3 Mode of Incongruence by Level of Incongruence matrix of scenes, with two representative scenes in each cell. The scenes have been demonstrated to have a known type and level of stimulus pull that is nearly orthogonal (Tyroler, Chelune, & O'Neill, 1980; Tyroler, Chelune, O'Neill, & Wright, 1981).

Following each scene, the subjects were asked to rate their global perception of the actress' communication for level of incongruency on

[1]Levy and Reid (1976) have found that right-handers who use a noninverted handwriting posture and left-handers who use an inverted ("hooked") posture, both producing the common lower left to upper right slant, show a left-hemisphere superiority for language tasks and a right-hemisphere superiority for spatial tasks. The reverse pattern of hemispheric specialization was generally observed for left-handers who wrote with a noninverted posture and right-handers with an inverted style.

a 7-point Likert scale. To aid the subjects in making their ratings, they were given a brief introduction to the nature of self-disclosing communication and the communication modalities through which this information is conveyed. After this introduction, the subjects were then given the folllowing definitions of congruent and incongruent communication and several examples:

> When a message is consistent (that is, when the sender presents a clear message that contains no contradictions or conflicting parts that could confuse the receiver or leave the message open to alternative interpretations), it is said to be *congruent*. When a message is inconsistent (that is, when it contradicts or qualifies itself, so that the receiver is confused or is forced to select one of several interpretations), it is said to be *incongruent*. Within a message, there can be varying degrees of how well the message matches itself, or different levels of congruence. (O'Hara, 1982, p. 76)

The ratings for the two representative scenes in each Mode by Level combination were combined so that scores ranged from 2 to 14, and these data were then analyzed for handedness effects. The most interesting finding of the study was a significant Group by Mode of Incongruency interaction, which is depicted in Figure 4. As can be seen,

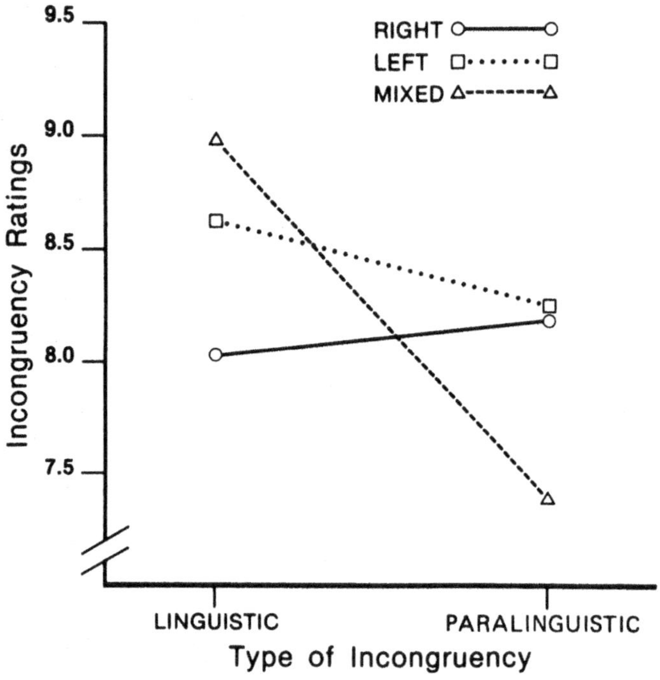

FIGURE 4. Interaction effects between handedness groups and their ratings of videotape stimuli with either linguistic or paralinguistic incongruencies.

the right-handed and left-handed groups showed little difference in their ratings of scenes that contained either linguistic or paralinguistic incongruencies. Both groups made equally graduated ratings across the three levels of incongruency in each mode, yielding mean ratings in each mode near the theoretical midpoint of 8.0 on the 2- to 14-point scale. In contrast, the mixed-handed group, with presumably more bilateral or diffuse hemispheric specialization, manifested a sharp discrepancy between their ratings of scenes when the incongruencies occurred in the linguistic versus paralinguistic modality.

The data indicate that the mixed-handed group was much more sensitive or critical of linguistic incongruencies than presumably comparable incongruencies in the paralinguistic modality. This is not to say that they were more accurate than the other two groups in detecting linguistic incongruencies (or conversely, less accurate in detecting paralinguistic inconsistencies), but rather that they tended as a group to assign more extreme incongruency ratings when they did detect discrepant linguistic cues than when they perceived discrepant paralinguistic cues in the actress' disclosures. This finding is consistent with previous neuropsychological research (Dean *et al.*, 1981; Kail & Siegel, 1978; Miller, 1971), which has demonstrated that individuals with diffuse hemispheric specialization tend to develop one modality, typically the linguistic mode, to the detriment of the other modality. Levy (1974) suggests that when two or more complementary processes are "crowded" into the same functional space, the individual develops a bias for that process that has the greatest reinforcing value, which in our verbally oriented society is usually the linguistic modality.

Implications for Understanding Individual Differences in Communication

Although the design of this study does not lend itself to issues of perceptual accuracy, the data do suggest that individual differences in the differential encoding of linguistic and paralinguistic cues may be related to variations in hemispheric specialization as indexed by handedness. If we assume that variations in the functional organization of the brain were responsible for the observed differences in the encoding of the linguistic and paralinguistic incongruities in the videotaped vignettes, then the potential impact of biological factors on interpersonal communication styles can be inferred and a variety of empirical questions formulated. Imagine Person X with a "right-handed" communication style attempting to share personally relevant and subjectively intimate information with Person Y with a "mixed-handed" communication style. Because Person X is apt to extend the range and nuances of his or her disclosures by strategically using paralinguistic cues to qualify, emphasize, or negate the linguistic content of the communications, one might hypothesize that Person Y may be predisposed or at risk to miss their intended meaning and respond concretely to only the linguistic content. This biologically based mismatch of communication styles could, in turn, affect the degree of disclosure reciprocity seen in the dyad and subsequent perceptions of attraction.

Variations in the degree of functional asymmetry of linguistic and paralinguistic processes may also affect appropriateness of self-disclosure. Because appropriateness is dependent on the ability to accurately encode social-situational nuances in a situation and modulate (decode) one's disclosures accordingly, one might expect individuals with clearly differentiated neural processing centers for linguistic and paralinguistic information to be more appropriate or flexible in their disclosures than persons with more diffusely organized language centers. Empirical evaluation of these hypotheses awaits future research at the interface between neuropsychology and the social phenomenon of interpersonal communicaton. Although social and situational variables are important determinants of behavior, their impact on the individual is relative and mediated by the brain's capacity to effectively process and respond to them.

SUMMARY

The fundamental premise of neuropsychology is that the brain is the organ of all behavior; that is, all behavior, overt as well as covert, is mediated at some level by the central nervous system. In this chapter, I have attempted to demonstrate how this extreme biological perspective can be extended to account for individual differences in the complex social process of interpersonal communication. By focusing on a single feature of close relationships, the exchange of personal information, as an exemplar, we have examined how the right and left hemispheres of the brain work together to analyze and synthesize messages at numerous levels to allow us to share personally relevant information with another.

Disturbances from illness or injury in how the brain normally functions result in relatively predictable changes in the communication process. Impairment of the left hemisphere disturbs the encoding and decoding of the linguistic aspects of language, whereas right-hemisphere impairment affects the expression and appreciation of the affective-paralinguistic components of language. The functional lateralization of these processing styles may be dependent on anatomical asymmetries in the language areas of the brain. However, the size and laterality of these anatomical asymmetries are relative and differentially distributed among individuals. The relative distribution of these anatomical asymmetries could affect the degree of functional cerebral space between the neural loci for the dissimilar but complementary linguistic and paralinguistic components of language, resulting in differences or biases in how normal individuals simultaneously process information in these modalities.

For those of us who seek to understand the nature of close relationships, many aspects must be considered concurrently within an interactive science that allows us to view relationships as a dynamic whole. However, to appreciate the complexities of relationships as a whole, we must understand their individual components. The purpose of this chapter has been to present a novel perspective of individual differences in but one of these key elements; namely the exchange of personal information. Although the early work of Jourard (1971a,b) and others examined individual differences in self-disclosing behavior in some detail, their focus was on the individual and limited to a social psychological level of analysis. Application of current neuropsychological theory to social communication suggests that self-disclosure in close relationships is not only a social behavior but also an interactive cognitive-behavioral activity that is mediated and modified by underlying neural mechanisms. To develop a truly comprehensive model of interpersonal communication that can adequately account for individual variations in self-disclosing behavior, one must not only consider relevant social-situational parameters but also look beneath the skin.

REFERENCES

Altman, I., & Taylor, D. A. (1973). *Social penetration: The development of interpersonal relationships.* New York: Holt, Rinehart & Winston.

Bandler, R., Grindler, J., & Satir, V. (1976). *Changing with families.* Palo Alto, CA: Science and Behavior Books.

Bem, D. J., & Funder, D. C. (1978). Predicting more of the people more of the time: Assessing the personality of situations. *Psychological Review, 85,* 485–501.

Benson, D. F., & Geschwind, N. (1972). Aphasia and related disturbances. In A. B. Baker (Ed.), *Clinical neurology* (pp. 1–26). New York: Harper & Row.

Berscheid, E., & Walster, E. H. (1978). *Interpersonal attraction* (2nd ed.). Reading, MA: Addison-Wesley.

Borod, J. C., & Caron, H. S. (1980). Facedness and emotion related to lateral dominance, sex and expression type. *Neuropsychologia, 18,* 237–241.

Bryden, M. P. (1982). *Laterality: Functional asymmetry in the intact brain.* New York: Academic Press.

Bryden, M. P., Ley, R. G., & Sugarman, J. H. (1982). A left ear advantage for identifying the emotional quality of tonal sequences. *Neuropsychologia, 20,* 83–87.

Chelune, G. J. (1976). The Self-Disclosure Situations Survey: A new approach to measuring self-disclosure. *JSAS Catalog of Selected Documents in Psychology, 6*(1367), 111–112.

Chelune, G. J. (1977). Disclosure flexibility and social-situational perceptions. *Journal of Consulting and Clinical Psychology, 45,* 1139–1143.

Chelune, G. J. (Ed.). (1979). *Self-disclosure: Origins, patterns, and implications of openness in interpersonal relationships.* San Francisco: Jossey-Bass.

Chelune, G. J., Robison, J. T., & Kommor, M. J. (1984). A cognitive interational model of intimate relationships. In V. J. Derlega (Ed.), *Communication, intimacy, and close relationships* (pp. 11–40). Orlando, FL: Academic Press.

Chelune, G. J., Rosenfeld, L. B., & Waring, E. M. (1985). Spouse disclosure patterns in distressed and nondistressed couples. *American Journal of Family Therapy, 13,* 24–32.

Connolly, C. J. (1950). *External morphology of the primate brain.* Springfield, IL: Charles C Thomas.

Dean, R. S., Schwartz, N. H., & Smith, L. S. (1981). Laternal perference patterns as a discriminator of learning difficulties. *Journal of Consulting and Clinical Psychology, 49,* 277–233.

Dee, H. L. (1971). Auditory asymmetry and strength of manual preference. *Cortex, 7,* 236–245.

Derlega, V. J. (Ed.). (1984). *Communication, intimacy, and close relationships.* New York: Academic Press.

Derlega, V. J., & Chaikin, A. L. (1975). *Sharing intimacy: What we reveal to others and why.* Englewood Cliffs, NJ: Prentice-Hall.

Derlega, V. J., & Grzelak, J. (1979). Appropriateness of self-disclosure. In G. J. Chelune (Ed.), *Self-disclosure: Origins, patterns, and implications of openness in interpersonal relationships* (pp. 151–176). San Francisco: Jossey-Bass.

Geschwind, N. (1974). The anatomical basis of hemispheric differentiation. In S. J. Dimond & J. Beaumont (Eds.), *Hemisphere function in the human brain* (pp. 7–24). New York: Halstead Press.

Geschwind, N. (1979). Specializations of the human brain. *Scientific American, 241,* 180–199.

Geschwind, N., & Levitsky, W. (1968). Human brain: Left-right asymmetries in the temporal speech region. *Science, 161,* 186–187.

Graves, R., Landis, T., & Goodglass, H. (1981). Laterality and sex differences for visual recognition of emotional and nonemotional words. *Neuropsychologia, 19,* 95–102.

Haggard, M. P., & Parkinson, A. M. (1971). Stimulus and task factors in the perceptual lateralization of speech signals. *Quarterly Journal of Experimental Psychology, 23,* 168–177.

Heilman, K. M., Scholes, R., & Watson, R. J. (1975). Auditory affective agnosia: Disturbed comprehension of affective speech. *Journal of Neurology, Neurosurgery and Psychiatry, 38,* 69–72.

Hinde, R. A. (1978). Interpersonal relationships: In quest of a science. *Psychological Medicine, 3,* 378–386.

Hinde, R. A. (1981). The basis of a science of interpersonal relationships. In S. Duck & R. Gilmour (Eds.), *Personal relationships* (Vol. 1, pp. 1–22). New York: Academic Press.

Jackson, D., & Weakland, J. (1961). Conjoint family therapy: Some considerations on technique and results. *Psychiatry, 24,* 30–45.

Jackson, J. H. (1878). On affections of speech from disease of the brain. *Brain, 1,* 304–330.

Jourard, S. M. (1971a). *Self-disclosure: An experimental analysis of the transparent self.* New York: Wiley-Interscience.

Jourard, S. M. (1971b). *The transparent self* (Rev. ed.). New York: Van Nostrand-Reinhold.

Kail, R. V., & Siegel, A. W. (1978). Sex and hemispheric differences in the recall of verbal and spatial information. *Cortex, 14,* 556–563.

Key, M. (1965). *Paralinguistic and kinesics.* Metuchen, NJ: Scarecrow Press.

Kinsbourne, M. (1982). Hemispheric specialization and the growth of human understanding. *American Psychologist, 37,* 411–420.

Ley, R. G., & Bryden, M. P. (1979). Hemispheric differences in processing emotions and faces. *Brain and Language, 7,* 127–138.

Ley, R. G., & Bryden, M. P. (1982). A dissociation of right and left hemispheric effects for recognizing emotional tone and verbal content. *Brain and Cognition, 1,* 3–9.

Levy, J. (1974). Psychobiological implications of bilateral asymmetry. In S. Dimond & J. G. Beaumont (Eds.), *Hemisphere function in the human brain* (pp. 121–183). New York: Halstead Press.

Levy, J., & Reid, M. L. (1976). Variations in writing posture and cerebral organization. *Science, 194,* 337–339.

Luria, A. R. (1970). *Traumatic aphasia.* The Hague: Mouton.

Luria, A. R. (1973). *The working brain.* New York: Basic Books.

McKeever, W. F., & Van Deventer, A. D. (1977). Familial sinistrality and degree of left-handedness. *British Journal of Psychology, 68,* 469–471.

Miller, E. (1971). Handedness and patterns of human ability. *British Journal of Psychology, 62,* 111–112.

Mischel, W. (1968). *Personality and assessment.* New York: Wiley.

Mischel, W. (1973). Toward a cognitive social learning reconceptualization of personality. *Psychological Review, 80,* 252–283.

Mischel, W. (1977). On the future of personality measurement. *American Psychologist, 32,* 246–254.

Monrad-Krohn, G. H. (1957). The third element of speech: Prosody in the neuropsychiatric clinic. *Journal of Mental Science, 103,* 326–331.

Moscovitch, M., & Olds, J. (1982). Asymmetries in emotional facial expressions and their possible relation to hemispheric specialization. *Neuropsychologia, 20,* 71–81.

Nebes, R. D. (1974). Hemispheric specialization in commissurotomized man. *Psychological Bulletin, 81,* 1–14.

O'Hara, C. C. (1982). Handedness and ratings of congruence in verbal and nonverbal channels of communication (Doctoral dissertation, University of Georgia, 1982). *Dissertation Abstracts International, 43,* 1994-b.

O'Hara, C. C., & Chelune, G. J. (1982). *Handedness and discrimination of verbal and nonverbal incongruent communication.* Paper presented at the 10th annual meeting of the International Neuropsychological Society, Pittsburgh, PA.

Pervin, L. A. (1976). A free response description approach of person-situation interaction. *Journal of Personality and Social Psychology, 34,* 465–474.

Phillips, G. M., & Metzger, N. J. (1976). *Intimate communication.* Boston: Allyn & Bacon.

Price, R. H. (1974). A taxonomic classification of behavior and situations and the problem of behavior-environment congruence. *Human Behavior, 27,* 567–585.

Price, R. H., & Bouffard, D. L. (1974). Behavior appropriateness and situational constraint as dimensions of social behavior. *Journal of Personality and Social Psychology, 30,* 579–586.

Rasmussen, T., & Milner, B. (1977). The role of early left-brain injury in determining lateralization of cerebral speech functions. *Annals of the New York Academy of Science, 299,* 355–369.

Ross, E. D. (1981). The aprosodias: Functional-anatomic organization of the affective components of language in the right hemisphere. *Archives of Neurology, 38,* 561–569

Ross, E. D. (1983). Right-hemisphere lesions in disorders of affective language. In A. Kertesz (Ed.), *Localization in neuropsychology* (pp. 493–508). New York: Academic Press.

Ross, E. D., & Mesulam, M. M. (1979). Dominant language functions of the right hemisphere? Prosody and emotional gesturing. *Archives of Neurology, 36,* 144–148.

Safer, M. A. (1981). Sex and hemispheric differences in access to codes for processing emotional expressions and faces. *Journal of Experimental Psychology: General, 110,* 96–100.

Sackheim, H. A., Gur, R. C., & Saucy, M. C. (1978). Emotions are expressed more intensely on the left side of the face. *Annals of the New York Academy of Science, 202,* 424–435.

Satir, V. (1967). *Conjoint family therapy* (Rev. ed.). Palo Alto, CA: Science and Behavior Books.

Schaefer, M. T., & Olson, D. H. (1981). Assessing intimacy: The PAIR Inventory. *Journal of Marital and Family Therapy, 7,* 47–60.

Springer, S. P., & Deutsch, G. (1981). *Left brain, right brain.* San Francisco: W. H. Freeman.

Squire, L. R., & Butters, N. M. (Eds.). (1984). *Neuropsychology of memory.* New York: Guilford.

Strauss, E., & Moscovitch, M. (1981). Perception of facial expressions. *Brain and Language, 13,* 308–332.

Tyroler, M. J. (1980). The effects of experience and affective sensitivity on the ability to discriminate and accurately reflect incongruent communication (Doctoral dissertation, University of Georgia, 1980). *Dissertation Abstracts International, 41,* 2351-B.

Tyroler, M. J., Chelune, G. J., & O'Neill, C. P. (1980). *Is what you hear really what is being said?* Paper presented at the 88th annual meeting of the American Psychological Association, Toronto, Canada.

Tyroler, M. J., Chelune, G. J., O'Neill, C. P., & Wright, J. (1981). *The Incongruency Discrimination Assessment: A measure of sensitivity to incongruent communication.* Paper presented at the 89th annual meeting of the American Psychological Association, Los Angeles.

Tucker, D. M., Watson, R. T., & Heilman, K. M. (1977). Discrimination and evocation of affectively intoned speech in patients with right parietal disease. *Neurology, 27,* 947–950.

von Bonin, G. (1962). Anatomical asymmetries of the cerebral hemispheres. In V. B. Mountcastle (Ed.), *Interhemispheric relations and cerebral dominance* (pp. 1–6). Baltimore: Johns Hopkins University Press.

Walster, E., Walster, G. W., & Berscheid, E. (1978). *Equity theory and research.* Boston: Allyn & Bacon.

Waring, E. M., & Chelune, G. J. (1983). Marital intimacy and self-disclosure. *Journal of Clinical Psychology, 39,* 183–190.

Waring, E. M., Tillman, M. P., Frelick, L., Russell, L., & Weisz, G. (1980). Concepts of intimacy in the general population. *Journal of Nervous and Mental Disease, 168,* 471–474.

3

Why Am I Telling You This?

Self-Disclosure in a Goal-Based Model of Personality

LYNN CAROL MILLER and STEPHEN J. READ

Bernice sat next to Bob on the plane. Bob smiled, and said "hello" as Bernice introduced herself. An hour later, Bernice listened attentively as Bob told her he was upset because he and his wife had just been divorced. Before their plane had touched down, Bob had asked Bernice to meet him for dinner.

This scenario raises a number of questions concerning disclosure in interpersonal relationships. Chief among them is: Why did Bob disclose so intimately to Bernice? One approach is to ask what traits or characteristics distinguish Bob from others who would not have disclosed in this situation. Perhaps Bob is generally a high discloser. Or, alternatively, we might ask what Bob's goals were in disclosing to Bernice. And, what were the plans, strategies, beliefs, and resources that might enable him to reach these goals?

On the surface, these may seem like very different sets of questions. In fact, the two sets of questions have much in common. For, as the present chapter argues, most personality characteristics can be understood as particular clusters of goals, plans for attaining those goals, resources necessary for the plans, and beliefs and knowledge about the world.

LYNN CAROL MILLER • Department of Psychology, Scripps College, Claremont, California 91711. **STEPHEN J. READ** • Department of Psychology, University of Southern California, University Park, Los Angeles, California 90089–1061.

This chapter is divided into four parts. We will start by reviewing some of the literature on individual differences in self-disclosure and by pointing out some of the inconsistencies and confusion in the present literature. In order to shed some light on findings in this literature, we will present a theoretical model for analyzing personality traits based on Schank and Abelson's (1977) analysis of the role of scripts, plans, and goals in social understanding. Then we will discuss individual differences in self-disclosure and measures related to predicting self-disclosure in light of our theoretical model. In doing so, the model will be applied both to a consideration of multiple personality characteristics of the same individual and to the interaction among the characteristics of the individuals in a dyadic relationship. We will conclude by discussing the implications of this type of model for personality research.

PREDICTING INDIVIDUAL DIFFERENCES IN DISCLOSURE

Early researchers in self-disclosure focused on the possibility that the tendency to disclose was a stable personality characteristic, measurable by means of a self-report instrument (Jourard, 1959). Measures of individual differences in disclosure, however, produced a conflicting and confusing array of results. For example, personality measures of disclosure have been positively related to self-disclosure in some field and laboratory studies (Jourard & Resnick, 1970; Pederson & Breglio, 1968; Taylor, 1968), but in an equal number of other studies, they have been found to be unrelated to (Burhenne & Mirels, 1970; Ehrlich & Graven, 1971; Vondracek, 1969) or even negatively related to self-disclosure (Doster & Strickland, 1971). The literature was in such a state of disarray that several reviewers concluded that personality research using disclosure measures should be abandoned (Cozby, 1973; Goodstein & Reinecker, 1974).

Rather than taking this extreme step, personality researchers asked, "Why are individual difference measures of self-disclosure sometimes predictive and sometimes not?" In addressing this question, researchers took a variety of approaches: focusing on the problems of disclosure scales themselves (Chelune, 1979; Cozby, 1973; Goodstein & Reinecker, 1974), looking at individual differences in variability of disclosure across contexts (Chelune, 1975), using multidimensional measures of disclosure (Chelune, 1979), focusing on the importance of situational factors (Cash, 1975), assessing the relationship of the target to the revealer such as friend, stranger, parent, or peer (Chaikin & Derlega, 1974; Jourard & Lasakow, 1958; Morton, 1978; Rubin & Shenker, 1978), and exploring the role of personality characteristics of the recipient of disclosure (Miller, Berg, & Archer, 1983). Although all of these approaches are potentially useful ones, they have been primarily descriptive in nature. Little of the prior work in this area has attempted to understand how underlying personality processes may influence individual differences in self-disclosing behaviors. The current work presents a framework for viewing such processes and suggests why self-report measures of self-disclosure are sometimes predictive of disclosing behaviors and sometimes not.

A GOAL-BASED MODEL OF PERSONALITY

A number of theorists (e.g., Miller, Galanter, & Pribram, 1960; Murray, 1938; Schank & Abelson, 1977) have argued that social interaction can be analyzed in terms of people's goals and the plans and strategies necessary to achieve those goals. One of the most explicit analyses of this has been presented by Schank and Abelson (1977). Schank and Abelson's analysis identifies two key components in analyzing social interaction—goals and the plans and strategies individuals use to attain these goals. Implicit in their analysis are two additional considerations: an individual's beliefs as they relate to these goals and strategies and the resources necessary to carry out the plans and attain these goals.

We argue that personality traits can be viewed as chronic, stable configurations of these four components: (1) an individual's goals, (2) the plans and strategies for attaining those goals, (3) the resources required for successfully carrying out the plans, and (4) beliefs about the world that affect the execution of their plans.

For a concrete example of what we mean, let us reexamine the example of Bob and Bernice. One thing that may distinguish Bob from others is that he is highly sociable. In terms of the present model we mean that Bob very much wants and likes to be with people, that he engages in various plans and behaviors to interact with them, that he possesses the skills and resources to successfully interact with them, and that he has certain beliefs and knowledge that are instrumental in carrying out his plans. An example can be found in Figure 1a. Before providing a more detailed analysis of this conception of a trait, it would first be helpful to more carefully explicate these four components.

COMPONENTS OF THE MODEL

Goals

For our present purposes, a goal is, quite simply, something that the individual desires or wants to attain because it is rewarding in its own right. As suggested in the earlier example of Bernice and Bob, Bob

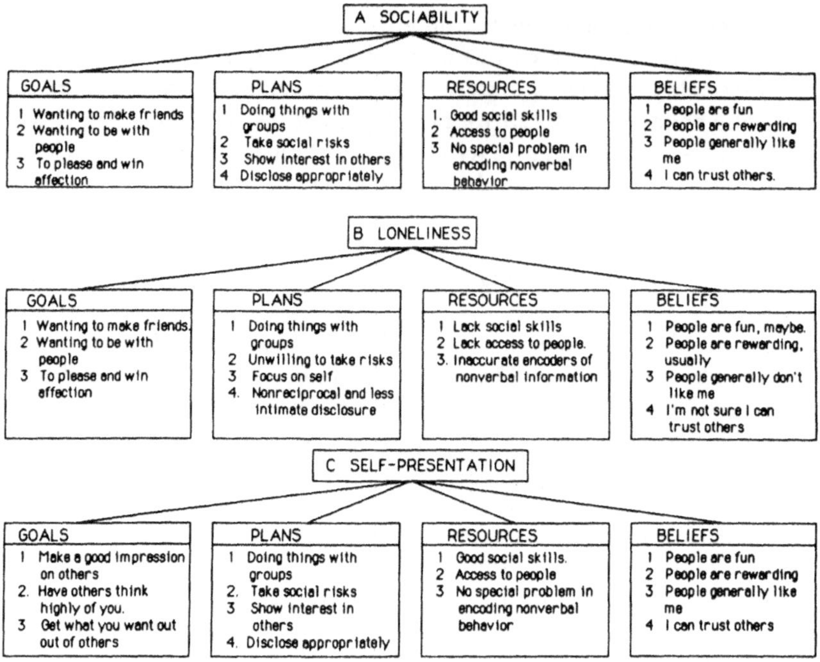

FIGURE 1. A comparison of sociability, loneliness, and self-presentation in terms of the model's four components.

may have had a number of goals in disclosing to Bernice, including wanting to meet and get to know her better, seeking sympathy, reducing his boredom on long trips, and so forth.

As several people (Murray 1938; Schank & Abelson, 1977; Wilensky, 1983) have pointed out, there are several possible relations among an individual's goals. First, the goals may be irrelevant to one another. In this case, there are few interesting issues.

Second, various goals may conflict with one another. For instance, the goal of being rich and successful may conflict with the goal of relaxing. Or the goal of being totally honest in what we say may very well conflict with the goal of maintaining friendships. These examples suggest one of the reasons why goals may conflict: The plans necessary for attaining two goals may be inconsistent with one another. Thus the plan of spending a weekend at the shore to relax may conflict with plans to work hard all weekend to maximize profits in order to be successful. In this case, both plans may require the same resource (time), but there may only be enough of the resource to carry out one of the plans. Here the individual must decide which goal is most important.

A third possibility is that various goals may be subsumed so that multiple goals can be attained at the same time. In getting married, for example, we get companionship and friendship (hopefully), sex, and depending on the marriage, we may get such things as money, intellectual stimulation, or children.

A fourth possible relationship among goals involves goals that enable or facilitate achieving other goals. For example, we may desire to become close to the boss (and engage in a variety of plans to achieve that goal) in order to achieve a higher goal (getting the raise instead of another employee) that in itself is a subgoal of the need to achieve. We can distinguish between end goals (ends in themselves or terminal goals) and means goals (which are subgoals to be achieved in pursuing a higher order goal or an end goal). For clarity, when we refer to *goals* we will be referring to end goals. Subgoals will be considered part of a set of plans or strategies used to attain the higher order goal.

Plans and Strategies

In addition to the goals of the interaction, there are the plans and strategies that Bob uses in the interaction in order to attain these goals. Plans are organized sequences of behavior aimed at the attainment of some end goal or set of goals. Oftentimes, a given plan of behavior is composed of several subsequences or subplans that are linked together into an overall plan in order to attain the goals in a particular situation. Let us consider the set of plans and strategies Bob used in addressing one of his possible goals: wishing to get to know Bernice.

Bob may actually have a number of strategies in his repertoire for accomplishing this goal of being friendly to another. For example, he may have kissing or agreeing with the other as strategies to use when being friendly to another. These strategies may vary in effectiveness. Some involve behaviors that are too intimate, given the relationship he has with Bernice. Fortunately, he has other strategies that are more appropriate given the nature of his relationship with Bernice. These include (a) introducing himself to attractive strangers, (b) saying "hello," and (c) inviting attractive women to restaurants.

Beliefs

An individual's beliefs and knowledge about the world are apt to be instrumental to the choice and successful completion of a plan. Among these may be such things as knowledge about the locations of objects (such as restaurant locations) necessary to a plan, evaluations of the morality and effectiveness of various plans, and knowledge about the likely behavior of physical and social objects (the plane is about to land; when the plane lands the passengers will depart; because I don't know this woman's name or address, I won't be able to see her again). Implicit in the preceding story of Bob and Bernice may be some of his beliefs about people ("people are basically worthwhile and trustworthy") and himself ("if I tell her this, she'll continue talking to me"), which may have influenced his behavior and set him apart from others on the plane who would not have disclosed. There are beliefs (end beliefs) that may relate more to goals *per se* (such as "people are basically good"), wheras other beliefs, such as "disclosing about myself is a good way to get others to like and pay attention to me," may have influenced the strategy or plans Bob adopted to reach his goals (these will be referred to as means beliefs).

Resources

Most plans of action carry with them numerous conditions that must be satisfied for the successful completion of the plan. Some of these conditions simply depend on the particular state of the world and are beyond the control of the individual trying to carry out the plan. However, most of the time, various plans require that the individual possesses certain resources necessary to successfully carry out the plans. Among resources commonly required in social interaction (Foa & Foa, 1976) are such things as money, information, time, and various skills and abilities. Bob may have differed from others in terms of the resources he possessed, including his ability to know and talk about his feelings to Bernice, his reasonable social skills, and time to spend interacting with her.

Summary

To reiterate, one way of viewing individual differences in social interaction is in terms of a specific stable cluster of (1) goals, (2) strategies, (3) beliefs, and (4) resources, abilities, and skills. Within each of these components, there are important individual differences. Traits can be viewed as a particular chronic configuration of individual differences across each of these areas. For instance, to be called sociable, an individual must have the goal of being with people. If she or he had no desire to be with people, then she or he would hardly be considered sociable. Further, a truly sociable individual must be able to successfully carry out various plans for social interaction. An individual who is not able to interact successfully (e.g., achieve his or her goal to be with others) will not typically be considered sociable but instead may be chronically lonely. Figure 1 contrasts sociability with chronic loneliness. As you can see, the sociable person and the lonely person have similar goals. However, these individuals have different traits because their beliefs, strategies, and resources differ considerably.

Likewise, individuals may have similar strategies but associate these strategies with the attainment of different goals. Thus one individual, Ellen, may be quite likely to self-disclose intimate information about herself when she is trying to impress others, whereas another woman, Louise, may typically self-disclose only when she is trying to make new friends. Given a chronic configuration of Ellen's goals, strategies, beliefs, and resources, as indicated in Figure 1c, the trait "positive self-presenter" might be a more useful way to describe Ellen's constellation of goals and strategies, whereas Louise's constellation of goals and strategies might be better summarized (see Figure 1a) as involving "sociability" (Cheek & Buss, 1981) or "need for affiliation" (Murray, 1938). In short, although both Ellen and Louise use similar strategies, because these strategies are associated with different chronic goals, Louise and Ellen could be said to possess different traits.

Limitations

Although we would argue that most traits can be analyzed in terms of the four components outlined previously, there are some apparent exceptions, such as stylistic traits and abilities. However, they can still be naturally integrated into the present model. For instance, various stylistic traits may modify the way in which individuals carry out their plans and strategies. And certain abilities such as being intelligent or socially skilled can be viewed as social resources that are useful in carrying out a wide range of social plans.

APPLICATION OF THE MODEL

Self-Disclosure

How then would this model describe individuals who are high or low disclosers? When we claim that an individual possesses a trait to self-disclose across a broad range of situations, we are claiming that he or she chronically uses a particular strategy (disclosing about him- or herself) to achieve a subset of one or more goals that are frequently salient to the individual (e.g., intimacy, impressing others, knowing oneself and others, desiring attention). A high discloser would also be apt to have the resources and knowledge to successfully carry out these plans (e.g., one could not disclose about his or her deepest feelings if he or she has never examined these feelings and does not know how he or she feels) and a set of beliefs and expectancies that is apt to correspond to these disclosing tendencies (e.g., getting how one feels out in the open makes one feel a lot better). An individual apt to be low in self-disclosing tendencies might be an individual who has a chronic set of goals that involve avoiding close contact with others (e.g., needing privacy), strategies for achieving such goals (e.g., topics to avoid in conversing with others), resources for achieving these goals (e.g., the person may have developed excellent skills for deflecting the conversation away from "intimate" areas), and a corresponding belief system (e.g., "People will laugh at me if they really knew me," "If I really let this person know how I feel, she'll think I'm a real wimp").

How does this conceptualization of self-disclosure differ from previous approaches to viewing individual differences in self-disclosure? In earlier approaches, the emphasis was on individual differences in a particular kind of strategy: disclosing across a range of topics that varied in intimacy (Jourard & Lasakow, 1958) or across a range of situations (Chelune, 1976). These approaches have placed little emphasis on individuals' goals, beliefs, or resources in social interaction.

For example, examination of typical disclosure measures reveals that little explicit attention was paid to the goals of disclosing. There are no self-disclosure items such as "I often disclose in order to impress others" or "Sometimes I disclose about what I've gone through in order to help someone through a similar experience." Perhaps Chelune's (1976) measure comes closer than Jourard's to tapping into a range of goals by looking at different situations, although it is still unclear what the goals are in those situations.

Miller *et al.* (1983) have perhaps developed the most specific measure of self-disclosure. The items appear to be intimate in nature and are associated with an experimentally appropriate target (e.g., friend). Although still not explicit, there is apt to be more agreement concerning the implied goal(s) of disclosing intimate information to a close friend than disclosing intimate information to a stranger. It is perhaps this greater specificity in terms of the experimental or field situation and the greater clarity regarding presumed goals of the situation that have yielded greater predictability (Miller *et al.*, 1983).

But, we might ask, if we are interested in predicting individual differences in self-disclosure, why concern ourselves with goals? Because differences in goals may well be related to differences in levels and nature of disclosure and might account for differences in predictability for individual difference measures in self-disclosure across situations. In order to examine this possibility, let us consider different paradigms in disclosure that may have yielded differences in implied goals.

Two Paradigms Considered

Some of the work on individual differences in self-disclosure can be categorized into two research paradigms, an interview paradigm and a person by person (P × P) paradigm that will be examined separately. In the interview paradigm, a subject who has filled out a self-disclosure questionnaire responds to an interviewer's questions. Using the Jourard Self-Disclosure Questionnaire (JSDQ), Vondracek (1969) found no relationship between self-disclosure scores and disclosing behaviors, whereas Doster and Strickland (1971) found that low scorers tended to disclose more than high scorers. Using the Self-Disclosure Situational Survey (SDSS), Chelune (1976) found that high-scoring men disclosed more in an interview than low-scoring men, but the result was reversed for women.

In the second paradigm, the P × P paradigm, two subjects matched in self-disclosure as measured by the JSDQ interact with one another. In two studies using this paradigm, high-disclosing pairs disclosed more than low-disclosing pairs (Jourard & Resnick, 1970; Taylor, 1968).

These two paradigms present a different pattern of results. First, though the P × P (or dyadic paradigm) produces the expected pattern of results (high disclosers disclose more than low disclosers), the results from the interview paradigm are mixed, in several cases yielding reversals of the expected pattern (e.g., Chelune's results for women).

One possible explanation for the differences across paradigms is simply that the interview situations have different goals than do dyadic situations. Interview situations, it would seem, would be more likely to emphasize forming a good impression with one's disclosures, whereas in dyadic interactions the goal is more likely to be getting to know others and letting them get to know you. An examination of self-disclosure measures suggests that neither measure taps into how willing individuals would be to disclose to *an interviewer*. Both measures seem to make *willingness to provide accurate information about oneself* more salient than explicit concerns with self-presentation and the impression one will make on others. It seems reasonable that if these measures tap into the goal of getting to know others that they should be more predictive in those situations where that goal is more salient.

A direct examination of the importance of goals in influencing the nature and amount of disclosure is provided in work by Berg and Archer (1982). They made one of three interaction goals salient: (1) providing information about oneself to one's partner so that one's partner could form an accurate impression, (2) having a typical conversation, and (3) making a positive impression. These different sets of goals produced differences in both the type and amount of disclosure. For example, when the goal is to "provide information," subjects provided the most fact-oriented or descriptive disclosures compared to other conditions with different goals. And, after having heard a confederate disclose intimate information, subjects who were in the make-a-positive-impression condition were more likely to express sympathy or affect in their disclosures (give more evaluative disclosures) than those in the other goal conditions.

In terms of predicting behavior, this analysis suggests that in order to enhance predictability, we would need a measure that assessed willingness to disclose, given a variety of possible goals, and we would need a way of specifying the nature of the strategy employed (type of disclosure), given different likely salient goals. For the vast majority of people, unless we have some sense of which goals related to disclosing behaviors are apt to generally be salient to them and the nature of the situation in terms of eliciting certain goals, we may be hard pressed to predict self-disclosing tendencies across situations.

Maximizing Knowledge of Goals

How could we maximize our knowledge of a person's goals, given our present use of disclosure measures? First, we can simultaneously consider several individual difference variables within the person that may better identify the goals and strategies of him or her in a particular social context. Regarding disclosure, two relevant variables may involve (a) willingness to disclose in dyadic interactions and (b) an expressed interest in getting to know one's partner and being interested in what he or she has to say.

In one study (Miller, 1982), patterns of these two personality variables within the same individual were used to predict responsiveness (e.g., as measured by subjective judgments of raters and such objective behaviors as head nods, smiles, "uh hums," etc.) and disclosure in social interactions among strangers. Individuals who (1) did not indicate an interest in others *and* (2) reported themselves on a disclosure self-report measure to be low disclosers (to same-sex strangers) were in fact the least responsive individuals and disclosed the least in social interactions compared to all other types of individuals.

A second approach to maximizing goal knowledge is to consider the goals and strategies of both individuals in the interaction. Knowledge of the various goal relationships should allow us to better predict both individual and relationship outcomes. For example, if two people with a high need for intimacy get together, we should expect their goals to be compatible and the interaction to run smoothly.

Oftentimes, however, goals conflict. If one person is low in the need for intimacy, whereas the other is high, we should expect a major goal conflict as one individual tries to become intimate, whereas the individual low in the need for intimacy rebuffs the other's advances. What is important in deciding whether there will be agreement or conflict depends on the extent to which the other's goals and plans are instrumental to the attainment of one's own goals or whether they conflict with them. Thus, the submissive individual's goals and plans are instrumental to the dominant individual's attainment of his or her goals, whereas the nonaffiliative individual's goals and plans can block the affiliative individual's attainment of his or her goals.

In this disclosure literature, a number of studies can be viewed as having examined characteristics of both participants that are relevant to individual and relationship goals. For example, researchers have sometimes paired (using the dyadic paradigm) individuals who are high or low on disclosure measures with other individuals who are high or low on such measures. These 2 × 2 dyadic designs provide us with information not typically available using other paradigms: We have some information about the strategies and goals of both individuals in the interaction. In these paradigms, the typical finding is that when one of the participants is a high discloser, the level of disclosure for the individuals of the pair is high compared to low/low disclosing groups (Miller, 1982).

Researchers in self-disclosure (e.g., Chaikin & Derlega, 1974; Derlega, Harris, & Chaikin, 1973) have argued that this "reciprocity effect" results because recipients are under a social obligation to return a disclosure of comparable value (or intimacy) to the one that they have received. In terms of our theoretical framework, the high discloser's disclosing behavior may activate a social norm (e.g., disclose when disclosed to) or may eliminate the salience of goals that are in conflict with disclosing (e.g., this "open" person may be less likely to reject me, so I'm more likely to risk disclosing). High disclosers may provide a low discloser with a clearer situational norm or goal (being intimate with another) and perhaps the means (by following the example of the high discloser) to achieve it. Several people have argued that some people, like the high disclosers mentioned previously, may act as a type of environmental press (Murray, 1938), making certain goals (e.g., desire to become intimate or do the socially appropriate thing) more salient than others.

APPLICATION TO A RELATED CHARACTERISTIC: OPENERS

Up to this point, we have argued that traits can be viewed as particular constellations of goals, plans (and strategies), resources, and beliefs. Self-disclosure measures, we have argued, focus most on strategies and provide relatively little insight into subjects' goals and beliefs. Presumably, however, additional information can be provided either by relevant additional characteristics of the disclosing individual or by characteristics of the recipients of such disclosure. Such additional information may help to more clearly specify likely dyadic goals. Our theoretical framework argues that characteristics of recipients relevant to disclosure in dyadic interactions should be examined. Let us look at one of these relevant recipient characteristics.

As indicated in Figure 2, the Opener Scale (Miller et al., 1983) incorporates many of the components of a goal-based model. As originally conceived, the items on this scale fall into three distinct categories: (1) goals (and ends-beliefs) involving an interest in listening to others (e.g., "I enjoy listening to people"); (2) strategies involving interpersonal skills (e.g., "I can keep people talking about themselves," I encourage people to tell me how they are feeling"); and (3) beliefs about how others react to and perceive the actor (e.g., "People frequently tell me about themselves," "People feel relaxed around me," "People trust me with their secrets"). These items have been shown to load on a single factor and to have adequate test–retest and internal reliability (Miller, Berg, & Archer, 1983, Study 1). As indicated in Figure 2, the items also strongly suggest some implied goals (e.g., a desire to nurture, become intimate, seek close relationships with others), plans and strategies (e.g., listen attentively), beliefs (e.g., people are interesting), and resources (e.g., time, social skills).

By endorsing items on the Opener Scale, "high" openers would be reporting that they have a number of goals, strategies, resources, and beliefs that we hypothesized would be consistent with engaging in a set of responsive behaviors, encouraging others to disclose, enabling people

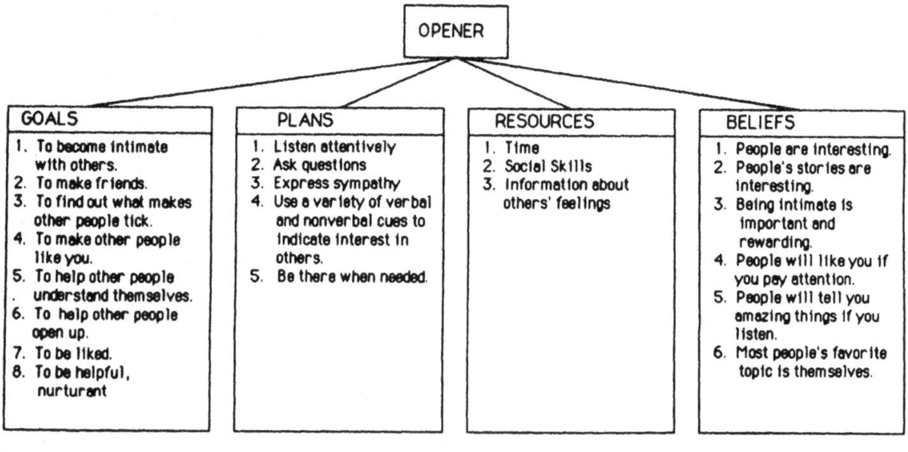

FIGURE 2. An analysis of the Opener Scale in terms of the model's four components.

to feel comfortable, and encouraging the development of friendships. In fact, data collected up to now support many of these hypotheses.

In one study (Miller *et al.*, 1983, Study 2), pairs of women interacted during a 10-minute tape-recorded session. One woman, chosen on the basis of her opener scores (high or low) asked a second woman questions given to her by the experimenter. This second woman, who was either dispositionally a high or low discloser (on the basis of her stated willingness to disclose to a same-sex stranger), answered the questions the first woman asked. The responses of this second woman were tape-recorded and rated for intimacy by independent raters, blind to the subjects' personality data. Were the high-opener women more successful at eliciting intimate disclosures from their low-disclosing partners? Yes. With high-opener partners, low disclosers revealed more intimately than they did with low-opener partners.

Another study (Miller *et al.*, 1983, Study 3) examined whether high openers might be well-liked and sought-after listeners. In a study among acquaintances and friends at a sorority house, women who were high openers were like more and disclosed to more intimately as determined by peer ratings from their sorority sisters. Openers in the Miller *et al.* study (1983) were especially likely to be disclosed to by women who had indicated that they were willing to disclose intimately to same sex friends (high disclosers). It is interesting to note here that disclosure measures involving a different target (and presumably different goals) of disclosure were not predictive.

In both sets of studies, individual difference measures of disclosure provided an incomplete picture. Additional information about the recipient's characteristics, however, led to significant predictions about disclosing in relationships. Given our theoretical model, these findings might suggest that openers may more clearly provide an atmosphere conducive to pursuing intimacy as an important goal in the relationship. These findings suggest that patterns of personality variables across individuals provide additional information about the likely goals and strategies to be used in a particular interaction. Not only are openers better liked by their acquaintances and more adept at eliciting disclosure compared to low openers, they also report having more close friends (Miller, 1982) and have been found to report being less lonely (Berg & Peplau, 1982).

Thus, regarding their ability to elicit disclosures from others and the ability to establish more intimate and closer relationships, high openers appear to meet with considerable success in reaching their apparent social goals. How do they accomplish these goals?

High openers seem to engage in different strategies in social interaction than low openers. In one study, Purvis, Dabbs, and Hopper (1984) matched same-sex pairs on Opener Scores; their nonverbal and verbal behaviors were recorded and subjective judgments of interpersonal involvement were made. High/high opener pairs tended to gaze at one another more and were judged as spending more time involved in each others conversations than were low/low opener pairs.

Additional research (Miller, 1982) on nonverbal and verbal behaviors examined the role that patterns of opener and disclosure scores played in influencing subjects' responsive behaviors (e.g., head nods, smiling, uh hums, reallys, yesses, OKs, etc.) and judgments of responsiveness made by independent raters. Women who were low openers and low disclosers were judged "least responsive," and behaviorally they engaged in fewer responsive behaviors than individuals with any other pattern of opener/discloser characteristics.

This series of studies offers converging evidence that low openers are less responsive and attentive listeners who are less adept at getting others to "open up." Presumably, low openers lack important goals, strategies, beliefs, and/or resources that would enable them to pursue and achieve this end. On the other hand, high openers appear to have the goals, plans, resources, and beliefs necessary to act as a strong environmental press (Murray, 1938), altering others' goals or the perceived acceptability of strategies (such as disclosing) in this interpersonal situation.

A BROADER THEORETICAL MODEL

Common Descriptive Language for Persons and Situations

Although we believe that the goal-based model of personality presented here is useful in better understanding individual difference findings in self-disclosure, it should be apparent that this model can be more broadly applied, forming the basis of a general model of personality and of the interaction between personality and the social situation. The present analysis of traits provides an explicit conceptual framework for a general model of personality. The other part of the framework, specifying the nature of social situations, has been provided by Argyle, Furnham, and Graham's (1981) analysis of situations. Several of the major aspects of situations that they identify have a parallel in our analysis of traits. In the following paragraphs, we will briefly review those components that are most relevant to our analysis.

First, according to Argyle *et al.*, the chief component of a situation is the goals whose satisfaction it affords. Second, situations have associated with them various rules that govern the appropriateness of behavior in that situation. Third, different situations have different roles that people can fill. Each role specifies particular behaviors that are appropriate for people filling those roles. Finally, associated with any given situation are elements and sequences of behavior that can be used to attain goals within that situation.

Thus, both personality and situation can be analyzed in a common language within an explicit conceptual framework for the analysis of person–situation interactions. We can think of potential person–situation interactions in terms of the interplay between the goals, plans, and resources of the individual and the goals, plans, and roles that are associated with the situation in which the individual finds him or herself.

The present approach bears a strong similarity to Murray's (1938) attempt to characterize person and situation in a common language. Murray referred to various characteristics of the individual that directed behavior as needs, while referring to aspects of the situation that activated those need as press. Thus, if an individual had a need for achievement or a need for affiliation, the situation would be characterized in terms of its press for achievement or its press for affiliation. However, the present formulation goes beyond Murray in its emphasis on the additional components of plans, resources, and beliefs and the way in which these additional characteristics of person and situation also interact. At this point, let us examine how these components are related to one another in a general process model of personality.

Beyond Description: A Process Model of Personality

An outline of the model is presented in Figure 3. The first step is the monitoring of both the external environment and internal states. When we monitor the environment, we pay attention to such things as other people's behavior, the nature of the situation, and our own behavior. When we monitor our internal states, we pay attention to a host of things such as our self-concept and our goals.

This monitoring has several results. One result is the activation of the goals that guide our behavior. A number of different factors affect the activation of goals. For instance, a perceived discrepancy between what we wish to be the case and what is the case often activates a goal. A threat to our self-concept may motivate us to try to reassert the way we view ourselves (Swann, 1983; Swann & Read, 1981a, b). Or noticing that we have failed to live up to our standards for behavior may motivate us to meet those standards. In addition, various goals may be activated when we perceive that the particular situation we are in is particularly appropriate for the attainment of some goal. For example, if we generally desire to become more intimate with people, then finding ourselves alone with a potential friend may make that goal much more salient.

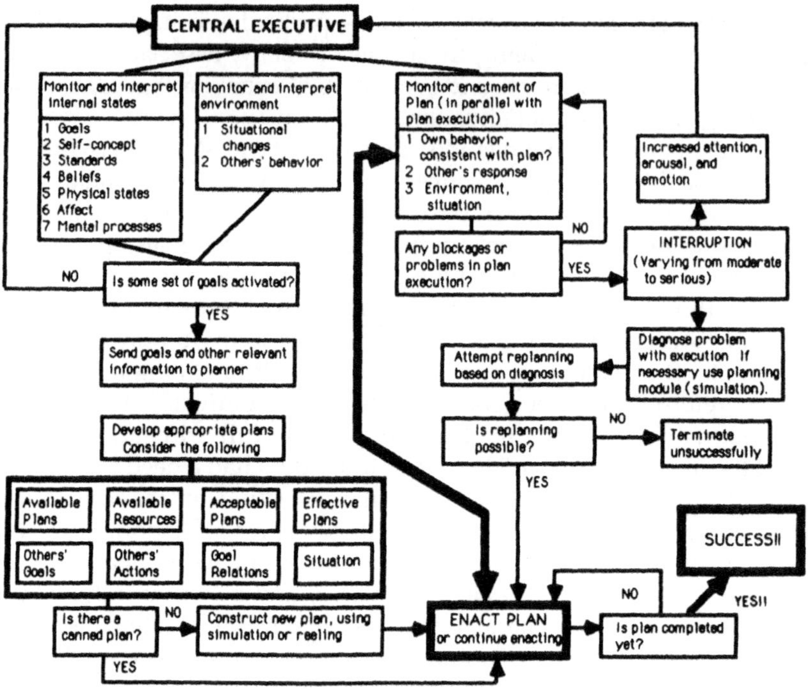

FIGURE 3. A flowchart representing the general process model.

An additional factor that plays an important role in the likelihood of activation of a goal is the importance of that goal to an individual. Presumably, the more important the goal, the greater the likelihood that it will be activated. Thus individual differences in the importance of various goals would seem to be important sources of behavioral variability across individuals. Finally, greater internal focus or self-awareness (e.g., Carver & Scheier, 1981; Duval & Wicklund, 1972) should increase the chance that goals are activated by internal cues, whereas greater focus on the environment should increase the chance that goals are activated by external cues.

Once some goal or set of goals is activated, we must decide what kind of action to take and what to do. As can be seen from the model in Figure 3, the goal or set of goals, along with relevant additional information, such as knowledge about the situation we are in, is used to develop an appropriate plan. To develop a plan, we must take into account a tremendous number of different factors. First, we need to consider what we know about the situation we are in. For instance, what goals are easily afforded (Argyle, Furnham, & Graham, 1981), and what resources are available. Second, if there are multiple goals, we must consider various relations among them, such as which are most important, which conflict, and which might possibly be achieved by the same plan. Third, we must assess the relationship among our goals and actions and the possible goals and actions of those with whom we are interacting. Fourth, we must assess what plans seem to be currently known and available for achieving our goals in this particular situation. Further, we need to know whether these plans are likely to be effective in achieving our goals and are socially and morally acceptable. Finally, we need to assess whether we possess the resources necessary to carry out possible plans. And if we do possess the resources but they are limited, we need to decide whether the benefits of attaining our goals are worth the expenditure of resources such as time, money, effort, and the like.

One way to look at this planning process is in terms of our earlier analysis of person–situation interactions. Essentially, the individual is trying to integrate his or her various personality characteristics (in terms of various goals, plans, resources, and beliefs) with the goals, plans, roles, and rules associated with the particular social situation.

People's expectancies about likely outcomes and the reactions of others play an important role in many parts of the planning process. For instance, an individual's expectancies influence which particular plan components are chosen and even whether a developed plan will be enacted. In fact, they may even effect whether people attempt to plan. An individual may give up without even attempting to construct a plan, saying, "Why bother. Every time I'm in this kind of situation I mess up!"

If we are fortunate, a canned plan or script (Schank & Abelson, 1977) may already exist, and we will not need to spend very much time in the planning process. We can just take the script and act it out.

However, frequently we do not have such canned plans available and must spend some time developing them. One way to develop plans is to mentally simulate the enactment of a possible plan or sequence of plans (Wilensky, 1983). That is, one can mentally try out different plans or parts of plans, see how they fit together, and simulate how both people and the environment will respond to those plans. Such simulations are often useful in identifying potential problems, such as undesirable interactions between components or unfavorable reactions from other people. (For a detailed and insightful analysis of human planning, see Wilensky, 1983.)

The completeness of this simulation probably depends greatly on the extent to which an individual is internally focused. The greater the degree to which an individual chronically focuses internally on his or her own mental processes (e.g., private self-consciousness [Carver & Scheier, 1981]) and thus focuses on this simulation and its development, the more complete and adequate the simulation should be.

Once we have developed a plan, we can start to enact it. During enactment, we continually monitor our performance, the responses of our interaction partners, and the nature of the situation. This monitoring occurs in parallel with the actual behavior. There are two reasons why this process is important. First, in most situations, it is not possible to develop a detailed plan ahead of time. Oftentimes, we can just sketch out the broad strokes and later fill out the details as we reach that part of the plan. In order to do that we need to continually monitor our performance. Second, rarely do our plans work out precisely as intended. Thus, we need to be able to deal with such problems as they arise.

Problems during the enactment of our plans produce an interruption (Mandler, 1975) that increases both our attention to what is happening and our emotional response. Further, this interruption leads us to try to diagnose the problems and then throws us back into a replanning mode where we use our diagnosis to try to come up with a new plan that can overcome the source of the interruption. If such replanning is possible, we proceed to enact the new plan. However, if replanning is impossible or impractical, we will stop, having failed to attain our goals.

Implications for Self-Disclosure

Past research on individual differences in self-disclosure may have presented a conflicting pattern of results for self-disclosure measures (Cozby, 1973) because previous disclosure measures were not concerned with subjects' explicit goals when disclosing. But, for newer measures, when the disclosure goals appear clearer, predictability for disclosure measures has been improved (Miller *et al.*, 1983).

As suggested in previous research (Miller *et al.*, 1983) and the present theoretical framework, additional personality information about the recipient as well as the discloser should provide us with clearer notions of the salient goals of individuals in particular situations. Such Person × Person approaches have already proven to be useful ones within this literature (Miller, 1982; Miller *et al.*, 1983). But, given the complexity of the individuals and situations that are influencing disclosure, we need to ask (1) which patterns should we examine, (2) which goals are apt to be salient in a particular setting, (3) how important are these goals to specific individuals, and (4) what plans are apt to be enacted (given a particular set of resources and beliefs).

Beyond these questions are some additional long-term issues. For example, given that we will probably need to consider concurrently many different components of personality for individuals and also consider the possible interactions of person and situational variables, our methods will need to keep pace with the complexity of our theoretical development. One promising approach might be to use computer simulations to concretely model the likely outcomes of various combinations of specific goals (varying in prominence), strategies, beliefs, and resources in various dyadic interactions. Such an approach may not be as far into the future as one might expect. For example, our approach employs a language similar to one that is currently being successfully applied in the development of computer simulations of human planning (Wilensky, 1983).

The present model also suggests that we may want to rephrase some of the research questions that we have been asking about individual differences in self-disclosure. Thus, instead of asking "which individuals are more likely to disclose?", we may want to ask the following questions: (1) "What are the different goals (e.g., seeking intimacy, self-knowledge, succorance, attention, friendship development, positive impression formation) that may lead to disclosing about oneself and how are they similar and different from one another?"; (2) "are there differences in disclosing patterns for different goals (e.g., disclosing positive self-information associated with wanting to appear competent)?"; and (3) "given a particular interaction goal, how do individuals differ in their beliefs, resources, and strategies regarding disclosure of particular kinds of self-related information?" For example, in assessing beliefs, we could determine how important it is for individuals to share intimate information with those whom they consider friends. We could also assess whether and what subjects know about various self-disclosing strategies that research suggests are effective in leading to certain goals (Archer & Burleson, 1980; Miller & Morgan, 1985). And we could assess the extent to which individuals use common, prototypical strategies (cf. Buss & Craik, 1983, 1984) or very distinctive strategies (cf. Allport, 1937), given particular goals and traits.

These new questions take us beyond the relatively simplistic views of individual differences regarding disclosure that were the basis for early measures of it (e.g., Jourard & Lasakow, 1958). Such early measures promoted several generations of self-disclosure research (cf. Archer, 1979; Cozby, 1973; Goodstein & Reinecker, 1974), but as our knowledge of self-disclosure and the processes associated with disclosing expanded rapidly, our disclosure measures (and our conceptualizations of such individual differences) may have lagged behind (cf. Cozby, 1973). Now we would like to propose that it may be time to rethink, as our model might suggest, (1) our goals in developing such measures, (2) our strategies for accomplishing such goals, (3) our knowledge of disclosure, and (4) the resources that we can bring to bear to develop a better understanding of why individuals differ in the level and patterns of their disclosing given a variety of interpersonal goals.

Implications for Personality

The present framework presents what may appear at first blush to be a somewhat "radical" approach to personality. After all, it takes traits and seems to chop them up into a number of components much as if we were looking at chemical compounds instead of traits and trying to ascertain the "essential" elements. What is more, we have chosen as components elements that seem to have an unfamiliar ring (goals, strategies, beliefs, and resources). Further, unlike many traditional nomothetic approaches to describing personality, this framework addresses processes as well as descriptions of personality and seems "idiographic" in nature.

However, what we are proposing has a long and venerable tradition in personality studies (Allport, 1937; Murray, 1938). For personologists, the framework presented here may seem like a wedding of a variety of historical as well as current theoretical approaches to personality. For example, Allport (1929) noted that the

> only really significant congruences in personality must be sought in the sphere of conation. It is the striving of a man which binds together the traits, and which shows how essentially harmonious they are in their determination of his behavior (pp. 14–27)

And, in advocating a dynamic theory, Allport (1937) noted that his theory of personality

> breaks with the nomothetic tradition completely, and regards motives as personalized systems of tensions, in which the core of impulse is not to be divorced from the images, ideas of goal, past experience, capacities, and style of conduct employed in obtaining the goal. The whole system is integral. . . . Only individualized patterns of motives have the capacity to select stimuli, to control and direct segmental tensions, to initiate responses and to render them equivalent, in ways that are consistent with, and characteristic of, the person himself. (pp. 320–321)

Murray's (1938) theory of personality focused on those traits (using a more nomothetic approach) that were motivational in nature. In so doing, he viewed traits as needs (e.g., need for dominance, affiliation, achievement). Such needs were viewed as constructs that stand

> for a force . . . which organizes perception, apperception, intellection, conation and action in such a way as to transform in a certain direction an existing, unsatisfying situation. A need is sometimes provoked directly by internal processes of a certain kind . . . but, more frequently . . . by the occurrence of one of a few commonly effective press (or by anticipatory images of such a press). Thus, it manifests itself by leading the organism to search for or to avoid encountering or, when encountered, to attend and respond to certain kinds of press. It may even engender illusory perceptions and delusory apperceptions. . . . Each need is characteristically accompanied by a particular feeling or emotion and tends to use certain modes (subneeds and actones) to further its trend. It may be weak or intense, momentary or enduring. But, usually it persists and gives rise to a certain course of overt behavior (or fantasy), which (if the organism is competent and external opposition not insurmountable) changes the initiating circumstance in such a way as to bring about an end situation which stills (appeases or satisfies) the organism (p. 124)

And, concepts such as "plans" and "goals" have frequently surfaced as central concepts in theories concerning personality (cf. Allston, 1970, 1975; Carbonnell, 1979; Carson, 1969; Mischel, 1973, 1977).

CONCLUSIONS

So, what does this new framework buy us in the study of personality? First, it allows us to view traits in both nomothetic and idiographic terms. That is, when we refer to individual differences in sociability we can talk about a configuration of goals, strategies, beliefs, and resources that most people would refer to as prototypically involving "sociability" (e.g., a nomothetic perspective). At the same time, the exact set of goals (and their organization and salience), strategies, resources, and beliefs for any particular individual are going to be unique (e.g., idiographic in nature). This model provides a language for discussing this unique organization.

Second, the present approach provides us with a unique framework to examine the relationship among different traits. For example, it draws our attention to the way in which conceptually different traits (e.g., loneliness and sociability) may be related to each other in terms of these components. And it emphasizes the need to look at the unique organization of traits within each individual (e.g., which ones are important to this person, what other traits conflict with which other traits, and so forth) if we wish to accurately predict behavior.

Third, most models of personality tend to be restricted in how they view personality. They seem to focus more on discussing personality in fairly descriptive terms (Cattell, 1965) or in "process" terms (Mischel,

1973). The present model provides a language that allows us to both describe personality (in terms of its components) and to talk about the process by which a trait guides behavior.

Fourth, the present model suggests a way in which various aspects of the self (e.g., self-awareness and the self-concept) may be concretely associated with various goals, strategies, resources, and beliefs. Thus, for example, although most of the time most individuals may be relatively unaware of the goals that are salient to them, some individuals, those high in private self-consciousness (Carver & Scheier, 1981), would presumably be more aware of their goals, beliefs, affective reactions, and plans than others. In addition, the present model specifies that the self-concept often plays an important role in initiating goals and specifying strategies of action regarding particular traits. Thus the present model explicitly examines the self-concept within a general model of personality.

Fifth, although earlier personality psychologists (Allport, 1937; Carson, 1969; Murray, 1938) realized that understanding the behavior of individuals required examining the role of the situation, a good common language for describing the interaction of person and situation remained elusive. The present model moves us closer to such a common language.

We opened this chapter with two characters, Bob and Bernice, as they began a new relationship. "Why did Bob disclose so intimately?", we asked. The present framework suggests a novel way of viewing this question, in terms of Bob's goals, plans, resources, and beliefs. Such a goal-based model of personality allows us new insights into past findings and raises some exciting new questions for future research. Our theory though, like Bob and Bernice's relationship, is in its infancy. We invite, you, the reader to join us in its development.

REFERENCES

Allport, G. W. (1929). The study of personality by the intuitive method. *Journal of Abnormal and Social Psychology, 24,* 14–27.

Allport, G. W. (1937). *Personality: A psychological interpretation.* New York: Henry Holt.

Allston, W. P. (1970). Toward a logical geography of personality: Traits and deeper lying personality characteristics. (pp. 59–92). In H. D. Krefer & M. K. Munitz (Eds.), *Mind, science, and history.* Albany, NY: State University of New York.

Allston, W. P. (1975). Traits, consistency and conceptual alternatives for personality theory. *Journal for the Theory of Social Behaviour, 5,* 17–48.

Archer, R. L. (1979). Role of personality and the social situation. (p. 28–58). In G. J. Chelune (Ed.), *Self-disclosure.* San Francisco, Jossey-Bass.

Archer, R. L., & Burleson, J. A. (1980). The effects of timing of self-disclosure on attraction and reciprocity. *Journal of Personality and Social Psychology, 38,* 120–130.

Argyle, M., Furnham, A. & Graham, J. A. (1981). *Social situations*. Cambridge, England: Cambridge University Press.

Berg, J. H., & Archer, R. L. (1982). Responses to self-disclosure and interaction goals. *Journal of Experimental Social Psychology, 18*, 501–512.

Berg, J. H., & Peplau, L. A. (1982). Loneliness: The relationship of self-disclosure and androgyny. *Personality and Social Psychology Bulletin, 8*, 624–630.

Burhenne, D., & Mirels, H. L. (1970). Self-disclosure in self-descriptive essays. *Journal of Consulting and Clinical Psychology, 35*, 409–413.

Buss, D. M., & Craik, K. H. (1983). The act frequency approach to personality. *Psychological Review, 90*, 105–126.

Buss, D. M., & Craik, K. H. (1984). Acts, dispositions, and personality. *Progress in Experimental Personality Research, 13*, 241–301.

Carbonnell, J. G. (1979). *Subjective understanding: Computer models of belief systems*. (Computer Science Tech. Rep. No. 150, Doctoral dissertation, Yale University.

Carson, R. C. (1969). *Interaction concepts of personality*. Chicago: Aldine.

Carver, C. S., & Scheier, M. F. (1981). *Attention and self-regulation: A control-theory approach to human behavior*. New York: Springer-Verlag.

Cash, T. F. (1975). Self-disclosure in the acquaintance process: Effects of sex, physical attractiveness and approval motivation (Doctoral dissertation, George Peabody College for Teachers, 1974). *Dissertation Abstracts International, 35*, 3572B.

Cattell, R. B. (1965). *The scientific analysis of personality*. Chicago: Aldine.

Chaikin, A. L., & Derlega, V. J. (1974). Liking for the norm-breaker in self-disclosure. *Journal of Personality, 42*, 117–129.

Cheek, J. M., & Buss, A. H. (1981). Shyness and sociability. *Journal of Personality and Social Psychology, 41*, 330–337.

Chelune, G. J. (1975). Self-disclosure: An elaboration of its basic dimensions. *Psychological Reports, 36*, 79–85.

Chelune, G. J. (1976). The Self-Disclosure Situations Survey: A new approach to measuring self-disclosure. *JSAS Catalog of Selected Documents in Psychology, 6* (1367), 111–112.

Chelune, G. J. (1979). Measuring openness in interpersonal communication. In G. J. Chelune (Ed.)., *Self-disclosure* (pp. 1–21). San Francisco, CA: Jossey-Bass.

Cozby, P. C. (1973). Self-disclosure: A literature review. *Psychological Bulletin, 79*, 73–91.

Derlega, V. J., Harris, M. S., & Chaikin, A. L. (1973). Self-disclosure and reciprocity, liking, and the deviant. *Journal of Experimental Social Psychology, 9*, 227–284.

Doster, J. A., & Strickland, B. R. (1971). Disclosing of verbal material as a function of information requested, information about the interviewer, and interviewee differences. *Journal of Consulting and Clinical Psychology, 37*, 187–194.

Duval, S., & Wicklund, R. A. (1972). *A theory of objective self-awareness*. New York: Academic Press.

Ehrlich, J. H., & Graven, D. B. (1971). Reciprocal self-disclosure in a dyad. *Journal of Experimental Social Psychology, 7*, 389–400.

Foa, E. B., & Foa, U. G. (1974). *Societal structures of the mind*. Springfield, IL: Thomas.

Goodstein, L. D., & Reinecker, V. M. (1974). Factors affecting self-disclosure: A review of the literature. In Brendan A. Maher (Ed.), *Progress in experimental personality research* (Vol. 7, pp. 49–77). New York: Academic Press.

Jourard, S. M. (1959). Self-disclosure and other-cathexis. *Journal of Abnormal and Social Psychology, 59*, 428–431.

Jourard, S. M., & Lasakow, P. (1958). Some factors in self-disclosure. *Journal of Abnormal and Social Psychology, 56*, 91–98.

Jourard, S. M., & Resnick, J. L. (1970). The effect of high-revealing subjects on the self-disclosure of low-revealing subjects. *Journals of Humanistic Psychology, 10*, 84–93.

Mandler, G. (1975). *Mind and emotion*. New York: Wiley.

Miller, G. A., Galenter, E., & Pribram, K. H. (1960). *Plans and the structure of behavior*. New York: Holt, Rinehart, & Winston.

Miller, L. C. (1982). *Patterns of two individual differences relevant to recipient and revealer roles in dyadic interactions*. Unpublished doctoral dissertation, University of Texas at Austin.

Miller, L. C., & Morgan, F. (1985). *Should I brag? Effects of negative, positive and boastful disclosures*. Unpublished manuscript, Scripps College, Claremont, CA.

Miller, L. C., Berg, J. H., & Archer, R. L. (1983). Openers: Individuals who elicit intimate self-disclosure. *Journal of Personality and Social Psychology, 44*, 1234–1244.

Mischel, W. (1973). Toward a cognitive social learning reconceptualization of personality. *Psychological Review, 80*, 252–283.

Mischel, W. (1977). On the future of personality measurement. *American Psychologist, 32*, 246–254.

Morton, T. L. (1978). Intimacy and reciprocity of exchange: A comparison of spouses and strangers. *Journal of Personality and Social Psychology, 36*, 72–81.

Murray, H. (1938). *Explorations in personality*. New York: Oxford University Press.

Pederson, D. M., & Breglio, V. J. (1968). The correlation of two self-disclosure inventories with actual self-disclosure: A validity study. *Journal of Psychology, 68*, 291–298.

Purvis, J. A., Dabbs, J., & Hopper, C. (1984). The "Opener": Skilled user of facial expression and speech pattern. *Personality and Social Psychology Bulletin, 10*, 61–66.

Rubin, Z., & Shenker, S. (1978). Friendship, proximity, and self-disclosure. *Journal of Personality, 46*, 1–22.

Schank, R. C., & Abelson, R. P. (1977). *Scripts, plans, goals, and understanding*. Hillsdale, NJ: Erlbaum.

Swann, W. B. (1983). Self-verification: Bringing social reality into harmony with the self. In J. Suls & A. G. Greenwald (Eds.), *Psychological perspectives on the self*. (Vol. 2, pp. 33–66). Hillsdale, NJ: Erlbaum.

Swann, W. B., & Read, S. J. (1981a). Self-verification processes: How we sustain our self-perceptions. *Journal of Experimental Social Psychology, 17*, 351–372.

Swann, W. B., & Read, S. J. (1981b). Acquiring self-knowledge: The search for feedback that fits. *Journal of Personality and Social Psychology, 41*, 1119–1128.

Taylor, D. A. (1968). The development of interpersonal relationships: Social penetration processes. *Journal of Social Psychology, 75*, 79–90.

Vondracek, F. W. (1969). The study of self-disclosure in experimental interviews. *Journal of Psychology, 72*, 55–59.

Wilensky, R. (1983). *Planning and understanding: A computational approach to human reasoning*. Reading, MA: Addison-Wesley.

4
Private Self-Consciousness and Self-Disclosure

MARK H. DAVIS and STEPHEN L. FRANZOI

What types of persons are more or less likely to self-disclose? That is, what individual differences exist between those who voluntarily reveal personal information to others and those who avoid such intimate self-revelation? Recent attempts to survey the evidence concerning this question have not been especially encouraging. For example, Archer (1979), in a review of the empirical attempts to link self-disclosure with personality characteristics of the discloser, stressed the relative dearth of strong and consistent results. Among the few features that do appear to be characteristic of disclosers are a lack of introversion, a lack of neuroticism, and a tendency toward impulsivity. However, despite numerous attempts to demonstrate links with many other measures of psychological functioning, Archer's conclusion was that at present a "hazy, confused portrait is all that can be distilled from some twenty years of research" (p. 38).

Most of these previous efforts attempted to link disclosure with some measure of personality *dysfunction*; that is, the theoretical rationale for the research was that self-disclosure was therapeutic and that greater disclosure should therefore be associated with measures of personality adjustment. However, not all personality characteristics can be so easily

MARK H. DAVIS • Department of Psychology, Eckerd College, St. Petersburg, Florida, 33733. **STEPHEN L. FRANZOI** • Department of Psychology, Marquette University, Milwaukee, Wisconsin 53233.

conceptualized on the adjustment-maladjustment continuum, and some of these characteristics may quite logically be expected to demonstrate a relationship with self-disclosure. Recently, for example, in a series of investigations we have identified a consistent relation between a particular personality trait and the tendency to disclose intimate self-knowledge to others. This trait, *private self-consciousness,* refers to the dispositional tendency to engage in a particular kind of psychological state termed private self-awareness. *Private self-awareness* is a psychological state in which one is attentive to the more private and covert aspects of oneself. These aspects can include one's emotional states, motives, and reflections about past experiences. Thus, the personality trait of private self-consciousness locates people on a continuum according to their private self-awareness tendencies. Since this personality construct was first introduced in the mid-1970s (Fenigstein, Scheier, & Buss, 1975), hundreds of studies have investigated its behavioral consequences.

In this chapter, we will be describing the association between private self-consciousness and the tendency to self-disclose, and we will be doing so in three stages. We will first summarize and briefly discuss a series of recent investigations in which we discovered a consistent positive relation between individual differences in private self-consciousness and the tendency to disclose in depth concerning private personal thoughts and feelings. Second, we will outline a variety of possible causal explanations for this observed relationship; some of these explanations are based on hypothesized motivational processes and some on nonmotivational processes. Finally, after presenting these explanations, we will compare their relative strengths and weaknesses and propose some general research strategies for better evaluating the adequacy of each as an explanation for the self-consciousness/self-disclosure linkage.

THE SELF-CONSCIOUSNESS/DISCLOSURE LINKAGE: INITIAL DEMONSTRATIONS

Our original examination of the self-consciousness and self-disclosure relation came about as part of a larger investigation in which we utilized a simple conceptual model linking personality variables, social behaviors, and psychological well-being. In part, this model assumes that personality characteristics often influence psychological well-being through the mediating variables of specific social behaviors. That is, measures of psychological well-being (for example, loneliness) are most influenced by specific, relevant social behaviors (such as self-disclosure), which in turn are to some degree influenced by dispositions of the individual (such as private self-consciousness). Of course, the general nature of this model allows an examination of numerous personality, social, and well-being variables other than these three examples. For the purposes of this chapter, however, we will limit our focus to a consideration of the self-consciousness and disclosure link.

HIGH-SCHOOL STUDENTS

Our first study testing the implications of this model was an investigation of the personality and social determinants of loneliness among adolescents (Franzoi & Davis, 1985). Participants were 442 high-school students who were administered a classroom survey that included a 10-item measure of private self-consciousness from the Self-Consciousness Scale (SCS: Fenigstein *et al.*, 1975), a shortened version of the Self-Disclosure Inventory (SDI: Miller, Berg, & Archer, 1983), and the UCLA Loneliness Scale (Russell, Peplau, & Cutrona, 1980). Using structural equation techniques (LISREL V), we successfully tested a theoretical model designed to describe the causal relations existing between the measures of loneliness, self-disclosure to peers and parents, and specific antecedent variables, among those being private self-consciousness. In our analysis, we found that high private self-conscious adolescents tended to self-disclose more to their same-age friends than did low private self-conscious adolescents. Further, this tendency toward peer self-disclosure resulted in the high-disclosing adolescents feeling less lonely than those who tended not to self-disclose. One year later at the same testing site, these findings were replicated (Davis & Franzoi, 1986). The general nature of these results is displayed visually in Figure 1.

In both studies, the findings were consistent with our expectation that private self-consciousness was especially potent as a predictor of *peer* self-disclosure as opposed to disclosure to parents. Such a pattern was expected because it seemed likely to us that a personality variable would be a more powerful influence on disclosure among persons roughly equal in age and status (such as peers), whereas disclosure to persons markedly different in age and status (such as parents) would be more affected by role requirements of the parent–child relationship and by specific characteristics of the parents. Our results indicated that the educational level of the parents and the adolescents' perceptions of their parents' love for them significantly influenced the adolescents' willingness to self-disclose to them. Thus, the conclusion suggested by these studies is that among U.S. adolescents, an habitual focus of attention on private self-aspects tends to increase the willingness to disclose private information primarily to peers.

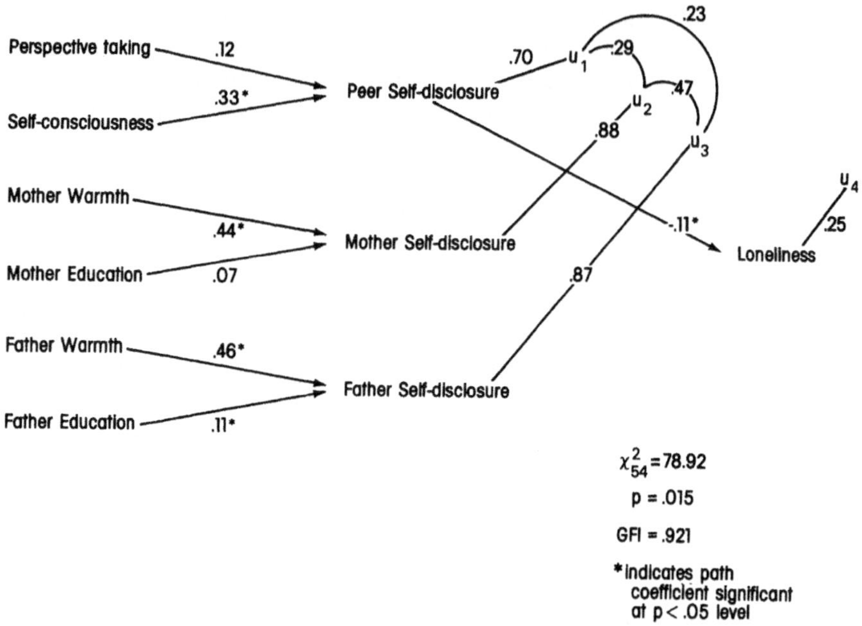

FIGURE 1. Results for the first high-school study. "Adolescent Self-Disclosure and Loneliness: Private Self-Consciousness and Parental Influences" by S. L. Franzoi and M. H. Davis, 1985, *Journal of Personality and Social Psychology, 48,* p. 775. Copyright 1985 by the American Psychological Association. Reprinted by permission.

College Students

Although these findings may be safely generalizable to American adolescents, it was less clear to us that the relation between private self-consciousness and self-disclosure could be applied to different age groups and different types of social relationships. With this in mind, we next conducted a study in which we collected information on the dating relationships of college couples (Franzoi, Davis, & Young, 1985). Our purpose was first to determine whether a slightly older sample's private self-consciousness scores would be related to willingness to self-disclose to an intimate other, and second, whether this self-disclosure would affect feelings of satisfaction in the dating relationship.

The survey sample consisted of 131 heterosexual couples, most of whom were dating one another exclusively, and some of whom (approximately 25%) were actually married or engaged. As in the adolescent studies, the SCS and SDI were included in the survey, along with a modified version of the Marital Adjustment Test (Locke, 1951) to measure each partner's satisfaction in the relationship. Following hierarchical regression analyses of the data, we found that for both males and females, one's level of self-disclosure was significantly and positively affected by one's own level of private self-consciousness and that degree of self-disclosure, in turn, positively influenced one's satisfaction with the relationship. Thus, an indirect influence of private self-consciousness on satisfaction could be clearly seen. Further, when the effects of disclosure on satisfaction were controlled, no positive effect of private self-consciousness on satisfaction was apparent, supporting the view that any effect of private self-consciousness on satisfaction is due to its impact on disclosure. These findings, in concert with the results from the adolescent loneliness studies, suggest that habitual private self-attention need not lead to social isolation but rather can facilitate an intimate social sharing that reduces loneliness and increases satisfaction with social relationships. Given the composition of our samples, this statement would seem to be safely applicable to roughly middle-class individuals in their early teens to mid-20s.

Of course, we are not alone in claiming that self-disclosure can have salutary effects on social functioning and psychological well-being. Self-disclosure has long been seen as an important contributor to intimate social relationships and mental health (e.g., Jourard, 1964). Although the linkage between amount of disclosure and psychological health does not seem to be entirely straightforward (inappropriately high levels of disclosure may be as damaging as too little disclosure), most would agree that at least moderate levels of disclosure are psychologically beneficial to the discloser. Given the generally desirable effects of self-disclosure on social and psychological well-being, then, it would seem that the facilitating effect of private self-consciousness on self-disclosure is largely a beneficial one and bodes well for those high in private self-consciousness. Given this link between private self-consciousness and self-disclosure, our attention has begun to turn toward the question of how this relation is produced. What is it about attention to private self-aspects that leads to heightened disclosure? Before addressing this question, however, one final point must be considered: the issue of alternative causal interpretations of the self-consciousness/self-disclosure association.

Alternative Interpretations

One way to interpret the stable and consistent association between private self-consciousness and self-disclosure is, as we have done thus far, to interpret it as evidence of a causal process by which self-consciousness affects self-disclosure. Although this may be the correct interpretation, there are two other causal possibilities that should be considered. One obvious alternative interpretation is that the hypothesized causal direction is simply reversed, with self-disclosure instead producing greater private self-consciousness. That is, it is possible that disclosing intimate private self-aspects to another results in an increased habitual attentiveness to private thoughts and feelings. For example, such a development could be imagined for one who enters into a psychotherapeutic relationship where the social definition of the situation is one in which the client is expected to self-disclose. Prior to entering into the therapeutic relationship, the person may not have been habitually self-attentive, but this type of active and ongoing self-revelation may result in a heightening of the person's habitual attentiveness to private self-aspects. Stated another way, persons who seldom, if ever, disclose to others about personal feelings, fears, or aspirations may never develop the self-examining style characteristic of those high in private self-consciousness. The second possibility is that there is a reciprocal causal relation between the two variables. That is, a dispositional tendency to analyze oneself may make one more likely to self-disclose to others, which may, in turn, strengthen the tendency to analyze oneself.

In the second year follow-up (Davis & Franzoi, 1986) to the first longitudinal study, we made an effort to evaluate these alternative explanations. Using the LISREL VI structural equation program, we estimated several different models that incorporated the three different causal assumptions outlined previously. The results of these analyses indicated quite clearly—at least for our sample—that the most reasonable assumption is that private self-consciousness *produces* greater self-disclosure. When a single path was estimated from self-disclosure to self-consciousness (reflecting a causal direction opposite to our hypothesized direction), the result was that the estimated path coefficients dropped to near zero. Such a path from disclosure to self-conciousness also proved inadequate when it was estimated simultaneously with a path in the opposite direction (the "reciprocal paths" model). In short, with this particular high-school sample, the only causal assumption that seemed appropriate was that dispositional self-consciousness produces heightened self-disclosure but that there is no reciprocal effect of disclosure on self-consciousness. Given the fact that private self-consciousness is considered to be a relatively stable personality trait, unaffected by situational press, these longitudinal findings make theoretical sense.[1]

[1]Further testing may find that the regular and personally penetrating self-disclosure that often occurs in a therapy situation, for example, may result in a temporary heightening of private self-attention for the client outside the therapist–client dyad. However, this effect would be situationally induced and would unlikely change the level of private self-

THE SELF-CONSCIOUSNESS/DISCLOSURE LINKAGE: THEORETICAL EXPLANATIONS

For the present, then, we feel secure in our assumption that private self-consciousness is one cause of self-disclosure. With this fact more or less established, our attention can now turn to the more interesting question of *why* this is so. That is, what is it about a dispositional tendency to self-reflect that contributes to a tendency to more fully disclose intimate self-relevant information? Several possible explanations for this finding can be advanced, and in the following pages we will describe five such explanations and discuss their similarities, differences, and implications for the self-consciousness/disclosure association. To simplify the ensuing discussion of these causal mechanisms, we will divide them into two classes of explanation: *nonmotivational* and *motivational* explanations.

Nonmotivational Explanations

The nonmotivational explanations to be discussed share a common feature: They all rest on the assumption that private self-consciousness affects self-disclosure because of the operation of some relatively automatic psychological process that makes it likely that high-private self-conscious individuals will self-disclose, when given the opportunity, more so than those who do not habitually self-reflect. These explanations do not hypothesize any desire or need to disclose on the part of those high in private self-consciousness. The heightened disclosure among such persons instead is assumed to result from some greater amount of self-information possessed by them or some greater salience of that information. The motivational explanations, on the other hand, attempt to identify some *desire* or *need* underlying this relation. We will present two different nonmotivational hypotheses: the "accumulation hypothesis" and the "salience hypothesis."

The Accumulation Hypothesis. The first nonmotivational explanation states that a high level of private self-consciousness simply makes one better equipped to self-disclose about private self-aspects. This notion was expressed quite clearly by Buss (1980) in his analysis of possible behavioral differences due to level of self-consciousness: "It is a reasonable hypothesis that, other things equal, people high in private self-consciousness tend to disclose more about themselves (private topics)

---

consciousness. Once the client had resolved the problems that initially brought him or her to seek therapy, his or her degree of private self-attention would most likely return to what is normal for the person.

simply because they have more to disclose" (p. 121). This was our original explanation for the observed relation (Franzoi & Davis, 1985), and in some ways it may be the most parsimonious.

The crux of this view is that people high in private self-consciousness, due to their greater introspection, eventually accumulate more extensive self-knowledge, and come to have fuller, more detailed, and more accurate self-understandings. Franzoi (1983) and Turner (1978a), for example, found that high-private self-conscious subjects listed more self-descriptive adjectives when describing themselves than did those who did not typically reflect on private self-aspects, suggesting that the former individuals have more self-information available. Regarding self-report accuracy, Scheier, Buss, and Buss (1978) found the correlation between self-reports of aggressiveness and aggressive behavior to be significantly greater for high- than for low-private self-conscious subjects. Bernstein and Davis (1982) found that, following observation of high- and low-private self-conscious target persons, observers were better able to match the former group with their self-descriptions than the latter group. Finally, Franzoi (1983) found significant discrepancies between the self-descriptions of low-private self-conscious individuals and descriptions of them by their close friends, yet no significant discrepancies between high self-conscious individuals and their friends. Based on these studies, it may be concluded that high-private self-consciousness does appear to be associated with a more detailed and accurate knowledge of private self-aspects. Because the content of this self-awareness (emotions, thoughts, aspirations, and doubts) is typical material for intimate self-disclosure, persons possessing such detailed and accurate self-knowledge would seem to be better equipped to self-disclose, whereas persons lacking such elaborate self-knowledge would be less able to share personal information with others.

The Salience Hypothesis. The second nonmotivational explanation is based on a slightly different hypothesized mechanism. The "accumulation" hypothesis is predicated on the notion of high-private self-conscious persons accumulating self-knowledge through their chronic tendency to attend to private self-aspects; therefore, when called upon, high self-conscious persons will have a greater depth of information on which to draw than will low self-conscious persons. The salience hypothesis, in contrast, does not rely on a previous accumulation of self-knowledge. Instead, this hypothesis explains the greater disclosure of those high in private self-consciousness in terms of the *immediate* salience of self-information during a disclosure-appropriate situation.

According to this explanation, high-private self-conscious individuals are simply more attentive to self-relevant information in their environment, and consequently, they are more likely to bring up personal anecdotes and illustrations in conversation than their less self-conscious counterparts. Thus, high-private self-conscious persons self-disclose more because they are probabilistically more likely to attend to and report on self-relevant information. Whether such persons already possess a detailed, articulated self-concept is largely irrelevant to this explanation; they are more likely to disclose because relevant self-information is simply more salient to them. Thus, the observed self-consciousness/self-disclosure association, according to this view, is due to the ongoing, moment-by-moment salience of self-information for persons high in private self-consciousness. It should be clear from this explanation, however, that the eventual result of this ongoing salience of self-information could well be the development over time of an extensive *accumulation* of self-knowledge. Thus, although conceptually distinct, the "accumulation" and "salience" hypotheses clearly do bear some relationship to one another.

Motivational Explanations

The two nonmotivational explanations offered thus far ignore any potential role for an individual's desire or need to self-disclose. Instead, they both share the view that some consequence of high levels of private self-consciousness (i.e., either accumulated self-knowledge or an ongoing self-salience) will naturally lead to increased self-disclosure—in the appropriate setting—independent of any motives or needs on the part of the disclosing individual. In a sense, the nonmotivational view assumes that disclosure will occur more or less "automatically" as a function of greater private self-consciousness. An alternative view is that some motivational process or processes are involved in the link between dispositional self-consciousness and self-disclosure. The question is: What might these motivations be?

Another way to phrase this question is: What function does self-disclosing serve for the high-private self-conscious person, and/or what function is served for the low self-conscious person by not disclosing? In a very real sense, motivational explanations of the relation between private self-consciousness and self-disclosure are motivational explanations of how individuals form positive and negative attitudes about self-disclosing based on their level of self-consciousness. That is, the motivational perspective assumes that underlying individual differences in private self-awareness tendencies are needs that are being served that cause individuals to develop positive or negative attitudes toward activities that are related to self-analysis, introspection, and general self-attention, such as self-disclosure. In this respect, the following motivational explanations draw much of their inspiration from the functional approach to attitude formation (e.g., Katz, 1960; Smith, Bruner, & White, 1956). As with the nonmotivational perspective, there is more than one possible explanation. We will present and briefly discuss three such explanations: expressive needs, self-knowledge needs, and self-defense needs.

Expressive Need Hypothesis. In a functional analysis of self-disclosure, Derlega and Grzelak (1979) suggest that self-disclosing may be a self-rewarding activity, satisfying expressive needs of the individual. That is, the act of self-disclosure itself may be a pleasant, rewarding experience because it fulfills an individual's *need* to express himself or herself to others. From this perspective, high-private self-conscious individuals may disclose more to their friends and to their romantic partners because it may be more *important* for them to act on this need: to share these internal, nonvisible aspects of themselves with others. Thus the first motivational explanation argues that those high in private self-consciousness have a greater desire specifically to disclose self-information than those low in self-consciousness.

One point to be considered is the following. The expressive needs hypothesis does not explicitly posit any desire among those high in private self-consciousness for greater or more accurate *self-knowledge*; this hypothesis instead deals solely with the desire to *express* oneself to others in some fashion. However, if persons high in private self-consciousness do indeed tend to reveal their private thoughts and feelings to others, they may also tend to place themselves in a position to receive feedback concerning the *validity* of their private self-theories. Thus it may be that increased self-understanding (resulting from the give-and-take of social intercourse) may be an added consequence of the highly self-conscious individuals' needs to express themselves to others. For this reason, the research cited earlier that indicates a greater self-knowledge among those high in self-consciousness (Bernstein & Davis, 1982; Franzoi, 1983; Scheier *et al.*, 1978; Turner, 1978a) may also be consistent with the expressive needs hypothesis.

Self-Knowledge Need Hypothesis. Alternatively, of course, it is possible that self-consciousness is directly associated with a heightened desire to understand oneself. That is, rather than explain the self-consciousness/self-disclosure relation in terms of a motivational desire to express themselves, an alternative view is that high-private self-conscious persons may instead have a greater desire to know and understand themselves. This motivational explanation can therefore account for the relation between self-consciousness and self-disclosure, if we assume that self-disclosure is one way to increase self-knowledge.

This view of self-disclosure is consistent with a number of theorists who have written on the topic. For example, Jourard (1964), one of the first psychologists to lay the theoretical foundation for later self-disclosure research, believed that disclosing one's "private side" to others does indeed result in greater self-understanding. Derlega and Grzelak (1979) have also argued that, in addition to satisfying expressive needs, self-disclosure provides the opportunity to increase personal clarification; the act of self-disclosing may allow one to more clearly perceive and understand internal, nonvisible states. Although personal clarification may occur without feedback from the one who is disclosed to, Derlega and Grzelak state that self-disclosing also opens the door for social validation (or disconfirmation) of one's self-perceptions and beliefs. Thus, according to this hypothesis, high-private self-conscious individuals are more likely to self-disclose to friends and lovers and eventually to acquire a more knowledgeable and articulated self-understanding, at least partially because of their desire to better understand themselves.

This perspective on self-disclosure and the feedback received from others is also consistent with earlier approaches that hold that self-understandings come, to a large degree, from the reflected appraisals of others. Cooley's (1922) notion of the looking-glass self and Mead's (1934) self theory are examples of such approaches. Thus, there is a strong theoretical grounding for the hypothesis that engaging in deep conversation with others, including intimate self-disclosure, is one way to achieve self-understanding.

Self-Defense Hypothesis. A final way to explain the relation between private self-consciousness and self-disclosure is in terms of a motive to protect oneself from exposure to painful or unpleasant stimuli. In describing this hypothesis, it may be useful to consider the self-consciousness/self-disclosure relation from the point of view of the low self-conscious person—the assumption will be that it may be more appropriate in this hypothesis to consider the *reluctance* of the low self-conscious person to disclose, rather than the heightened desire by high self-conscious persons to do so. According to this view, low-private self-conscious individuals have a desire to avoid engaging in self-revealing activities, and the relation between private self-consciousness and self-disclosure is explained by this reluctance.

Underlying the third motivational explanation, then, is the assumption that low-private self-conscious individuals are concerned with defending their current level of self-esteem by avoiding activities that might result in the questioning of their self-conceptions. From this perspective, low-private self-conscious individuals do not attend to their private self-aspects for the same reason that they do not discuss personal, intimate matters with friends and lovers: a reluctance to explore and reveal hidden, and perhaps unpleasant, personal qualities. This hypothesis is derived from the conception of people as being primarily driven by a need to maintain the most positive self-esteem possible and, as such, forms a natural contrast with the second motivational explanation that conceives of people being primarily driven by a need for self-knowledge.

To date, some of the available evidence on behavioral differences due to level of private self-consciousness can be most easily explained by the self-defense hypothesis. Turner (1978b), for example, in a study of the speed of processing self-relevant information, found that high-private self-conscious individuals made faster judgments concerning the self-relevance of socially undesirable trait adjectives than did low-private self-conscious individuals but did not differ from them in response time to socially desirable trait adjectives. These findings led Turner to conclude that positive or socially desirable components of the self-concept are readily available for both high and low self-conscious individuals, but only individuals high in private self-consciousness have ready access to their negative or socially undesirable characteristics. This study would appear to be quite consistent with the self-defense hypothesis; the low-private self-conscious subjects were selective in their self-knowledge, only differing from their high self-conscious counterparts in knowledge of negative self-aspects.

A second study that appears to be parsimoniously explained by the self-defense hypothesis investigated the nature and quality of the private self-aware state in high- and low-private self-conscious individuals. Employing experiential sampling methodology that enabled them to randomly sample subjects' thoughts and feelings as they went about their normal daily activities, Franzoi and Brewer (1984) found evidence suggesting that high- and low-private self-conscious individuals react differently to the private self-aware state. Not only did low-private self-conscious subjects spend less time attending to private self-aspects, but when they were privately self-aware, their degree of private self-awareness was positively related to their evaluation of affect experienced in this state of awareness. If the affect was unpleasant, the degree of private self-awareness tended to be low, but if the affect was pleasant, the degree of private self-awareness tended to be higher. This effect, which Franzoi and Brewer termed "selective self-attention," did not occur among the high-private self-conscious subjects; for them, the degree of private self-awareness was unrelated to whether their private thoughts and feelings were positive or negative. Consistent with the "self-defense" hypothesis, then, these findings suggest that individuals low in private self-consciousness may be less willing to engage in private self-awareness when their dominant affect in that state is negative.

Motives, Goals, and Plans

Elsewhere in this volume, Miller and Read (Chapter 3) present a view of self-disclosure as it might relate to a goal-based model of personality. One key tenet of their model is that most personality traits can be seen as enduring configurations of an individual's goals, plans and strategies for attaining the goals, resources required for these plans, and beliefs that are relevant to executing the plans. It is possible, and we think useful, to draw some connection between the five hypotheses presented in this chapter and the goal-based model they outline.

There are several points of contact between their proposed model and our hypothesized links between self-consciousness and self-disclosure; the first of these concerns their notion of goals. There are doubtless many goals for which the disclosure of intimate self-knowledge is a feasible strategy, and in fact, Miller and Read list a number of these. Given our special interest in explaining the self-consciousness/self-disclosure link, our treatment of the motivational hypotheses has focused on a set of three goals that seem most likely to be related to dispositional levels of private self-consciousness. That is, self-defense, self-knowledge, and self-expression were treated as three goals that are relevant to one's self-consciousness level: Those high in private self-consciousness are more likely to desire the goals of self-knowledge and self-expression, and those low in self-consciousness are more likely to value the goal of self-defense. In Miller and Read's terminology, then, the act of self-disclosing constitutes a plan or strategy employed by those high in self-consciousness to attain one or more of those goals. Just as there are other goals for which self-disclosure is a viable strategy, however, there are certainly strategies other than self-disclosure that would also be useful in the attainment of these goals.

Possible connections also exist between our approach and the other two components of the goal-based model. For example, if the logic of the accumulation hypothesis (one of the two nonmotivational hypotheses) is correct and those high in private self-consciousness do amass a relative wealth of detailed self-knowledge, then those high in self-consciousness can be seen as possessing a *resource* (self-knowledge) that is useful in enacting any self-disclosure strategy. In contrast, the lack of detailed self-knowledge would seem to be a substantial barrier in the path of successful self-disclosure. Thus greater self-consciousness may affect not only one's goals but also one's resources for acting on those goals. Finally, it is also possible to find a point of contact between our hypotheses and the fourth element of the goal-based model—beliefs related to the strategy. It seems reasonable to assume, for instance, that if those high in self-consciousness engage in disclosure (a plan) to further self-knowledge or self-expression (a goal), then they probably hold the *belief* that such behavior is effective in the achievement of that goal. That is, they are likely to hold cognitions such as "telling others about my thoughts and feelings is a way to learn more about myself."

THE SELF-CONSCIOUSNESS/DISCLOSURE LINKAGE: EVALUATING THE HYPOTHESES

Five possible explanations for the observed link between private self-consciousness and self-disclosure have been reported. This list of hypotheses is not intended to be an exhaustive account—there may well be other possible explanations as well. However, these five do seem to represent several of the most well-grounded and most likely mechanisms by which the observed relation could be produced.

Although each of these explanations has been presented separately and described as though it operated in isolation, we do not mean to imply that any single one of these explanations is necessarily wholly responsible for the self-consciousness/self-disclosure link. It is important to recognize that it is entirely possible—indeed, likely—that more than one hypothesized process is contributing to the effect. It could be, for example, that multiple processes operate within the individual; for example, a person discloses for self-expressive reasons, consequently accumulates a richer self-knowledge, and is therefore better equipped to disclose in subsequent disclosure settings. Focusing exclusively on the three motivational explanations and invoking a proposition from the functional attitude theorists (e.g., Katz, 1960; Smith *et al.*, 1956), it could also be that different motivational processes operate for different people: some persons disclosing for self-expressive needs, others disclosing equally intimately for self-knowledge needs, and still others not disclosing in order to defend their self-esteem.[2] Although such multiple determinants of disclosure are possible, for ease of explication we have treated each hypothesis separately and will continue to do so for the time being.

Existing Evidence

How can one best evaluate the adequacy of these various explanations? One obvious strategy is to examine the results of previous studies concerning self-consciousness and/or self-disclosure to locate evidence that might tend to support or disconfirm particular explanations. However, in the present case, such a strategy is of limited usefulness because much of the previous research is consistent with all of the

[2]One implication of this particular view of the self-consciousness/self-disclosure relation is that if self-disclosing is indeed beneficial to one's mental health, in order to promote a greater willingness to self-disclose in low-private self-conscious individuals, it will be necessary to convince them either that revealing personal feelings to others will, in the long run, enhance their self-esteem or that some other salient need will be satisfied (e.g., need for affiliation).

hypothesized mechanisms thus far proposed. For example, considerable evidence exists that indicates that those high in private self-consciousness have more articulated self-concepts (Turner, 1978a; Franzoi, 1983) and more accurate views of themselves (Bernstein & Davis, 1982; Franzoi, 1983; Scheier *et al.*, 1978). This association of high private self-consciousness with better self-understanding probably is partly due to the self-consciousness/disclosure relation we are attempting to explain. However, the fact that disclosure might lead to self-knowledge is *irrelevant* to the key question at hand: *Why* do they disclose in the first place? After all, disclosure can lead to self-knowledge whether those high in self-consciousness disclose in order to learn more about themselves (self-knowledge need) or for some other reason (e.g., self-salience; expressive need). The finding of a clear association between self-consciousness and self-knowledge simply does not allow us to really differentiate among these five explanations.

There is one kind of research that does lend itself somewhat to drawing distinctions among these explanations, and it was mentioned earlier. This is the work of Turner (1978b), which found that although those high and low in private self-consciousness did not differ in response speed while making judgments of self-relevance for socially *desirable* traits, they did show a difference for socially undesirable traits. Those high in private self-consciousness were faster processors of undesirable trait information than were those low in self-consciousness. Such a pattern seems more easily accounted for by the motivational explanation of self-defense, which proposes a reason for the low self-conscious person to avoid unpleasant information, than by other explanations (such as self-knowledge needs) that do not. Likewise, the evidence from Franzoi and Brewer (1984) concerning "selective self-attention" is most gracefully accounted for by the self-defense notion.

In the absence of much evidence that would allow a meaningful evaluation of these competing explanations, we will turn our attention instead to an examination of some implications of these differing views. By identifying assumptions that are inherent in each explanation, some possible ways to evaluate the relative adequacy of each explanation may result. Thus the focus for the remainder of this chapter will be on briefly identifying potential research strategies that will allow a meaningful comparison of these five explanations.

Testing between Motivational and Nonmotivational Views

One possible way to evaluate the validity of the nonmotivational versus motivational explanations for self-disclosure focuses on a fundamental difference between these two approaches: the hypothesized tendency to seek out or enter disclosure-appropriate situations. That is, one implication of the motivational explanations—but not the nonmotivational ones—is that those high in private self-consciousness will more likely seek out or at least be more willing to enter situations where self-disclosure is appropriate, expected, or required than those low in self-consciousness. They may do this in order to share their private self-aspects with others (expressive need hypothesis) or to have a chance to learn more about themselves (self-knowledge need hypothesis). Similarly, low-private self-conscious individuals may be more likely to avoid entering situations where self-disclosure is possible because of their reluctance to engage in activities that explore private, and perhaps unpleasant, personal qualities that may adversely affect their self-esteem (self-defense hypothesis). Because the nonmotivational explanations do not explain self-disclosure in terms of the fulfillment of any needs or wishes, they do not predict that those high in private self-consciousness will act differently than those low in this disposition when choosing whether or not to enter a disclosure-relevant setting.

Therefore, one way to test for the relative efficacy of motivational versus nonmotivational approaches would be to provide subjects with the opportunity to enter self-disclosure situations. Because the motivational explanations are based on the notion that there is either a greater desire among the high self-conscious individuals to disclose or a greater desire among the low self-conscious individuals to avoid disclosure, one would expect that high-private self-conscious persons would take advantage of this opportunity more so than those low in self-consciousness. Thus, placed in a situation where self-disclosing is one of a number of behavioral options possible, the motivational approach would predict that the high-private self-conscious individuals would be more likely to avail themselves of the opportunity to disclose. The nonmotivational explanations, because they do not posit any desire to engage in disclosure, would not predict any difference between high and low self-conscious persons in their tendency to enter such settings.

Testing among Nonmotivational Views

Although the previous strategy may be useful in distinguishing generally between the motivational and nonmotivational approaches, it may also be necessary to evaluate the relative efficacy of one nonmotivational view over the other. In this case, key questions become "What different implications flow from these two hypothesized processes?" and "How can such differing implications be used to compare the two explanations?" One implication is that the "accumulation" argument suggests that high-private self-conscious persons will have more to tell about themselves than low self-conscious persons because they have accumulated more information through self-scrutiny. The "salience" argument, on the other hand, implies that high self-conscious persons are simply more likely to think of (and presumably talk about) self-information, whereas the sheer amount of self-information that has been built up over the years may be irrelevant. That is, the difference between the accumulation and the salience ideas may be the difference between *depth* of disclosure and *frequency* or *likelihood* of disclosure. The "accumulation" argument would predict that high-private self-conscious people would be able to disclose in greater depth, whereas the "salience" argument might predict that high self-conscious persons would simply self-disclose more readily or frequently, perhaps at relatively superficial levels.

Thus, to provide a test between the accumulation and salience hypotheses, it might be advantageous to measure disclosure in two different ways. One way would be to measure the intimacy of the disclosure, and the other would be to measure the likelihood of initiating disclosure in a setting where both self-relevant and non-self-relevant matters are equally appropriate. The salience hypothesis would predict that high self-conscious persons would be more likely to initiate disclosure about themselves but not necessarily reveal very much intimate information. In contrast, the accumulation explanation would predict that the high self-conscious persons would engage in more intimate and more detailed disclosure due to their wealth of self-knowledge. It is difficult to know precisely what the accumulation hypothesis would predict with regard to the question of initiating self-disclosure; however, the prediction of the salience position seems clear. Therefore, a finding of greater depth of disclosure among those high in self-consciousness would tend to support the accumulation hypothesis; a finding that high and low self-conscious persons differ only in likelihood of initiating disclosure would be consistent with the salience hypothesis.

Testing among Motivational Views

One strategy for evaluating the validity of the three motivational hypotheses is quite straightforward: Simply ask people about their motives. The motivational explanations all hypothesize a difference between those low and high in self-consciousness in terms of some need—either a need for self-expression, for self-knowledge, or self-defense. If the expressive need hypothesis is accurate, then those high in self-consciousness (relative to those low in self-consciousness) should report that they place a high value or feel a strong need to express themselves to others or to share information about themselves with other people. If the self-knowledge need hypothesis is correct, then those high in private self-consciousness should exhibit a similar pattern to questions concerning the importance of "truly understanding yourself" or how strongly they desire to know themselves fully and accurately. If the self-defense hypothesis is correct, those low in private self-consciousness may well be more likely to feel that "too much self-examination can be painful or damaging" or that "one should not think too much about one's own shortcomings." In each of these instances, a finding of significant differences between those high and low in self-consciousness would be consistent with the specific motivational hypothesis in question. Of course, greater confidence would be placed in a significant difference between high and low self-conscious individuals if it could be buttressed by other evidence.

One approach to obtaining such evidence might be to examine the differences between those high and low in self-consciousness with regard to other self-related behaviors that are clearly connected to one of the motivational hypotheses. For example, consider a class of behaviors that are clearly related to a quest for self-knowledge and less clearly related to self-expressive needs (e.g., buying and reading psychological self-help books). If a pattern were found such that high self-conscious persons consistently engaged in more such behaviors than those low in self-consciousness, it could be viewed as supportive of the self-knowledge hypothesis. It would not, of course, disprove the other hypotheses but would constitute one piece of the larger evidentiary pattern. Likewise, consider a class of behaviors that seem clearly related to self-expression but less clearly so to self-knowledge (e.g., painting, sculpting, and composing music). A finding that these activities are more common among high than low self-conscious persons would be consistent with the self-expressive rather than the self-knowledge hypothesis.

Although this method may help to distinguish between the self-expressive and self-knowledge hypotheses, it is much less useful in distinguishing between the self-knowledge and self-defense explanations. This is because both of these latter two hypotheses can provide credible explanations for the same behavioral differences between high and low self-conscious individuals. For example, from the self-knowledge need perspective, high-private self-conscious people may read a self-improvement book to gain greater insight into their behavior patterns and motives, whereas low self-conscious persons may be relatively indifferent to this type of self-knowledge. Likewise, from the self-defense perspective, low self-conscious people may avoid such a book because they may be forced to focus on unpleasant personal qualities that will threaten their self-esteem, whereas high self-conscious individuals may not view transient negative self-affect as a specific threat, and thus, may be more likely to read such books.

Because of this difficulty, attempts to differentiate between these two explanations will probably be best served by controlled laboratory manipulations. For example, one experimental approach might be to place high and low self-conscious subjects in a situation in which they have a choice of interacting or not with another person; this other person will possess some information concerning an ability or characteristic of the subject. The manipulation will consist of the subject's expectation regarding the kind of information she or he can expect from the other person. Some subjects will have an expectation that the self-information to be conveyed by the other person is probably positive; some will have an expectation that it is probably negative; some will have no expectation regarding the positivity of the information. If the dominant motive among those high in self-consciousness is for self-knowledge, then it might be expected that high self-conscious subjects will choose to interact with the knowledgeable other regardless of the likely valence of the information, and those low in self-consciousness would be relatively unlikely to so choose. If the dominant motive is one of self-defense, however, then a different pattern may be expected. Both high and low self-conscious subjects should choose to interact with the other as long as the information is likely to be positive; if unpleasant information is expected, those low in private self-consciousness may be especially unwilling to interact with the other and run the risk of threatening self-esteem.

CONCLUSION

It is clear that any comprehensive evaluation of these five hypotheses must await empirical tests, some examples of which have been suggested here. Because these tests have yet to be conducted, specific conclusions about the relative superiority of one hypothesis over another are certainly premature. Generally speaking, however, we do have one strong expectation about the pattern of results likely to emerge from future investigations: The expectation is that in the final analysis it will be found that not one but several of these explanations have some validity. Whether multiple mechanisms operate within most individuals or whether each individual's behavior is primarily characterized by one dominant mechanism remains to be seen; what seems probable is that some evidence will be found for the operation of more than one of these five hypotheses.

It should be clear, then, that a complete evaluation and understanding of these hypotheses cannot result from any single empirical approach. It is, in fact, unlikely that any two or three approaches will suffice. Only when a complete pattern of results is assembled, obtained through the use of the full range of research techniques, will it be possible to meaningfully evaluate these hypotheses. Given the strong likelihood that more than one of the mechanisms is valid, the most valuable outcome likely to emerge from these proposed investigations will be some understanding of when and under which circumstances particular explanations may be the most appropriate.

REFERENCES

Archer, R. L. (1979). Role of personality and the social situation. In G. J. Chelune (Ed.), *Self-disclosure* (pp. 28–58). San Francisco: Jossey-Bass.

Bernstein, W. M., & Davis, M. H. (1982). Perspective-taking, self-consciousness, and accuracy in person perception. *Basic and Applied Social Psychology, 3,* 1–19.

Buss, A. H. (1980). *Self-consciousness and social anxiety.* San Francisco: W. H. Freeman.

Cooley, C. H. (1922). *Human nature and the social order* (Rev. ed.). New York: Scribner's.

Davis, M. H., & Franzoi, S. L. (1986). Adolescent loneliness, self-disclosure, and private self-consciousness: A longitudinal investigation. *Journal of Personality and Social Psychology, 51,* 595–608.

Derlega, V. J. & Grzelak, J. (1979). Appropriateness of self-disclosure. In G. Chelune (Ed.), *Self-disclosure: Origins, patterns, and implications of openness in interpersonal relationships* (pp. 151–176). San Francisco: Jossey-Bass.

Fenigstein, A., Scheier, M. F., & Buss, A. H. (1975). Public and private self-consciousness: Assessment and theory. *Journal of Consulting and Clinical Psychology, 13,* 522–528.

Franzoi, S. L. (1983). Self-concept differences as a function of private self-consciousness and social anxiety. *Journal of Research in Personality, 17,* 275–287.

Franzoi, S. L., & Brewer, L. C. (1984). The experience of self-awareness and its relation to level of self-consciousness: An experiential sampling study. *Journal of Research in Personality, 18,* 522–540.

Franzoi, S. L., & Davis, M. H. (1985). Adolescent self-disclosure and loneliness: Private self-consciousness and parental influences. *Journal of Personality and Social Psychology, 48,* 768–780.

Franzoi, S. L., Davis, M. H., & Young, R. D. (1985). The effects of private self-consciousness and perspective-taking on satisfaction in close relationships. *Journal of Personality and Social Psychology, 48,* 1584–1594.

Jourard, S. M. (1964). *The transparent self.* New York: Van Nostrand.

Katz, D. (1960). The functional approach to the study of attitudes. *Public Opinion Quarterly, 24,* 163–204.

Locke, H. J. (1951). *Predicting adjustment in marriage: A comparison of a divorced and a happily married group.* New York: Holt.

Mead, G. H. (1934). *Mind, self, and society.* Chicago: University of Chicago Press.

Miller, L. C., Berg, J. H., & Archer, R. L. (1983). Openers: Individuals who elicit intimate self-disclosure. *Journal of Personality and Social Psychology, 44,* 1234–1244.

Russell, D., Peplau, L. A., & Cutrona, C. B. (1980). The revised UCLA loneliness scale: Concurrent and discriminant validity evidence. *Journal of Personality and Social Psychology, 39,* 472–480.

Scheier, M. R., Buss, A. H., & Buss, D. M. (1978). Self-consciousness, self-report of aggressiveness, and aggression. *Journal of Research in Personality, 12,* 133–140.

Smith, M. B., Bruner, J. S., & White, R. W. (1956). *Opinions and personality*. New York: Wiley.

Turner, R. G. (1978a). Consistency, self-consciousness, and the predictive validity of typical and maximal personality measures. *Journal of Research in Personality*, *12*, 117–132.

Turner, R. G. (1978b). Self-consciousness and speed of processing self-relevant information. *Personality and Social Psychology Bulletin*, *4*, 456–460.

5

Gender and Self-Disclosure

Strategies for Exploring the Issues

CHARLES T. HILL and DONALD E. STULL

INTRODUCTION

The relationship between gender and self-disclosure is a topic of research for which some of the clearest predictions have been made, yet some of the most puzzling results have been obtained. In this chapter we review strategies that we and others have used in efforts to solve the puzzle. Our goal is to explore issues that have been addressed in the past and to identify issues that need to be addressed in the future.

THE PUZZLE

The earliest research on self-disclosure found that men revealed less about themselves than women (e.g., Jourard & Lasakow, 1958). Jourard (1971a) explained this finding in terms of sex roles: The male role requires men to "appear tough, objective, striving, achieving, unsentimental, and emotionally unexpressive" (p. 35). Further studies of self-disclosure, however, did not always find a sex difference (see Cozby, 1973; Goodstein & Reinecker, 1974). Some studies have even

CHARLES T. HILL • Department of Psychology, Whittier College, Whittier, California 90608. **DONALD E. STULL** • Department of Sociology, University of Akron, Akron, Ohio 44325.

found greater disclosure by men than by women under certain circumstances, such as in the initial development of an opposite-sex relationship (e.g., Davis, 1978; Derlega, Winstead, Wong, & Hunter, 1985; Stokes, Childs, & Fuehrer, 1981).

In attempts to understand these inconsistent findings, researchers have employed strategies that explore possible mediating factors. These strategies will be discussed in terms of (1) situational factors, (2) sex-role attitudes, (3) sex-role identity, (4) sex-role norms, and (5) self-disclosure measures.

STRATEGY 1: SITUATIONAL FACTORS

This strategy assumes that various situational factors may account for inconsistencies in gender differences in self-disclosure. The logic of the approach is as follows: A number of situational factors have been found to affect self-disclosure. There often are gender differences in the way in which these factors affect disclosure; hence interactions with these factors may mediate gender differences. These situational factors include topic of disclosure, sex of target (disclosure recipient), and relationship to target.

Topic of Disclosure

Researchers usually measure the extent of self-disclosure in terms of the "breadth" of disclosure, the "depth" of disclosure, or a combination of both. *Breadth* refers to the range of topics discussed, whereas *depth* refers to the degree of intimacy of the topics discussed (Altman & Taylor, 1973). Breadth and depth are usually assumed to increase concurrently. In particular, self-disclosure is considered to be greater when more topics or more intimate topics are discussed. If men and women differ in the topics on which they tend to self-disclose, then the topics studied will influence whether or not sex differences are obtained.

A number of studies have found sex differencese as a function of disclosure topic, although the precise topics have varied somewhat from study to study. Women have disclosed more about themselves, their homes, and relationships with family and friends (Haas, 1979; Komarovsky, 1967); feelings, things they were afraid of, and accomplishments at school or work (Rubin, Hill, Peplau, & Dunkel-Schetter, 1980); social-emotional topics (Rubin, 1974; Rubin & Shenker, 1978); weaknesses (Hacker, 1981); and topics rated higher on intimacy (Morgan, 1976; Stull, 1981). Men, on the other hand, have disclosed more about cars, sports, work, and politics (Komarovsky, 1967); sports, money, and business

(Haas, 1979); political views, things they were proud of, and things liked about a dating partner (Rubin *et al.*, 1980); and strengths (Hacker, 1981). In some studies, no sex differences have been found on task topics (Rubin, 1974) or nonintimate topics (Morgan, 1976; Stull, 1981).

The topics on which sex differences have been found tend to support the notion that traditional sex-role expectations encourage women to be concerned about social-emotional matters, whereas men are supposed to be emotionally unexpressive (see Millett, 1975; Pleck & Sawyer, 1974). However, there are some inconsistencies. For example, men have disclosed more about work (Komarovksy, 1967), yet women have disclosed more about accomplishments at school or work (Rubin *et al.*, 1980). To some extent, these inconsistencies reflect differences in the ways in which the topics are described or categorized by researchers, but they also indicate the importance of additional mediating factors.

Sex of Target

A number of studies have found differences between opposite-sex and same-sex disclosure (e.g., Annicchiarico, 1973; Brooks, 1974; Certner, 1970; Hyink, 1975; Inman, 1978; Jourard, 1971a). Often female–female disclosure is highest, male–male disclosure is lowest, and opposite-sex disclosure is in between. For example, Komarovsky (1974) reported that male seniors confided more to a girlfriend than to a same-sex friend. On the other hand, Cash (1975) found that both men and women disclosed more to a woman than to a man. In addition, gender differences than occur in same-sex disclosure may disappear in opposite-sex disclosure (Aries, 1976; Piliavin & Martin, 1986).

The finding that gender differences may be smaller in opposite-sex relationships than in same-sex relationships may be due in part to effects of reciprocity. The phenomenon of disclosure reciprocity occurs when one person's self-disclosure influences another person to disclose at a similar level (see Chaikin & Derlega, 1974; Rubin, 1976). Rubin *et al.* (1980) argued that high disclosures by women encourage their male partners to disclose more, whereas low disclosures by men encourage their female partners to disclose less. This results in both men and women disclosing at intermediate levels, with a smaller sex difference than in same-sex relationships.

Relationship to Target

Greater disclosure to friends than to strangers has been reported in several studies (Chaikin & Derlega, 1974; Jourard, 1971a,b; Jourard & Lasakow, 1958; Morton, 1978; Rickers-Ovsiankina, 1956). However, these effects are qualified by sex differences. Stokes *et al.* (1981) found that women disclosed more to best friends, whereas men disclosed more than women to strangers. Rosenfeld, Civikly, and Herron (1979) and Colwill & Perlman (1977) also reported that men disclosed more than women to strangers, although this was not supported by Lombardo, Franco, Wolf, and Fantasia (1976).

Relative social status may also be important in self-disclosure. Intimate disclosure tends to flow from those low in power to those with high power in organizational settings (Goffman, 1967; Slobin, Miller & Porter, 1968). Hence, gender differences in self-disclosure should be accentuated when men have more power than women, reduced when men and women have equal power, and perhaps even reversed when women have more power than men. However, Brooks (1974) found that males disclosed more to a high-status interviewer, whereas females disclosed more to a low-status interviewer, indicating that effects of social status may be influenced by gender and possibly other factors such as the type of role relationship.

Most studies of target effects have focused on targets' social characteristics. However, recent research has examined personality characteristics of targets who are more likely to elicit disclosure (see chapters by Miller and Reed [3], Davis & Franzoni [4], Berg [6], and Fitzpatrick [7] in this volume). If men and women differ in such personality characteristics, or in a tendency to seek out targets with these characteristics, these may mediate sex differences in disclosure as well.

In general, research on situational factors influencing self-disclosure clearly demonstrates the need to take these factors into account whenever gender differences in disclosure are examined. At the same time, there are enough inconsistencies in the ways in which these situational factors interact to indicate that other kinds of factors are operating as well. This has led us and other researchers to explore individual differences in the tendency to self-disclose as a function of variations in either sex-role attitudes or sex-role identity.

STRATEGY 2: SEX-ROLE ATTITUDES

If traditional sex roles inhibit men's self-disclosure, as argued by Jourard (1971a) and other authors cited before, then men who endorse statements prescribing traditional sex-role behaviors should be more inhibited in their self-disclosure than men who do not endorse such prescriptions. At the same time, because traditional sex roles are not thought to inhibit women's self-disclosure, presumably it should not be influenced by their sex-role attitudes.

This prediction was explored in Rubin *et al.*'s (1980) study of dating couples, using a measure of sex-role traditionalism called the "TRAD" scale. This scale assesses agreement or disagreement with traditional and liberal statements about appropriate sex-role behaviors, for example, "One of the most important things a mother can do for her daughter is to prepare her for being a wife" and "Women could run most businesses as well as men could." Rubin *et al.* (1980) hypothesized that couples with more traditional attitudes would have greater sex differences in disclosure than couples with less traditional attitudes. They assumed that men's disclosure would be inhibited in traditional couples but not in liberal couples, whereas women's disclosure would be high regardless of sex-role attitudes. Instead, they found that both men and women reported less disclosure in couples with more traditional sex-role attitudes. This finding was explained in terms of disclosure reciprocity, such that the lack of responsiveness from traditional boyfriends inhibited the women's disclosure.

In the original data analyses by Rubin *et al.* (1980), traditionalism scores were averaged for each couple because the partners tended to have similar scores. A reanalysis of the data (Hill, 1980) indicated that both men and women's disclosure scores were more highly correlated with the men's traditionalism scores than with the women's traditionalism scores. Moreover, when men's traditionalism scores were held constant statistically, the effects of the women's scores vanished. This finding supports Rubin *et al.*'s argument that the lesser disclosure of traditional men inhibited their partner's disclosure and makes clear that it is primarily the men's sex role traditionalism that affects couple disclosure.

We reasoned that a clearer test of gender differences in the effects of sex-role attitudes could be obtained by studying same-sex relationships. If traditional sex-role attitudes inhibit men's disclosure but not women's, then sex-role attitudes should affect disclosure in male–male friendships but not in female–female friendships. We tested this prediction in a study in which 106 same-sex roommate pairs were given the TRAD scale and the disclosure scale (expanded with additional topics relevant to roommates) used by Rubin *et al.* (1980). Surprisingly, no correlation was found between the TRAD scale and self-disclosure for either male or female roommates (Stull, 1981). Instead, men's disclosure was less than women's disclosure regardless of sex-role attitudes.

This result was unexpected but would be consistent with Pleck's (1976) notion of the modern male role. In contrast to the traditional male role's emphasis on physical achievements, the modern male role is thought to emphasize interpersonal skills. The capacity for emotional intimacy is also encouraged but closely restricted to romantic heterosexual relationships and excluded elsewhere; it is acceptable for a modern male to open up to his wife or girlfriend but not to other men. Based on Pleck's ideas, we reasoned that having more liberal sex-role attitudes should increase men's disclosure to their girlfriends but not change their disclosure to other men. Hence sex-role attitudes should affect disclosure in opposite-sex dating relationships (what Rubin *et al.*, 1980, found) but not in same-sex friendships (what Stull, 1981, found).

To test this explanation, we conducted another study (Hill, 1981a) in which 75 women and 30 men in a sociology class were asked to complete the TRAD scale and to indicate the extent of their self-disclosure to their best friend of the same sex and to their best friend of the opposite sex. For each target, the disclosure topics used in the Stull (1981) roommate study were assessed. Consistent with previous studies of sex of partner, the women reported more same-sex disclosure than the men, but no sex difference in opposite-sex disclosure was found. However, contrary to expectations, the TRAD scale was not significally correlated with either same-sex or opposite-sex disclosure for either men or women.

This latter result was puzzling. We thought that perhaps a better test of individual differences in sex roles could be made by using more than one sex-role measure. So we repeated the study the following semester (Hill, 1981b) in another section of the same sociology class but using four sex-role measures instead of just one. These included two measures of sex-role attitudes (the TRAD scale and the Attitudes toward Women Scale developed by Spence & Helmreich, 1978) and two measures of sex-role identity (to be described in the next section). The 75 women and 29 men completed the same disclosure scales that were used before. Surprisingly, the TRAD scale was correlated with both same-sex ($r = -.39$) and opposite-sex ($r = -.31$) disclosure for the men but not significantly correlated with either type of disclosure for the women ($-.04$ and $-.08$, respectively). Virtually identical results were obtained for the Attitudes Toward Women Scale, which is similar to the TRAD scale (except that it is scored in the opposite direction which changes negative to positive correlations).

These effects for both same-sex and opposite-sex disclosure confirmed the original predictions we made for the Stull (1981) study, rather than our revised prediction that only opposite-sex disclosure would be affected. It was unclear, however, why these results were statistically significant, whereas the previous two studies (Hill, 1981a; Stull, 1981) obtained no effects for the TRAD scale. One problem with all of these studies is that most of the theorizing about gender differences in self-disclosure has focused on the inhibiting effects of male-role prescriptions (e.g., Jourard, 1971a), yet the two measures of sex-role attitudes that have been used in research focus primarily on female role prescriptions.

In recent years, several measures of attitudes toward the male role have been developed (Brannon & Juni, 1984; Doyle & Moore, 1978; Downs & Engleson, 1982; Mosher & Sirkin, 1984; Orlofsky, 1981; Snell, 1983; Snell, Belk, & Hawkins, 1984). At this point, it is not clear how these various scales relate to one another, either conceptually or empirically; further research is needed in this regard. However, at least one scale has been found to be related to self-reports of self-disclosure—the Restrictive Emotionality subscale of the Masculine Role Inventory (Snell, 1983). In general, researchers need to explore the multidimensionality of sex-role attitudes in studying correlations with self-disclosure.

STRATEGY 3: SEX-ROLE IDENTITY

While we were conducting research involving sex-role atittudes, other researchers were using measures of sex-role identity. We thought that the latter approach might prove enlightening and began a systematic literature review. We quickly learned, however, that this line of research was very complex.

Whereas measures of sex-role atittudes focus on behaviors deemed appropriate or inappropriate for men and women, measures of sex-role identity assess self-descriptions in terms of personality traits originally thought to be "masculine" or "feminine." Although the latter terms are still used, some researchers now feel that the terms *instrumental* and *expressive* would be more accurate (see Cook, 1985). In addition, the expression *sex-role self-concept* is often used instead of *sex-role identity*. Different measures have been developed, as well as different methods of scoring the measures. We will describe the rationale for each approach and summarize the relevant disclosure findings.

EARLY MEASURES

At first, psychological masculinity and femininity were viewed as opposite poles of a single dimension. From this perspective, it might be expected that persons high on feminine expressiveness would disclose more than persons on the masculine end of the scale. However, one early study found no relationship between the Masculinity–Femininity scale of the Adjective Check List and self-reports of disclosure for a sample of women (Heilbrun, 1973). Another study reported greater disclosure in an interview by women who identified more with their father than by women who identified more with their mother (Doster, 1976). This latter result suggested that a masculine identification might promote disclosure instead of discouraging it, an idea that was initially puzzling to us but that later made sense in light of findings to be described.

Androgynous Group Comparisons

More recent measures of sex-role identity view masculinity and femininity as separate dimensions. Persons who report having both masculine and feminine characteristics are called androgynous and are thought to be more flexible in adapting to various situations. The most widely used measure is the Bem Sex Role Inventory or BSRI (Bem, 1974, 1977, 1979, 1981). Bem initially (1974) scored androgyny as an adjusted difference between a person's masculinity and femininity scores. Those with a difference score near zero were considered androgynous, whereas those with a large difference score were either sex typed or sex-reversed depending on their gender. That is, men who were higher on masculinity than on femininity were sex-typed, whereas women who scored in that manner were sex-reversed.

A second measure was developed by Spence, Helmreich, and Stapp (1975), called the Personal Attributes Questionnaire or PAQ. This measure is similar to the BSRI but was designed to avoid "socially undesirable" feminine items. It also has a Masculine versus Feminine Scale containing traits that formed a third factor in factor analyses. Spence *et al.* argued that in scoring androgyny, a distinction should be made between persons high on both masculinity and femininity and persons low on both. They used a fourfold classification scheme based on median splits on the two dimensions, with the categories *androgynous* (high on both dimensions), *sex-typed* (high on masculinity—low on femininity for men and the reverse for women), *cross-sex-typed* (the opposite of sex-typed), and undifferentiated (low on both dimensions). Bem subsequently (1977) reanalyzed her data using the fourfold classification and confirmed that the distinction between androgynous and undifferentiated persons was useful. As a result, many studies have used a one-way analysis of variance comparing the four BSRI groups.

Because androgynous persons are thought to be more flexible, they are expected to be "better adjusted" in various ways (see Cook, 1985). Because self-disclosure has been assumed to be associated with better mental health (Jourard, 1971a), researchers predicted that androgynous groups would disclose more than other groups. This prediction was supported in one study using the difference-score measure of androgyny

(Switkin, 1974) and in three studies using the four-group classification approach (Fielden, 1982; Ickes & Barnes, 1978; Stokes *et al.*, 1981). However, an additional study found this true for men but not women (Fischer, 1981), whereas another reported it for women but not men (Rosenfeld *et al.*, 1979). Even more contradicting was a study that found sex-typed men to disclose more than androgynous men, with no effects for women (Small, Gross, Erdwins, & Gessner, 1979). No effects were obtained by Banikiotes and Merluzzi (1981) for men and by Baffi (1979) for women. All of these studies used the BSRI. An additional study using the ANDRO scale (which is based on rescoring the Personality Research Form) also found no effects (Denton, 1982).

Separate Dimensions

One of the difficulties in interpreting four-group comparisons is that androgynous men have higher femininity scores than sex-typed men, whereas androgynous women have higher masculinity scores than sex-typed women. Hence it might be useful to examine effects of masculinity and femininity as separate dimensions (see Taylor & Hall, 1982).

Several studies have found positive correlations between self-disclosure and masculinity. That is, those with higher masculinity scores disclosed more. Although this seems contrary to the notion that the traditional male role defines being masculine in terms of inhibiting disclosure, it can be interpreted in terms of the idea that self-disclosure may reflect masculine assertiveness. Unfortunately, however, the correlations with masculinity have not been consistent for both sexes across studies. Using the BSRI Masculinity scale, a positive correlation has been found for men (Naurus & Fischer (1982), for men but not women (Bem, 1977), for women but not men (Pearson, 1980), for both men and women (Hill, 1981b), and for neither men nor women (Axel, 1979; Bender, Davis, Glover, & Stap, 1976). Using the Personal Attributes Questionnaire Masculinity scale, no effects have been found for either sex in two studies (Bender, *et al.*, 1976; Hill, 1981b). In addition, one study found a negative correlation for men but not women using the BSRI (Winstead, Derlega, & Wong, 1986), and another reported a negative correlation for women but not men using the PAQ (Grigsby & Weatherley, 1983).

We expected positive correlations between self-disclosure and femininity scales, but those correlations are inconsistent, too. Using the BSRI Femininity scale, positive correlations have been found for men (Naurus & Fischer, 1982), for men but not women (Pearson, 1980), for both men and women (Hill, 1981b), for men and women combined (Bender *et al.*, 1976), and for neither men nor women (Axel, 1979; Bem, 1977; Winstead *et al.*, 1984). With the PAQ Feminity scale, correlations have been reported for both sexes separately (Hill, 1981b), for both sexes combined (Bender *et al.*, 1976), and for neither sex (Grigsby & Weatherley, 1983).

Androgyny as an Interaction Effect

Recently, it has been argued that if Bem is correct in assuming that androgyny is something more than simply having both masculine and feminine traits, it should be conceptualized as the interaction of masculinity and femininity rather than merely their sum. Hence, it should be measured as the interaction term in a multiple regression analysis (Stokes *et al.* 1981). Lubinski (1983) argues that it should be a hierarchical regression in which the main effects of masculinity and femininity are controlled first; that way the interaction term is not confounded by correlations with the main effects. This has been explored in four disclosure studies, using four different measures of disclosure and two different gender identity measures. All four studies found no effect of the interaction term (Berg & Peplau, 1982; Hill, 1981b; Stokes, 1983; Winstead *et al.*, 1986). It does not appear to be useful to measure androgyny as an interaction term, at least in research on self-disclosure. Taylor and Hall (1982) reach a similar conclusion regarding other areas of research.

More generally, we find that looking for individual differences in self-disclosure as a function of sex-role identity produces no more consistent results than we obtained in research on sex-role attitudes. Further studies of sex-role identity and self-disclosure need to focus on specifying factors that might mediate relationships between sex-role identity and self-disclosure.

STRATEGY 4: SEX-ROLE NORMS

Another line of research has explored sex-role expectations concerning appropriate self-disclosure, by studying how subjects evaluate self-disclosures made by others. In this research, it is assumed that sex roles prescribe different norms of disclosure for men and women. Hence, disclosures by men should be evaluated differently than disclosures by women. Differential evaluations thus provide information about sex-role norms. In addition, there may also be differences in evaluation as a function of the gender or the sex-role identity of the evaluator.

One of the earliest evaluation studies was an experiment by Derlega and Chaikin (1976) in which subjects read a case study about a man or woman who did or did not self-disclose something quite personal. Both male and female subjects rated the male stimulus person as being better adjusted when he failed to disclose than when he did disclose; the female stimulus person, on the other hand, was rated as better adjusted when she did disclose than when she did not. A similar study was conducted by Chelune (1976) in which subjects listened to a tape recording. The male speaker was liked most when he was a low discloser, whereas the female was liked most when she was a high discloser. There was a tendency to see high disclosure to a stranger as less emotionally healthy than low disclosure, but this did not differ by sex of speaker. Instead, male speakers were generally rated more emotionally healthy than females regardless of disclosure level. Hence, there do appear to be differing norms for men and women concerning the appropriateness of the self-disclosure.

In a related study by Cunningham (1981), subjects read disclosure scripts supposedly written by another subject. The sex of the author was varied, as well as the sex-role congruency (appropriateness) of the disclosure topics. Male subjects rated male authors as being in poorer mental health when the disclosure contents were "feminine" than when-they were "masculine." No differences were found, however, in male subjects' ratings of female authors or female subjects' ratings of either male or female authors. Sex-role congruency was also examined in a counseling analogue study by Feldstein (1979). Subjects were interviewed by a male or female authors. Sex-role congruency was also examined in a counseling analogue study by Feldstein (1979). Subjects were interviewed by a male or female counselor who displayed masculine or feminine behaviors (e.g., assertiveness vs. warmth). Male subjects indicated greater satisfaction and higher counselor regard for feminine counselors than for masculine counselors, regardless of counselor sex. Female subjects, in contrast, gave higher ratings to masculine counselors.

These studies suggest that the norms of appropriate disclosure by men and women depend in complex ways upon situational factors such as the topic of disclosure, the relationship between the discloser and the recipient (e.g., therapist–client versus other relationships), and the gender of the evaluator.

Sex-Role Identity Interactions

Other studies have looked for variations in subjects' evaluations of others' disclosure as a function of subjects' sex-role identity. In her gender schema theory, Bem has argued (1979, 1981) that androgynous and sex-typed individuals differ in their processing of gender-relevant information. Although other research has supported this prediction (Cook, 1985), the results from disclosure studies are inconsistent.

Bergey (1977) had teachers evaluate written descriptions of disclosures by children. In general, teachers referred more girls than boys for counseling. In addition, female teachers with low masculine self-concepts referred more children than did high masculine females. However, no effects were reported for females' feminine scale, and male teachers did not vary in their referrals as a function of sex-role identity.

In a second study, Merluzzi and Merluzzi (1981) found a three-way interaction between therapist expertness, therapist disclosure level, and subject sex-role self-concept on ratings of therapist trustworthiness when subjects read transcripts of a brief interview. Sex-typed subjects rated nonexpert therapists as more trustworthy when therapist disclosure was low than when it was high, whereas androgynous subjects' ratings were not affected by either therapist expertness or therapist disclosure level. However, ratings of perceived therapist expertise and attractiveness were not influenced by subjects' sex-role self-concept; high-disclosing therapists were rated as less expert but more attractive by both sex-typed and androgynous subjects.

No effects of sex-role identity were found in other studies by Banikiotes, Kubinski, and Pursell (1981), Clavier (1979), and Das (1982). The inconsistent results for this line of research are in keeping with the findings of other studies of sex-role identity and disclosure described in Strategy 3.

STRATEGY 5: SELF-DISCLOSURE MEASURES

A major source of difficulty in comparing studies of self-disclosure is variation in the way in which disclosure is measured (see Chelune, 1979). A primary distinction is between self-report and behavioral measures, but there are differences within each of these types as well. The self-report measures vary in terms of (a) whether they ask about past disclosure or willingness to disclose, (b) recipients (same-sex vs. opposite-sex, strangers vs. intimates, peers vs. parents), and (c) topics. The behavioral measures may be based on judges' ratings of intimacy of subjects' disclosures, ratings of the intimacy of the topics on which the disclosures occur, and/or simply a word count.

In examining the studies referenced in this chapter, we paid close attention to differences among the disclosure measures used in the hope that this might explain inconsistencies in the results. However, no clear patterns have emerged. Among the studies of sex-role attitudes, conflicting results have been obtained using the same disclosure measures (e.g., Hill, 1981a,b). Among the sex-role identity studies, both positive results and no results have been obtained for various disclosure measures. There does not appear to be any consistent variation in the results of the studies.

However, one possibility merits further research. The studies finding a positive relationship between masculinity and self-disclosure have used self-report measures of disclosure, which suggests that the positive correlation may be an artifact of using self-reports. Winstead *et al.* (1984) note that masculinity is related to self-confidence and high self-esteem and that persons high on masculinity may feel confident about telling others about themselves or claiming to do so. Winstead *et al.* found a negative correlation between masculinity and intimacy of actual disclosures between strangers, although this was only for men paired with other men. There was no correlation for other combinations of the sexes. Grigsby and Weatherly (1983), on the other hand, found a negative correlation for women but not for men in actual disclosure to same-sex strangers, using the PAQ measure of masculinity instead of the BSRI. In addition, Axel (1979) found no correlation between BSRI masculinity and actual disclosure in an interview for either men or women. Thus a negative correlation for actual disclosure is not always found, which suggests that it may be mediated by other factors.

It is also possible that differences between self-report and actual disclosure might account for inconsistencies in gender differences found in other studies of self-disclosure that do not measure sex-role attitudes or sex-role self-concept. To explore this, 52 additional studies of gender differences (which are not listed among the references at the end of this chapter but which were cited by the listed references) were examined and coded for the type of disclosure measure used, as well as the type of disclosure recipient, type of subjects, and results. (A list of these studies is available from the authors.) After all of these studies were located and analyzed, no consistent differences were found in the results as a function of whether self-report or behavioral measures of self-disclosure were used. Nor were there any obvious patterns of interaction between the type of disclosure measure and the other factors examined. Although these studies represent a small proportion of the more than 1,400 disclosure studies that have been conducted, these are the studies cited most often, and it seems unlikely that an analysis of all of the studies would be worth the effort in the absence of further theoretical specification of ways in which the factors should interact.

It is often assumed that self-report measures of disclosure are less reliable and valid than behavioral measures because early studies reviewed by Cozby (1973) found that scores on the JSDQ did not predict disclosure in laboratory settings. However, that interpretation assumes that past disclosure in ongoing intimate relationships ought to predict current disclosure between strangers in a single encounter in a laboratory. There is good reason to believe that single encounters between strangers differ in their dynamics from ongoing relationships; in particular, reciprocation may occur over longer time periods in ongoing relationships than in encounters between strangers (Hill & Stull, 1982). In addition, there are other factors that influence disclosure, including the characteristics and the personality of the disclosure recipient (Miller, Berg, & Archer, 1983).

Hence, self-report measures of past disclosure may have some validity as measures of past disclosure in specific relationships, even if they do not always predict laboratory disclosure. In support of this view are additional studies that sometimes find a correlation between the JSDQ and laboratory disclosure (reviewed by Miller *et al.*, 1983) and other studies of dyads that show moderate agreement between same-sex roommates (Rubin & Shenker, 1978) and between dating couples (Rubin *et al.*, 1980) on measures of total disclosure given and received. Self-reports of disclosure have also been found to be related to whether or not dating couples continue dating (Hill, Rubin, & Peplau, 1976) and to the extent of agreement or disagreement between members of dating couples (Hill, Peplau, & Rubin, 1981).

Thus if there are systematic differences between self-report and behavioral measures in the sex-role results obtained, these differences may reflect differences between accumulative exchanges in ongoing relationships and single encounters between strangers. Therefore, future research comparing self-report and behavioral measures needs to take into account the relationship with the disclosure recipient as well as the time frame over which the disclosure is measured.

CONCLUSIONS

In our own research on sex-role attitudes and self-disclosure, we have been frustrated due to the inconsistencies in the results that we have obtained. We had hoped that a careful review of other research relevant to sex-roles and self-disclosure would resolve the issues, but the other strategies have produced results just as inconsistent.

One of the problems is that self-disclosure is far more complex than anyone realized when this research was begun. The original prediction that traditional male-role expectations inhibit men's disclosure is too simple because it does not take into account the many situational factors that affect disclosure. We now know what many of these factors are, but we still cannot specify how these factors interact with one another and with gender. Future studies need to incorporate these situational factors and test hypotheses about interactions among them.

A second problem is methodological. Our measures of sex-role attitudes focus primarily on female role prescriptions, whereas the predictions focus more on men's disclosure. More attention needs to be given to the multidimensionality of sex-role attitudes. There are also many measures of sex-role identity, many ways of scoring them, and conceptual disagreement as to what they all mean (see Cook, 1985). Progress is needed in determining the best way to measure sex-role identity and in specifying factors that mediate between sex-role identity and self-disclosure. In addition, there are differing ways of assessing self-disclosure, which appear to tap differing aspects of disclosure dispositions, behaviors, and time frames. These differences need to be considered when predictions are made and results are compared.

The most fundamental problem, however, is conceptual. When self-disclosure was first measured by Jourard (e.g. 1971b) and his colleagues, it was conceptualized as a personality trait. Hence, it was measured as a unitary construct. Later researchers distinguished between the depth and breadth of disclosure (Altman & Taylor, 1973), and variations in sex differences as a function of the topic of disclosure were found (reviewed under Strategy 1). Yet self-disclosure has still largely been conceptualized and measured as a unidimensional construct.

More attention needs to be given to differences in the kinds of disclosures that are made and the purposes for which they are made in given types of social interaction. A clue to the importance of this is suggested in the finding that the hypothesized sex difference in self-disclosure is reversed in certain circumstances. Men may self-disclose more than women in the initial development of an opposite-sex relationship (Davis, 1978; Derlega *et al.*, 1985; Stokes *et al.*, 1981) in order to initiate the development of intimacy. This is consistent with the traditional male-role prescription that the man should be the initiator in the relationship. In addition, many women have been encouraged by their mothers to ask a man questions in order to get him to talk about himself. Future research should explore who *asks* for disclosure under what circumstances, as well as who discloses.

Further clues are provided in research on power strategies. Men tend to use more direct approaches, whereas women are more indirect (Johnson, 1976). Thus men may express their feelings and desires when it serves to exert power, whereas women may refrain from expressing their wishes explicitly when they think it more effective to use a more subtle influence approach. For example, by asking a man what he thinks, a woman can structure his choices in ways that let him think that he has made the decision, when she is merely delegating part of the decision to him. She may ask him which movie he wants to see, and he makes that decision, but in posing the question she has already decided the larger issue of whether to go to a movie or do something else (see Peplau, 1979). In addition, both men and women may withhold personal information if that information could give power to others.

More generally, research on communication in couples (see Brehm, 1985) implies that communications can serve a variety of functions, such as hurting or controlling as well as informing or expressing affection. More attention needs to be given to such differences in the way in which self-disclosure can be used. The research by Gottman (1979) on differences between men and women's communication patterns in distressed and nondistressed couples provides a good example of the fruitfulness of this approach.

Acknowledgments

The authors would like to thank John Berg, Val Derlega, Anne Peplau, and Pam Hill for comments on earlier drafts. Diane Ramirez assisted in the coding of the set of 52 gender-difference studies.

REFERENCES

Altman, I., & Taylor, D. A. (1973). *Social penetration: The development of interpersonal relationships.* New York: Holt, Rinehart & Winston.

Annicchiarico, L. K. B. (1973). Sex differences in self-disclosure as related to sex and status of the interviewer (Doctoral dissertation, University of Texas at Austin, 1973). *Dissertation Abstracts International, 34,* 2296B.

Aries, E. (1976). Interaction patterns and themes of male, female, and mixed groups. *Small Group Behavior, 7,* 7–18.

Axel, R. A. (1979). The relationship of discloser-disclosee sex and discloser self-ascribed sex-role to self-disclosing behavior (Doctoral dissertation, New York University, 1979). *Dissertation Abstracts International, 40(3-B),* 1347–1348.

Baffi, C. R. (1979). The influence of sex role identification on college males' performance in achievement and self-disclosure tasks (Doctoral dissertation, University of Maryland, 1979). *Dissertation Abstracts International, 40(5-B),* 2331.

Banikiotes, P. G., Kubinski, J. A., & Pursell, S. A. (1981). Sex role orientation, self-disclosure, and gender-related perceptions. *Journal of Counseling Psychology, 28,* 140–146.

Banikiotes, P. G., & Merluzzi, T. V. (1981). Impact of counselor gender and counselor sex role orientation on perceived counselor characteristics. *Journal of Counseling Psychology, 28,* 342–348.

Bem, S. L. (1974). The measurement of psychological androgyny. *Journal of Consulting and Clinical Psychology, 42,* 155–162.

Bem, S. L. (1977). On the utility of alternative procedures for assessing psychological androgyny. *Journal of Consulting and Clinical Psychology, 45,* 196–205.

Bem, S. L. (1979). Theory and measurement of androgyny: A reply to the Pedhazur-Telenbaum and Locksley-Colten critiques. *Journal of Personality and Social Psychology, 37,* 1047–1054.

Bem, S. L. (1981). Gender schema theory: A cognitive account of sex typing. *Psychological Review, 88,* 354–364.

Bender, V. L., Davis, Y., Glover, O., & Stapp, J. (1976). Patterns of self-disclosure in homosexual and heterosexual college students. *Sex Roles, 2,* 149–160.

Berg, J., & Peplau, L. A. (1982). Loneliness: The relationship of self-disclosure and androgyny. *Personality and Social Psychology Bulletin, 8,* 624–630.

Bergey, S. F. (1977). Teachers' response to self-disclosure of children (Doctoral dissertation, University of Pennsylvania, 1977). *Dissertation Abstracts International, 37(7-A),* 4220.

Brannon, R., & Juni, S. (1984). A scale for measuring attitudes toward masculinity. *Psychological Documents, 14* 6–7 (ms. 2012).

Brehm, S. S. (1985). *Intimate relationships.* New York: Random House.

Brooks, L. (1974). Interactive effects of sex and status on self-disclosure. *Journal of Counseling Psychology, 21,* 469–474.

Cash, T. F. (1975). Self-disclosure in the acquaintance process: Effects of sex, physical attractiveness, and approval motivation (Doctoral dissertation, George Peabody College for Teachers, 1975). *Dissertation Abstracts International, 35,* 3572B.

Certner, B. C. (1970). *The exchange of self-disclosures in same-sexed and heterosexual groups of strangers.* (Unpublished doctoral dissertation, University of Cincinnati.)

Chaikin, A. L., & Derlega, V. J. (1974) *Self-disclosure.* Morristown, NJ: General Learning Press.

Chelune, G. J. (1976) The self-disclosure situations survey: A new approach to measuring self-disclosure. *JSAS Catalog of Selected Documents in Psychology, 6,* 111–112 (Ms. 1367).

Chelune, G. J. (Ed.). (1979). *Self-disclosure.* San Francisco: Jossey-Bass.

Clavier, D. E. (1979). Psychological androgyny and individual differences in an inequitable exchange of self-disclosure (Doctoral dissertation, Florida State University, 1979). *Dissertation Abstracts International, 40(6–A),* 2981.

Colwill, N. L., & Perlman, D. (1977). Effects of sex and relationship on self-disclosure. *JSAS Catalog of Selected Documents in Psychology, 7,* 40 (Ms. 1470).

Cook, E. P. (1985). *Psychological androgyny.* New York: Pergamon Press.

Cozby, P. C. (1972). Self-disclosure, reciprocity, and liking. *Sociometry, 35,* 151–160.

Cozby, P. C. (1973). Self-disclosure: A literature review. *Psychological Bulletin, 79,* 73–91.

Cunningham, J. A. (1981). Effects of intimacy and sex-role congruency of self-disclosure (Doctoral dissertation, University of Utah). *Dissertation Abstracts International, 42(6–B),* 2597.

Das, B. D. (1982). Self disclosure, androgyny, and the attribution of maladjustment (Doctoral dissertation, Illinois Institute of Technology, 1981). *Dissertation Abstracts International, 42(8–B),* 3396.

Davis, J. D. (1978). When boy meets girl: Sex roles and the negotiation of intimacy in an acquaintance exercise. *Journal of Personality and Social Psychology, 36,* 684–692.

Denton, E. A. (1982). The effects of gender and sex role orientation on written self-disclosure (Doctoral dissertation, University of Tennessee). *Dissertation Abstracts International, 42(11–B),* 4617.

Derlega, V. J., & Chaikin, A. L. (1976). Norms affecting self-disclosure in men and women. *Journal of Consulting and Clinical Psychology, 44,* 376–380.

Derlega, V. J., Winstead, B. A., Wong, P. T. P., & Hunter, S. (1985). Gender effects in an initial encounter: A case where men exceed women in disclosure. *Journal of Social and Personal Relationships, 2,* 25–44.

Doster, J. A. (1976). Sex role learning and interview communication. *Journal of Counseling Psychology, 23,* 482–485.

Downs, A. C., & Engleson, S. A. (1982). The Attitudes Toward Men Scale (AMS): An analysis of the role and status of men and masculinity. *JSAS Catalog of Selected Documents in Psychology, 12,* 45 (Ms. 2503).

Doyle, J. A., & Moore, R. J. (1978). Attitudes toward the Male's Role Scale (AMR): An objective instrument to measure attitudes toward the male's sex role in contemporary society. *JASA Catalog of Selected Documents in Psychology, 8*, 35, (Ms. 1678).

Feldstein, J. C. (1979). Effects of counselor sex and sex-role and client sex on clients' perceptions and self-disclosure in a counseling analogue study. *Journal of Counseling Psychology, 26*, 437–443.

Fielden, P. M. (1982). Sex-role and gender influences upon self-disclosing behavior (Doctoral dissertation, University of Alabama, 1982). *Dissertation Abstracts International, 43(5–A)*, 4617.

Fischer, K. I. (1979). Studies in the relationships of psychosocial competence, gender and sex role orientation to appropriate flexibility and amount of self-disclosure (Doctoral dissertation, University of Delaware). *Dissertation Abstracts International, 42(5–B)*, 2054–2055.

Goffman, E. (1967). The nature of deference and demeanor. In E. Goffman (Ed.), *Interaction ritual* (pp. 47–95). Garden City, NY: Anchor.

Gottman, J. M. (1979). *Marital interaction*. New York: Academic Press.

Goodstein, L. D., & Reinecker, V. M. (1974). Factors affecting self-disclosure: A review of the literature. In B. A. Maher (Ed.), *Progress in experimental personality research, 7* (pp. 49–77). New York: Academic Press.

Grigsby, J. P., & Weatherley, D. (1983). Gender and sex-role differences in intimacy of self-disclosure. *Psychological Reports, 53*(3, Part 1), 891–897.

Haas, A. (1979). Male and female spoken language differences: Stereotypes and evidence. *Psychological Bulletin, 86*, 616–626.

Hacker, H. M. (1981). Blabbermouths and clams: Sex differences in disclosure in same-sex and cross-sex friendship dyads. *Psychology of Women Quarterly, 5*(3), 385–401.

Heilbrun, A. B. (1973). History of self-disclosure in females and early defection from psychotherapy. *Journal of Counseling Psychology, 20*, 250–257.

Hill, C. (1980). Unpublished reanalyses of data from Rubin, Hill, Peplau, and Dunkel-Schetter.

Hill, C. (1981a). Unpublished data collected at the University of Washington, Spring 1981.

Hill, C. (1981b). Unpublished data collected at the University of Washington, Autumn 1981.

Hill, C. T., & Stull, D. E. (1982). Disclosure reciprocity: Conceptual and measurement issues. *Social Psychology Quarterly, 45*, 238–244.

Hill, C. T., Rubin, Z., & Peplau, L. A. (1976). Breakups before marriage: The end of 103 affairs. *Journal of Social Issues, 32*(1), 147–168.

Hill, C. T., Peplau, L. A., & Rubin, Z. (1981). Differing perceptions in dating couples: Sex roles versus alternative explanations. *Psychology of Women Quarterly, 5*, 418–434.

Hyink, P. W. (1975). The influence of client ego strength, client sex and therapist sex on the frequency, depth, and focus of client self-disclosure (Doctoral dissertation, Michigan State University, 1975). *Dissertation Abstract International, 35*, 4652B.

Ickes, W., & Barnes, R. D. (1978). Boys and girls together—and alienated: On enacting stereotyped sex roles in mixed-sex dyads. *Journal of Personality and Social Psychology, 36*, 669–683.

Inman, D. J. (1978). Self-disclosure and interview reciprocity (Doctoral dissertation, Louisiana State University & Agriculture & Mining College, 1978). *Dissertation Abstracts International, 38*, 3398B.

Johnson, P. (1976). Women and power: Toward a theory of effectiveness. *The Journal of Social Issues, 32*(3), 99–110.

Jourard, S. M. (1971a). Some lethal aspects of the male role. In S. M. Jourard (Ed.), *The transparent self* (rev. ed., pp. 34–44). New York: Van Nostrand.

Jourard, S. M. (1971b). *Self-disclosure: An experimental analysis of the transparent self.* New York: Wiley-Interscience.

Jourard, S. M., & Lasakow, P. (1958). Some factors in self-disclosure. *Journal of Abnormal and Social Psychology, 56,* 91–98.

Komarovsky, M. (1967). *Blue-collar marriage.* New York: Random House.

Komarovsky, M. (1974). Patterns of self-disclosure of male undergraduates. *Journal of Marriage and the Family, 36,* 677–686.

Lombardo, J. P., Franco, R., Wolf, T. M., & Fantasia, S. C. (1976). Interest in helping activities and self-disclosure to three targets on the Jourard Self-Disclosure Scale. *Perceptual and Motor Skills, 42,* 299–302.

Lubinski, D. (1983). The androgyny dimension: A comment on Stokes, Childs, and Fuehrer. *Journal of Counseling Psychology, 30*(1), 130–133.

Merluzzi, T. V., & Merluzzi, B. (1981). Androgyny, stereotypy and the perception of female therapists. *Journal of Clinical Psychology, 37,* 280–284.

Miller, L. C., Berg, J. H., & Archer, R. L. (1983). Openers: Individuals who elicit intimate self-disclosure. *Journal of Personality and Social Psychology, 44,* 1234–1244.

Millet, K. (1975). The shame is over. *Ms.*, January 1975, pp. 26–29.

Morgan, B. S. (1976). Intimacy of disclosure topics and sex differences in self-disclosure. *Sex Roles, 2,* 161–166.

Morton, T. L. (1978). Intimacy and reciprocity of exchange: A comparison of spouses and strangers. *Journal of Personality and Social Psychology, 36,* 72–81.

Mosher, D. L., & Sirkin, M. (1984). Measuring a macho personality constellation. *Journal of Research in Personality, 18,* 150–163.

Naurus, L. R., & Fischer, J. L. (1982). Strong but not silent: A reexamination of expressivity in the relationships of men. *Sex Roles, 8,* 159–168.

Orlofsky, J. L. (1981). Relationship of sex role attitudes and personality traits and the Sex Role Behavior Scale-1: A new measure of masculine and feminine role behaviors and interests. *Journal of Personality and Social Psychology, 40,* 927–940.

Pearson, J. C. (1980). Sex role and self-disclosure. *Psychological Reports, 47,* 640.

Peplau, L. A. (1979). Power in dating relationships. In J. Freeman (Ed.), *Women: A feminist perspective* (2nd ed., pp. 106–121). Palo Alto, CA: Mayfield.

Piliavin, J. A., & Martin, R. R. (1978). The effects of the sex composition of groups on style of social interaction. *Sex Roles, 4*(2), 281–296.

Pleck, J. H. (1976). The male sex role: Definitions, problems, and sources of change. *Journal of Social Issues, 32*(1), 155–164.

Rickers-Ovsiankina, M. (1956). Social accessibility in three age groups. *Psychological Reports, 2,* 283–294.

Rosenfeld, L. B., Civikly, J. M., & Herron, J. R. (1979). Anatomical and psychological sex differences. In G. J. Chelune (Ed.), *Self-disclosure* (pp. 80–109). San Francisco: Jossey-Bass.

Rubin, Z. (1974). Lovers and other strangers: The development of intimacy in encounters and relationships. *American Scientist, 62*(2), 182–190.

Rubin, Z. (1976). Naturalistic studies of self-disclosure. *Personality and Social Psychology Bulletin, 2,* 260–263.

Rubin, Z., & Shenker, S. (1978). Friendship, proximity, and self-disclosure. *Journal of Personality, 46,* 1–11.

Rubin, Z., Hill, C. T., Peplau, L. A., & Dunkel-Schetter, C. (1980). Self-disclosure in dating couples: Sex roles and the ethic of openness. *Journal of Marriage and the Family, 42,* 305–317.

Slobin, D. I., Miller, S. H., & Porter, L. W. (1968). Forms of address and social relations in a business organization. *Journal of Personality and Social Psychology, 8,* 289–293.

Small, A., Gross, R., Erdwins, C., & Gessner, T. (1979). Social attitude correlates of sex role. *Journal of Psychology, 101,* 115–121.

Snell, W. E., Jr. (1983). *The masculine role inventory: Components and correlates.* Unpublished doctoral dissertation, The University of Texas at Austin.

Snell, W. E., Jr., Belk, S. S., & Hawkins, R. C. II. (1984). *The stereotypes about male sexuality scale: Components, correlates, antecedents, and counselors' perceptions.* Paper presented at the annual meeting of the Southwestern Psychological Association, San Antonio, Texas.

Spence, J. T., & Helmreich, R. L. (1978). *Masculinity & femininity: Their psychological dimensions, correlates & antecedents.* Austin: The University of Texas Press.

Spence, J. T., Helmreich, R., & Stapp, J. (1975). Ratings of self and peers on sex role attributes and their relation to self-esteem and conceptions of masculinity and femininity. *Journal of Personality and Social Psychology, 32,* 29–39.

Stokes, J. (1983). Androgyny as an interactive concept: A reply to Lubinski. *Journal of Counseling Psychology, 30,* 134–136.

Stokes, J., Childs, L., & Fuehrer, A. (1981). Gender and sex roles as predictors of self-disclosure. *Journal of Counseling Psychology, 28,* 510–514.

Stull, D. E. (1981). *Sex differences in self-disclosure: A comparison of men's and women's same-sex relationships.* (Unpublished master's thesis, University of Washington).

Switkin, L. R. (1974). Self-disclosure as a function of sex roles, experimenter-subject distance, sex of experimenter and intimacy of topics (Doctoral dissertation, St. Louis University, 1974). *Dissertation Abstracts International, 35(5–B),* 2451.

Taylor, M. C., & Hall, J. A. (1982). Psychological androgyny: Theories, methods, and conclusions. *Psychological Bulletin, 92,* 347–366.

Winstead, B. A., Derlega, V. J., & Wong, P. T. P. (1984). Effects of sex-role orientation on behavioral self-disclosure. *Journal of Research in Personality, 18*(4), 541–553.

6

Responsiveness and Self-Disclosure

JOHN H. BERG

In recent years, the concept of responsiveness has been used in investigations of self-disclosure (e.g., Berg & Archer, 1980, 1983; Davis & Perkowitz, 1979), social exchange phenomena (e.g., Berg, Blaylock, Camarillo, & Steck, 1985; Clark & Mills, 1979; Kelley, 1979), and friendship formation (e.g., Berg & Clark, 1986; Berg & McQuinn, 1986). It is the intent of this chapter to explore the applicability of responsiveness to self-disclosure phenomena in a more extensive and systematic fashion than has been heretofore possible. In doing this, I will first review usages of the term *responsiveness* and the research that supports its existence as an independent construct. In so doing, a distinction will be made between two general forms of responsiveness: *conversational responsiveness* and *relational responsiveness*. The consequences of responsive action and the aspects of an action that lead to its being judged as responsive are then presented. Following this presentation of the concept of responsiveness, various aspects of self-disclosure and findings in the self-disclosure literature will be examined as they relate to responsiveness. Finally, the limitations of present findings dealing with responsiveness and self-disclosure will be noted, and directions for future investigation will be discussed.

JOHN H. BERG • Department of Psychology, University of Mississippi, University, Mississippi 38677.

RESPONSIVENESS

Classes and Aspects of Responsive Actions

The term *responsiveness* was first applied to self-disclosure settings by Davis and Perkowitz (1979). In their study of communicative interactions, Davis and Perkowitz defined responsiveness in terms of the extent that replies to another's communication met three demands implicit in that communication. These are (a) that the other respond in some way, (b) that the response address the content of preceding communication, and (c) that the response be characterized by a suitable degree of elaboration (i.e., that that the initial speaker intended to elicit). Davis and Holtgraves (1984) have noted a fourth implicit demand of communication—that the latency for the response be appropriate (as determined by cultural norms, individual preferences, or rhythmic patterns of the communicating dyad). The reply made to another is considered to be responsive to the degree that the other *perceives* it as meeting these four demands.

A somewhat different usage of the term *responsiveness* was made by Clark and Mills (1979) in their studies of communal (close) and exchange (not close) relationships. They held that communal relationships operated in accordance with a norm of mutual responsiveness by which they meant that each person benefited the other because the other needed some particular resource and without any expectation that the other make repayment. In fact, they present evidence indicating that if such return payment is made, it can have the effect of undermining the relationship. A very similar point was made by Kelley (1979) when he noted that one of the primary characteristics of a close personal relationship was that participants would demonstrate increased responsiveness. By this he meant that each person would consider the other's outcomes (rewards and costs) as well as their own when allocating resources or deciding how to act.

Miller and Berg (1984) employ the term *responsiveness* in a way that appears to bridge these other usages. They view responsiveness as "the extent to which and the way in which one participant's actions address the previous actions, communications, needs, or wishes of another participant in that interaction" (p. 191). They then go on to distinguish two general classes of actions through which one person indicates that he or she is addressing the other's previous behaviors, communications, needs, or wishes. These are *conversational responsiveness* ("behaviors made by the recipient of another's communication through which the recipient indicates interest in and understanding of that communication" [p. 193] and *relational responsiveness* ("behaviors involving the attainment or distribution of rewards through which a person indicates that he or she is concerned with and is taking account of another's outcomes or needs" [p. 193].

In general, what Miller and Berg (1984) describe as conversational responsiveness appears to correspond to the way responsiveness is used by Davis (1982; Davis & Holtgraves, 1984; Davis & Perkowitz, 1979), whereas relational responsiveness bears many similarities to the usages of Clark and Mills and of Kelley (Clark & Mills, 1979; Kelley, 1979; Mills & Clark, 1982). What is common to both conversationally and relationally responsive acts is that both are means through which one person indicates understanding of another and concern with him or her. Also, both are based on and address the other's past behaviors, and both require knowledge of the other's needs and/or interests. Conversational responsiveness does this primarily in the domain of communication exchanges, whereas relational responsiveness deals primarily with exchanges involving more tangible commodities. By applying this same concept, highlighting a concern with addressing another's interests and past actions to both types of exchanges, one begins to move closer to having a common language for describing different aspects of interpersonal interaction and one that points to similarities in the intentions that motivate these different actions. For this reason and because it appears to subsume other usages, the definition of responsiveness employed by Miller and Berg (1984) will be adopted here.

Consequences of Responsiveness

Regardless of which definition of responsiveness is employed, responsive actions may be expected to lead to certain consequences. Davis (1982; Davis & Perkowitz, 1979) has described a number of effects that are expected to follow responsive acts. Among these are (a) maintenance of interaction between people, (b) maintenance of interaction focus, (c) increases in the degree to which interactions becomes predictable for the target of the responsive act and a corresponding reduction in interaction stress for him or her, (d) increased attraction for the person acting responsively, and (e) an increased perception that the people involved in the interaction have or will develop a closer relationship. One way to judge whether or not an action is responsive is then to determine whether it leads to the previously mentioned effects.

The preceding list of consequences is also a list of potential goals that are motivating the responsive person. (See Chapter 3 by Miller and Read for an extended discussion of such interaction goals.) To the preceding list, several additional consequences that will follow from responsive acts (and hence additional goals that may motivate such acts) can be added.

First, because responsiveness will serve to maintain interaction and interaction focus, it can serve the goals of allowing a responsive person to discover more about the other and encouraging the other to become more intimate. In line with this is the finding of Miller, Beng, and Archer (1983) that individuals scoring high on an individual difference measure of responsiveness (the Opener Scale) were able to elicit more intimate self-disclosure from persons who generally did not disclose in a structured laboratory interview and were more often chosen as recipients of self-disclosure in a field setting. Presumably, the responsive actions of these high "openers" conveyed to the other that she was liked, that the opener was interested in and concerned with her, and so encouraged the other to disclose more.

Determinants of Responsiveness

In discussing the determinants of responsiveness, two issues need to be considered. The first involves the need to specify more precisely the aspects of a person's actions that result in their being perceived as responsive. A second issue concerns the need to describe the conditions in which a person is most likely to act in a responsive manner. This section will briefly review previous thought and work dealing with each of these issues.

Aspects of Responsive Actions. One distinction between Miller and Berg's (1984) usage of responsiveness and the manner in which it has been applied by other researchers is their explicit recognition that responsiveness may be indicated and perceived through variations in three different facets of action: content, style, and timing. In terms of relational responsiveness, content will deal with the extent to which a person provides another needed or desired resources and the extent to which he or she considers the outcomes the other will receive when allocating joint resources. It is this dimension of content that Clark and Mills (1979) and Kelley (1979) refer to when they speak of responsive acts. In terms of conversational responsiveness, content will deal with the degree to which the things a person says address another's interests and previous communications. The three demands of communication exchanges that Davis and Perkowitz (1979) originally proposed as the conditions that define responsiveness (probability of a response, the extent to which previous communicative content is addressed, and degree of elaboration) would all seem to reflect variations of content.

The dimension of style refers to the way in which an action is performed. For relational responsiveness, this would involve such things as providing another with a certain response willingly and enthusiastically as opposed to reluctantly. Although no research directly addresses this issue, it seems unlikely that giving even a highly desired resource would be viewed as responsive or that many of the positive consequences of responsive acts would follow if that resource were given only begrudgingly. Perhaps it is for this reason that people will often accompany the giving of other resources with expressions of affection or admiration (Foa & Foa, 1980). For conversational responsiveness, style will involve the use of eye contact, smiles, head nods, and backchannel communicators typically refered to as "listener cues." For a speaker, style will involve variations in the affect with which something is said and will involve various nonverbal and paraverbal aspects of communication and the use of qualifying words that can indicate differences in intensity. In many ways, the distinction between content and style is akin to the distinction drawn by communication theorists between the content and relational components of communication or the literal meaning and the connotative meaning (metacommunication) (Bateson, 1972; Norton & Montgomery, 1982). It is through this stylistic relational or connotative component that participants communicate to one another how literal meanings are to be taken, filtered, or understood, and through which they define their relationship. This distinction between content and style also resembles distinctions that have been made in the self-disclosure literature. For example, Morton (1978) distinguishes descriptive intimacy from evaluative intimacy. The former refers to the intimacy of the factual information a disloser reveals (content), whereas the latter deals with the intensity of the affect or the strength of the judgment he or she expresses (style). In a similar vein, Chelune (1975) notes that self-disclosures will vary not only in their duration, amount, and intimacy (content) but also in the affective manner of their presentation (style).

The third aspect of an action that needs to be considered when judging its responsiveness is timing or when that action occurs in relation to another's preceding communication or the time when one discovers the other has some need. Davis and Holtgraves (1984) recognized this when they added the appropriateness of response latency to the three demands of conversation originally proposed by Davis and Perkowitz (1979). It is proposed here that variations in the timing of an action will intensify the effects of either responsive or unresponsive content and style. Thus it would be predicted that responsive content that immediately follows another's statement will be seen as indicating more attraction and will result in greater liking than that same content occurring later. Similarly, it is expected that unresponsive content will result in decreased liking when it immediately follows another's communication compared to the later occurrence of that same content. In attempting to test this prediction, however, one needs to keep in mind that actions that are rather automatically elicited by preceding actions or communications are likely to have very short response latencies. Such automatic actions are not, however, considered to be responsive as the term is used here (cf. Miller & Berg, 1984).

An important task for future research will be to map out the potential interactions and influences that the facets of content, style, and timing have on each other and their relationship to more global judgments of responsiveness. Although such a task is beyond the scope of this chapter, it is appropriate to briefly note some of the research suggesting that responsiveness be viewed in terms of these three dimensions. Because it is conversational responsiveness that is most relevent to this volume's focus on self-disclosure, work dealing with relational responsiveness will not be reviewed.

Responsive Content. Of the three dimensions hypothesized to influence perceptions of responsiveness, content has received the greatest amount of empirical attention. In the first published investigation of responsiveness, Davis and Perkowitz (1979) varied responsive content in two different ways. In their first experiment, a confederate was given the option of answering a question or of not answering after the subjects had answered a question. In a second study, confederates were always required to answer but were given the choice of answering the same question subjects had previously answered or a different question. In this way, either the probability of a response or the relevence of the response to preceding content was varied. Both manipulations produced the expected effects. The greater the proportion of times the confederate responded or the more often this response dealt with the same content as the subject's answer, the more the subject felt a relationship existed, liked the confederate, and perceived him or her as being responsive. Berg and Archer (1980) varied content in a slightly different way. In this study, subjects read about an encounter between two women in which the first disclosed either intimately or nonintimately. The other woman replied by making either an intimate or nonintimate disclosure of her own on a different topic or by expressing concern for the initial speaker. In terms of content, the most responsive reply would be the statement of concern, followed by a disclosure of matching intimacy, and finally by a disclosure of different intimacy. As would be predicted from the concept of responsiveness, liking for the second woman also followed this pattern. Finally, Davis and Holtgraves (1984) varied the responsiveness of candidates' answers to debate questions. This was done by varying the questions the candidates were asked so that the content of the answer, although linguistically the same, either directly or only tangentially addressed the question asked. As predicted, in comparison to the candidate's giving directly relevant answers, the less responsive candidate was perceived as less attractive, less competent, motivated, and knowledgeable, and as not understanding either the question or the issues it addressed.

Responsive Style. When a speaker is able to receive feedback from a listener, even if such feedback is limited to nonverbal or monosyllabic utterances (head nodding, yeses, or um humm), the listener becomes more likely to understand the communicated message because such responses inform the speaker about the listener's interest, understanding, and his or her affective state. They consequently allow conversation to become more coordinated and effective (Kraut, Lewis, & Sweeny, 1982). Thus, in addition to indicating interest and understanding, such stylistic behaviors should facilitate conversations, reduce their stress, and encourage future interactions. They should also promote intimacy. As was noted before, it is variations in precisely these sorts of cues that are involved in responsive style.

Ellsworth and Ross (1975) manipulated one of these responsive listener cues (gaze). A male or female subject disclosed to a same-sex partner who had been previously instructed to gaze continually at the discloser, gaze when the discloser said something intimate, avoid looking at the speaker, or avoid looking when he or she said something intimate. Their results indicated that both male and female disclosers perceived themselves to have been more intimate in the former two conditions than in the latter two. Thus disclosers saw the situation as more intimate if the other behaved with a responsive style.

Miller *et al.* (1983) developed a scale to identify persons who would be able to elicit intimate self-disclosure from others (the Opener Scale). Women scoring either high or low on this scale then asked five standardized questions to other women who had been classified as either dispositionally high or low self-disclosers. It was found that the high openers elicited more intimate self-disclosure from interviewees who were low in their tendency to self-disclose. In a second study, it was found that these high openers were most often the recipients of self-disclosure from members of their sorority and were better liked than their sorority sisters who were low openers. These findings are consistent with Miller *et al.*'s belief that the high openers are more responsive. The fact that both high and low openers asked the same questions in the interview study suggests that they differ primarily in terms of stylistic factors.

A direct test of this is provided in a study by Purvis, Dabbs, and

Hopper (1984) who examined the nonverbal behavior of pairs of high and low openers during a conversation. It was found that the high-opener pairs gazed at each other more, smiled more, and employed more head nods and backchannel communications than the low-opener pairs.

In addition to the dimensions of responsiveness tapped by the Opener Scale, a second responsive style is hypothesized by Norton and Montgamery (1982). They describe an "open style" of communication that is indicated through both verbal and nonverbal factors. In describing the effects an open style of communication will have, they note that

> at minimum, the person with an open style seems to grant permission to explore specified aspects of the personal domain. At maximum, the person with an open style invites radically intense and reciprocal interaction. (p. 402)

Norton and Montgomery go on to report data indicating that this communication style is significantly related to the extent subjects report having disclosed to various targets.

That both this open style and responsiveness as measured by the Opener Scale have similar effects on listener responsiveness is suggested in a study by Miller (1982). In this experiment, subjects were classified as high or low for both opener status and willingness to self-disclose. In subsequent conversations, it was found that individuals who were low on *both* traits smiled less, used fewer backchannel communicators and head nods, and were rated as less responsive by independent raters than persons who were high on either one or both traits.

Timing and Responsiveness. To date, only one study (Piner, Berg, & Miller, 1986) has addressed the manner in which timing may affect conversational responsiveness. The results of this study indicate that as described before, timing will interact with content in such a way that it magnifies the effects of responsive and unresponsive content. In this study, subjects read of a first encounter between two women, one of whom disclosed either a serious problem or one that was quite minor. The second woman replied to this in one of three ways: (a) she talked about herself and other issues, (b) she said the same things about herself but preceded them by expressing concern for the first woman, or (c) said the same things but followed them with an expression of concern. An indication of sympathy should be responsive in terms of its content when the initial problem was rather serious. If the problem was trivial, immediately expressing sympathy implies that the respondent really did *not* understand the first woman's meaning or situation. Thus, if timing acts to magnify the effects of content, we should expect large differences in the expected consequences when concern comes immediately after disclosure of serious or trivial difficulties. Much less of a difference between disclosure of serious or trivial problems would be predicted in the other conditions. This is, in fact, what was found. For example, when concern was expressed immediately, subjects felt it was significantly more likely the women would become close friends when the problem intially disclosed had been serious than when it had been trivial. However, no differences for problem severity were found if concern was not expressed or was expressed late.

Summary. From the data reviewed here, it does in fact seem that judgments of responsiveness are influenced by three conceptually different facets of action. Variations in content, style, and timing of actions have been shown to influence judgments of responsiveness and to lead to differences in the consequences actions produce. The next issue that needs to be addressed is to specify *when* a person is most likely to vary different aspects of his or her actions so that they are more responsive.

Conditions Leading to Responsive Acts. Although it is a truism to state that responsiveness, like all behavior, is a function of both personal and situational factors, what the particular individual differences and/or the particular situations are that lead to responsiveness is not so obvious. Because an extensive discussion of the influence of personality characteristics and situational contexts on conversational responsiveness is available in Davis (1982), only a brief presentation of major points will be made here.

As implied before, one important factor concerns an individual's interaction goals. As Miller and Read note in this volume (Chapter 3), many personality or individual difference variables may be conceptualized as representing differences in the goals people have. They also provide a description of the goals that are presumably held by one type of person who has been shown to be highly responsive (the high opener). This individual has as salient goals making friends and becoming intimate with people and finding out more about and being liked by the people with whom he or she is interacting. These goals are precisely the results that will follow from responsive action, so it should not be surprising that persons who value these goals act in the most responsive ways (Miller, 1982; Miller *et al.*, 1983; Purvis *et al.*, 1984).

Persons who are high self-monitors (Snyder, 1974) are also likely to highly value some of the goals that lead to acting responsively. Because self-monitoring and self-disclosure are discussed in detail by Coates and Winston in their chapter (see Chapter 11), it is sufficient here to note just two points. First, high self-monitors are hypothesized to be particularly concerned with presenting themselves in a manner that will result in their being liked and with acting appropriately. As persons who value such goals, they should be expected to act in a responsive manner. Research has, in fact, shown this to be true. For example, Shaffer, Smith, and Tomarelli (1982) found that high self-monitors were more likely to formulate replies to another's self-disclosure that were more responsive in terms of both content and style. The replies of high self-monitors addressed the same topical content as preceding disclosures to a greater degree than the replies of low self-monitors. They also revealed factual information that was of comparable intimacy, whereas the replies of low self-monitors did not. As for style, high self-monitors replied with a degree of affect that closely approximated the affect of the preceding communication, whereas low self-monitors did not vary their affect.

Berg and Archer (1982) performed an experiment that directly examined the influence of subjects' interaction goals on both the extent of responsiveness and the manner in which it was demonstrated. Subjects were asked to adopt one of three interaction goals: (a) giving their partner an accurate impression of themselves, (b) having a conversation, or (c) being liked by their partner. Although the influence of these different interaction goals on the form of responsiveness will be discussed at a later point, it should be noted here that the subjects who were most responsive were those who had the goal of maximizing their attractiveness. Although it remains to be empirically demonstrated, similar increases in responsiveness should occur if subjects are given the goal of finding out as much as they can about another, keeping him or her talking about a particular topic, or becoming intimate. It would not, however, be expected that responsiveness would be expressed in exactly the same ways to achieve all of these goals (i.e., sometimes different content may best indicate interest and understanding of the other; sometimes variations in style and/or timing may do this).

Besides a person's interaction goal(s), a second condition that will influence the probability of responsive behavior's being enacted is the amount of attention that is given to the other and particular aspects of his or her behavior. Obviously, one cannot produce actions that indicate interest in and understanding of another's past behaviors or indicate concern for his or her interests or needs unless one has attended to the other's previous behaviors. Here again, both individual differences and situational factors should be important. For example, self-monitoring has been shown to increase the extent to which subjects attend to and recall information about an interaction partner (Bercheid, Graziano, Monson, & Dermer, 1976). Although there is some disagreement on the point, one might then speculate that the increased responsiveness of high self-monitors, noted before, is due, at least in part, to their attending more to the behavior of others.

Miller and Mueller (1983) developed an individual difference measure to directly assess differences in the degree to which respondents attend to others' conversational behavior. Scores on this measure of conversational attentiveness were significantly related to subjects' ability to accurately recall what had been said during a 10-minute videotaped interview. It remains to be demonstrated, however, that persons high in such conversational attentiveness are also persons who act in responsive ways. Similarly, other traits and interaction styles that affect responsiveness (e.g., opener status and open communication style) may do this because they affect attention. This should be determined in future work. Another general factor that will determine when and how responsive acts occur is the extent to which a respondent possesses a resource that can satisfy the need or has behaviors in his or her response repertoire that can adequately convey interest and understanding. This may involve whether or not a person is able to give the time necessary to meet the other's need as well as the degree to which the person has access to sufficient quantities of different resources. It also involves whether a person has sufficient knowledge about a particular subject to produce a response that adequately addresses the previous communication. Even in terms of the more stylistic aspects of conversational responsiveness, an individual may not have appropriate responses in his or her repertoire. For example, Miller, Lechner, and Rugs (1985) find that younger children are viewed as less responsive and produce fewer responsive listener behaviors (e.g., uh huhs, head nods, smiles) than older children. Or consider the example of the conversation between the American and the person from Latin America. The latter keeps moving closer, whereas the American keeps backing away. Both individuals have distancing behaviors that are inappropriate and unresponsive in the other's eyes.

APPLICATIONS TO SELF-DISCLOSURE PROCESSES

In the preceding sections of this chapter, I have attempted to lay out the basic components of a theory of responsiveness. In several places, I have made reference to the role responsiveness is thought to play in conversations and self-disclosure exchanges. In the remaining pages, I will be more explicit about this and will explore the role of responsiveness in accounting for disclosure reciprocity and disclosure liking effects. Finally, the concept of responsiveness will be used to help explicate the role of self-disclosure in counseling. For simplicity, when the term *responsiveness* is used without any preceding qualifier, it is conversational responsiveness that is being referred to.

Disclosure Reciprocity

Disclosure reciprocity is by far the most consistent finding in the self-disclosure literature (see reviews by Archer, 1979; Chaikin & Derlega, 1974a; and Cozby, 1973). As these reviewers and others have noted, the best predictor of the intimacy of Person A's disclosure will be the intimacy of the self-disclosure he or she has received from Person B. It is worth noting, too, that attempts to explore disclosure reciprocity have confined themselves almost exclusively to the intimacy of the facts contained in the two communications or what Morton (1978) has called *descriptive intimacy*.

The tendency for a disclosure recipient to match the intimacy of the factual information he or she has received has been attributed to modeling (e.g., Rubin, 1975), attempts to show liking (e.g., Worthy, Gary, & Kahn, 1969), and attempts to maintain equitable social exchange or a "norm of reciprocity" (e.g., Derlega, Harris, & Chaikin, 1973). Although studies comparing these various approaches favor the social exchange or normative explanation as specifying the necessary condition for reciprocity, none of the proposed explanations can be ruled out as specifying contributory factors. The concept of responsiveness is another such contributory factor. In fact, in some situations, including the ones in which reciprocity is often studied, the only way a subject may be able to demonstrate responsiveness is by varying the intimacy of his or her disclosure to match that of the person who disclosed to him or her.

To understand this last statement, consider the paradigm typically employed to study disclosure reciprocity. A subject arrives and is told that he or she and another subject (typically an experimental confederate) will be taking part in a study on impression formation in which they will take turns describing themselves to one another and following this will indicate the impressions they have formed. The confederate is always selected to describe himself or herself first, which he or she does in either an intimate or a nonintimate fashion. Subjects are then asked to disclose (or at least indicate their willingness to disclose) to the confederate. Often the topics subjects are asked to select from are quite different from those the confederate talked about. The factual information in these self-descriptions is subsequently scored in terms of its intimacy. In most studies, reciprocity is measured by comparing the intimacy of subjects exposed to intimate and nonintimate confederates. If subjects' disclosures in the former condition contain more intimate facts than in the latter, disclosure reciprocity is said to have occurred.

Now consider what the interaction goals of a subject in the preceding situation are likely to be and how he or she might best achieve these goals. One goal is likely to have been given by demands of the experimental situation. This is to convey to the other information so that the other can form an impression. In this sense, the interaction resembles what Jones and Thibaut (1958) have called *noncontingent interactions.* In noncontingent interactions, the behavior of participants is determined largely by role requirements and situational demands; in this case, the demand to relay information. However, this is not the only goal subjects are likely to have. It also seems likely that they would want the impression the other forms to be a favorable one, and, as Davis and Perkowitz (1979) have noted, communication exchanges carry with them the implicit demand that participants be responsive to one another's communications.

How may these different goals all be achieved? Certainly in those studies in which subjects are asked to disclose on topics that are different from those used by the confederate, the subject cannot directly address the content of the confederate's disclosure. However, even in those studies in which the subject is not directly prevented from talking about the same things as the confederate, doing so is likely to conflict with the goal of relaying the information needed by the other to form an impression. One way in which a subject may be able to achieve these various goals would be, to use the terms of Davis and Perkowtz (1979), by varying the elaboration of his or her reply. Or put another way, the subject may address the latent or emotional content of the other's communication. He or she might thus describe himself or herself in ways or on topics that are equally intimate or equally nonintimate. In so doing, the subject can potentially achieve both his or her goal of conveying information so that the other can form an impression and the goal of being responsive and thus having this impression be a positive one.

The preceding line of reasoning implies at least two things. First, it implies that if the demand to relay information was removed or lessened, other types of behaviors besides or in addition to talking about facts of different degrees of intimacy would be employed to demonstrate responsiveness. Second, it implies that when placed in the situation that is typically used to study disclosure reciprocity, the greatest amount of reciprocity will be shown by those individuals who are most motivated to act in responsive ways.

In recent years, preliminary support has been found for both of the preceding predictions. First, it will be recalled that earlier in this chapter I referred to an experiment by Berg and Archer (1982) as providing support for the proposition that having the maximization of one's attractiveness as an interaction goal would lead to an increased degree of responsiveness. At this time, evidence from this study indicating that subjects' primary interaction goal will affect the form in which responsiveness is shown as well as the extent to which it occurs will be discussed.

Berg and Archer (1982) measured three aspects of subjects' replies to the intimate and nonintimate disclosures of an experimental confederate, their descriptive intimacy (the extent to which they revealed intimate factual information), their evaluative intimacy (the extent to which strong affect or judgments are expressed), and their degree of topical reciprocity (the extent to which replies addressed the same subject matter as the original disclosure). Note that each of these may be differentially effective in achieving different interaction goals within the disclosure reciprocity paradigm. Topical reciprocity, for example, might be an effective means of achieving the goal of being liked by the other, but it would be less effective in achieving the goal of telling the other what is needed to form an impression. Similarly, varying degrees of descriptive and evaluative intimacy might serve the goal of appearing responsive (because they may address the latent content of received communications or represent variations in a response's degree of elaboration). Only descriptive intimacy, however, achieves the goal of conveying information. By varying the degree of descriptive intimacy, a subject who finds himself or herself in the situation represented by the typical disclosure reciprocity paradigm may satisfy both the goal of conveying factual information and the goal of appearing responsive.

Berg and Archer (1982) attempted to vary the salience of various interaction goals through their instructions to subjects. For one third of the subjects (information exchange condition), the instructions that are typically employed in the reciprocity paradigm described before were used, and subjects were asked to concentrate on telling their partner what she needed to know to form an accurate impression. A second third of the subjects (conversation condition) were asked to call to mind conversations they had in the past when formulating their reply. Subjects in this condition should feel much less of a demand to convey information; so comparisons between this and the information exchange condition should yield information about the way this demand influences subjects' replies. The final third of the subjects (conversation plus liking condition) were asked not only to recall conversations but also to attempt to create a positive impression on their partner, allowing an evaluation of the manner in which the goal of being liked will influence replies to another. In all three of these conditions, half the subjects received an intimate disclosure from their confederate partner and half received a nonintimate disclosure.

Results indicated that interaction goals affected all three of the aspects of communication that were examined. As predicted, subjects' replies were higher in descriptive intimacy in the information exchange than in the other two conditions. In addition, replies to an intimate partner were higher in descriptive intimacy than replies to a nonintimate partner. In the information exchange condition, no differences emerged as a function of received disclosure for either evaluative intimacy or topical reciprocity. It thus appears that, as expected, subjects in this condition were attempting to achieve their interaction goals primarily through using and varying descriptive intimacy.

There was a larger amount of topical reciprocity in both the conversation and conversation plus liking conditions than in the information exchange condition. Thus, also as predicted, the demand to convey information that is implicit in the typical instructions for disclosure reciprocity experiments appear to actively suppress this form of responsiveness. The descriptive intimacy and evaluative intimacy of subjects' replies varied as a function of confederate intimacy in both these conditions with greater amounts of both types in replies to the intimate as compared to the nonintimate confederate. These latter findings were more pronounced in the conversation plus liking condition. This also should be expected because the interaction goal most salient to subjects in this condition—being liked—should lead them to attempt to appear as responsive as possible. Thus, in addition to reciprocating in terms of topical content, they showed the greatest degree of reciprocation in terms of the intimacy of the facts they revealed and the amount of emotion they expressed.

Future work should examine the effects of making other interaction goals salient to subjects on both the form and extent of subsequent responsiveness. It should also examine nonverbal and stylistic effects in addition to verbal responses. A start in this latter direction was made in a study by Kaplan, Firestone, Klein, and Sodikoff (1983). Subjects in this experiment participated as interviewees with either a liked or a disliked interviewer. Because the study was said to be investigating the interviewing process, one can again assume that a situational demand to convey information was felt by subjects. In addition to manipulating interviewer likability, Kaplan *et al.* also varied the intimacy of the interviewer's disclosure to subjects and the amount of interviewer gaze. Dependent variables were the intimacy of subjects' disclosures, subjects' body orientations, and their degree of gazing at the interviewer.

For verbal behavior, the traditional reciprocity effect was found. For the nonverbal behaviors, however, a somewhat different pattern emerged. When the interviewer was liked, subjects matched him or her in terms of the stylistic behaviors measured. This would seem consistent with the probable desire of these subjects to appear responsive and indicate liking. For subjects with a disliked interviewer, just the opposite pattern emerged for the nonverbal measures. Thus, although the nonverbal behavior of subjects with a liked interviewer may have been an invitation to approach or a sign of liking, the unresponsive mismatching of nonverbal behaviors with a disliked interviewer most likely was indicative of suspicion or a desire to avoid. It would be interesting to observe what would happen if subjects in this situation were explicitly given the goal of creating a favorable impression. Would all subjects with this goal begin to match the interviewer's stylistic behaviors, or would there be increased nonverbal signals to approach only for a liked interviewer?

The second implication of the present view linking responsiveness and disclosure reciprocity that I noted before was that reciprocity should be greatest among those persons who are motivated to be responsive. The greater reciprocity of subjects in the conversation plus liking condition of Berg and Archer's (1982) study is consistent with this idea. Further support comes from a study by Shaffer *et al.* (1982) that was also mentioned earlier. Recall that high self-monitors are held to be especially concerned with creating a positive impression. Consequently, they should also be the persons most motivated to act in a responsive manner. When Shaffer and his colleagues examined how high and low self-monitors responded to another's intimate or nonintimate disclosure, they found that the high self-monitors showed the greatest degree of reciprocity for both the intimacy of the information they revealed and the emotion that was expressed. In addition, they also addressed the same content as had the disclosures they received to a greater extent than did the low self-monitors. In fact, if one examines the two intimacy measures, it is *only* the responsive high self-monitors who showed any reciprocity effects.

The Disclosure-Liking Relationship

It would be inaccurate to speak of a single disclosure-liking effect. Actually, research has found evidence for several kinds of relationships between self-disclosure and attraction. Liking another person may lead subjects to disclose to that person (Jourard, 1959; Kohen, 1975). Under certain circumstances, self-disclosure to another has also been found to lead to attraction for the target of that disclosure (Adams & Shea, 1981; Berg & Archer, 1983, Study 1). Receiving intimate disclosure from another can signal that one is liked by that person (Worthy *et al.*, 1969). Finally, receiving disclosure from another may result in attraction for that person (Archer, Berg, & Runge, 1980; Certner, 1973; Worthy *et al.*, 1969). This section will be concerned with only this last pattern, and when the disclosure-liking effect is referred to, it is the possibility that the receipt of disclosure will produce liking that is being considered.

Even limiting the range of potential relationships in this manner still leaves a rather muddled and inconsistent literature. The traditional wisdom would hold that greater attraction will result from the receipt of moderately intimate disclosure than very intimate or very superficial disclosure, and several studies support this idea (Cozby, 1973; Davis & Sloan, 1974; Mann & Murphy, 1975). However, as discussed by Kleinke (1979), many variables beside the degree of intimacy have been shown to mediate the disclosure-liking effect (e.g., appropriateness of the disclosure, attributions made for the disclosure, sex-role orientation of the recipient, and the recipient's own tendency to disclose). I propose that responsiveness is another such mediating variable. Specifically, intimate disclosure should be most likely to result in liking for the discloser when it is perceived as being responsive.

I attempted to show in the preceding section how a desire to appear responsive might interact with a situational demand to convey self-information to produce instances of disclosure reciprocity. As would be expected from this, research has demonstrated that reciprocal disclosure of high intimacy leads to greater liking than a nonreciprocal low-intimacy disclosure (e.g., Berg & Archer, 1980; Chaikin & Derlega, 1974b). Yet the *matching* of intimacy is only one way in which responsiveness may be demonstrated. In some situations, a high-intimacy disclosure may itself indicate responsiveness (i.e., that the discloser is interested in the other).

One condition that is likely to result in an intimate disclosure being viewed as responsive is when that disclosure deals with the same topical content as a subject's previous disclosure. Experiments by Berg and Archer (1983, Study 2) and Daher and Banikiotes (1974, 1976) both provide empirical support for this idea. Note that this goes beyond the claim that disclosures dealing with the same content as preceding disclosures will lead to greater attraction. Instead, it is suggested that intimate disclosure will lead to greater attraction than nonintimate disclosure primarily when content or subject matter is the same as a previously received disclosure. For example, in the Berg and Archer (1983) study, subjects first disclosed to a female confederate concerning either their own and their parents' personalities or their relationship with a close friend. When she subsequently disclosed to the subject, the confederate appeared to choose the topics of personalities on which to do so. In addition, she spoke about her personality and those of her parents in either an intimate or a nonintimate fashion. High intimacy led to a significant increase in liking when the topics were the same. If they were different, there was no difference in liking for the intimate and nonintimate confederate. Daher and Banikiotes (1974, 1976) report an almost identical pattern of results.

The response indicating sympathy and a willingness to discuss the issues initially raised by another in Berg and Archer's (1980) experiment, in addition to being more responsive, was also rated as being high in intimacy. Even following low-intimacy disclosure, this response resulted in greater attraction for the respondent than a matching low-intimacy disclosure on different topics. It may be that once a person has shown some minimal amount of responsiveness by choosing to address the content of previous communication, it becomes easier to earn "extra credit" for increased intimacy.

To the extent that disclosure flexibility (Chelune, 1975) is a characteristic of responsive individuals, a study by Neimeyer and Banikiotes (1981) provides some added support. Persons high in disclosure flexibility are better able to modulate their disclosure on the basis of subtle social cues and in this sense may resemble the high self-monitors discussed earlier. Neimeyer and Banikiotes (1981) formed dyads of individuals who were of various disclosure flexibility levels and had them engage in a structured interview. At the conclusion of this exercise, greater attraction was reported in dyads where both partners were high in disclosure flexibility than in other combinations. Although results regarding the intimacy of conversations are not reported, the nature of disclosure flexibility makes it appear likely that those subjects who are highly flexible would have engaged in intimate disclosure only when such disclosure would be responsive.

More indirect support for the view that intimate disclosure leads to increased liking when it is perceived as being responsive comes from a reinterpretation of studies that have examined the effects of timing and personalism of intimate disclosure. As Kleinke (1979) notes, the attributions made about the motives of either an intimate or a nonintimate discloser will have a large influence on how one evaluates that discloser and on liking for him or her. The application of the concept of personalism would predict that greater liking for an intimate discloser would result when one feels that he or she has been specifically chosen to receive that intimate disclosure. It would also predict that less liking would occur when one perceives that he or she has been specifically omitted from those whom the discloser trusts with this intimate information.

Several studies have found evidence consistent with the personalism hypothesis. For example, Wortman, Adesman, Herman, and Greenberg (1975) and Archer and Burleson (1979) provide evidence indicating that the discloser of intimate information will be liked more when this information is disclosed late as opposed to early in a conversation. Presumably, this was because, in the late disclosure condition, the revealer is seen as more discriminating and his or her intimate disclosure is viewed as the result of a developing friendship with the subject (i.e., as personalistic). When the intimate disclosure is made very early, the discloser may appear to be the sort of person who would share intimacies with anyone. Notice, however, that it is very easy to reinterpret this data as the result of the later disclosure appearing more responsive than the early disclosure. In other words, subjects could infer that a change occurred in the other's behavior because of something they had previously said.

The crux of the difference between an interpretation based on responsiveness and one based on personalism is the emphasis on past action. For responsiveness, it is imperative that the subject has previously *acted* in some fashion that could have invited intimacy in some way. For example, a subject may have indicated initial liking for the discloser, made a previous self-disclosure of at least moderate intimacy, or talked about similar topics as are now the basis for the intimate disclosure. The concept of personalism carries no such requirement for previous behavior. A person may feel that he or she has been singled out to receive an intimate (or nonintimate) disclosure because he or she is a member of a certain class rather than because of anything he or she has done. If the responsiveness interpretation is correct, one would expect some measurable differences. For example, subjects should feel that they were more in control of the interaction. All past studies finding evidence for a disclosure-liking effect (e.g., Archer *et al.*, 1980; Archer & Burleson, 1980; Certner, 1973; Worthy *et al.*, 1969; Wortman *et al.*, 1976) have either included a "get acquainted" session between subjects and confederates prior to the exchange of disclosures or had the subjects disclose first. As such, they would all be consistent with a responsiveness explanation that would hold that subjects felt they acted in some way that invited the other to become intimate.

Although the distinction between a responsiveness and a personalism explanation might seem like splitting hairs, it does help to understand one finding that has always been rather problematic for those arguing in favor of a personalism interpretation of the disclosure-liking effect. In the first investigation of the personalism hypothesis, Jones and Archer (1976) made subjects aware of a confederate's personal problems and allowed them to view the confederate either disclosing or not disclosing this problem to two other people. Subjects then had a brief get-acquainted session with the confederate following which he either did or did not disclose this problem to the subject. Results indicated that the confederate was most liked when he treated the subject differently than others (i.e., disclosed to the subject but not to others or disclosed to others but not to the subject). In the case where the subject has been singled out for nondisclosure, this should appear to be a personalistic affront. Why then was this individual liked?

Jones and Archer (1976) attempted to explain this by hypothesizing that subjects in the personalistic nondisclosure condition were experiencing relief when they were not burdened as others had been with this intimate problem. Another interpretation is possible however. In both conditions where the confederate's behavior was different to the subject, he appeared to *change* after having had a brief meeting with the subject. It thus became possible for the subject to infer that this change occurred as a result of their meeting.

Any definitive answer regarding the efficacy of personalism and responsiveness explanations of the disclosure-liking effect must await future research. Although a preference between the two is to some extent a question of individual taste at present, I would note that the responsiveness explanation does have the advantage of parsimony. It is able to account for the previous work dealing with personalism and also for that in which both topical similarity and disclosure intimacy have both been varied.

Self-Disclosure in Counseling

Several chapters in this volume discuss the role of self-disclosure in counseling. As they document, self-disclosure is important for two reasons. First, client difficulties with disclosure may be the primary cause of some client problems (e.g., loneliness). Second, counselors may employ self-disclosure to facilitate disclosure and self-exploration on the part of the client that is necessary for successful counseling. This section will examine how responsiveness may be used to understand the role of self-disclosure as both a client variable that may be causally related to distress and as a counselor variable that may be used to facilitate therapeutic progress.

Problems in Responsiveness as the Cause of Distress. The extent to which a person both discloses to and receives disclosure from others has been linked to client problems of loneliness (e.g., Franzoi & Davis, 1985; Solano, Batten, & Parish, 1982, Study 1), marital satisfaction-dissatisfaction (e.g., Hendrick, 1981), the relational competence needed to maintain social support networks (Hansson, Jones, & Carpenter, 1984), and self-alienation (e.g., Jourard, 1971). Other work, however, suggests that the problem may lie not only in the amount of disclosure given or received but with the way in which self-disclosure is regulated (Davidson, Balwick, & Halverson, 1983; Solano *et al.*, 1982, Study 2) or with affective and stylistic variables that occur with self-disclosure (e.g., Chelune, Sultan, Vosk, Ogden, & Waring, 1984; Jones, Hobbs, & Hockenbury, 1982). In other words, distressed individuals may fail to use self-disclosure in a way that is responsive and/or may not use responsive actions to encourage others to disclose to them. Consequently, they may disclose at inappropriate levels and fail to receive intimate disclosure from others.

Some preliminary support for this idea stems from the finding of Berg and Peplau (1983) that for women, loneliness was inversely related

($r = -.57$) to scores on the Opener Scale. It will be recalled that the Opener Scale attempts to measure individual differences in conversational responsiveness. In addition, Jones *et al.* (1982) report that lonely individuals display less partner attention while conversing than do nonlonely persons. Jones *et al.* (1982) further demonstrated that training could result in an increase in these responsive cues and a subsequent reduction in reports of loneliness.

Work relating loneliness to other personality and social skill variables finds that loneliness is associated with social anxiety, distrust and dislike of others, and decreased interest in and attention to others (Jones, 1981; Jones, Freeman, & Goswick, 1981). Solano *et al.* (1982) found that lonely persons displayed more rigid and extreme patterns of self-disclosure than nonlonely individuals. All of these reactions and behaviors are factors inconsistent with the goals of a responsive person and should all be negatively related to a tendency to act responsively. The distress experienced by these individuals would thus be due, in part, to deficits in responsive action.

In studying distressed and nondistressed couples, Chelune *et al.* (1984) found that they differed not in their amounts of self-disclosure but primarily in the extent to which they elaborated on this and in the congruence between verbal content and the affective manner in which the content is presented. It is tempting to speculate that these correspond to differences in terms of both responsive content and responsive style in distressed and nondistressed marriages.

Other studies have linked differences in marital satisfaction primarily to differences in disclosure reciprocity (Davidson *et al.*, 1983; Levinger & Senn, 1967). Earlier I argued that disclosure reciprocity might itself constitute a form of responsiveness (because it addresses the latent content of a communication or represents differences in the degree of elaboration). While I was then dealing primarily with the laboratory work on disclosure reciprocity, Hill and Stall (1982) note that on a long-term basis disclosure reciprocity will be just as important in extended relationships as it is in early encounters. Such differences as do exist in the time frame for reciprocity would be related to the timing component of responsiveness.

Responsiveness and Disclosure as Counselor Variables. An extensive literature exists dealing with the manner in which self-disclosure may be employed by a counselor to facilitate self-disclosure and self-exploration on the part of clients (see Doster & Nesbitt, 1979, for a review). Explorations of counselor self-disclosure generally deal with either the use of counselor disclosure as a model for appropriate client behavior and as a means for establishing a therapeutic relationship or with the reinforcement value counselor disclosure may have for the client. The concept of responsiveness is relevent to both of these issues.

First, as regards the use of counselor disclosure as a model, the bulk of empirical evidence suppports the belief that self-disclosure on the part of a counselor will have a facilatory effect on clients' subsequent disclosure (e.g., Bundza & Simonson, 1973; Doster & Brooks, 1974; Graff, 1970; Truax & Carkhuff, 1967). However, as Hendrick notes in her chapter in this volume (Chapter 14), positive relationships between counselor and counselee disclosure are not invariably found (e.g., Schoeninger, 1955; Weigel, Dinges, Dyer, & Straumfjord, 1972), and the efficacy of counselor disclosure will often depend on additional factors such as the status of the counselor (Simonson & Bahr, 1974), client expectations (Derlega, Lovell, & Chaikin, 1976), intimacy of counselor disclosure (Mann & Murphy, 1975), and therapist style (Simonson, 1976), to name only a few.

This large array of third variables makes it clear that no simple answer can be given to the question of whether or not a therapist should or should not self-disclose. As Hendrick notes, the question that should more properly be asked is *when* should a counselor self-disclose. Given that the goals of counselor disclosure (facilitation of client disclosure and the development of a warm and trusting relationship) are generally the same as the expected consequences of responsive action, one answer is that counselor disclosure should be used when it is likely to be viewed as responsive. Some evidence that is consistent with this view is provided by Neimeyer and Fong (1983). These researchers rated the disclosure flexibility of counselors and if, as claimed above, high-disclosure flexibility is related to using disclosure in ways that are responsive, one would expect the more flexible counselors to be more effective. This was in fact what Neimeyer and Fong found.

Work investigating the influence of clients' dispositional tendencies toward disclosure and counselor disclosure can also be interpreted in the present framework. Hays (cited in Doster & Nesbitt, 1979) found that initially low disclosers increased their level of disclosure when exposed to either moderate or high levels of interviewer disclosure, whereas interviewees who were high disclosers *decreased* their level of disclosure with a nondisclosing interviewer. It is tempting to speculate that both these effects are due to interviewees' attempts to demonstrate responsiveness by modeling interviewer disclosure levels that differed from their own. The influence of individual differences in disclosure may also have contributed to the finding that, across subjects (who vary in disclosure levels), moderate levels of counselor disclosure have been shown to be most beneficial (Mann & Murphy, 1975).

The second approach to studying the effects of counselor disclosure has involved consideration of the reinforcement value of disclosure. I argued before that disclosure would be more likely to have such reinforcement value when it was perceived as being responsive. The same argument may be made in the present context. Consistent with this view is the finding of Hoffman-Graff (1977) that interviewers who disclosed content similar to that of interviewees were perceived as more emphathic, warm, and credible. These are precisely the sorts of perceptions responsive actions should lead to, and the disclosure of similar content is a rather unambiguous manipulation of responsive content.

Other research involving differences between self-disclosing and self-involving therapists is also highly relevant. Although this distinction is also discussed by Hendrick in Chapter 14, several aspects of it should be noted here as well. McCarthy (1982) expresses the distinction between self-disclosing and self-involving responses, noting that

> self-disclosure responses are statements referring to the past history or personal experiences of the counselor and self-involving responses are direct present expressions of a counselor's feelings about or reactions to client statements and/or behaviors. (p. 125)

This distinction suggests that all self-involving statements must be responsive in terms of content because they will always directly address a client's previous verbalizations. As would be expected if the crucial factor were counselor responsiveness, past studies have found that self-involving counselors are more favorably perceived (e.g., more expert, attractive, and trustworthy) than self-disclosing counselors (McCarthy, 1979; McCarthy & Betz, 1978). In addition, the self-involving counselors were better able to facilitate client self-exploration. In a later study, McCarthy (1982) qualifies these findings somewhat. In this experiment, she compared reactions of clients to low self-disclosing, high self-disclosing, and self-involving counselors and found that both high-disclosing and self-involving counselors were superior to low-disclosing counselors and did not differ from one another. In her earlier studies, McCarthy had examined only low-disclosing interviewers.

Before going any further, however, a consideration of the manner in which high- and low-disclosing as well as self-involving statements were operationalized is in order. In low-intimacy disclosing statements, the counselor agreed with the client's previously expressed experience (e.g., "I remember having to make it on my own when I was growing up"). The high-disclosing statements agreed both with the client's experience and also contained a feeling the client had not yet identified (e.g., "I remember having to make it on my own too and it felt so lonely"). Self-involving comments were statements about the counselor's feelings about the client's behavior (e.g., "I appreciate the way you are relating to me right now"). Notice that all three of these responses address the preceding client communication and thus all may be considered responsive to some extent. The high-disclosing and self-involving responses, however, also reveal a private feeling of the counselor. Because of this, they may both be considered more intimate, and it was noted before that increased intimacy will result in more favorable impressions than low intimacy primarily when statements address the content of received communication (Berg & Archer, 1983; Daher & Banikiotes, 1974, 1976).

As noted several times before, variations in content are not the only ways in which responsiveness may be shown. In addition to content, other studies suggest that a responsive style may be facilitative of interviewee disclosure and be rewarding to clients. Neimeyer and Fong's (1983) finding that counselors high in disclosure flexibility were more effective than those low in flexibility is consistent with this view as is the finding of Ellsworth and Ross (1975) that, for women, direct gaze was associated with increased liking for an interviewer as well as increased interviewee intimacy. Finally, those studies that demonstrate that clients disclose more intimately and have more favorable impressions of counselors with a "warm" style (e.g., Bundza & Simonson, 1973; Simonson, 1976) provide further evidence suggesting the centrality of responsiveness.

CONCLUSION

This chapter has attempted to present the basic aspects of a theory of responsiveness and has reviewed evidence that indicates the importance and utility of responsiveness in relation to self-disclosure. With this single construct, evidence concerning disclosure reciprocity, disclosure-liking effects, and disclosure in counseling that has been difficult for current theories to explain has been accounted for. Much, however, remains to be done and in concluding, I will point out some promising directions for future work.

First, as regards the concept of responsiveness itself, I again note the need for work investigating the possible relations and interactions among the three aspects of responsive action. For example, does an increase in responsive style compensate for less responsive content? It will also be important for future research to explore the relationship between conversational and relational responsiveness. Are those persons who are more conversationally responsive (e.g., the high opener) also more relationally responsive? Will situational variations that lead to one class of responsive action also lead to the other?

An important question in regard to disclosure reciprocity concerns how the ways used to express responsiveness change as a relationship develops. Altman (1973) notes that reciprocity for nonintimate information will decline steadily throughout a relationship's development, whereas reciprocity of intimate information will show a curvilinear effect, being maximal during the middle stages of relationship development. Several studies (e.g., Derlega *et al.*, 1973; Morton, 1978) have found support for this prediction as regards descriptive intimacy. As reciprocation of descriptive intimacy drops off, is it replaced with corresponding increases in other expressions of responsiveness (e.g., topical reciprocity)? Does evaluative intimacy show the same pattern as descriptive intimacy? As regards relational responsiveness, some work regarding this has already been done. Berg (1984) and Berg and McQuinn (1986) have found that roommates and dating couples will exchange more selective and more particularistic resources as their relationships develop. They also become less concerned with maintaining strict equality between the amount of things they do for one another. It is thus reasonable to expect to find similar differences in the way conversational responsiveness is expressed as a relationship grows.

As regards the influence of responsiveness in mediating disclosure-liking effects, an important direction for future work involves distinguishing the effects of responsiveness from those of personalism. In attempting to do this, a researcher might expose subjects to low- and high-intimacy disclosures that are attributed to the particular type of person the subject is (personalistic) or to some particular thing the subject has done (responsive). By comparing these conditions to each other and to one in which the target has disclosed this information to several other people but not to the subject, the effects of responsiveness and personalism might be teased apart. It will also be important to investigate how differences in the three facets of responsive action may interact with the intimacy of a received disclosure. To date, this has been done only for content (Berg & Archer, 1983; Daher & Banikiotes, 1974, 1976).

The role of responsiveness in counseling situations will be of interest to many readers of this book. Promising directions for the future should involve further explorations of the effects of self-involving statements in a counseling context. For example, would the same effects occur if responsiveness was varied through manipulations of style and timing as is found when the counselor addresses the content of a client's statement?

In conclusion, the study of responsiveness appears to be a very fruitful direction for future explorations. This is especially true because responsiveness is in many ways an integrative concept that may aid in bringing conceptual unity and simplicity to what have been very divergent and complex areas.

REFERENCES

Adams, G. R., & Sheam, J. A. (1981). Talking and loving: A cross-lagged panel investigation. *Basic and Applied Social Psychology, 2,* 81–88.

Altman, I. (1973). Reciprocity of information exchange. *Journal for the Theory of Social Behavior, 3,* 249–261.

Archer, R. L. (1979). The role of personality and the social situation. In G. J. Chelune (Ed), *Self-disclosure* (pp. 1–27). San Francisco: Jossey-Bass.

Archer, R. L., & Burleson, J. A. (1980). The effects of timing and responsibility of self-disclosure on attraction. *Journal of Personality and Social Psychology, 38,* 120–130.

Archer, R. L., Berg, J. H., & Runge, T. E. (1980). Active and passive observers' attraction to a self-disclosing other. *Journal of Experimental Social Psychology, 16,* 130–145.

Bateson, G. (1972). *Steps to an ecology of mind.* New York: Ballantine Books.

Bundza, K. A., & Simonson, N. R. (1973). Therapist self-disclosure: Its effect on impressions of therapist and willingness to disclose. *Psychotherapy: Theory, Research, and Practice, 10,* 215–217.

Berg, J. H. (1984). The development of friendship between roommates. *Journal of Personality and Social Psychology, 46,* 346–356.

Berg, J. H., & Archer, R. L. (1980). Disclosure or concern: A second look at liking for the norm-breaker. *Journal of Personality, 48,* 245–257.

Berg, J. H., & Archer, R. L. (1982). Responses to self-disclosure and interaction goals. *Journal of Experimental Social Psychology, 18,* 501–512.

Berg, J. H., & Archer, R. L. (1983). The disclosure-liking relationship: Effects of self perception, order of disclosure, and topical similarity. *Human Communication Research, 10,* 269–282.

Berg, J. H., & Clark, M. S. (1986). Differences in social exchange between intimate and other relationships: Gradually evolving or quickly apparent? In V. J. Derlega & B. A. Winstead (Eds.), *Friendship and social interaction* (pp. 101–128). New York: Springer-Verlag.

Berg, J. H., & McQuinn, R. D. (1986). Attraction and exchange in continuing and noncontinuing dating relationships. *Journal of Personality and Social Psychology, 50,* 942–952.

Berg, J. H., Blaylock, T., Camarillo, J., & Steck, L. (1985, March). *Taking another's outcomes into consideration.* Paper presented at the meeting of the Southeastern Psychological Association, Atlanta.

Berg, J. H., & Peplau, L. A. (1982). Loneliness: The relationship of self-disclosure and androgyny. *Personality and Social Psychology Bulletin, 8,* 624–630.

Berscheid, E., Graziano, W. G., Monson, T., & Dermer, M. (1976). Outcome dependency: Attention, attribution, and attraction. *Journal of Personality, 48,* 89–102.

Bundza, K. A., & Simonson, N. R. (1973). Therapist self-disclosure: Its effects on impressions of therapist and willingness to disclose. *Psychotherapy: Theory, Research, and Practice, 10,* 215–217.

Certner, B. E. (1973). Exchange of self-disclosures in same sexed groups of strangers. *Journal of Consulting and Clinical Psychology, 40,* 292–297.

Chaikin, A. L., & Derlega, V. J. (1974a). *Self-disclosure*. Morristown, NJ: General Learning Press.
Chaikin, A. L., & Derlega, V. J. (1974b). Liking for the norm-breaker in self-disclosure. *Journal of Personality, 42*, 117–129.
Chelune, G. J. (1975). Self-disclosure: An elaboration of its basic dimensions. *Psychological Reports, 36*, 79–85.
Chelune, G. J., Sultan, F. E., Vosk, B. N., Ogen, J. K., & Waring, E. M. (1984). Self-disclosure patterns in clinical and nonclinical couples. *Journal of Clinical Psychology, 40*, 213–215.
Clark, M. S., & Mills, J. (1979). Interpersonal attraction in exchange and communal relationships. *Journal of Personality and Social Psychology, 37*, 12–24.
Cozby, P. C. (1973). Self-disclosure: A literature review. *Psychological Bulletin, 79*, 73–91.
Daher, D. M., & Banikiotes, P. G. (1974). Disclosure content, disclosure level and interpersonal attraction. *Personality and Social Psychology, 1*, 76–78.
Daher, D. M., & Banikiotes, P. G. (1976). Interpersonal attraction and rewarding aspects of disclosure content and level. *Journal of Personality and Social Psychology, 33*, 492–496.
Davidson, B., Balswick, J., & Halverson, C. (1983). Affective self-disclosure and marital adjustment: A test of equity theory. *Journal of Marriage and the Family, 45*, 93–102.
Davis, D. (1982). Determinants of responsiveness in dyadic interactions. In W. Ickes & E. G. Knowles (Eds.). *Personality, roles, and social behavior* (pp. 85–140). New York: Springer-Verlag.
Davis, D., & Holtgraves, T. (1984). Perceptions of unresponsive others: Attributions, attraction, understandability, and memory of their utterances. *Journal of Experimental Social Psychology, 20*, 383–408.
Davis, D., & Perkowitz, W. T. (1979). Consequences of responsiveness in dyadic interactions. Effects of probability of response and proportion of content related responses. *Journal of Personality and Social Psychology, 37*, 534–550.
Davis, J. D., & Sloan, M. L. (1974). The basis of interviewee matching of interviewer self-disclosure. *British Journal of Social and Clinical Psychology, 13*, 359–367.
Derlega, V. J., Harris, M. S., & Chaikin, A. L. (1973). Self-disclosure and reciprocity, liking, and the deviant. *Journal of Experimental Social Psychology, 9*, 227–284.
Derlega, V. J., Lovell, R., & Chaikin, A. L. (1976). Effects of therapist disclosure and its perceived appropriateness on client self-disclosure. *Journal of Consulting and Clinical Psychology, 44*, 866.
Doster, J. A., & Brooks, S. J. (1974). Interviewer disclosure modeling, information revealed, and interviewee verbal behavior. *Journal of Consulting and Clinical Psychology, 42*, 420–426.
Doster, J. A., & Nesbitt, J. G. (1979). Psychotherapy and self-disclosure. In G. J. Chelune (Ed.), *Self-disclosure* (pp. 177–224). San Francisco: Jossey-Bass.
Ellsworth, P., & Ross, L. (1975). Intimacy in response to direct gaze. *Journal of Experimental Social Psychology, 11*, 592–613.
Foa, E. B., & Foa, V. G. (1980). Resource theory: Later-personal behavior in exchange. In K. J. Gergen, M. S. Greenberg, & R. E. Willis (Eds.), *Social exchange: Advances in theory and research* (pp. 77–102). New York: Plenum Press.
Franzoi, S. L., & Davis, M. H. (1985). Adolescent self-disclosure and loneliness: Private self-consciousness and parental influences. *Journal of Personality and Social Psychology, 48*, 768–780.
Graff, R. W. (1970). The relationship of counselor self-disclosure to counselor effectiveness. *The Journal of Experimental Education, 38*, 19–22.

Hansson, R. O., Jones, W. H., & Carpenter, B. N. (1984). Relational competence and social support. In P. Shaver (Ed.), *Review of personality and social psychology* (pp. 265–284). Beverly Hills: Sage.

Hays, C. F. (1972). *The effects of initial disclosure level and interviewer disclosure level upon interviewee's subsequent disclosure level.* Unpublished doctoral dissertation, University of Colorado.

Hendrick, S. S. (1981). Self-disclosure and marital satisfaction. *Journal of Personality and Social Psychology, 40,* 1150–1159.

Hill, C. T., & Still, D. E. (1982). Disclosure reciprocity: Conceptual and measurement issues. *Social Psychology Quarterly, 45,* 238–244.

Hoffman-Graff, M. A. (1977). Interviewer use of positive and negative self-disclosure and interviewer-subject sex pairing. *Journal of Counseling Psychology, 24,* 184–190.

Jones, W. H. (1981). Loneliness and social contact. *Journal of Social Psychology, 113,* 195–196.

Jones, E. E., & Archer, R. L. (1976). Are there special effects of personalistic self-disclosure? *Journal of Experimental Social Psychology, 12,* 180–193.

Jones, E. E., & Thibaut, J. W. (1958). Interaction goals as bases of inference in interpersonal perception. In R. Tagiuri & L. Petrullo (Eds.), *Person perception and interpersonal behavior* (pp. 151–178). Stanford: Stanford University Press.

Jones, W. H., Freeman, J. E., & Goswick, R. A. (1981). The persistence of loneliness: Self and other determinents. *Journal of Personality, 49,* 27–48.

Jones, W. H., Hobbs, S. A., & Hockenbury, D. (1982). Loneliness and social skills deficits. *Journal of Personality and Social Psychology, 42,* 682–689.

Jourard, S. M. (1959). Self-disclosure and other cathexis. *Journal of Abnormal and Social Psychology, 59,* 428–431.

Jourard, S. M. (1971). *The transparent self* (2nd ed.). New York: D. Van Nostrand.

Kaplan, K. J., Firestone, I. J., Klein, K. W., & Sodkoff, C. (1983). Distancing in Dyads: A Comparison of Four Models. *Social Psychology Quarterly, 46,* 108–115.

Kelley, H. H. (1979). *Close relationships: Their structures and processes.* Hillsdale, NJ: Lawrence Erlbaum Associates.

Kleinke, C. L. (1979). Effects of personal evaluations. In G. J. Chelune (Ed.), *Self-disclosure* (pp. 59–79). San Francisco: Jossey-Bass.

Kohen, J. (1975). Liking and self-disclosure in opposite sex dyads. *Psychological Reports, 36,* 695–698.

Kraut, R. E., Lewis, S. H., & Sweeny, L. W. (1982). Listener responsiveness and the coordination of conversation. *Journal of Personality and Social Psychology, 43,* 718–731.

Levinger, G. & Senn, D. J. (1967). Disclosure of feelings in marriage. *Merrill-Palmer Quarterly of Behavior and Development, 13,* 237–249.

Mann, B., & Murphy, K. C. (1975). Timing of self-disclosure, reciprocity of self-disclosure, and reactions to an initial interview. *Journal of Counseling Psychology, 22,* 304–308.

McCarthy, P. R. (1979). Differential effects of self-disclosing versus self-involving counselor statements across counselor-client gender pairings. *Journal of Counseling Psychology, 26,* 438–541.

McCarthy, P. R. (1982). Differential effects of counselor self-referent responses and counselor states. *Journal of Counseling Psychology, 29,* 125–131.

McCarthy, P. R., & Betz, N. E. (1978). Differential effects of self-disclosing versus self-involving counselor statements. *Journal of Counseling Psychology, 25,* 251–256.

Miller, L. C. (1982). *Patterns of two individual differences relevant to recipient and revealer roles in dyadic interactions.* Unpublished doctoral dissertation, University of Texas at Austin.

Miller, L. C., & Berg, J. H. (1984). Selectivity and urgency in interpersonal exchange. In V. J. Derlega (Ed.), *Communication, intimacy, and close relationships* (pp. 161–206). New York: Academic Press.

Miller, L. C., Berg, J. H., & Rugs, D. (1984, September). *Selectivity in exchange: When you give me what I need.* Paper presented at the 93rd annual convention of the American Psychological Association, Toronto, Canada.

Miller, L. C., Berg, J. H., & Archer, R. L. (1983). Openers: Individuals who elicit intimate self-disclosure. *Journal of Personality and Social Psychology, 44,* 1234–1244.

Miller, L. C., Lechner, R. E., & Rugs, D. (1985). Development of conversational responsiveness: Preschoolers' use of responsive listener cues and relevant comments. *Developmental Psychology, 21,* 473–480.

Miller, L. C., & Mueller, J. (1983). *Conversational attentiveness and memory for what people actually said.* Unpublished manuscript.

Mills, J., & Clark, M. S. (1982). Exchange and communal relationships. In L. Wheeler (Ed.), *Review of personality and social psychology* (Vol. 3, pp. 121–144). Beverly Hills: Sage.

Morton, J. L. (1978). Intimacy and reciprocity of exchange: A comparison of spouses and strangers. *Journal of Personality and Social Psychology, 36,* 72–81.

Neimeyer, G. J., & Banikiotes, P. G. (1981). Self-disclosure flexibility, empathy, and perceptions of adjustment and attraction. *Journal of Counseling Psychology, 28,* 272–275.

Neimeyer, G. J., & Fong, M. L. (1983). Self-disclosure flexibility and counselor effectiveness. *Journal of Counseling Psychology, 30,* 258–261.

Norton, R., & Montgomery, B. M. (1982). Style, content, and target components of openness. *Communication Research, 9,* 399–431.

Piner, K. E., Berg, J. H., & Miller, L. C. (1986). *The influence of timing on responsiveness.* Paper presented at the 32nd Annual Meeting of the Southeastern Psychological Association, Orlando, Florida.

Purvis, J. A., Dabbs, J., & Hopper, C. (1984). The "opener": Skilled user of facial expression and speech pattern. *Personality and Social Psychology Bulletin, 10,* 61–66.

Rubin, Z. (1975). Disclosing oneself to a stranger: Reciprocity and its limits. *Journal of Experimental Social Psychology, 11,* 233–260.

Schoeninger, D. W. (1955). *Client experiencing as a function of therapist self-disclosure and pretherapy training.* Doctoral Dissertation, University of Wisconsin. *Dissertation Abstracts International, 26,* 5551.

Shaffer, D. R., Smith, J. E., & Tomarelli, M. T. (1982). Self-monitoring as a determinant of self-disclosure reciprocity during the acquaintance process. *Journal of Personality and Social Psychology, 45,* 163–175.

Simonson, N. R. (1976). The impact of therapist disclosure on patient disclosure. *Journal of Counseling Psychology, 23,* 3–6.

Simonson, N. P., & Bahr, S. (1974). Self-disclosure by the professional and paraprofessional therapist. *Journal of Consulting and Clinical Psychology, 42,* 359–363.

Snyder, M. (1974). The self-monitoring of expressive behavior. *Journal of Personality and Social Psychology, 30,* 526–537.

Solano, C. H., Batten, P. G., & Parish, E. A. (1982). Loneliness and patterns of self-disclosure. *Journal of Personality and Social Psychology, 43,* 524–531.

Truax, C. B., & Carkhuff, R. R. (1967). Client and therapist transparency in the psychotherapeutic encounter. *Journal of Counseling Psychology, 12,* 3–9.

Weigel, R. G., Dinges, N., Dyer, R., & Straumfjord, A. A. (1972). Perceived self-disclosure, mental health, and who is liked in group treatment. *Journal of Personality and Social Psychology, 19,* 47–52.

Worthy, M., Gary, A. L., & Kahn, G. M. (1969). Self-disclosure as an exchange process. *Journal of Personality and Social Psychology, 13,* 59–63.

Wortman, C. G., Adesman, P., Herman, E., & Greenberg, R. (1976). Self-disclosure: An attributional perspective. *Journal of Personality and Social Psychology, 33,* 184–191.

7
Marriage and Verbal Intimacy

MARY ANNE FITZPATRICK

INTRODUCTION

In the latter part of the 20th century, the sharing of personal feelings and information has become the hallmark of a close relationship. In North America, the gradual exchange of intimate information about one's inner self is considered the major process through which relationships between people develop. Most theories of relational growth equate the development of relationships with the exchange of increasingly more intimate information (Bochner, 1983). Although such theoretical work stresses the centrality of self-disclosure (e.g., Altman & Taylor, 1973), very little recent research has actually examined what function self-disclosure has in established relationships. One classic exception to this rule is the work of Komarovksy (1964) who shows that self-disclosure and open communication, although central to satisfactory functioning in some marriages, are clearly not all that important to couples in many stable blue-collar marriages. The degree to which self-disclosure and expressiveness in communication between partners is vital to marital functioning in various other social class groupings remains an open question.

The role that self-disclosure plays in close relationships may not be as clear-cut as originally theorized. Cultural (e.g., Sennett, 1978) and

---

MARY ANNE FITZPATRICK • Department of Communication Arts, University of Wisconsin, Madison, Wisconsin 53706. The research reported in this chapter was supported by grants from the Wisconsin Alumni Research Foundation and the National Institutes of Health, Biomedical Research Division.

historical (e.g., Shorter, 1975) analysts argue that modern relationships are strained literally to the breaking point by demands for expressivity and openness between married partners. Recently, psychologists have begun to question the predominance of self-disclosure as a defining feature of close relationships. Definitions of close relationships that emphasize interdependence are emerging as alternatives to definitions that focus on feelings and their expression (e.g., Fitzpatrick, 1977; Kelley *et al.*, 1983). Close relationships can be defined as relationships in which a significantly greater range and diversity of linkages exist between people rather than as relationships in which the defining feature is the expression of intimate thoughts and feelings. When close relationships are defined according to their levels of interdependence, then self-disclosure becomes only one of many possible manifestations of the range and diversity of the linkages between partners. This position does not suggest that self-disclosure is not important but rather that it is differentially important in various marriages.

In considering self-disclosure in marriage, my fundamental premise is that marriage is not a monolithic institution, for the range and diversity of the linkages that define various marital relationships vary enormously. The variations are by no means random, however, nor are they so highly individualized as to be out of the purview of the scientist. Distinctive marital styles show up repeatedly in any sample of couples, and the couples within each style are remarkably similar in the ways in which they communicate with one another. Between marital styles or types, however, enormous differences emerge in the degree to which couples engage in and value self-disclosure.

In this chapter, I will outline a typological approach to marital interaction and show how couples in different types of marriages prefer and use different communication styles with one another. Further, I will show that the underlying psychological processes that direct the experience of emotion in close relationships affect the degree and kind of self-referential messages that marital partners exchange with one another.

A TYPOLOGICAL APPROACH TO MARITAL INTERACTION

Dimensions of Marriage

A typological approach to marital interaction presupposes that interaction styles vary in different types of relationships and thus lead to different outcomes (Fitzpatrick, 1976, 1984). Any married couple can be categorized into a specific marital type. The scheme for categorizing couples is based on three underlying conceptual dimensions. The first is *interdependence* that stresses the connectedness of relational partners physically, temporally, and psychologically. Although all relationships exhibit some form of interdependence, it is assumed that the negotiation of an appropriate degree of autonomy and interdependence is an ongoing dialectic in all human relationships (Bochner, 1976; Hess & Handel, 1959). In a marriage, each spouse attempts to define the ways he or she wants to be dependent on the other. The level of interdependence in a marriage is measured by the amount of sharing and companionship as well as by the couple's organization of time and household space. The more interdependent the couple, the higher the level of companionship, the more time they spend together on a regular basis, and the more they organize their space to promote togetherness.

The second dimension is *ideology* that taps the beliefs, standards, and values that individuals hold concerning relationships. The values that individuals hold concerning marriage and family life are a major factor guiding not only interactions with the spouse but also the judgments individuals make concerning the outcomes of their interactions. Values concerning marriage can range from those stressing the importance of stability and predictability to those emphasizing the excitement of spontaneity and relational uncertainty.

The third dimension is *conflict*. Although it is inevitable that individuals in ongoing relationships experience conflict, people approach the resolution of differences in a variety of ways, ranging from total conflict avoidance to active and open engagement in conflict. This dimension is measured by the willingness of participants to engage in conflict with the spouse and the general level of assertiveness between partners.

In most classical typological approaches, these three major conceptual dimensions would be divided into high and low values, and eight possible marital definitions would be hypothesized. Within this polythetic typological scheme, a different approach is taken. A questionnaire, the Relational Dimensions Instrument (RDI), designed to measure the conceptual dimensions of interest, was developed. Table 1 lists some representative statements from the questionnaire. The responses of a number of samples (see Fitzpatrick, 1984, for a description of the sampling procedures utilized) of married individuals have been cluster-analyzed. Subsequently, the clusters have been named. Using these procedures, only three of the eight logically possible cells are filled. No currently married individual, for example, defines his or her marriage as one in which high conflict occurs with low levels of interdependence, regardless of the ideological orientation of the individual. Although other

TABLE 1. Representative Statements from the Relational Dimensions Instrument

Interdependence

Sharing

We tell each other how much we love or care about each other.
My spouse/mate reassures and comforts me when I am feeling low.
I think that we joke around and have more fun than most couples.

Autonomy

I have my own private workspace (study, workshop, utility room, etc.)
I think it is important for one to have some private space that is all his or her own and separate from one's mate.

Undifferentiated Space

I feel free to interrupt my spouse/mate when he or she is concentrating on something if he or she is in my presence.
I open my spouse/mate's personal mail without asking permission.
I feel free to invite guests home without informing my spouse/mate.

Temporal Regularity

We eat our meals (i.e., the ones at home) at the same time every day.
In our house, we keep a fairly regular daily time schedule.
We serve the main meal at the same time every day.

Ideology

Ideology of Traditionalism

A woman should take her husband's last name when she marries.
Our wedding ceremony was (will be) very important to us.
Our society, as we see, it needs to gain faith in the law and in our institutions.

Idealogy of Uncertainty and Change

In marriage/close relationships, there should be no constraints or restrictions on individual freedom.
The ideal relationship is one marked by novelty, humor, and spontaneity.
In a relationship, each individual should be permitted to establish the daily rhythm and time schedule that suits him or her best.

Conflict

Conflict Avoidance

If I can avoid arguing about some problems, they will disappear.
In our relationship, we feel that it is better to engage in conflicts than to avoid them.
It is better to hide one's true feelings in order to avoid hurting your spouse/mate.

Assertiveness

My spouse/mate forces me to do things that I do not want to do.
We are likely to argue in front of our friends or in public places.
My spouse/mate tries to persuade me to do something that I do not want to do.

cultures may have different definitions of marriage, it appears that in North American culture, there are three basic approaches that individuals take to marriage: traditional, independent, and separate.

THREE BASIC MARITAL DEFINITIONS

Traditionals exhibit interdependence in their marriage, for they have a high degree of companionship and sharing. This companionship is reinforced by the traditional's use of time and sharing. A regular daily time schedule as well as a lack of autonomous physical space in the home facilitates interaction between these spouses. A traditional places greater emphasis on stability than on satisfaction in marriage, and he or she holds conventional values about relationships. Such conventionality includes agreement with such statements as the following: A woman should take her husband's last name when she marries, and spouses should care deeply about one another but not become overly demonstrative. Traditionals describe their communication style as nonassertive, although they are willing to engage their spouses in conflicts when the issues are serious ones.

Independents maintain a high level of companionship and sharing in their marriages, but it is of a qualitatively different kind than that of the traditionals. Although independents try to stay psychologically close to their spouses, independents are also careful to maintain separate physical spaces to achieve some control over the accessibility each has to the other. An additional limitation on accessibility and hence interaction is that independents have trouble maintaining regular daily time schedules. Independents are at the opposite end of the ideological continuum from the traditionals. Independents, for example, espouse a belief that relationships should not constrain an individual's freedom. Finally, independents report some assertiveness in their marriages and are apt to engage in conflicts with their spouses on a variety of issues, both large and small.

Separates maintain much less interdependence in their marriage than the other basic types. Separates are disengaged from one another in that they control accessibility both physically and psychologically. The major index of interdependence in this type of marriage is temporal regulation, in that separates keep regular daily schedules. Separates are ideologically bivalent in that they can agree with both the importance of stability and the importance of satisfaction. In reference to their communication style, separates report some assertiveness in their marriage, but they always try to avoid open conflict.

Couple Types

Couple or marital types are defined by comparing the relational definitions of husbands and wives. The couple's rather than individuals' self-reports and communication behaviors are compared and discussed because the former are a more meaningful analytic unit. In the study of personal and social relationships, dyadic-level constructs such as couple or marital type can yield information about the relationship between partners that is significantly more predictive of communication patterns and outcomes than is an individual-level assessment.

The pure couple types (traditional, independent, separate) are those in which the husband and wife share the same definition of the marriage. Approximately 60% of those couples who have completed the Relational Dimensions Instrument agree on a definition of their marriage. To say that the couple type is a more meaningful unit of analysis than is the individual relational definition means that knowing how an individual views his or her marriage is less informative than knowing how both partners view the marriage. For example, the pattern of communication in the relationship between a traditional and an independent is significantly different than that in a pure traditional or a pure independent marriage. Such a difference is apparent only when couples are used as the unit of analysis rather than the individual.

The remaining 40% of the couples fall into the mixed category. The mixed types are those in which the husband holds one definition of the marriage and the wife another (e.g., separate/traditional). The overall 40% disagreement rate on dimensions of marriage is relatively consistent with the literature. In research on relationships in general (Duck, 1980) and on marriage in particular (Bernard, 1972), such discrepancies on the reports of partners concerning the relationship are relatively common. The major mixed type of couple uncovered in this program of research is the marriage in which the husband is a separate and his wife is a traditional. In a separate/traditional marriage, the husband maintains some distance in the relationship, although his wife is more interdependent and expressive. Both spouses support conventional ideological orientations to the marriage, although the husband is somewhat more likely to doubt these views.

Building a typology of marriage is an elegant and useless exercise unless the types of marriages relate to other dimensions of interest. The combination of relational dimensions that create the marital types predicts the sex-role orientations of husbands and wives (Fitzpatrick & Indvik, 1982), their accuracy in predicting the responses of their spouses (Fitzpatrick & Indvik, 1979), their achieved level of marital adjustment and satisfaction (Fitzpatrick & Best, 1979), and their communication behavior in both high conflict and casual marital discussions (Fitzpatrick, 1981; Fitzpatrick, Fallis, & Vance, 1982; Fitzpatrick, Vance, & Witteman, 1984; Sillars, Pike, Redman, & Jones, 1983; Witteman & Fitzpatrick, 1986). The range and diversity of the interaction differences among these couple types indicates that the typology is not artifactual. These couple types represent a description of patterned yet significantly different ways that individuals organize their marriages and their communication behaviors with the spouse.

Not only do these couple types exist in the minds of married individuals and influence their behavior with the spouse, but these couple types appear to be psychologically real to other individuals as well. Giles and Fitzpatrick (1985) found that when presented with patterns of communication found in actual couples of various types, individuals do relate these patterns to the conceptual dimensions that define the typology. The next section considers self-disclosure within marriage.

SELF-DISCLOSURE IN MARRIAGE

Self-disclosure is a process of revealing oneself to others. In the interest of capturing the richness of the phenomenon, some theorists have broadened the definition of self-disclosure to include any self-revelatory statement (e.g., Derlega & Grzelak, 1979). Such broad definitions of self-disclosure have been particularly useful when examining the functions of self-disclosure across a number of different relationships at various stages of development. Many researchers agree that disclosure helps in the initial development process of relationships by promoting mutual liking and reducing uncertainty about the partner's social status and personality characteristics (Berger & Bradac, 1982). Self-disclosure appears to decrease as relationships move through various stages of deterioration (Baxter, 1985). When one turns to established relationships, however, the role of self-disclosure in the maintenance of relationships is less clear.

Ongoing relationships may be maintained by illusions about the other, exaggerations of similarity, expectations of goodness, and less than full disclosure. In a classic longitudinal study of married couples, Raush and his colleagues (Raush, Barry, Hertel, & Swain, 1974) expressed surprise at the use of what they considered communication pathology. Some of the happily married couples in their experiment avoided unpleasant topics, lied about their feelings, and disqualified their own or their spouse's statements. These data clearly indicate that optimal communication from one point of view (openness, honesty, self-disclosure) is not what is perceived as a good or functional relational style by all couples. The research suggests that the communication exchanges that maintain functional marriages are not necessarily characterized by high mutual self-disclosure.

Not only the empirical work but also some theoretical models (e.g., Bochner, 1983) question the role of self-disclosure in *maintaining* intimate relationships. Conversation in established relationships needs to serve a number of functions other than revealing the self to the other. For example, a growing expectation in an established relationship is that each person can trust the other to protect his or her vulnerability. These vulnerabilities are revealed early in relationships through the process of self-disclosure. To protect the vulnerability of the spouse, however, it is sometimes necessary to conceal thoughts or feelings one has about the spouse that the speaker now knows may hurt or anger the other. Revelation balanced against concealment is one example of the types of simultaneously contradictory functions that conversation serves in ongoing relationships.

Marital dialogue serves many functions. These functions often are in dialectical opposition to one another, as when the need to validate the spouse is in conflict with the need to be open and honest. The multifunctional nature of marital talk can be examined by considering the underlying psychological processes governing such talk. An examination of the underlying processes that govern communication in marriage can help to predict and explain the message choices that spouses make in interaction and the outcomes that these choices produce in specific marriages. With this view, self-disclosure becomes one of many possible messages that lead to different outcomes for different couples.

At the core of the typological approach to marital interaction is a move away from an emphasis on one particular style of marital interaction. The typological perspective examines how couples communicate and what outcomes are promoted by such message exchanges. Within the various marital types, couples are expected to place differential emphasis on the various functions of communication in maintaining a marriage. Consequently, the degree and kind of self-disclosure in the various types of marriages is expected to differ.

Couple Types and Self-Disclosure

When, how, why, and with what effect may couples in the various marital types be expected to self-disclose to one another? To begin to answer this question, a definition of self-disclosure that discriminates factual and affective disclosures is used (see Morton, 1978). In one study of the interactions between 50 couples conducted in my laboratory (Fitzpatrick, *et al.*, 1984), there were significant differences across the couple types in the proportion of time couples affectively disclosed to one another, with independents disclosing more than the traditionals who disclosed more than the separates. Significant differences obtained also for the degree to which couples exchanged objective information about the self with one another. Specifically, the separate/traditionals disclosed a significantly higher proportion of factual information to one another than did any other couple type during these dialogues. These couples spent twice the conversational floor time disclosing facts about themselves than did the other couples.

Communication of Facts

Facts and feelings about the self need to be analytically separated in both the conceptual definitions and measurement of self-disclosure. The exchange of "objective information" about the self may be more common in early stages of a relationship. Information-processing structures such as self-schemata (Markus, 1977), cognitive structures that represents one's general knowledge about one's own personality, appearance, and behavior, may control what individuals perceive, notice, and remember about themselves. Information that is relevant (and either consistent or inconsistent) with one's self-schema is more likely to be noticed and remembered (Hastie, 1981). Such information may also be more likely to show up in talk with the relational partner. In the early stages of the development of a relationship, the exchange of schema-relevant information about the self may predominate because it helps partners to reduce uncertainty about each other's attitudes, values, and personality characteristics and to develop understanding and shared views of one another (Berger & Bradac, 1982).

Once partners feel they understand one another, the exchange of such objective or factual information about the self probably decreases. Only separate/traditional couples spent any appreciable amount of time exchanging objective self-information with one another during their interactions. Separate/traditionals are so extremely sex-typed in their orientation toward male and female roles that they see males and females as living in different cultures (Fitzpatrick *et al.*, 1984). Unlike partners in many marriages, these couples do not presume to understand one another. These husbands and wives do not share identical mental worlds, yet they try to make points of contact with one another in their conversations. Throughout their marriage, separate/traditionals keep up a steady exchange of objective information about themselves.

Communication of Feelings

As relationships progress, the amount of emotional information that can be exchanged between partners may be limitless. In initial interaction, a speaker only has facts or feelings about the self to reveal. As a relationship becomes established, not only how the speaker feels about him or herself but also how the speaker feels about the partner and the relationship become part of an individual's self-definition. The development of a relationship involves a change in identity for the individuals involved. Ongoing relationships, like marriage, involve the adoption of new roles and expanded definitions of the self. Marriage becomes part of how each person defines himself or herself (Weiss, 1975).

The self-definition of an individual in an established relationship soon starts to include not only how the individual feels about himself or herself but also how he or she feels about the partner and the relationship. As relationships between people develop, a greater range of topics for self-referential talk emerges. Self-disclosure in ongoing relationships continues to involve the disclosure of feelings about the self, but it now also can involve feelings about the partner and the relationship. Individuals in ongoing relationships may discuss their emotional reactions to one another, and these reactions may become a major part of the relationship.

Within the context of a marriage, an individual can experience a number of emotional states that can possibly be communicated to the spouse. An emotional state can be positive or negative. Further, this positive or negative affect can be, according to Sprecher (1985), directed toward the self (happiness or depression), directed toward the partner (lust or anger), or directed toward the relationship (commitment or dissatisfaction).

These emotional states are predicted to be experienced at different rates in the various couple types. The level of interdependence reached in the marriage, the ideology held by couples on relationship issues, and their openness to conflict affect self-disclosure between married partners. Specifically, the type, valence (positive or negative information), and rate of self-disclosure among married couples is hypothesized to vary depending on these factors. The interdependence established by couples directly affects the experience of emotion in close relationships. The *experience* of an emotion is, however, a necessary but not a sufficient condition for the expression of that emotion to the spouse. The ideological orientation that an individual holds concerning marriage and family life affects the meaning that he or she assigns to an emotion-producing stimulus. Further, this ideological orientation and openness to conflict predict the *expression* of what is experienced.

COMMUNICATION OF EMOTION IN MARRIAGE

Few would argue with the commonsense notion that emotion in close relationships is an important area that needs to be studied. Many would be surprised to find, however, that relatively little attention has been paid, until recently, to this topic (Bowers, Metts, & Duncanson, 1985; Bradbury & Fincham, 1986). In this section, the communication of the emotional states that can be experienced within a marriage is the focus. Affective self-disclosure is defined as the communication of emotion between long-term relationship partners. This disclosure can involve feelings about the self, the partner, and/or the relationship.

This section differentiates between the experience of emotion and the expression of that emotion to the spouse and shows that different underlying psychological processes can be used to account for experience and expression. The analysis of emotional experience in close relationships developed by Ellen Berscheid (1983) will be examined and subsequently applied to the marital typology.

THE EXPERIENCE OF EMOTION

In an intriguing analysis, Berscheid (1983) has applied Mandler's (1984) theory of emotion to close relationships. A necessary condition for the experience of emotion is the presence of physiological arousal. Physiological arousal is said to occur when an individual is interrupted in the completion of an organized behavioral sequence. After the interruption occurs and alternative routes to complete the sequence are blocked, then emotion is experienced. The valence (positivity or negativity) of the experienced emotion depends on the context in which the interruption occurs. Positive affect results if the interruption is seen as benign or controllable, leads to the accomplishment of a goal sooner than expected, or removes something previously disruptive. Because interruptions are usually uncontrollable, however, most of them lead to negative affect.

When this model is applied to close relationships, such as marriage, by Berscheid (1983), the concept of interdependence is central to understanding what the individual may or may not experience as interrupting. Between spouses, there are a number of sequences of events in which each event in one person's causal chain is causally connected to an event for the other. That is, couples develop a series of organized behavioral sequences that necessitate the spouse as a partner in the action in order to achieve successful completion. The sequences that require the spouse for completion are called interchain sequences (e.g., lovemaking, marital conversations). The event in each person's chain is causally connected to an event in the spouse's chain, and each needs the actions of the other to complete the sequence.

Individuals also have intrachain sequences or ongoing goal-directed activities that need to be completed once they have begun. Interchain causal connections are viewed as necessary, but not sufficient, conditions for emotion to occur. Autonomic arousal and emotion occur when some interchain connection interfaces or interrupts the completion of an individual's intrachain sequence. For example, a highly organized intrachain sequence may involve a wife regaling her colleagues with the story about her recent corporate takeover. The story may be well rehearsed and often told, and one element of the story carefully builds on another. Usually, during this performance, her husband interjects a comment in the middle of the story, "Don't forget to tell them about the lawyer from the Securities and Exchange Commission." This is an organized behavioral sequence for the couple in which his comment interchains with her intrachain sequence (the story) and serves to help her to complete her narrative successfully. No "hot" emotion would be expected to occur as a consequence of this event. Suppose, however that this wife tells her story and her husband interjects and says, "Tell them how the next day the *Wall Street Journal* claimed you paid too much for the stock." This statement represents an interruption to her intrachain sequence. This interruption stops the completion of her story, is probably physiologically arousing, and will also give rise to negative emotion on the part of the wife toward her husband. If the husband of this tycoon had commented on the favorable *Wall Street Journal* report, the experience would have been interrupting, but it would have been interpreted as positive because the interchain connection actually augmented or facilitated her goal-directed performance.

Berscheid (1983) defines an individual's emotional investment in a relationship as the extent to which there are interchain causal connections to one's own intrachain sequences. Because connections of this sort lead to the experience of emotion in marriage, emotional investment refers to the potential amount of emotion that might be experienced. In certain types of relationships with very well-meshed sequences, however, one may tend to underestimate one's own emotional investment in a relationship because the experience of emotion does not occur very frequently.

The use of the term *interdependence* in Berscheid's (1983) model is very similar to its use in the typology as a defining feature of marriage. The occurrence of organized behavioral sequences was measured indirectly in the typology by the level of sharing in the marriage as well as the couple's organization of time and space in the household. Using this model of emotion and the levels of interdependence achieved by couples, it is possible to generate predictions concerning the degree of meshing in organized behavioral sequences in the various couple types.

Couple Types and Characteristic Emotional Experience

Symmetrical and Assymmetrical Emotional Experience. The more highly interdependent the couple, the greater the number of meshed intrachain sequences. In other words, husbands and wives simultaneously engage in highly organized intrachain sequences, and the events in each person's chain facilitate the performance of the other's sequence. A great number of meshed intrachain sequences occur for the traditionals. Meshing makes it possible for many interconnected and highly organized event sequences to be performed by traditionals without the smallest interruptive hitch. The connections between the traditionals are symmetrical in that each partner facilitates the completion of the organized behavioral sequences for the other person. The connections between these couples are also facilitative. Because of their meshed and mutually facilitative intrachain sequences, the traditionals are significantly less likely than the other couple types to experience emotion in reference to either the partner or the relationship on a daily basis. Under the tranquil exterior of the traditional marriage, however, lies a very committed partnership. The traditionals have a high degree of emotional investment in the relationship, although these couples do not experience emotion on a daily basis. The paradox of the traditional form of interdependence is that the mutual facilitation of intrachain sequences by each spouse for the other goes unnoticed (and does not produce even positive emotion) until the facilitation ceases.

The separates have a marriage in which there are very few meshed intrachain sequences. This means that there are few or no causal connections between the intrachain sequences simultaneously enacted by the individuals in this marriage. Separates are disengaged from one another. These couples neither facilitate nor inhibit the organized behavioral sequences of one another. Because they are like children at parallel play, the separates are not expected to experience much emotion in reference to the partner or to the relationship. This lack of emotional experience with respect to the marriage is qualitatively different than that of the tranquil exterior of the traditional relationship. There are few connections between the searpate spouses. Under the surface of the separate marriage, neither spouse is emotionally invested in the marriage because the potential to experience emotion in interaction with one's spouse is small.

The independents represent couples with a number of nonmeshed sequences. The causal connections between the intrachain sequences interfere with the enactment of behavioral sequences for one spouse or the other. The independents experience a greater range and intensity of emotions on a daily basis than do the other couples. These couples have been shown to engage in conflict significantly more than other couples, and they have also reported having more fun, good times, and laughter than the other couples (Fitzpatrick, 1984). These couples probably experience negative emotion in reference to the spouse and to the marriage because the experience of interruption is most often regarded as negative.

The emotional state of each participant in the pure couple types is symmetrical, in that the facilitation or interference in the completion of behavioral sequences is balanced equally between husbands and wives. Husbands and wives have the same level of interdependence in the marriage and hence are more similar in the emotional experiences that the marriage can generate. The mixed couple types show that asymmetries do exist. In the separate/traditional relationship, for example, the traditional wife facilitates the completion of a number of intrachain sequences for her husband, although he does not facilitate the completion of a number of intrachain sequences for her. Emotionally, this separate needs his wife more than she needs him. Although neither one may experience emotion on a daily basis as a consequence of the relationship, the husband is more emotionally invested in the marriage than is the wife. This husband may hold the power in a number of the spheres of their life together, but the wife has more power to precipitate emotion in her husband (by interrupting her facilitation of his intrachain sequences) than he does in his wife. The emotional paradox of this marriage is that if the marriage ends, the "separate" male may experience greater distress. He loses the facilitation provided by his wife, of which he is unaware until it ceases. His traditional wife may be surprised to find herself less distressed at the end of the marriage because so few of her behavioral sequences were facilitated by her husband.

The Meaning Analysis. Although the level of interdependence in the marriage governs the degree to which emotion can be experienced in it, the assignment of meaning to the interrupting stimuli is controlled by the second major typological dimension, that is, ideology. Once the interruption has caused arousal, two decisions are made. The first concerns the class to which an emotion belongs; that is, whether the interruption can be attributed to the self, the partner, or to the relationship. Emotion directed toward the self occurs when individuals decide that they interrupted one of their own organized behavioral sequences. The emotion is directed toward the partner when the meaning analysis places the onus on the partner for the interruption. Finally, emotion is directed toward the relationship when the individual decides that the marriage *per se* is interfering in the accomplishment of higher-order plans or goals. The second decision involves whether the interruption can be considered positive or negative.

Based on the typology, no predictions can be made on the experience of emotion concerning the self. There may be no differences among the types in the experience of emotion in regard to the self. Or, at this point, we do not have enough information on the individuals in these marriages to make statements about how they feel about themselves. Differences among the types, however, in their emotional reactions to both partners and to the relationships can be specified.

The Traditionals are expected to experience few interruptions, and those that they do experience when related to the partner or the marriage will be experienced as positive ones. Even when traditionals are interrupted in an important organized behavioral sequence, the interruption will be perceived as benign because marriage or the relationship to the partner is a higher-order plan within the traditional ideological framework. The meaning analysis engaged in by the traditionals would show that an interruption by the spouse, although interfering with the completion of a lower-order plan, actually facilitates the completion of a higher-order plan (that is, the maintenance of the relationship between parties). Thus the interruption is likely to lead to positive feelings toward the relationship. In support of these predictions, we find that traditionals report much satisfaction and commitment to the marriage (Fitzpatrick & Best, 1979).

Interruptions occur frequently for the Independents, giving the marriage an emotional tone that is largely negative. These interruptions are viewed negatively because a meaning analysis of the interruptive behavior of the spouse would not show that this behavior fits into any higher-order plan. The Independents believe that marriage should not constrain the achievement of an individual's goals or plans. Independents attribute the interruption to the relationship, and experience much negative affect and dissatisfaction toward the marriage (see Fitzpatrick & Best, 1979). Furthermore, the overall number of interruptions is high because Independents have nonmeshed intrachained sequences. When these interruptions are ascribed to the partner, the independent may be more willing to view them positively. Independents are hypothesized to have strong positive feelings toward the partner and strong negative feelings toward the relationship.

Interruptions occur rarely for the separates because the points of contact are few. When these interruptions do occur, however, the separates ascribe them to the relationship but may view them as positive or negative. The separates are ambivalent about the importance of the marriage in their higher-order plans, sometimes giving it high importance, other times less importance. Thus, sometimes the interruption by the spouse will be viewed as positive because it aids the attainment of higher-order goals; at other times, such an interruption will be viewed negatively as interfering with higher-order goals for individualism. Emotional ambivalence is usually resolved in one direction or another (Gergen & Jones, 1963). Negative information appears to be more heavily weighted in all types of social interaction (Kellermann, 1984). We predict that the separates will remember the negative emotional reactions to the relationship and indicate more dissatisfaction and a lack of commitment to the marriage.

Table 2 lists the predictions for the experience of positive and negative emotions in the pure couple types. Future research will be directed toward assessing these predictions. Particular attention will be paid to how the emotion directed toward the self is altered by the interdependence and ideology supported in the marriage.

In the next section, we examine norms of expressivity in marriage. The expression of emotion is controlled not only by the experience of an emotion but also by the appropriate norms governing the expression of emotion in a close relationship.

TABLE 2. The Experience of Emotion in the Pure Couple Types

	Valence of emotion[a]	
	Positive	Negative
Traditional: Meshed intrachain sequences		
Self	3	3
Partner	3	1
Relationship	4	1
Independent: Unmeshed intrachain sequences		
Self	3	3
Partner	4	5
Relationship	1	5
Separate: Nonmeshed intrachain sequences		
Self	3	3
Partner	1	1
Relationship	1	1

[a]For ease of comparison both within and between types, a number coding for these theoretical predictions was utilized. *Very likely* (5); *likely* (4); *neither likely nor unlikely* (3); *unlikely* (2); *very unlikely* (1).

Norms Governing the Expression of Emotions

Individuals manage their emotions, and the mere experience of emotion does not necessarily translate into immediate intentional communication of that emotion, even to one's spouse. Ekman (1980) argues that all socities specify a variety of cultural display rules for the expression of emotions. These rules include masking and neutralizing what one feels as well as intensifying or deintensifying the actual emotional state one is experiencing. It appears that individuals in all societies learn norms governing emotional expressivity. These norms are appropriate standards of behavior that indicate when and what an individual can and should express. Couples in the various types have different norms governing the expression of emotion to one another. Both the gender roles embedded in the definition of each marital type and the individual's openness to conflict supply the norms governing emotional expressivity in these couples.

The norms governing emotional expressivity within and outside marriage are tied to definitions of appropriate sex-role behavior (For an extensive discussion of this issue, see Hill and Stull, Chapter 5 this volume). Research that examines communication differences between males and females or husbands and wives needs to take into account the orientation that each has to appropriate male and female behavior. For some individuals, masculininity inhibits expressivity both directly with its emphasis on reserve and indirectly because it identifies interpersonal communication with the feminine role (Komarovsky, 1964). Folk wisdom suggests that men are less expressive than women, and social scientists have written of what they see as the "tragedy of the inexpressive male" (Balswick & Peek, 1971). Men, the argument goes, are socialized not to show any weakness and become so skilled at hiding their feelings and thoughts that not even their closest associates know when they are depressed, anxious, or afraid. Women, on the other hand, are socialized to show their emotions and to discuss their feelings with their friends and romantic partners.

Much recent evidence, however, indicates that in close relationships, the pattern of the silent male and the talkative female may not be as prevalent as in social life in general. Reis and his associates (Reis, Senchak, & Solomon, 1985) show that although men may inhibit their disclosure in conversations with other men and with women with whom they are not well acquainted, men do disclose at relatively high levels to their opposite-sex romantic partners. Thus close relationships with women are one context (perhaps the only context) in which males can be expressive.

The sex roles of the traditional are very conventional ones in that the male is expected to be task-oriented, concerned with problem solving, and dominant, whereas his wife is nurturant and concerned with the relationship (Fitzpatrick & Indvik, 1982). The women in this marriage type see themselves as very feminine, and the males see themselves as masculine. Communicatively, this would suggest that the traditional husband would not discuss his feelings with his wife nor with others. Contrary to expectations, the traditional husband can share his positive feelings about his spouse as well as his own anxieties and worries with his wife. However, this is the limit of the expressivity of this male, and his wife is the traditional husband's only confidant. She appears to be able to draw the husband out and helps him to express his feelings.

The traditional ideology specifies that spouses should fulfill marriage roles defined as important by society. Traditionals approach marriage like "structuralists" (e.g., Parsons, 1951) in that they define their marital roles according to culturally based categories about appropriate behavior for husbands and wives. Recently, two new family roles have emerged in American culture—the therapeutic and the companionship roles. Both of these roles specify that it is the duty of spouses to listen to one another, to help with each other's worries and anxieties, and to be pleasant companions with similar leisure time interests (Nye, 1976). A commitment to these new roles specifies that a spouse, even a husband, must communicate with his wife. He is to be assisted in this endeavor by an understanding wife. Thus, what appears at first to be an anomaly, the traditional husband disclosing to his wife, is actually now part of the appropriate role behavior for males when married. This communication is limited, however, by the views of the traditionals on conflict. Traditionals believe in exercising restraint in expressing negative feelings to the spouse.

In contrast, independents believe in less conventional sex roles, and these husbands and wives are more likely to see themselves as androgynous (having positive masculine and feminine traits) than the other couple types. Androgynous people are more flexible in adopting interpersonal behaviors not usually associated with their own sex. Both husbands and wives in these couples are able to express their feelings, including those feelings that society traditionally limits to the opposite sex. Thus the husband can express his vulnerability and the wife, her anger.

The ideology of the independents values spontaneity and change in relationships. Couples who adhere to this viewpoint attempt to construct their own husband and wife roles, according to their individualized preferences. These couples approach marriage like "interactionists" (e.g., Turner, 1970) in that they attempt to negotiate and create rules in the course of the marriage rather than to follow culturally prescribed roles. All the values of the independents stress disclosing to the spouse, whether the disclosure is positive or negative.

The disengagement of the separates from one another means that they rarely experience emotion in the relationship. When they do, their extreme preferences to avoid conflict and limit their expressiveness indicates that these couples engage in a minimum of affective self-disclosure. The separates are extremely conventional in their sex-role orientations. The separate husband sees himself as masculine sex-typed, yet his wife sees herself as unable to engage in typical feminine behaviors. Unlike the traditional relationship where the wife draws her husband out and helps him to express his emotions, this separate wife lacks this interpersonal skill.

Research on aspects of these predictions other than marital satisfaction (emotion directed toward the relationship) is not complete, but the results to date do not contradict the model. Forty-three couples were asked about self-disclosure in their marriage (Fitzpatrick, 1976). Although we did not ask about disclosure concerning all types of emotions (self, partner, and relationship), we did ask about the disclosure of positive feelings concerning the partner and negative feelings about the self. Traditionals can tell their spouse about the positive feelings they have toward them and are relatively uninhibited in so telling. Traditionals also see the marriage as one in which negative self-feelings can be exchanged.

Independents are less likely to express positive feelings to their spouses than the Traditionals but more likely than the Separates. Independents express any negative feelings they have about themselves to their mates but do not see the mate doing the same. In a behavioral study, Independents were found to self-disclose to their spouses more than either Traditionals or Separates (Fitzpatrick *et al.*, 1984). Separates do not express positive feelings to their spouses. In fact, they admit inhibiting the expression of positive feelings about the spouse that they actually do experience. Separates do not tell the spouse negative feelings they are having about themselves, nor do they perceive that their spouses disclose those feelings to them.

One way to test for the existence of norms governing interaction is to examine how individuals operate both with the spouse and with others in their social group. In a study asking couples about aspects of self-disclosure with individuals other than the spouse, Traditionals reported being very reserved with outsiders. Traditionals refrain from telling people either their opinions or their personal feelings (Fitzpatrick, 1977). Independents, on the other hand, are very open in discussing their thoughts and feelings with individuals other than the spouse. Separates can be open with others in discussing their opinions yet not their feelings.

In a study by Fitzpatrick and Dindia (1986), the self-disclosure of facts and feelings between spouses was compared to that between same- and opposite-sex individuals meeting for the first time. Using the social relations model (Kenny & La Voie, 1984), the analyst can statistically discriminate between the effects of individuals as speakers or as listeners and the effects that may be due to the particular adjustments that conversants make to one another. In this study, we found that most of the variance in self-referential communication was accounted for by the adjustment made by conversants to one another. Very little variance was due to individual personality characteristics or listening style. Indeed, the greater the intimacy of the material exchanged, the more likely it is that some set of characteristics of the relationship between the interactants explains the variation. The major relationship characteristics that predict affective self-disclosure not only with spouses but with others as well was the ideology held by the individuals concerning relationships and their acceptance of conflict. This finding suggests that norms governing interaction, particularly those measured with the dimensions of the typology, reference a core set of interpersonal attitudes that govern self-disclosure with others.

CONCLUSIONS AND DIRECTIONS FOR FUTURE RESEARCH

This chapter has generated predictions about self-disclosure in ongoing relationships based on a typology of marriage and a basic model of emotional processes. The juxtaposition of the typology with Berscheid's model can be used to explain a variety of emotional communication patterns in addition to self-disclosure. Such a juxtaposition can also generate predictions concerning a number of observed emotional responses in the presence of the spouse such as facial expressions, body movements, goal-directed behaviors, and so forth.

The typology answers some basic questions concerning communication in close relationships. First, the typology argues that individuals use communication in diverse ways based on implicit assumptions about what constitutes appropriate or desirable communication in maintaining a marital relationship. Second, these implicit assumptions determine the functional relationship between communication and satisfaction (Fitzpatrick, 1976), In the post-1960s culture, open and supportive communication was considered the essence of a good relationship. Research with the typology, however, clearly indicates that openness in disclosing oneself to the spouse is not an effective marital communication strategy for all couples.

Traditionals value self-disclosure in marriage, and they behaviorally disclose to their spouses. The kind of openness in a Traditional marriage limits self-disclosure to positive feelings and topics about the partner and the relationship. This pattern of self-disclosure leads to a very satisfying and adjusted relationship between the partners. For traditional couples, it is inaccurate to assume that open communication is a critical mediator of marital satisfaction. Many roles are defined by conventional belief in this type of marriage; hence there is less need to negotiate openly with the spouse. Furthermore, these couples may have less negative affect to exchange with the spouse than others have.

Independents also value self-disclosure and have been found to disclose substantially more to their spouses than do the other couples. The openness of the Independents is less restrained in that these couples are willing to disclose both positive and negative feelings to one another. This kind of openness is related to tension and conflict in the relationship. The independents, albeit very cohesive as a couple, exhibit dissatisfaction with the marriage, disagree with one another on a variety of topics, and have serious conflicts with the spouse. The expressivity of these couples is related to marital dysfunctioning. For the independents, however, relationships are meaningful only to the extent that they are dedicated both to psychological closeness and to growth and change. Open communication and the confrontation of conflict are a sign of relational vitality for these couples, although they pay a price in satisfaction for the intensity of the relationship.

The open style of communication is likely to violate the autonomy, privacy, and emotional distance of the separates. Separates do not value openness and disclosure in marriage and also do not self-disclose to their spouses. The reserve of the separates does not appear to be a communication strategy that promotes satisfaction in marriage. The separates, who agree with their spouse on a number of marital and family issues, are dissatisfied with their marriage, are not very cohesive as a couple nor affectionate with one another. Neither the extreme openness of the Independents nor the extreme reserve of the separates leads to positive outcomes for their marriage. Moderation in the degree and kind of self-disclosure seems to lead to more satisfaction in marriage.

The literature needs a more pluralistic view of what constitutes "good" communication in marriage and other close relationships. The potentially oppressive result for couples seeking help is that "good communication" may require conformity to someone else's idea of what constitutes a satisfying relationship. Within prescriptive communication programs, couples are urged to confront conflicts, self-disclose, and speak in terms that are descriptive, consistent, and direct. Indeed, couples, regardless of their ideological orientation or levels of interdependence in marriage, are urged to become Independents. The independent relationship matches the dominant ideology of relationships promulgated in the literature of interpersonal communication and may even match the marital type of most researchers in close relationships. The Independent relationship is not the only marital type nor even necessarily the most satisfying.

Acknowledgments

The author would like to thank Isabelle Bauman, University of Wisconsin, John Waite Bowers, University of Iowa, and the editors of this volume of their helpful comments on this chapter.

REFERENCES

Altman, I., & Taylor, D. A. (1973). *Social penetration: The development of interpersonal relationships*. New York: Holt, Rinehart & Winston.

Balswick, J., & Peek, C. (1971). The inexpressive male: A tragedy of American society. *Family Coordinator, 20*, 263–268.

Baxter, L. (1985). Accomplishing relationship disengagement. In S. Duck & D. Perlman (Eds.), *Personal relationships* (pp. 243–265). Beverly Hills: Sage.

Berger, C. R., & Bradac, J. J. (1982). *Language and social knowledge: Uncertainty in interpersonal relations*. London: Edward Arnold.

Bernard, J. S. (1972). *The future of marriage*. New York: Bantam.

Berscheid, E. (1983). Emotion in close relationships. In H. Kelley, E. Berscheid, A. Christensen, J. J. Harver, T. L. Huston, G. Levinger, E. McClintock, L. A. Peplau, & D. K. Peterson (Eds.), *Close relationships* (pp. 110–168). New York: W. H. Freeman.

Bochner, A. (1976). Conceptual frontiers in the study of communication in families: An introduction to the literature. *Human Communication Research, 2*, 381–397.

Bochner, A. P. (1983). The functions of human communication in interpersonal bonding. In C. C. Arnold & J. W. Bowers (Eds.), *Handbook of rhetorical and communication theory* (pp. 544–621). Boston: Allyn & Bacon.

Bowers, J. W., Metts, S. M., & Duncanson, W. T. (1985). Emotion and interpersonal communication. In M. L. Knapp & G. R. Miller (Eds.), *Handbook of interpersonal communication* (pp. 500–550). Beverly Hills: Sage.

Bradbury, T. N., & Fincham, F. D. (1986). Assessment of affect. In K. D. O'Leary (Ed.), *Assessment of marital discord*. Hillsdale, NJ: Lawrence Erlbaum.

Derlega, V. J., & Grzelak, J. (1979). Appropriateness of self-disclosure. In G. J. Chelune (Ed.), *Self-disclosure* (pp. 151–176). San Francisco: Jossey-Bass.

Duck, S. W. (1980). Personal relationship research in the 1980's: Toward an understanding of complex human sociality. *Western Journal of Speech Communication, 44*, 114–119.

Ekman, P. (1980). Asymmetry in facial expression. *Science, 209*, 833–834.

Fitzpatrick, M. A. (1976). *A typological approach to communication in relationships*. Unpublished doctoral dissertation, Temple University.

Fitzpatrick, M. A. (1977). A typological approach to communication in relationships. In B. Rubin (Ed.), *Communication yearbook 1* (pp. 263–275). New Brunswick, NJ: Transaction Books.

Fitzpatrick, M. A. (1981). A typological approach to enduring relationships: Children as audience to the parental relationships. *Journal of comparative Family Studies, 12,* 81–94.

Fitzpatrick, M. A. (1984). A typological approach to marital interaction: Recent theory and research. In L. Berkowitz (Ed.), *Advances in experimental social psychology,* (Vol. 18, pp. 1–47). New York: Academic Press.

Fitzpatrick, M. A., & Best, P. (1979). Dyadic adjustment in traditional, independent, and separate relationships: A validation study. *Communication Monographs, 46,* 167–178.

Fitzpatrick, M. A., & Dindia, K. (1986). *Self-disclosure in spouse versus stranger interaction.* Unpublished manuscript. Center for Communication Research, University of Wisconsin-Madison.

Fitzpatrick, M. A., & Indvik, J. (1979). *Why you see may not be what you have: Communicative accuracy in marital types.* Paper presented at the Speech Communication Association Convention, San Antonio.

Fitzpatrick, M. A., & Indvik, J. (1982). The instrumental and expressive domains of marital communication. *Human Communication Research, 8,* 195–213.

Fitzpatrick, M. A., Fallis, S., & Vance, L. (1982). Multifunctional coding of conflict resolution strategies in marital dyads. *Family Relations, 31,* 61–70.

Fitzpatrick, M. A., Vance, L., & Witteman, H. (1984). Interpersonal communication in the causal interaction of marital partners. *Language and Social Psychology, 3,* 81–95.

Gergen, K. J., & Jones, E. E. (1963). Mental illness, predictability, and affective consequences for stimulus factors in person perception. *Journal of Abnormal and Social Psychology, 67,* 95–104.

Giles, H., & Fitzpatrick, M. A. (1985). Personal, couple and group identities: Towards a relational context for language attitudes in linguistic forms. In D. Schiffrin (Ed.), *Meaning, form and use in context: Linguistic applications* (pp. 253–277). Washington, DC: Georgetown University Press.

Hastie, R. (1981). Schematic principles in human memory. In E. T. Higgins, C. P. Herman, & M. P. Zanna (Ed.), *Social cognition: The Onatario Symposium* (Vol. 1, pp. 155–177). Hillsdale, NJ: Lawrence Erlbaum.

Hess, R., & Handel, G. (1959). *Family worlds.* Chicago: University of Chicago Press.

Kelley, H., Berscheid, E., Christensen, A., Harvey, J. H., Huston, T. L., Levinger, G., McClintock, E., Peplau, L. A., & Peterson, D. R. (Eds.) (1983). *Close relationships.* New York: W. H. Freeman.

Kellermann, K. (1984). The negativity effect and its implication for initial interaction. *Communication Monographs, 51,* 37–55.

Kenny, D. A., & La Voie, L. (1984). The social relations model. In L. Berkowitz (Ed.), *Advances in experimental social psychology* Vol. 18, pp. 48–101). New York: Academic Press.

Komarovsky, M. (1964). *Blue collar marriage.* New York: Random House.

Mandler, G. (1984). *Mind and body: The psychology of emotion and stress.* New York: W. W. Norton.

Markus, H. (1977). Self schemata and processing information about the self. *Journal of Personality and Social Psychology, 35,* 63–78.

Morton, T. L. (1978). Intimacy and reciprocity of exchange: A comparison of spouses and strangers. *Journal of Personality and Social Psychology, 36,* 72–81.

Nye, F. I. (1976). *Role structure and an analysis of the family.* Beverly Hills: Sage.

Parsons, T. (1951). *The social system*. New York: Free Press.
Raush, H. L., Barry, W. A., Hertel, R. K., & Swain, M. A. (1974). *Communication, conflict and marriage*. San Francisco: Jossey-Bass.
Reis, H., Senchak, M., & Soloman, B. (1985). Sex differences in interaction meaningfulness. *Journal of Personality and Social Psychology, 48*, 1204–1217.
Sennett, R. (1978). *The fall of public man*. New York: Basic Books.
Shorter, E. (1975). *The making of the modern family*. New York: Basic Books.
Sillars, A. L., Pike, G. R., Redman, K., & Jones, T. S. (1983). Communication and conflict in marriage: One style is not satisfying to all. In R. Bostrom (Ed.)., *Communication yearbook 7* (pp. 414–431). Beverly Hills: Sage.
Sprecher, S. (1985). *Emotion in close relationships*. Unpublished doctoral dissertation, University of Wisconsin-Madison.
Turner, R. H. (1970). *Family interaction*. New York: Wiley.
Weiss, R. S. (1975). *Marital separation*. New York: Basic Books.
Witteman, H., & Fitzpatrick, M. A. (1986). Compliance-gaining in marital interaction: Power bases, processes, and outcomes. *Communication Monographs, 53*, 130–143.

8

Self-Disclosure and Relationship Disengagement

LESLIE A. BAXTER

Altman and Taylor's (1973) book, *Social Penetration*, has served as the foundation for much of the research on self-disclosure in developing relationships. However, Altman and Taylor posited the dynamics of depenetration in their volume as well as the process of social penetration. They viewed depenetration, or disengagement as it shall be referred to in this chapter, as a simple reversal of the relationship growth process, arguing that self-disclosure breadth, depth, and valence decreased to strangerlike status as relationship parties grew more distant. To date, Altman and Taylor's so-called "reversal hypothesis" has met with inconsistent support. Some studies have reported reduced depth of disclosure as relationships disengaged (Baxter, 1979a, 1983; Baxter & Wilmot, 1983; Lloyd, 1983; Wheeless, Wheeless, & Baus, 1984; Wilmot & Baxter, 1983), but other research has noted an increased depth of disclosure (Tolstedt & Stokes, 1984). No reduction in the breadth of disclosure has been noted in some studies (Baxter, 1979a; Baxter & Wilmot, 1983), in contrast to the reduced breadth of disclosure found in other research (Tolstedt & Stokes, 1984). Although a shift toward affectively neutral disclosure has been noted in some work (Ayres, 1982), other research has reported an increase in negatively valenced disclosures (Tolstedt & Stokes, 1984). Certainly, methodological differences in these various

LESLIE A. BAXTER • Communications Department, Lewis and Clark College, Portland, Oregon 97219.

investigations account at least in part for the discrepancies that exist. However, it is the argument in this chapter that the "reversal hypothesis," despite the elegance of its simplicity, fails to conceptualize important complexities of self-disclosure in the disengagement process that may lead to a prediction of reversal in some instances but not in others. The chapter is framed in a rhetorical/strategic theoretical perspective in contrast to the social exchange perspective (Altman & Taylor, 1973; Knapp, 1984) and the stochastic structural perspective (Cappella, 1984; Gottman, 1979), which are often associated with the self-disclosure construct.

To present an overview, the chapter first introduces complexity in distinguishing two important types of self-disclosure, personal and relational, in contrast to the globalized conception of self-disclosure that characterizes the "reversal hypothesis." Then a second complexity is introduced in the need to consider self-disclosure as it operates in different stages of relationship disengagement, in contrast to the holistic view of disengagement that dominates extant research. The chapter then presents an overview of the basic tenets of a rhetorical/strategic perspective and concludes by using this theoretical perspective as a tool by which to examine the role of self-disclosure in the relationship disengagement process.

DEFINITION OF KEY CONCEPTS

SELF-DISCLOSURE

Despite variations and inconsistencies in conceptual definitions of self-disclosure (Bochner, 1982), most researchers would accept the centrality of the depth component of the construct, that is, the intimacy value or personalness of the information disclosed. The depth dimension has traditionally referred to the personalness of the disclosure with regard to self, that is, information about one's past, present, or future that is not readily known by others. However, McAdams (1984) has argued that it is useful to distinguish disclosure about one's individual self from a second type of intimate disclosure that he terms *reflexive-relational*. The topic of reflexive-relational disclosure is the interaction episode itself or the relationship in which the parties are involved. Reflexive-relational disclosure is identical to what communication theorists refer to as "explicit metacommunication" (cf. Wilmot, 1980). Because the meaning of any single communicative action is often contingent on implicit contextual cues such as the episode or relationship in which the action is embedded, explicit metacommunication performs a clarification function by explicitly commenting on the context. Because these two types of intimate self-disclosure may function differently in the disengagement process, McAdams's (1984) distinction between self-disclosure about one's individual self and reflexive-relational disclosure is a useful one. For the sake of brevity, these two forms of intimate self-disclosure will hereafter be referred to as "personal self-disclosure" and "relational self-disclosure," respectively.

Relationship Disengagement

Central to this chapter is a view of relationship disengagement as a *process*. As others have noted, (cf. Duck, 1982) breakup research unfortunately has more often framed disengagement as a single, holistic event in time rather than a through-time process. Unlike the event conception that focuses on the antecedents and consequences of the dissolution event, a process conceptualization focuses on the dynamics of how relationships come apart. Several theorists have advanced models of the various stages of relationship disengagement (e.g., Duck, 1982; Knapp, 1984; Lee, 1984). From a rhetorical/strategic perspective, the following three stages of the disengagement process hold particular relevance:

1. *Private decisionmaking*. During this stage, the individual privately contemplates his or her dissatisfactions with the other party and with the relationship, reaching the decision to end the relationship.
2. *Decision implementation*. During this stage, the disengager seeks to accomplish the dissolution of the relationship through actions directed at the other party.
3. *Public presentation*. The dissolution of the relationship becomes officially public to social network members during this phase.

The disengagement process is rarely as linear and compartmentalized as this three-stage progression would suggest. However, these stages provide a useful organizing framework by which to discuss the role of self-disclosure in disengagement.

TENETS OF A RHETORICAL/STRATEGIC PERSPECTIVE

This chapter is framed in a rhetorical or strategic perspective that reflects the author's grounding in the communications discipline. The central premise of a rhetorical/strategic perspective is that communication is goal-directed strategic activity. In general, goal-directed strategic action refers to the rational means–ends nature of communication regardless of whether the parties are engaged in conscious strategic choice making. In fact, during most interpersonal exchanges, people are probably unaware of their goals and communicative choices (Berger & Douglas, 1982; Langer, 1978). However, conscious intent is likely in some situations, specifically those perceived as novel, effortful, and unpredictable (Baxter & Philpott, 1985; Langer, 1978). In the context of a relationship, the novelty, effort, and unpredictability criteria suggest that change points in the relationship's definition are situations conducive to conscious, intentional action (Miell & Duck, 1986). Because relationship disengagement involves a change in the relationship's definition that is new, often effortful, and plagued with uncertainties, the process is probably frequented with communication that is conscious and intentional.

The second important tenet of a rhetorical/strategic perspective is that individuals usually have multiple goals in any given encounter. These goals can relate in any of several ways, ranging from full compatibility, that is, pursuit of any goal facilitates accomplishment of other goals, to full interference, that is, pursuit of any goal blocks achievement of other goals (Argyle, Furnham, & Graham, 1981). What are the types of goals that persons seek to accomplish in their relationships? This chapter examines communicative action that seeks to accomplish one or more of the following goals relevant to the disengagement process: information acquisition, face-saving on behalf of self or the other party, relationship dissolution by the two parties, and public recognition of the relationship's dissolution. Whereas face-saving is a secondary goal across all stages of disengagement, the other goals tend to be localized in only one stage. As elaborated later, the goal of information acquisition is most salient during the private decision-making stage; relationship dissolution becomes the primary goal during the decision implementation stage; and public recognition of the dissolution becomes salient during the public presentation phase.

The third and final tenet of a rhetorical/strategic perspective is that a person's strategic actions are constrained by individual and situational factors. Individuals systematically vary in the likelihood of holding certain goals. Even if goals were identical, individuals vary systematically in their repertoire of strategic options and in their skill at implementing given communicative strategies. Similarly, the goals as well as the strategic resources available to a person in a given encounter may vary as a function of several situational exigencies, including the relationship in which the interaction is embedded, especially its degree of psychological closeness and its degree of interdependence, the anticipated and actual response of the other party, and the situational norms for appropriate action. In short, strategic choice making is best described as bounded choice making for interactants.

These three tenets of a rhetorical/strategic perspective are elaborated later in understanding self-disclosure during relationship disengagement. Even without further elaboration of the perspective, however, it is possible to discern how it complements current approaches to close relationships. The specific phenomena that comprise rewards and costs from a social exchange perspective correspond to the types of goals that a person holds from a rhetorical/strategic perspective. However, the strategic action component lacks a direct counterpart in the social exchange perspective; social exchange theory does not specifically address how reward and cost principles play themselves out among interacting parties (Bell & Daly, 1984). The interpersonal attraction arena provides a concrete illustration of how the social exchange and rhetorical/strategic perspectives compare. Both perspectives are interested in uncovering the bases of interpersonal attraction, for example, attitude similarity, although a social exchange theorist would refer to these as "rewards," whereas a rhetorical/strategic theorist would refer to them as "interaction goals." However, the rhetorical/strategic theorist goes one step further at the strategic action level to ask such questions as how interactants communicatively discern one another's attitudes, how they make their similarity known to one another, and how they communicate that they find one another attractive.

The stochastic structural approach is a second common framework for understanding relationships. This approach is characterized by study of the organization and patterning of interaction between the relationship parties, that is, the probabilities with which various types of interaction behaviors are sequenced (e.g., Cappella, 1984; Dindia, 1982; Gottman, 1979). Again consider the interpersonal attraction arena with a hypothetical sample of conversations between pairs of interacting strangers. Imagine that the second party's response to his or her partner's prior Type A act is Type B Act 60% of the time, Type C act 30% of the time, and Type D act 10% of the time. Whereas a stochastic structuralist would be attracted analytically to the A–B pattern as the most probable sequence pair, a rhetorical strategist would be interested in the full range of responses (B, C, and D) as strategic choices that are differentially selected because of variations in goals and/or individual/situation constraints. "Strategy" implies choice; hence the rhetorical/strategic perspective becomes relevant in this instance only because Act B does not follow Act A 100% of the time.

The remainder of the chapter examines self-disclosure choices as strategic action. A portion of the self-disclosure research concerned with relationship initiation and growth has emphasized the goals or functions of self-disclosure (cf. Derlega, 1984), hence providing a useful forerunner to the present view. However, relationship disengagement involves strategic action as much if not more than earlier stages of relationship development. Although some relationships may simply fade away in reciprocal inattention (Davis, 1973; Rose, 1984), most relationship dissolutions are accomplished only through communicative work by the relationship parties. Most dissolutions are desired initially by only one of the relationship parties (Baxter, 1979b, 1984; Hill, Rubin, & Peplau, 1976; Spanier & Thompson, 1984), requiring interaction work of some sort between the two parties. Further, all parties, whether the "breaker-upper" or the "broken-up-with" (Hill *et al.*, 1976), must communicatively manage the public presentation of the relationship dissolution to social network members. In addition to the strategic work involved in accomplishing the primary goal of dissolution (or continuation in the instance of the person who is broken up with), the secondary goals of face-saving and information acquisition require communicative action, as well.

THE STRATEGIC ACCOMPLISHMENT OF DISENGAGEMENT

The rhetorical/strategic analysis of disengagement can most effectively be approached by using the organizing framework of the three disengagement stages presented previously.

The Private Decision-Making Stage

As the label for this stage implies, this phase of disengagement involves a private assessment of the other party and of the relationship as a source of satisfaction and dissatisfaction. The person's primary goal is to decide what to do about the dissatisfactions—whether to do nothing, to stay in the relationship and seek its improvement, or to dissolve the relationship. Indecision, uncertainty and ambivalence often characterize this disengagement stage (Duck, 1982). The presence of uncertainty suggests that the potential disengager will hold a primary goal of uncertainty reduction and will take strategic action directed at acquiring additional information to alleviate this uncertainty (Berger & Bradac, 1982).

Several types of uncertainty can exist. Because the most difficult dissolution to accomplish involves unilateral as opposed to bilateral desire to terminate the relationship, the person might strategically acquire information to discern the other party's satisfaction level with the relationship. If this information acquisition effort uncovers that the other party is also dissatisfied and would not resist a dissolution, the projected costs associated with the dissolution diminish substantially. The person might also like to acquire information on the likelihood that the other party would be willing to improve the relationship in those areas that are problematic to the disengager. A third area in which additional information might be helpful to the dissatisfied but ambivalent person is social network perceptions of the other party, oneself, and the relationship. The discovery that one's friends really do not care for the other party and would welcome a dissolution would reduce the projected cost of the dissolution.

The most efficient strategy for acquiring additional information relevant to all three types of uncertainties is relational self-disclosure. In fact, disclosive relationship talk is a prevalent normative value in this culture (Bellah, Madsen, Sullivan, Swidler, & Tipton, 1985; Katriel & Philipsen, 1981). The individual's repertoire of strategies by which to acquire additional information about the other party or the relationship contains the strategy of Disclosive Directness, that is interrogating another to solicit disclosive information or disclosing onself in order to induce a reciprocal disclosure from the other (Baxter & Wilmot, 1984; Berger & Bradac, 1982). Relational self-disclosure has also been found in the repertoire of strategies with which people cope with their relationship dissatisfactions (Dindia & Baxter, 1985).

Although relational self-disclosure may be the most efficient way to gather additional information, such "bald-on-record" (Brown & Levinson, 1978), behavior potentially carries the greatest risk to the parties' "face" (Brown & Levinson, 1978). Despite the primary salience of the uncertainty reduction goal during this stage of disengagement, it is quite likely that the identity-based goal of face-saving is an important secondary goal, certainly with regard to the person's own face but perhaps to the face of the other party as well. Anthropologists Brown and Levinson (1978) have developed a useful extension of Goffman's (1967) classic work on the "face" construct, suggesting that two distinct types of face can be identified in contrast to Goffman's unitary conceptualization of the concept. Specifically, they distinguish *positive face* from *negative face*. Positive face refers to one's desire to be liked and valued, whereas negative face refers to one's desire to be unimpeded with complete autonomy and freedom of action. Thus the identity-based use of self-disclosure on behalf of self involves selective disclosure to insure that one is likable and to insure that one's freedom of action is not impeded upon. When the identity-based goal is other directed, the selective disclosure is for purposes of assuring the other party that she or he is liked and to assure that the other is not stripped of autonomy and control of action. Interrogating another or trying to induce a reciprocal disclosure applies pressure to the other party, thereby threatening the other's negative face. In the instance of expressed relationship dissatisfaction, disclosures would likely be negatively valenced, thus threatening the other's positive face and the potential disengager's positive face, as well, if the other reciprocated the disclosure with a negative or critical response.

Relevant research suggests that relational self-disclosure to one's partner during this period of uncertainty is not common, despite the value that our culture attaches to relationship talk (Lee, 1984; Spanier & Thompson, 1984). At first glance, this would suggest that relationship parties are sacrificing efficient information acquisition for the secondary goal of face-saving. However, individuals potentially have extensive repertoires of strategies by which to acquire information about the other party and about the relationship, only one of which involves relational self-disclosure (Baxter & Wilmot, 1984; Berger & Bradac, 1982). These alternative strategies are generally nondisclosive, indirect means of gathering information that overall may involve less risk to face because they ideally camouflage the user's intentions (Brown & Levinson, 1978). However, this camouflage may be somewhat limited in practice; Spanier and Thompson (1984) found that 70% of the broken-up-with marital partners in their sample displayed substantial foresight and were not surprised when their partners finally requested separation or divorce.

These alternative information acquisition strategies vary substantially in form (see Baxter & Wilmot, 1984), but two of them involve reduced personal self-disclosure. First, reduced personal self-disclosure constitutes what Baxter and Wilmot call an "endurance test" by which to discern the other party's perseverance of commitment to the relationship. By subjecting the other party to depersonalized strangerlike talk, the potential disengager discerns the intensity of the other's commitment. Second, reduced personal self-disclosure accomplishes what Baxter and Wilmot refer to as an "indirect suggestion test." Depersonalized talk hints at a possible disengagement, thereby affording the potential disengager an opportunity to "test the waters" in the other party's reaction. Because a reduction in personal self-disclosure is subject to multiple possible interpretations, from intended breakup to "having a bad day," the parties' face is jeopardized less than would be the case with a "bald-on-record" disclosure about the unsatisfactory state of the relationship.

It seems likely that direct, relational self-disclosure would be a strategy of last resort during this phase of disengagement, employed only if one of three conditions were present: (1) alternative strategies have failed to realize their potential of simultaneously maintaining face and acquiring addition information, (2) the potential disengager lacks sufficient skill in enacting indirect information acquisition strategies, or

(3) the secondary goal of face-saving becomes relatively unimportant to the potential disengager when compared to the goal of uncertainty reduction. To date, research on the use of information acquisition strategies in uncertainty reduction has been largely limited to the context of developing relationships. Additional research effort is needed that directly examines the use of these strategies during the private decision-making stage of disengagement. However, on the basis of the argument developed in this section, the "reversal hypothesis" appears to be a likely consequence of indirect information acquisition strategies, two of which involve reduced personal self-disclosure. Only when indirect strategies are ineffective or absent from the potential disengager's skill repertoire, or when the secondary goal of face-saving becomes unimportant, does the "reversal hypothesis" appear jeopardized through an increased use of relational disclosure.

At the conclusion of the decision-making stage, the dissatisfied person must determine how to cope with his or her dissatisfaction in the relationship—either to stay in the relationship and seek its improvement or to dissolve the relationship. Once a decision has been made, closure has been brought to this phase of the disengagement process.

The Decision Implementation Stage

The Domain of Dissolution Strategies. It is during the decision implementation phase that relationship parties communicatively negotiate the unbonding of their relationship. Substantial research has examined the domain of strategies employed by disengagers (for a detailed review see Baxter 1986). In order to focus on the role of self-disclosure during this stage, two basic strategy prototypes will be discussed.

1. *Distance cuing*. This strategy indirectly signals to the other party that a dissolution is desired by significantly reducing the valence, breadth, and depth of personal self-disclosure. This strategy potentially works because of the relational information that is carried implicitly in personal self-disclosure behavior. Based on Grice's (1975) principle of implicature, individuals alter the relational frame of a message if it violates what is expected. Because people's implicit theories of relationships clearly associate intimate individualistic self-disclosure with relational closeness (Wilmot & Baxter, 1983, 1984), a disengager could use the avoidance of personal self-disclosure as a cuing mechanism to encourage the other party to redefine the relationship as one of reduced closeness.

2. *Relationship talk cuing*. This strategy is an assemblage of various disengagement strategies, all of which involve relational self-disclosure directed at the other party. Although the tone of this disclosure may vary from hostile to supportive and the disengager may vary in how

much of his or her dissatisfaction is detailed, the broken-up-with party is nonetheless presented with the disengager's feelings about the relationship.

These two strategies resemble the strategies of reduced personal self-disclosure and increased relational self-disclosure from the decision-making stage; however, their use is put to a different purpose during the implementation stage—dissolution of the relationship as opposed to information acquisition.

"Distance cuing" and "relational talk cuing" hold implications for the parties' face. Because of the likelihood that relationship talk cuing might be met with negative affect and criticism from the broken-up-with party, the disengager's positive face is threatened in the use of this strategy. Because it relies on more indirectness, the disengager's positive face is less at risk with the strategy of distance cuing. Relationship talk cuing typically exacts greater effort to enact than does distance cuing, hence making the former strategy more costly to the disengager's negative face than the latter strategy. In short, the strategy of distance cuing places the disengager's face at less risk than does the strategy of relationship talk cuing. Unfortunately, face-saving for self is often at odds with face-saving on behalf of the other party. Relationship disengagement doubtless holds threat to the positive face of the broken-up-with party under any circumstances (Hill *et al.*, 1976). However, positive face is probably more threatened with distance cuing as opposed to relationship talk cuing; at least the latter strategy respects the other in recognizing that he or she is entitled to a direct, face-to-face statement of the situation. If the broken-up-with party desires to continue the relationship, disengagement blocks his or her relational goal and thus threatens the other's negative face regardless of how the disengagement goal is strategically accomplished. However, the other party's negative face is probably more threatened by distance cuing as opposed to relationship talk cuing; at least the latter strategy affords the other an opportunity to challenge, threaten, or persuade the disengager to stay in the relationship, thereby empowering the other party with some possible actions.

The "reversal hypothesis" would predict that the strategy of distance cuing would dominate this stage of disengagement, for this is the strategy that comes closest to a reversal of self-disclosure. Although distance cuing is a frequent strategic choice by disengagers (Baxter, 1979a, 1984; Lee, 1984), this strategy choice is contingent on several situational and individual constraint factors.

Situational and Individual Constraints on Strategy Selection. The situational constraint factor that has been studied the most extensively is the prior closeness of the relationship. Consistently, disengagers are less likely to employ distance cuing than direct relationship talk cuing as the prior relationship closeness increases (Baxter, 1982; Cody, 1982; DeStephen, 1984; Lee, 1984). The rhetorical/strategic perspective accounts for this consistent finding in examining the multiple goal structure of the disengager and the extent to which distance cuing accomplishes these goals. First, the disengager has the primary goal of dissolving the relationship. For relationships of greater prior closeness, the indirect strategy of distance cuing may be quite inefficient, jeopardizing this goal. Davis (1973) has argued that people in close relationships have succeeded in "sewing together" every dimension of their separate lives, unlike members of a more superficial relationship in which interdependence is evident only in restricted domains of the parties' lives. Johnson (1982) has supported this assertion in reporting the results of his research program on dating, finding that only 14% of those persons who were occasionally dating would have to reach decisions regarding the splitting up of possessions in contrast to 98% of the married respondents. Distance cuing does not suffice in dissolving relationships with complex webs of interdependence; direct relational self-disclosure is required in order to accomplish dissolutions of closer relationships.

Further, the distance cuing strategy probably is not of maximum efficiency in accomplishing dissolutions of even the less interdependent relationships. If the other fails to notice the cuing, or notices it but fails to attach the correct interpretation to the cuing, the disengager's dissolution goal is blocked. In fact, disengagements that are implemented through the distance cuing strategy do appear to be more protracted than disengagements handled through greater directness (Baxter, 1984; Baxter & Philpott, 1980).

If the distance cuing strategy at a minimum delays accomplishment of the dissolution goal, why is it selected at all by disengagers? Distance cuing is probably employed in less close relationships because it serves the disengager's goal of maintaining his or her own face. Further, the inefficiency of the strategy may be apparent to disengagers only in retrospect (Baxter, 1979b). Thus, distance cuing probably is used in less close relationships because it is perceived by disengagers as an integrative strategy that accomplishes both dissolution and face maintenance for self. Further, if the desire for dissolution is reciprocal and the relationship lacks complex interdependencies, distance cuing may in fact be quite successful for the disengager (Baxter, 1984; Davis, 1973; Rose, 1984).

The efficiency argument accounts for different likelihoods of use of distance cuing in superficial as opposed to close relationships, but what accounts for the greater use of direct relational self-disclosure in closer relationships? This question is an interesting one, for the relationship talk cuing strategy does not maintain the disengager's face, unlike distance cuing. Clearly, the disengager is placing a higher priority on the other's face than on his or her own face in using direct relational self-disclosure. Although the disengager's face is jeopardized in using this strategy, the immediate loss of face with the other party may be relatively modest and short-lived when compared to the potential long-term loss of face with social network members if one failed to employ relationship talk cuing. The closer the relationship, the more likely that the other party knows the members of the disengager's social network and can inform them of the disengager's conduct in the breakup. The disengager ultimately is accountable to his or her social network, and the members of that network may perceive that the disengager owes concern for the other's face based on the prior closeness of the relationship and the size of the face offense inherent in seeking dissolution. Initiating the breakup of a close relationship is a highly face-threatening act to the other party (Hill *et al.*, 1976), and the culture obligates the "polite" person to give appropriate compensation for face-threatening acts (Brown & Levinson, 1978). Failure to display such compensation in the form of direct relational self-disclosure may make the disengager less likable among the social network members.

In addition to the reactions of the social network to the disengager's strategic choice, Davis (1973) has offered a second reason why the disengager should be concerned with the other's face in close relationships. The closer the relationship, the more the parties have learned of one another's deepest and darkest secrets, thus affording substantial "betrayal potential" to the parties in their ability to publicize this information in the social network. News of the desired dissolution may provide the other party with motivation to betray the disengager's confidences and thereby damage the disengager's positive face among social network members. Other-oriented action in the form of relational self-disclosure may ameliorate such a revengeful reaction from the other party.

The attributed cause of the relationship's demise can also affect the disengager's choice of implementation strategy. When the cause of the relationship's breakup is attributed to sources external to the relationship (e.g., job relocation), as opposed to causes internal to the relationship, disengagers appear less likely to employ the strategy of distance cuing and are more likely to employ nonhostile relationship talk cuing (Baxter, 1982). Because the other party in no way is responsible for the externally induced demise, disengagers probably attempt to prevent the other party from undue face loss by using the strategy that best accomplishes compensatory facework on behalf of the other. Reciprocally, disengagers appear less likely to employ nonhostile relationship talk cuing and are more likely to employ distance cuing when the other's personality and behavior is the perceived cause of the relationship's demise (Cody, 1982). Thus disengagers generally appear less motivated to do facework on the other's behalf if the other is culpable.

What are the differences in strategy selection as a function of the unilateral versus bilateral desire to exit the relationship? Davis (1973), among others, has suggested that a mutual desire to terminate the relationship often produces reciprocal distance cuing and a general fading away of the relationship. Baxter (1984) supported this expectation in finding indirectness somewhat more likely in bilateral as opposed to unilateral dissolutions, but two additional studies (Baxter, 1979a, 1982) have found no relationship between mutuality of desire to end a relationship and strategy selection. If a relationship is relatively superficial without an extensive interdependence web, distance cuing in fact can accomplish this dissolution. Further, mutual reliance on distance cuing implies mutual disregard for one another's face needs. Clearly, the interdependence condition and/or face regard precluded a simple fading away effect in the majority of studies that have considered the mutuality factor.

The last situational factor to receive attention is the anticipation of continued future contact with the other party, albeit in a relationship of substantially reduced closeness. Perras and Lustig (1982) found that disengagers used indirect distance cuing less frequently under conditions of anticipated contact as opposed to no future contact. Baxter (1982) found a trend in the same direction. The anticipation of future contact with the other party introduces another goal for the disengager. In addition to dissolving the current relationship, the disengager has to lay the foundation for a future relationship with the other. Distance cuing is problematic as an integrative strategy that simultaneously must deal with both of these goals. The disengager probably must resort to some form of relational self-disclosure to meet both goals.

Strategy repertoire and goal structure may be constrained by characteristics of the disengager, including age and gender. The first of these factors, disengager age, is probably related to strategy repertoire. Preadolescents appear to have a smaller disengagement strategy repertoire in contrast to the larger repertoire sizes for older adults (Baxter & Philpott, 1981a, 1982). Given that preadolescents have a more limited range of relationship experiences than their older counterparts, this finding is hardly surprising. The second individual-level factor is the gender of the disengager. Unfortunately, results are inconsistent across studies. Females have been reported as the first to initiate dissolution (Hill *et al.*, 1976; Spanier & Thompson, 1984; Wright, 1982), but no consistency has emerged with regard to sex differences in how the dissolution is strategically accomplished. Some studies have reported that females are likely to use direct relational self-disclosure more than males (Lloyd, 1983; Wright, 1982), whereas other studies report no overall sex differences in strategy selection (Baxter, 1979a, DeStephen, 1984). In approaching gender in terms of psychological sex-role orientation as opposed to biological sex, masculine, feminine, and androgynous persons have displayed no significant differences in the sizes of their dissolution repertoires. However, masculine sex-role types may be the least inclined of the sex-role-orientation types to hold the goal of facework on the other's behalf and most inclined to hold a goal of maintenance of self's face, based on differences in expressed strategy preferences (Baxter & Philpott, 1981a,b).

The discussion thus far of the decision implementation stage is oversimplified in that it may create the false impression that the disengager successfully accomplishes the relationship's dissolution in a single strategic action. To the contrary, the typical relationship dissolution is generally quite protracted, necessitating multiple strategic actions on the part of the disengager (Baxter, 1984; Baxter & Philpott, 1980; Kressel, Jaffee, Tuchman, Watson, & Deutsch, 1980; Lee, 1984). Even if the initial "bid" for disengagement is through the indirect strategy of distance cuing, it can reasonably be predicted that subsequent "negotiation rounds" will bring the disengager to the more direct strategy of relational self-disclosure. The broken-up-with party may misinterpret or ignore the indirect hints afforded by reduced personal self-disclosure in the distance cuing strategy, thus forcing the disengager to become more direct in the disengagement message. Although the other party may misinterpret or ignore the distancing signals, he or she is more likely to receive the distancing cues and initiate a direct relationship talk with the disengager to determine what is occurring in the relationship (Baxter & Philpott, 1980). As mentioned earlier, the broken-up-with party most likely desires a continuation of the relationship and thus has substantial relational investment at stake. At a minimum, the broken-up-with party will seek verification that the distance cuing indeed indicates the disengager's desire to dissolve the relationship. If the other party's desire to continue the relationship is sufficiently strong, he or she will use the relationship talk as a basis of persuading the disengager to reconsider the disengagement (Miller & Parks, 1982). Although some disengagers experience ambivalence in their dissolution goal at this point (Baxter, 1984; Kressel *et al.*, 1980), the more likely outcome is continued strategic action "rounds." Unfortunately for the relationship parties, anger, hurt, and frustration increase proportionately as the dissolution time span increases and their relationship talk becomes increasingly negatively valenced (Baxter & Philpott, 1980; Lee, 1984).

Although only a few of several possible situational and individual constraint factors have been examined in the research to date, the findings suggest that global reduction of self-disclosure is far from the automatic reversal phenomenon originally posited by Altman and Taylor (1973). Distance cuing is likely under some circumstances, consistent with the reversal hypothesis. However, other situational and individual conditions promote an increased likelihood of strategies that involve relational self-disclosure, the opposite finding from that predicted by the reversal hypothesis. Once the two relationship parties have reached agreement on the disengagement of their relationship, the final stage of public presentation is entered.

THE PUBLIC PRESENTATION STAGE

A personal relationship is both constructed and deconstructed not only through the actions of the relationship parties but through social network recognition, as well. The decision implementation stage unbonds the relationship from the inside; the public presentation stage unbonds the relationship from the outside.

Both the disengager and the broken-up-with party bear the informational burden of making public the dissolution of their relationship. In addition, each party has a self-presentational goal to maintain his or her own face with the social network (Harvey, Weber, Yarkin, & Stewart, 1982). Both goals require selective self-disclosure to others.

The informational burden varies depending on the closeness of the relationship that is being dissolved. In general, both the social requirement to explain the dissolution and the anticipated disapproval of the dissolution should increase as a function of the prior closeness of the dissolving relationship (Johnson, 1982). Social network members have more invested in the married couple than the occasional-dating couple, for example, and would experience more disruption from dissolution of the more involved relationship.

Despite a general increase in disapproval with more relationship involvement, not all social network members respond alike to the dissolution. Friend appear less disapproving of marital breakups than do kin members, for example (Goode, 1956; Spanier & Thompson, 1984). Kin members have different role relationships with the relationship parites than do nonkin members of the social network, perhaps with greater investments to lose in the dissolution. Further, marital problems are likely to be more apparent to close friends than to parental families, producing greater understanding and acceptance of the dissolution among friends as opposed to kin (Spanier & Thompson, 1984).

The self-presentational goal of maintaining one's face should vary in difficulty more or less along the same lines as the goal of informing others. One's face should be less affected the more superficial the relationship being dissolved. Further, the facework task should be easier with people who approve of the dissolution as opposed to those who disapprove.

However, the facework goal involves a rhetorical "balancing act" of some complexity regardless of the relationship's closeness and the receptivity of the social network member. This task is particularly challenging for the broken-up-with party. Public knowledge that one was left makes suspect his or her basic likability in addition to confirming one's loss of negative face as a victim. The broken-up-with party must rhetorically repair his or her tarnished face by suggesting that his or her likability was not the real cause of the relationship's demise and that one was not victimized in the dissolution, perhaps by attributing blame for the relationship's demise to the disengager. However, the broken-up-with party must exert caution in denigrating the disengager to prevent others from perceiving one as overly negative or lacking in judgment in one's ability to select relationship partners (Duck, 1982). Of course, a similar risk to positive face occurs if one goes too far in the other direction by demonstrating to others that one is a poor "credit risk" (La Gaipa, 1982) for future relationships based on an admission of total blame in causing the dissolution. Thus the person must rhetorically balance the account presented for others' consumption.

The disengager must display the same rhetorical care in accounting for the relationship's demise. Excessive denigration of the other subjects one to criticism, but absorption of total blame reaps a similar cost to one's positive face. However, the disengager's face is less tarnished when confronting others because of the fact that he or she by definition is not the person left. La Gaipa (1982) has suggested an additional complexity that is unique to the disengager: He or she has to dissolve the relationship publicly while simultaneously displaying a commitment to relationships in the abstract. Rhetorically, the disengager cannot risk loss of positive face by being perceived as against relationship bonding in principle.

In addition to their separate rhetorical presentations to social network members, the relationship parties must exhibit care in how their postdissolution joint appearances are managed. Former spouses who have no contact with one another appear to be in the vast minority (Spanier & Thompson, 1984). Thus, joint appearances are likely to occur with some frequency in the presence of social network members. Postdissolution relationships are problematic to manage because the parties retain many of the communicative behaviors they established with the other as a result of the knowledge they acquired over time about the other party quite apart from the affective dimension of the former association (Baxter, 1983). When relationships are developing, communicative patterns become established because of increased familiarity with the other as well as increased positive affect toward the other. Because the familiarity-based communication patterns co-occur with the positive affect-based communication patterns during relationship growth, it is all too easy for people to mistake the former as evidence of the latter (Baxter, 1983). Thus, when a postdissolution pair is observed using shorthand phrases or vocabulary apparently unique to them, it could easily be mistaken as evidence of reconciliation instead of affectively neutral communication efficiency.

Just as the parties must carefully manage their joint appearances, so must they exhibit care in the other extreme of total avoidance of one another. Extreme avoidance of the other constitutes an implicit admission that one was and continues to be a victim controlled by the other's actions, thereby threatening one's negative face.

This third stage of disengagement is a fascinating one in terms of the careful rhetorical balances that must be maintained by the relationship parties. It is also the least researched stage from a rhetorical/strategic perspective; conjecture abounds and data do not. The paucity of empirical work devoted to this stage is unfortunate, for the successful rhetorical management of public presentation is central to long-term recovery from the relationship dissolution.

CONCLUSIONS

This chapter has examined the validity of the reversal hypothesis, that is, the posited reduction in disclosure breadth, depth, and valence as relationships disengage. Rather than viewing self-disclosure as a more or less automatic outcome of broader relational forces, the chapter is framed in a rhetorical/strategic perspective in which disclosure is regarded as goal-directed strategic action. An important distinction is made between personal self-disclosure, that is, personal revelations about oneself, and relational self-disclosure, that is, disclosive talk about the state of the relationship. In general, the research reviewed in the chapter suggests that reduced self-disclosure is but one strategic path that a disengaging relationship can take. Whether or not the disengagement progresses through reversal or, in contrast, displays a period of intensified self-disclosure about the relationship is a function of the disengagement stage under consideration and various situational and individual factors that influence the goals and strategic actions of the relationship disengager.

REFERENCES

Altman, I., & Taylor, D. (1973). *Social penetration: The development of interpersonal relationships.* New York: Holt, Rinehart, & Winston.

Argyle, M., Furnham, A., & Graham, J. A. (1981). *Social situations.* New York: Cambridge University Press.

Ayres, J. (1982). Perceived use of evaluative statements in developing, stable, and deteriorating relationships with a person of the same or opposite sex. *Western Journal of Speech Communication, 46,* 20–31.

Baxter, L. (1979a). Self-disclosure as a relationship disengagement strategy: An exploratory investigation. *Human Communication Research, 5,* 215–222.

Baxter, L. (1979b, February). *Self-reported disengagement strategies in friendship relationships.* Paper presented at the annual convention of the Western Speech Communication Association.

Baxter, L. (1982). Strategies for ending relationships: Two studies. *Western Journal of Speech Communication, 45,* 223–241.

Baxter, L. (1983). Relationship disengagement: An examination of the reversal hypothesis. *Western Journal of Speech Communication, 47,* 85–98.

Baxter, L. (1984). Trajectories of relationship disengagement. *Journal of Social and Personal Relationships, 1,* 29–48.

Baxter, L. (1986). Accomplishing relationship disengagement. In S. Duck & D. Perlman (Eds.), *Understanding personal relationships.* London: Sage.

Baxter, L., & Philpott, J. (1980, November). *Relationship disengagement: A process view.* Paper presented at the annual convention of the Speech Communication Association.

Baxter, L., & Philpott, J. (1981a, November). *Communicator age and sex-role orientation differences in preferred relationship termination strategies.* Paper presented at the annual convention of the Speech Communication Association.

Baxter, L., & Philpott, J. (1981b, February). *The effects of relational goal, communicator age and communicator sex-role orientation on communication competence.* Paper presented at the annual convention of the Western Speech Communication Association.

Baxter, L., & Philpott, J. (1982). Attribution-based strategies for initiating and terminating friendships. *Communication Quarterly, 30,* 217–224.

Baxter, L., & Philpott, J. (1985, February). *Conditions conducive to awareness of communication activity.* Paper presented at the annual convention of the Western Speech Communication Association.

Baxter, L., & Wilmot, W. (1983). Communication characteristics of relationships with differential growth rates. *Communication Monographs, 50,* 264–272.

Baxter, L., & Wilmot, W. (1984). Secret tests: Strategies for acquiring information about the state of the relationship. *Human Communication Research, 11,* 171–201.

Bell, R. A., & Daly, J. A. (1984). The affinity-seeking function of communication. *Communication Monographs, 51,* 91–115.

Bellah, R., Madsen, R., Sullivan, W., Swidler, A., & Tipton, S. (1985). *Habits of the heart: Individualism and commitment in American life.* Berkeley: University of California Press.

Berger, C. R., & Bradac, J. (1982). *Lanaguge and social knowledge: Uncertainty in interpersonal relations.* London: Edward Arnold.

Berger, C. R., & Douglas, W. (1982). Thought and talk: "Excuse me, but have I been talking to myself?" In F. Dance (Ed.), *Human communication theory* (pp. 42–60). New York: Harper & Row.

Bochner, A. (1982). On the efficacy of openness in close relationships. In M. Burgoon (Ed.), *Communication yearbook 5* (pp. 109–124). New Brunswick, NJ: Transaction Books.

Brown, P., & Levinson, S. (1978). Universals in language usage: Politeness phenomena. In E. N. Goody (Ed.), *Questions and politeness: Strategies in social interaction* (pp. 56–289). New York: Cambridge University Press.

Cappella, J. (1984). The relevance of the microstructure of interaction to relationship change. *Journal of Social and Personal Relationships, 1*, 239–264.

Cody, M. (1982). A typology of disengagement strategies and an examination of the role intimacy, reactions to inequity and relational problems play in strategy selection. *Communication Monographs, 49*, 148–170.

Davis, M. (1973). *Intimate relations*. New York: Free Press.

Derlega, V. J. (1984). Self-disclosure and intimate relationships. In. V. J. Derlega (Ed.), *Communication, intimacy, and close relationships* (pp. 1–9). Orlando, FL: Academic Press.

DeStephen, D. (1984, November). *Relational termination: The effect of sex and type of relationship on the selection of relational termination strategies*. Paper presented at the annual convention of the Speech Communication Association.

Dindia, K. (1982). Reciprocity of self-disclosure: A sequential analysis. In M. Burgoon (Ed.), *Communication yearbook, 6* (pp. 506–528). Beverly Hills, CA: Sage Publications.

Dindia, K., & Baxter, L. (1985). *Strategies used by marital partners in maintaining and repairing their relationship*. Unpublished manuscript.

Duck, S. (1982). A topography of relationship disengagement and dissolution. In S. Duck (Ed.), *Personal relationships 4: Dissolving personal relationships* (pp. 1–30). New York: Academic Press.

Goffman, E. (1967). *Interaction ritual: Essays on face to face behavior*. Garden City, NY: Doubleday/Anchor.

Goode, W. J. (1956). *After divorce (women in divorce)*.New York: Free Press.

Gottman, J. (1979). Marital interaction: Experimental investigations. New York: Academic Press.

Grice, H. P. (1975). Logic and conversation. In P. Cole & J. L. Morgan (Eds.), *Syntax and semantics, Volume 3: Speech acts* (pp. 41–58). New York: Academic Press.

Harvey, J., Weber, A., Yarkin, K., & Stewart, B. (1982). An attributional approach to relationship breakdown and dissolution. In S. Duck (Ed.), *Personal relationships 4: Dissolving personal relationships* (pp. 107–126). New York: Academic Press.

Hill, C. T., Rubin, Z., & Peplau, L. A. (1976). Breakups before marriage: The end of 103 affairs. *Journal of Social Issues, 32*, 147–168.

Johnson, M. P. (1982). Social and cognitive features of the dissolution of commitment to relationships. In S. Duck (Ed.), *Personal relationships 4: Dissolving personal relationships* (pp. 51–73). New York: Academic Press.

Katriel, T., & Philipsen, G. (1981). "What we need is communication": "Communication" as a cultural category in some american speech. *Communication Monographs, 48*, 301–317.

Knapp, M. L. (1984). *Interpersonal communication and human relationships*. Boston: Allyn & Bacon.

Kressel, K., Jaffee, N., Tuchman, B., Watson, C., & Deutsch, M. (1980). A typology of divorcing couples: Implications for mediation and the divorce process. *Family Process, 19*, 101–116.

La Gaipa, J. (1982). Rules and rituals in disengaging from relationships. In S. Duck (Ed.), *Personal relationships 4: Dissolving personal relationships* (pp. 189–210). New York: Academic Press.

Langer, E. (1978). Rethinking the role of thought in social interaction. In J. Harvey, W. Ickes, & R. Kidd (Eds.), *New directions in attribution research* (Vol. 2, pp. 35–58). Hillsdale, NJ: Erlbaum.

Lee, L. (1984). Sequences in separation: A framework for investigating endings of the personal (romantic) relationship. *Journal of Social and Personal Relationships, 1,* 49–73.

Lloyd, S. A. (1983). *Typological description of premarital relationship dissolution.* Unpublished doctoral dissertation, Oregon State University.

McAdams, D. P. (1984). Motives and relationships. In V. J. Derlega (Ed.), *Communication, intimacy, and close relationships* (pp. 41–70). Orlando, FL: Academic Press.

Miell, D., & Duck, S. (1986). Strategies in developing personal relationships. In V. J. Derlega & B. A. Winstead (Eds.), *Friendship and social interaction.* New York: Springer-Verlag.

Miller, G. R., & Parks, M. (1982). Communication in dissolving relationships. In S. Duck (Ed.), *Personal relationships 4: Dissolving personal relationships* (pp. 127–154). New York: Academic Press.

Perras, M., & Lustig, M. (1982, February). *The effects of intimacy level and intent to disengage on the selection of relationship disengagement strategies.* Paper presented at the annual convention of the Western Speech Communication Association.

Rose, S. M. (1984). How friendships end: Patterns among young adults. *Journal of Social and Personal Relationships, 1,* 267–277.

Spanier, G. B., & Thompson, L. (1984). *Parting: The aftermath of separation and divorce.* Beverly Hills, CA: Sage Publications.

Tolstedt, B. E., & Stokes, J. P. (1984). Self-disclosure, intimacy, and the depenetration process. *Journal of Personality and Social Psychology, 46,* 84–90.

Wheeless, L., Wheeless, V., & Baus, R. (1984). Sexual communication, communication satisfaction, and solidarity in the developmental stages of intimate relationships. *Western Journal of Speech Communication, 48,* 217–230.

Wilmot, W. (1980). Metacommunication: A re-examination and extension. In D. Nimmo (Ed.), *Communication yearbook 4* (pp. 61–69). New Brunswick, NJ: Transaction Books.

Wilmot, W., & Baxter, L. (1983). Reciprocal framing of relationship definitions and episodic interaction. *Western Journal of Speech Communication, 47,* 205–217.

Wilmot, W., & Baxter, L. (1984, February). *Defining relationships: The interplay of cognitive schemata and communication.* Paper presented at the annual convention of the Western Speech Communication Association.

Wright, P. (1982). Men's friendship, women's friendships, and the alleged inferiority of the latter. *Sex Roles, 8,* 1–20.

9

The Relation of Loneliness and Self-Disclosure

JOSEPH P. STOKES

> Loneliness . . . is the exceedingly unpleasant and driving experience connected with inadequate discharge of the need for human intimacy, for interpersonal intimacy. (Sullivan, 1953, p. 290)
>
> Loneliness appears to be a largely subjective experience associated with a perceived lack of interpersonal intimacy. (Chelune, Sultan, & Williams, 1980, p. 462)
>
> The phenomenological experience of loneliness appears to be at least as much a function of the intimacy and privacy of one's social intercourse as the sheer quantity of time spent in the presence of others. (Franzoi & Davis, 1985, p. 768)
>
> Individuals . . . attribute their loneliness feelings above all to the lack of an opportunity to talk about personally important, private matters with someone else. (Sermat & Smyth, 1973, p. 332)

These quotations emphasize the obvious, almost tautological, relation of loneliness and interpersonal intimacy. Although situational factors can lead to feelings of loneliness in the presence of an intimate relationship (consider, for example, a happily married couple who have moved to a city where they know no one), the type of loneliness that is the most painful and the most psychologically disturbing is driven by lack of intimacy, that is, a lack of closeness, of feeling cared about and understood. Actually, *perceived* lack of intimacy is more accurate, for

---

JOSEPH P. STOKES • Department of Psychology, University of Illinois at Chicago, Chicago, Illinois 60680.

both loneliness and intimacy are subjectively experienced states that correlate imperfectly with objective characteristics of one's social environment and with behavioral indicants of social relationships and interactions. Some studies have failed to find any relation between loneliness and social activity (Chelune *et al.*, 1980) or frequency of interacting with others (Jones, 1981). In a brief review of this literature, Jones (1982) emphasized the importance of distinguishing the qualitative and quantitative aspects of social intercourse. Cutrona (1982) found that subjective satisfaction with relationships predicted loneliness better than quantitative measures of social involvement did. Although it is not surprising that rated satisfaction with relationships would predict loneliness, the measure for which includes items that ask about satisfaction with relationships, these and other data emphasize the limits of quantitative measures of interaction and suggest the importance of perceived intimacy as it relates to the subjective experience of loneliness. As Anacharis said about 2500 years ago, "[It is] better to have one friend of great worth than many friends worth nothing at all" (Diogenes Laertius, 1972, Vol. 1, p. 109).

Researchers interested in intimacy and loneliness cannot be satisfied with the empirical verification of the obvious connection of perceived intimacy and loneliness. We need a more objective, more behavioral measure of at least one of these constructs. Loneliness, it would seem, is necessarily subjective, so perhaps we should look for a measure of intimacy that is not based entirely on self-reported perceptions. Most operational definitions of intimacy have emphasized verbal aspects of intimacy—that is, self-disclosure. Waring, Tillmann, Frelick, Russell, and Weiss (1980) reported that couples in the general population see self-disclosure as the primary determinant of intimacy. Waring (1981) assumed that facilitating a couple's self-disclosure would increase the intimacy of their relationship. Social penetration theory (Altman & Taylor, 1973), perhaps the most extensive theoretical work on the development of intimacy in relationships, views various aspects of self-disclosure as central to the development of intimacy.

Given the relation of self-disclosure to intimacy and of intimacy to loneliness, it is surprising that more research has not focused on the relation of self-disclosure and loneliness. Research on self-disclosure, stimulated largely by Jourard's influential work, has been voluminous, if nothing else. Loneliness, on the other hand, had been relatively neglected as a research topic until the late 1970s. This chapter is intended to explore the nature of loneliness and self-disclosure, as well as their relation to one another. The following sections will review historical thinking on the relation of loneliness and self-disclosure, discuss the nature of each variable, summarize empirical data relating the two variables, speculate on the nature of their relation, and present a heuristic model that links loneliness and self-disclosure. The model will differentiate openness as a personality characteristic from self-disclosing behavior. Similarly, loneliness as a characterological or individual difference variable is differentiated from loneliness as a situational variable that reflects a lack of intimate relationships. The model also emphasizes the recipient's response to one's self-disclosure in determining the relation of that self-disclosure to feelings of loneliness.

Although they did not study the issue empirically, several influential thinkers in psychology have written about a possible link between loneliness and self-disclosure. The following section reviews briefly the ideas relating loneliness and self-disclosure of four important psychologists: Harry Stack Sullivan, Erik Erickson, Carl Rogers, and Sidney Jourard. The ideas of some contemporary researchers studying loneliness are also summarized briefly.

IDEAS ON THE RELATION OF LONELINESS AND SELF-DISCLOSURE

Sullivan

Sullivan (1953) viewed people as having a driving need for intimacy and saw highly developed intimacy with another as "the principal source of satisfaction in life" (p. 34). He saw the degree to which this need for intimacy was satisfied during various developmental periods as an important determinant of adult insecurity and loneliness. The need for intimate interchange during preadolescence, according to Sullivan, is usually most appropriately satisfied by finding a chum, a peer with whom one shares intimate information. Sullivan emphasized the importance of chumships and suggested the primary role of self-disclosure in the chum relationship.

> I would hope that preadolescent relationships were intense enough for each of the two chums literally to get to know practically everything about the other one that could possibly be exposed in an intimate relationship, because that remedies a good deal of the often illusory, usually morbid, feeling of being different, which is such a striking part of rationalizations of insecurity in later life. (Sullivan, 1953, p. 256)

Thus, for Sullivan, an ideal chumship is characterized by intimate self-disclosure. The chumship satisfies intimacy needs during preadolescence and lays the groundwork for low levels of insecurity and loneliness during adulthood. It would be useful to test these hypotheses, preferably with a longitudinal study.

Erikson

Erikson (1963) postulated that a sense of self-identity must precede the capacity for intimacy, which to some degree entails a fusing of one's identity with that of another. A sense of self-identity is needed to face the fear of ego loss and self-abandon in intimate situations such as close friendships and sexual unions. If the fear of ego loss leads to avoidance of intimacy, the individual may experience "a deep sense of isolation and consequent self-absorption" (p. 264), that is, loneliness.

Erikson suggested that adolescent love is largely concerned with defining one's identity "by projecting one's diffused ego image on another and by seeing it thus reflected and clarified. This is why so much of young love is conversation" (p. 262). In this context, "projecting one's diffused ego image on another" sounds like self-disclosure. Although he did not use the words *loneliness* or *self-disclosure,* Erikson seems to have postulated a causal sequence whereby self-disclose builds ego identity, which in turn allows for the development of intimacy and prevents loneliness.

Rogers

In writing about loneliness, Carl Rogers (1970) emphasized the relation of loneliness and self-disclosure and maintained that self-disclosure followed by a caring, accepting response from another that can alleviate feelings of loneliness. Underlying loneliness, according to Rogers, is a conviction on the part of the lonely that their real selves, the selves that are hidden from others, are fundamentally flawed and unlovable. The solution is for the lonely individuals to take the risk of revealing more of themselves to others. Rogers described how self-disclosure that is well received in an encounter group can affect feelings of loneliness:

> The lonely person can voice and bring into the open aspects of himself of which he has been ashamed or which he felt were too private to reveal. To his surprise he finds that the members of the group feel far more warmly toward the real self than toward the outer front from which he has been facing the world. They are able to love and care for this real self, imperfect and struggling though it may be. When two such real selves reach out to each other in a group, there is the I-thou encounter that Buber has so well described. In that instance loneliness is dissolved. (p. 115)

Jourard

Jourard (1968) suggested that a healthy, well-functioning person is relatively high as a self-discloser. "The authentic being manifested by healthier personalities takes the form of unself-conscious disclosure of self in words, decisions, and actions." (p. 47). Jourard also maintained that the healthier personalities will find love and friendship and will "have access to relief from existential loneliness in which we all live" (p. 59). Less healthy personalities do not truly encounter other people and form strong relationships. "Hence, the feeling of loneliness, of not being known and understood, chronically nags at them like a boil on the buttocks or a stone in the shoe" (p. 50).

Recent Ideals on the Relation of Loneliness and Self-Disclosure

Many contemporary researchers studying loneliness have mentioned the importance of self-disclosure in relation to loneliness. A few of their ideas are summarized in this section.

In discussing the relation of social skills deficits to loneliness, Rook and Peplau (1982) noted that "existing social skills training programs appear to place greatest emphasis on skills needed to initiate relationships" (p. 365). They mentioned self-disclosure as a skill that might be needed for "deepening," as opposed to initiating, relationships. Because the ability to "deepen" relationships is certainly related to loneliness, a relation between loneliness and self-disclosure is suggested. Perhaps self-disclosure is most salient in "deepening" those superficial relationships the lonely complain about.

Similarly, in discussing his program of therapy for the lonely, Young (1982) emphasized the role of self-disclosure in building the kind of intimate relationships that can decrease feelings of loneliness. "The first step toward intimacy is often the sharing of private thoughts and feelings with another person" (p. 399).

Henry (1980) suggested a mechanism, similar to the one described by Rogers, whereby loneliness and self-disclosure might be related. He described how people, by the age of adolescence, become afraid of unacceptable impulses and are not able to reveal their inner selves to others. In a process that he likens to Freud's resistance, people resolve that no one, including themselves, will ever find out what they are really like. We become facades to one another. The result of this process, which is characterized by low levels of self-disclosure, is loneliness. Unfortunately, this interesting mechanism seems relatively impervious to empirical testing.

Sermat (1980) asked people to describe experiences of loneliness. Three fourths of the respondents spontaneously attributed their loneliness to problems in personal, intimate communications with others.

> They seemed to feel the lack of any opportunity to share those thoughts, feelings, and concerns that were most important to them with someone who would understand, accept, and care about what they wanted to say. (p. 306).

Some respondents felt a kind of existential loneliness related to the "realization of one's basic separateness from other people, the impossibility of sharing feelings and experiences fully with anyone" (p. 306). Perhaps this existential loneliness is something researchers should try to measure.

In listing cultural norms that "contribute to the creation of necessary conditions for loneliness" to occur, Kiefer (1980) included "norms that limit the kinds of information that might legitimately be exchanged between one individual and another in a given context" (p. 427). She suggests, therefore, that limits on the appropriateness of self-disclosure are necessary for loneliness to occur. If people hold norms that prevent them from communicating their ideas, needs, or feelings to another, the result may be feelings of deprivation and loneliness. Certainly, norms about what is appropriate to talk about influence self-disclosure; the idea that such norms can influence loneliness might be a useful research focus for this literature. Work on social norms for alcohol use (e.g., McKirnan, 1980) might provide a model for such research.

THE NATURE OF THE VARIABLES

In considering the relation of loneliness and self-disclosure we need to be clear about the nature of each variable. Definitions of loneliness (cf. Peplau & Perlman, 1982) usually emphasize that loneliness is an unpleasant, distressing experience that results from perceived deficiencies in one's social relationships. Without disputing this definition, Weiss (1973) focused on the source of the perception of deficiencies when he differentiated situational and characterological theories of loneliness. Situational theories place the source of these perceived deficiencies in the objective environment. Certainly no one would argue that situational factors do not play a role in the experience of loneliness. Young adults who begin jobs in new cities or recently divorced people are very likely to experience significant loneliness attributable to their situations. As mentioned earlier, however, the evidence that the social environments of the lonely are really restricted is at best mixed.

One can take a more characterological view (cf. Stokes, 1985a) and argue that loneliness is, at least in part, a trait or individual difference variable. Given identical objective situations, people will feel differentially lonely. This characterological view of loneliness emphasizes individual differences: Certain people are prone to negative affect in general and loneliness in particular because of who they are, how they view themselves, and how they view social situations. These people are generally disposed to experience negative moods and insecurity (see the discussion of negative affectivity in the next section); feelings of loneliness are one reflection of this general tendency.

The same distinction between situational and characterological factors can be made with respect to self-disclosure. Obviously situational factors play a big part in self-disclosing behavior. Disclosure to an acquaintance whom one rather dislikes is probably not going to be so complete or intimate as disclosure to a trusted loved one. On the other hand, characterological differences also seem, at least intuitively, to be important with respect to self-disclosure. Some people are simply more inclined than others to self-disclose. (See Miller and Read, Chapter 3, in this volume for another approach to individual differences in self-disclosure.)

Definitions of self-disclosure usually emphasize either information conveyed to another person or the process of making oneself known to others. We might consider, however, the degree to which measures of self-disclosure tap a personality variable. Cozby (1973) acknowledged that self-disclosure refers to "both a personality construct and a process which occurs during interaction" (p. 73). Mahon (1982) defined self-disclosure as "a personal variable people bring to encounters with others" (p. 344). It seems reasonable to assume that people vary in the degree to which they are open and accessible to others and that measures of self-disclosure reflect, to some degree at least, this individual difference. Viewing self-disclosure as an individual difference variable in no way negates the importance of situational factors. Situational factors certainly influence the expression of other variables (e.g., extroversion) that are commonly considered traitlike individual difference constructs.

To the degree that loneliness and self-disclosure can be considered individual difference variables, their relation might reflect the fact that they tend to covary in personality types. The correlation of loneliness and self-disclosure might be attributable to their relations to other individual difference variables. A variable such as self-esteem, for example, might be related to both loneliness and self-disclosure. In order to examine further the relation of loneliness and self-disclosure, let us consider the possibility that each variable is an individual difference variable.

Loneliness as an Individual Difference Variable

Research has consistently linked loneliness to a variety of individual difference variables. Lonely people have been shown to have lower self-esteem (Goswick & Jones, 1981; Hojat, 1982; Jones, Freemon, & Goswick, 1981; Levin, 1985; Russell, Peplau, & Cutrona, 1980); to be less extroverted and less prone to social risk taking (Hojat, 1982; Jones *et al.*, 1981; Russell *et al.*, 1980; Stokes, 1985a); to be more depressed (Bragg, 1979; Levin, 1985; Russell, Peplau, & Ferguson, 1978) and neurotic (Hojat, 1982; Stokes, 1985a); and to hold more cynical, pessimistic, and rejecting attitudes toward others (Brennan & Auslander, 1979; Jones *et al.*, 1981; Levin, 1985) than nonlonely people.

Individual differences may influence one's perception of a situation; people certainly differ in the degree to which they feel uncared for and lonely in response to a given social situation. Jones *et al.* (1981) found that lonely people expressed a more negative outlook on human nature and a more negative view of specific others with whom they interacted than did nonlonely people. Perhaps feelings of loneliness are one manifestation of a general tendency to perceive situations negatively and to fear the worst.

Watson and Clark (1984) suggested that trait anxiety, neuroticism, and other personal variables can be viewed as reflecting an overriding, integrative construct that they call negative affectivity.

> Negative affectivity (NA) [is] a mood-dispositional dimension. . . . High-NA individuals tend to be distressed and upset and have a negative view of self, whereas those low on the dimension are relatively content and secure and satisfied with themselves. (Watson & Clark, 1984, p. 465).

> High-NA individuals are more likely to report distress, discomfort, and dissatisfaction over time and regardless of the situation, even in the absence of any overt or objective source of stress. . . . [They dwell] particularly on their failures and shortcomings. They also tend to focus on the negative side of others and the world in general. Consequently, they have a less favorable view of self and other people and are less satisfied with themselves and with life. (Watson & Clark, 1984, p. 483)

The evidence that consistently links loneliness to neuroticism and self-esteem provides support for including loneliness as one of the variables encompassed by negative affectivity. This view emphasizes that loneliness is an individual difference, traitlike variable, although the importance of situational factors in inducing transitory loneliness cannot be dismissed entirely.

Loneliness might be related to another individual difference variable, one that is possibly uncorrelated with negative affectivity. People differ in their requirements for companionship. Some people, for example, are comfortable going to movies or dining out alone and find such experiences enjoyable and satisfying; others do not want to watch television at home alone. My guess is that people who enjoy doing certain activities alone are relatively low on negative affectivity (that is, they have relatively high self-esteem and are relatively nonneurotic), but the desired level of companionship may be an individual difference variable that is unrelated to negative affectivity. Researchers interested in loneliness might consider individual differences in desired levels of company and companionship.

Individual Differences and Self-Disclosure

The correlational evidence linking loneliness to individual difference variables like self-esteem and neuroticism is consistent. For self-disclosure, however, consistent relations to individual difference variables have not been established. After reviewing the literature relating self-disclosure to psychological characteristics, Goodstein and Reinecker (1974, p. 59) concluded that "almost every specific finding is contradicted by another investigation involving similar design and the same or similar measures." This discussion of the literature relating self-disclosure to individual differences variables will, therefore, be brief, because very few conclusions can be drawn and because other reviews of this literature, which are probably familiar to readers of this volume, are available (e.g., Archer, 1979; Chaikin & Derlega, 1974; Cozby, 1973; Goodstein & Reinecker, 1974).

Several studies have assessed the relationship of self-disclosure and mental health, which is often measured by a neuroticism scale. The results are mixed and inconclusive, with about an equal number of studies finding a positive correlation, a negative correlation, and no correlation (see Cozby, 1973, for a thorough review). Even within the same study (Pedersen & Higbee, 1969), contradictory results have been obtained depending on whether the 60-item or the 25-item version of The Jourard Self-Disclosure Questionnaire (JSDQ), two supposedly equivalent measures, was used. As Cozby and others have pointed out, there are serious problems with the JSDQ, and most of the research that has used it to measure self-disclosure is of questionable value.

There are, however, two relations of individual difference variables and self-disclosure that seem fairly well established. The first is that paper-and-pencil measures of self-disclosure like the JSDQ are related positively to measures of sociability and extroversion (see Cozby, 1973, for a review of these studies) and negatively to the Social Introversion

Scale of the Minnesota Multiphasic Personality Inventory (MMPI) (see Goodstein & Reinecker, 1974). Remember that social risk taking and extroversion are reliably related to loneliness as well. Possibly any relation of loneliness and self-disclosure could be mediated by extroversion; that is, extroverts are both more self-disclosing and less lonely.

The second reliable finding links behavioral measures of self-disclosure to need for approval. Two studies (Brundage, Derlega, & Cash, 1977; Burhenne & Mirels, 1970) used behavioral measures of self-disclosure and found a negative correlation between self-disclosure and need for approval as measured by the Marlowe-Crowne Social Desirability Scale (Crown & Marlowe, 1960). Burhenne and Mirels (1970) also included the JSDQ in addition to the behavioral measure of self-disclosure. The JDSQ and the social desirability scale were uncorrelated. A third study (Anchor, Vojtisek, & Berger, 1972) found a relation between social desirability and behavioral self-disclosure, although in this study the relation was curvilinear with moderate scores on social desirability being associated with greater self-disclosure than either low or high scores. The special nature of the sample in this study (24 hospitalized psychotic men), however, limits the generalizability of the findings.

These findings suggest that measures of self-disclosure, especially behavioral measures, tap individual differences in openness or accessibility to others. In thinking about self-disclosure and its relation to other variables, researchers should be clear about whether they are conceiving self-disclosure as a process that has occurred or as an individual difference, traitlike variable, which probably should be renamed openness or accessibility. If self-disclosure is seen as a process, researchers need to look at how self-disclosing behavior (including *receiving* self-disclosures) relates to feelings of loneliness. Assuming that self-disclosure is a trait variable, researchers interested in loneliness and self-disclosure might focus on how that personality characteristic relates to loneliness.

In either case, traditional measures of self-disclosure that ask "what have you disclosed" or "what would you be willing to disclose" are unsatisfactory. The JSDQ, for example, is notorious for being unable to predict actual self-disclosure (see Cozby, 1973; Goodstein & Reinecker, 1974; or almost any other review of research on self-disclosure). Scores on the JSDQ and measures like it probably say more about one's history of close relationships than about self-disclosure as a process or trait. Conceiving self-disclosure as a process suggests manipulating or at least measuring self-disclosing behavior. If self-disclosure is viewed as a personality characteristic, researchers need a more valid measure of openness or accessibility.

EMPIRICAL FINDINGS RELATING LONELINESS TO SELF-DISCLOSURE

Studies that have reported for males and females the correlation between a measure of self-reported self-disclosure and a measure of self-reported loneliness are summarized in Table 1. The similarily of these studies to one another in several important ways enhances their comparability. All of the studies used college students as subjects, with the exception of Davis and Franzoi (1985) and Franzoi and Davis (1985) who used high-school students. What is often a serious limitation in psychological research, the use of college students is less problematic in the study of loneliness than in other research areas because loneliness is a particularly salient problem for students (cf. Cutrona, 1982). College-age people are involved in developing relationships and building new networks of friends, especially if they are attending school away from home. Many college students are living away from home for the first time and find themselves relatively isolated from family and close friends. In addition, the development of intimate, romantic relationships often takes on new importance during late adolesence. The proverbial college sophomores are a good population in which to examine issues of loneliness and the development of relationships.

Another consistency of the studies listed in Table 1 is that all of them measured loneliness with some version of the UCLA Loneliness Scale. Chelune *et al.* (1980), Jones *et al.* (1981), Solano *et al.* (1982), and Stokes (1985a) used the original UCLA Loneliness Scale (Russell *et al.* 1978). Berg and Peplau (1982) used the revised UCLA Loneliness Scale (Russell *et al.* 1980), which they expanded to 28 items and modified in some unspecified way. Stokes and Levin (1985) also used the revised UCLA Loneliness Scale. Davis and Franzoi (1985), Franzoi and Davis (1985), and Stokes (1985b) used a four-item short form of the UCLA scale.

The original UCLA Loneliness Scale consists of 20 statements such as "I lack companionship" and "It is difficult for me to make friends." Respondents indicate how often each statement is true for them on a 4-point scale (*never, rarely, sometimes, often*). Russell *et al.* (1978) and Perlman and Peplau (1981) reported good reliability (coefficient alpha above .90) and evidence of validity for this scale. This original scale included only negatively worded items. The revised version (Russell *et al.*, 1980) balanced the direction of the wording of items by including items that were worded positively (e.g., "I feel in tune with people around me"). Russell *et al.* (1980) presented additional evidence for the reliability and validity of the UCLA scale and reported the correlation of the original

TABLE 1. Empirical Studies Relating Loneliness and Self-Disclosure

Study	UCLA loneliness measure	Self-disclosure measure[a]	Target[b]	Correlations: Male	Correlations: Female
Berg & Peplau (1982)	Modified revised	MTI	SS friend	−.06	−.31
			OS friend	−.07	−.11
		SDSS	Varied	.02	−.57
Chelune, Sultan, & Williams (1980)	Original	SDSS	Varied	—	−.29
Davis & Franzoi (1985)	Short form	Short MTI	Peer, mother, father	−.15	−.34
				−.18	−.20
				−.32	−.31
Franzoi & Davis (1985)	Short form	Short MTI	Peer, mother, father	−.11	−.27
				−.11	−.09
				−.03	−.09
Jones, Freemon, & Goswick (1981)	Original	JSDQ	Varied	−.14	−.19
Solano, Batten, & Parish (1982)	Original	JSDQ	Mother, father, SS friend, OS friend	−.08	−.26
				−.10	−.08
				−.26	−.33
				−.33	−.48
Stokes (1985a)	Original	TI	SS friend	−.01	−.23
Stokes (1985b)	Short form	MTI	SS friend, OS friend	−.20	−.34
				−.29	−.12
Stokes & Levin (1985)	Revised	MTI	Any friend	−.35	−.42

[a] MTI = Miller Topics Inventory (past disclosure); SDSS = Self-Disclosure Situations Survey (willingness to disclose); JSDQ = Jourard Self-Disclosure Survey (past disclosure); TI = Topics Inventory (willingness to disclose).
[b] SS = same sex; OS = opposite sex.

and revised forms is .91, a finding that suggests these two forms may be used interchangeably. Russell *et al.* (1980) also suggested the four-item short form of the scale that Davis and Franzoi (1985), Franzoi and Davis (1985), and Stokes (1985b) used. Franzoi and Davis reported that the short form correlates .61 for males and .70 for females with the longer revised UCLA Loneliness Scale.

The various forms of the UCLA Loneliness scale correlate in the .7 to .8 range with a single-item rating of loneliness, a fact that suggests both the validity and limitations of the scale. The main limitation is that scores are subject to the influence of social desirability and impression management.

Measures of self-disclosure used in the studies in Table 1 are more varied and probably more problematic than the measures of loneliness. The measures of self-disclosure vary as to the target of the disclosure and as to whether they ask about actual self-disclosures in the past or about willingness to disclose in the future. Self-disclosure measures will be described as each study is discussed.

Berg and Peplau (1982) measured self-disclosure in two ways. The Miller Topics Inventory (Miller, Berg, & Archer, 1983) asks respondents to indicate the degree to which they have disclosed in the past 10 fairly intimate topics (e.g., "what is most important to me in life" and "what I like and dislike about myself"). Scores are derived for two target people—same-sex friend and opposite-sex friend. The second self-disclosure measure was the Self-Disclosure Situation Survey (SDSS; Chelune, 1976), a 20-item inventory that assesses willingness to disclose in a variety of situations to a variety of target people. The SDSS does not specify specific topics for disclosure but asks respondents essentially to rate how much personal information they would disclose to specific targets in varied situations. Berg and Peplau (1982) found no relationships between loneliness and the self-disclosure measures for males. For females, however, loneliness was associated with less reported willingness to disclose ($p < .001$).

Chelune *et al.* (1980), using only female subjects, also found a negative relation between loneliness and willingness to disclose as measured by the SDSS. In their original research report, Chelune *et al.* had trichotomized self-disclosure and found that willingness to self-disclose was related inversely to loneliness ($p < .001$). The correlation coefficient in Table 1 resulted from a reanalysis of their data.

The work by Franzoi and Davis (1985; Davis & Franzoi, 1985) measured disclosure to three targets (mother, father, and friend) on four intimate topics (e.g., "things I have done which I feel guilty about"). Of the correlations between loneliness and self-disclosure to various targets, only the correlation of disclosure to peers for females was statistically significant ($p < .01$).

The Jourard Self-Disclosure Questionnaire (JSDQ; Jourard, 1971) asks about past disclosure on specific topics to specific target people, usually mother, father, same-sex friend, and opposite-sex friend. Using the JSDQ as a measure of self-disclosure and presumably summing over target people, Jones *et al.* (1981) found negative but nonsignificant relations between self-disclosure and loneliness for both males and females.

Solano *et al.* (1982) also used the JSDQ but analyzed their data separately for each of the four target people. Levels of past disclosure to parents were not related to loneliness; past disclosure to friends generally was. Although the correlation of loneliness and same-sex self-disclosure for males did not reach the conventional level of statistical significance, Solano *et al.*'s emphasis on sex differences in their findings seems unwarranted. The correlations of loneliness and same-sex self-disclosure for males (−.26) and females (−.33) were of similar magnitude. For self-disclosure to opposite-sex friends, the correlations with loneliness were statistically significant for both males and females, although the correlation coefficient was larger for females (−.48) than for males (−.33).

Stokes (1985a) measured willingness to self-disclose by asking respondents to indicate the degree to which they would be willing to discuss each of 14 topics with their same-sex best friends. The topics were selected to cover a wide range of intimacy as rated by Davis (1976) (e.g., "schools I've attended," "my feelings regarding my sexual performance"). Stokes (1985b) measured past self-disclosure to same-sex and opposite-sex best friends on the 10 topics used in Miller *et al.* (1983). Stokes and Levin (1985) used the same topics, but the target was specified as "any of your friends." Taken together, the data from these three studies suggest a moderate negative relation between self-disclosure and loneliness.

Two studies not included in Table 1 support the idea that self-disclosure and loneliness are negatively related. Mahon (1982) measured loneliness with the revised UCLA Loneliness scale and self-disclosure with the JSDQ. Summing self-disclosure over the four target people, she found a correlation of −.336 ($p < .005$) between loneliness and reported self-disclosure for her college student sample, which was 57% female. Mahon did not report the correlation of loneliness and self-disclosure separately for males and females.

Using a sample of college students, Ginter (1982) dichotomized his subjects into high and low loneliness groups based on scores on the revised UCLA Loneliness Scale. These two groups differed reliably ($p < .001$) on total self-disclosure as measured by the SDSS.

Considered collectively, the data in Table 1 plus the results of Mahon (1982) and Ginter (1982) make a strong case for an empirical relation between various measures of self-disclosure and loneliness. Of the 37 correlation coefficients reported in Table 1, 35 are negative, a proportion that cannot be attributed to chance. Although many, even most, of the individual correlations reported in Table 1 are not statistically significant, the overall pattern is clear. The magnitude of the correlation coefficients is not impressive, but then neither are the measures of self-disclosure, all of which are of the self-report, paper-and-pencil variety. My hunch is that stronger, more behavioral measures of self-disclosure would correlate more highly with loneliness. In fact, Solano *et al.* (1982) found that during a structured interaction, lonely subjects were less effective than nonlonely subjects at making themselves known to their partners.

The data in Table 1 also suggest that when friends are included as targets of self-disclosure, the relation between loneliness and self-disclosure is stronger for females than for males. The correlation for females is of greater magnitude than the correlation for males in 11 of the 12 relevant comparisons in Table 1.

Stokes and Levin (1985) reported that social network variables tend to predict loneliness better for men than for women, a finding we attributed to the fact that friendships of men are more group-oriented than friendships of women, which focus more on dyadic relationships (Bell, 1981). In this context, then, it makes sense that a variable like self-disclosure, which presumably reflects qualities of close dyadic relationships, would predict loneliness better for women than for men.

THE NATURE OF THE RELATION OF LONELINESS AND SELF-DISCLOSURE

Possible Causal Relations

Although intuitive reasoning and empirical data suggest a link between loneliness and self-disclosure, the nature of the relation is unclear. There are at least three possibilities: (1) self-disclosure leads to reduced loneliness, (2) loneliness leads to a decrease in self-disclosure, or (3) some third variable influences both self-disclosure and loneliness. Sermat and Smyth (1973) suggested that lack of self-disclosure leads to loneliness when they reported that three fourths of their subjects attributed loneliness to a "lack of opportunity to talk about personally important, private matters with someone else" (p. 332). Similarly, Rogers (1970) postulated that deep individual loneliness "cannot be ameliorated unless the individual takes the risk of being more of his real self to others"

(p. 113). Being more of one's real self to others would probably involve self-disclosure.

Jones *et al.* (1981) suggested three ways in which feelings of loneliness might lead to reduced self-disclosure. First, the behaviors, moods, and cognitive states associated with loneliness might interfere with developing relationships, which in turn would reduce opportunities for intimate self-disclosure. Second, loneliness might lead to a hypersensitivity to rejection, which could inhibit self-disclosure. Rogers (1970) supported this idea when he maintained that the lonely are convinced that their real self, the self that would be revealed through intimate self-disclosure, is one that no one would love. Third, emotions associated with loneliness could disrupt the effective use of social skills, including self-disclosure. Davis and Franzoi (1985) tested the idea that loneliness leads to decreased self-disclosure but found no support for this hypothesis in their adolescent sample.

Several writers have suggested that loneliness would motivate people to increase their self-disclosure, a conception that has some intuitive appeal but no empirical support. Komarovsky (1974), for example, wrote that "the desire to escape loneliness . . . generate[s] the need to share feelings and thoughts with others" (p. 679), a need that could be met by increased self-disclosure. More likely, failure to meet this need leads to the feelings of loneliness. Sullivan (1953) postulated that loneliness can motivate increased self-disclosure and other attempts at intimacy in spite of the anxiety aroused. He recognized also that loneliness in other situations might be paralyzing and could lead to feelings of hopelessness and futility, which would probably inhibit attempts to establish intimacy through self-disclosure.

To assume that self-disclosure and loneliness are related in a unidirectional causal way is simplistic and naive. More likely they influence each other or are part of the same package, such that loneliness and low levels of self-disclosure tend to co-occur with no particular causal relation. Comments of Alan Watts (1972) about cause and effect are relevant:

> Here is someone who has never seen a cat. He is looking through a narrow slit in a fence, and, on the other side, a cat walks by. He sees first the head, then the less distinctly shaped furry truck, and then the tail. Extraordinary! The cat turns round and walks back, and again he sees the head, and a little later the tail. This sequence begins to look like something regular and reliable. Yet again, the cat turns round, and he witnesses the same regular sequence: first the head, and later the tail. Thereupon he reasons that the event head is the invariable and necessary cause of the event tail, which is the head's effect. This absurd and confusing gobbledygook comes from his failure to see that head and tail go together: They are all one cat. (p. 27)

In the case of self-disclosure and loneliness, the "package" of which they are a part probably focuses on relationships. A person with good, trusted, dependable friends and an intimate relationship characterized by constant caring and complete acceptance (remember this is a hypothetical situation!) would likely self-disclose with abandon—or at least to a level limited only by self-awareness and comfort with him- or herself—and would not feel lonely except perhaps in some existential sense. Alternately, a person at the opposite extreme, that is, one who had no relationships with other people, would have no opportunity to self-disclose and would likely feel lonely.

Role of an Intimate Relationship

Weiss (1982) emphasized the importance of an intimate relationship in alleviating loneliness. "Loneliness is delayed only by a relationship in which there is assurance of the continued accessibility of someone trusted" (p. 77). As Weiss points out, having someone to pass time with is not enough, and transitory relationships can make loneliness worse.

On the other hand, Horowitz, French, and Anderson (1982) found that self-reported problems with intimacy did not distinguish the lonely from the nonlonely. When sorting interpersonal problems using the Q-sort technique into categories from *least familiar as a problem of mine* to *most familiar as a problem of mine,* college student subjects who were lonely reported problems with socializing and making friends. Lack of differences on problems of intimacy in this age group may reflect lack of experience with intimacy.

Not surprisingly, other studies have found that loneliness is related to the degree of close and romantic relationships. Jones (1982) reported that students who have never had a steady dating partner are more lonely than those who have. Russell *et al.* (1980) found that loneliness was related to the degree of romantic involvement and to the number of close friends. Cutrona (1982) found that students who remained lonely throughout their freshman year at college most often said that "finding a boyfriend/girlfriend" was the only way to overcome their loneliness. Jones (1982) cited unpublished studies that failed to find correlations between loneliness and global indexes of friendship, such as a total number of friends. It is the special, intimate relations that count most.

The existence or lack of at least one intimate relationship might explain the covariation of self-disclosure and loneliness. Having a friend or romantic partner with whom one feels mutual liking and closeness seems conducive to both intimate self-disclosure and low levels of loneliness.

Pilot Study—Mediating Role of Relationships

Some data I collected indicate that close relationships may mediate the correlation of self-disclosure and loneliness. About 500 students in introductory psychology courses completed a short questionnaire with three parts. The first part was a self-disclosure questionnaire that included the 10 topics used by Miller *et al.* (1983) in their self-disclosure index. Respondents were asked to rate the degree to which they had discussed each topic on a 3-point scale: (1) never talked about it, (2) discussed it in general terms but not in detail, (3) discussed in detail. The target person was either "your closest friend of the same sex" or "your closest friend of the opposite sex." The self-disclosure score was the sum of the ratings for the 10 topics.

The second part of the questionnaire was the four-item short form of the revised UCLA Loneliness Scale recommended by Russell *et al.* (1980). The third part of the questionnaire asked respondents about current relationships. Respondents rated their degree of agreement (*disagree strongly, disagree mildly, agree mildly,* or *agree strongly*) to two statements: (1) "I am currently involved in a romantic relationship with someone of the opposite sex" and (2) "I have at least one special friend (not a romantic partner) I feel close to and whom I can talk to freely about almost anything."

One hypothesis was that the relation between loneliness and self-disclosure to the opposite-sex best friend would be greatly attenuated when responses to the item asking about current involvement in a romantic relationship were partialled out. Similarly, the second hypothesis maintained that partialling out variance in loneliness accounted for by the items asking about having a special nonromantic friendship would greatly decrease variance in loneliness accounted for by self-disclosure to the same-sex best friend. Stepwise multiple regression was used to measure the variance in loneliness accounted for by self-disclosure before and after the relationship items were included as predictors in the regression equation.

First let us consider self-disclosure to same sex-best friends, which accounted for about 8.8% of the variance in loneliness ($N = 252$, $F[1, 251] = 24.29, p < .001$). If responses to the item asking about having one special nonromantic friend are forced into the prediction equation before the same-sex self-disclosure score, self-disclosure then accounts for only 3.1% of the variance in loneliness. On the other hand, forcing the item about current romantic involvement reduced the variance in loneliness accounted for by self-disclosure to a same-sex best friend only slightly (to 8%). These results are at least consistent with the idea that the relation of self-disclosure to a same-sex friend and loneliness is largely mediated by the quality of the relationship one has with (a) nonromantic friend(s).

The same pattern of results holds with disclosure to opposite-sex closest friend, which by itself accounted for 3.7% of the variance in loneliness ($N = 262$, $F[1, 261] = 10.10$, $p < .001$). Partialling out variance accounted for by being currently involved in a romantic relationship reduced this percentage of variance in loneliness accounted for to 2%. Partialling out responses to the item asking about a nonromantic friend reduces to 2.5% the percentage of variance in loneliness accounted for.

The pattern of results reported in the previous two paragraphs holds also when data from males and females are analyzed separately, although the zero-order correlation between loneliness and opposite-sex self-disclosure is not statistically significant for females. These data support the idea that the correlation between loneliness and self-disclosure is at least partially mediated by the relationships, both romantic and nonromantic, one has with others. Satisfactory, intimate relationships lead to both increased self-disclosure and decreased feelings of loneliness.

A Heuristic Model

The heuristic model presented in Figure 1 illustrates one way that self-disclosure and loneliness might be related. Developmental factors, including genetic predispositions and history of relationships, determine personality characteristics of an individual. These personality characteristics, especially the one I have called openness/accessibility, are influential in leading to self-disclosing behavior. This model is explicit, then, about differentiating openness as a personality characteristic from self-disclosing behavior.

The relation of self-disclosure to loneliness is mediated by the response of the recipient of the self-disclosures. Self-disclosure, especially disclosures of negative information, that are met with acceptance

FIGURE 1. A heuristic model.

and with reciprocation lead to feelings of closeness and intimacy. Disclosures that are rejected produce feelings of loneliness. Rejection in this context might be either explicit, as when the recipient responds, "I don't want to hear about your personal problems," or implicit, as when the recipient does not respond to the self-disclosure or subsequently withdraws from the relationship. The response to the self-disclosing behavior also influences the likelihood of subsequent self-disclosure.

Thus the acceptance and reciprocation of a self-disclosure are reinforcing and increase the probability of self-disclosure in the future, particularly when the same recipient is involved. Rejection of the self-disclosure has the opposite effect. The response to the self-disclosing behavior thus influences both feelings of loneliness and subsequent self-disclosing behavior. An inverse relation between self-disclosure and loneliness is implied.

The model just described is simplistic and incomplete. Certainly loneliness is too complex a phenomenon to be produced only by negative, rejecting responses to self-disclosing behavior. I suggested earlier that loneliness be viewed in large part as a personality characteristic, possibility a part of what Watson and Clark (1984) have called "negative affectivity." This reasoning implies that loneliness should be included as a personality characteristic that is determined by genetic predispositions and early developmental history. Thus loneliness is included in two places in the model in Figure 1, once as characterological loneliness, possibly a subset of negative affectivity, and once as a situational variable that varies inversely with perceived intimacy in relationships. Let us now consider factors involved in early relationships, especially relationships with parental figures, that might be important in leading to characterological loneliness and other aspects of negative affectivity.

Importance of Parent–Child Attachment

Drawing on the work of Bowlby (1973), Rubenstein and Shaver (1980) hypothesized that adult loneliness can be traced to childhood experiences of separation, loss, or neglect. Bowlby suggested that humans have evolved proximity-seeking mechanisms and that being alone, for an infant or child, is a cue to danger. This cue is manifested as separation anxiety when young children are separated from parents, especially mothers. If a young child is confident that an attachment figure will be available when needed, the child develops a relative resistance to separation anxiety. Bowlby maintained that this feeling of confidence is built up gradually and may influence individuals throughout their lives. This reasoning suggests that early relationships with parents play a role in determining feelings of loneliness in adults.

In a large survey printed in newspapers in two cities, Rubenstein and Shaver (1980) found support for these ideas. Respondents who reported having warm, helpful parents and who viewed their parents as "trusted and secure bases of support" tended not to be lonely. A conflicted relationship with parents who could not be counted on for support was associated with moderate levels of loneliness. The absence of a parent, especially if it resulted from divorce, produced the highest degree of loneliness. Rubenstein and Shaver interpreted their findings as suggesting that chronic "separation anxiety" leaves one vulnerable to loneliness.

An anecdote from Rubenstein and Shaver (1982) suggests the importance of parental comfort in alleviating feelings of loneliness. When asked to imagine a solution to her loneliness,

> one 30-year-old woman imagined snuggling up against and "barrowing under" a vaguely defined older male figure who was lying down. When asked to discuss this image, . . . she recalled . . . that when she was young, her father, who worked late during the week, would come home early on Friday evenings, change clothes, and lie down on the floor under an afghan and let me snuggle up next to him while he watched TV. (p. 221)

Rubenstein and Shaver (1982) reported that most of the solutions to loneliness images they recorded were reminiscent of parent-child relations.

Paloutzian and Ellison (1982) reported data that implicate childhood experiences and relationships with parents as determiners of loneliness in adulthood. In a questionnaire study with college students, Paloutzian and Ellison asked about early childhood experiences in parent–child relationships (e.g., "I told my parents about my problems as I was growing up") and family togetherness (e.g., "We did a lot of fun things together as a family"). Both reports of better relationships with parents and perceived family togetherness were related inversely to loneliness. Similarly, Franzoi and Davis (1985) and Davis and Franzoi (1985), using high-school students as subjects, found inverse relations between measures of perceived parental warmth and loneliness.

Brennan (1982) has argued that family processes influence loneliness in adolescents in at least two ways. Adolescents pushed prematurely into independence may feel insecure and alone. On the other hand, adolescents who remain overly dependent on parents may fail to develop mature peer and cross-sex relationships and be susceptible to loneliness. Brennan further asserted that lonely adolescents report a pattern of negative, nonsupportive relationships with their parents. "Lonely youths report parental disinterest, limited nurturance, parental violence and rejection, low level of encouragement for success, and negative labeling" (p. 280).

Importance of Feeling Accepted

The model presented here emphasizes the response of the recipient of a self-disclosure in mediating the relations of self-disclosure and loneliness. The writings of Rogers, summarized earlier in this chapter, suggested that loneliness can be alleviated when one feels understood, accepted, and cared about. Probably the reason intimate relationships alleviate loneliness is that in such relationships one is both relatively fully known and accepted. In such relationships, one has self-disclosed intimately, and the self-disclosures generally have been met with positive, accepting responses. People whose religious beliefs emphasize a personal relationship with God see themselves as fully known and accepted. Such people tend not to be lonely (Paloutzian & Ellison, 1982).

At the core of the experience of loneliness is a feeling of not being understood; lonely people think that no one can really understand them or their experiences. Related to this is lonely people's fear that they will be rejected by others. The risk and vulnerability associated with self-disclosure are real (see Derlega, 1984). Thus the lonely are less likely to risk the kind of self-disclosures that can help interested others understand them or respond emphatically. Sermat (1980) suggested that "one of the contributing factors to loneliness is the individual's unwillingness to enter into interpersonal situations that involve the risk of being rejected, embarrassed, or disappointed" (p. 311). Lonely people may be less able or less willing to take the social risks that might lead to alleviation of the lonely feelings. Moustakas (1961) echoes this theme: "Even the slightest criticism hurts [the lonely]. [They] often perceive nonexistent deprecation in surface or tangetial remarks" (p. 30). The lonely person is "not open enough to attach himself [or herself] to new persons and find value in new experiences" (Moustakas, 1961, p. 31).

Peplau, Miceli, and Morasch (1982) hypothesized that loneliness and lonely people's fear of rejection keeps the lonely from learning about social problems experienced by their peers. "Fearing that public comparisons would expose their failings, lonely people may conceal their feelings of dissatisfaction from others and avoid discussions about social matters" (p. 140). By avoiding self-disclosure on social matters, the lonely are unable to develop realistic standards for relationships and may continue to feel incompetent in social situations.

Cutrona (1982) summarized correlational data (see Russell *et al.*, 1980) that indicated that lonely students were sensitive to rejection. "A picture emerges of the lonely college student as an individual who lacks social self-confidence, is unassertive, and is sensitive to rejection" (p. 303). This description does not sound like someone who would be disclosing a lot of intimate, risky information.

Jones *et al.* (1981) provided empirical evidence that the lonely anticipate rejection. They collected data from a psychology class at the beginning and end of the semester. The data included sociometric choices and ratings on various dimensions, such as friendliness, from four perspectives: (1) self-ratings, (2) how subjects expected to be rated by others, (3) actual ratings by others, and (4) ratings of others. Initially loneliness was related to negative self-ratings and to expectations of negative ratings from others. Lonely men but not lonely women tended to rate others negatively, and some evidence suggested that the lonely were actually evaluated less favorably by others. At the posttest, the lonely continued to rate themselves negatively and to expect negative ratings from others. Lonely and nonlonely subjects were not actually judged differently by others, however, at the posttest.

People predisposed to feeling lonely (that is, the characterologically lonely) may be relatively impervious to the reinforcing effects of positive responses to their self-disclosures. Because of their high levels of negative affectivity, the characterologically lonely achieve feelings of closeness and intimacy only with difficulty. They are guarded against self-disclosing and are sensitive to rejection; negative responses to their self-disclosure are especially salient and painful. Such responses lead to feelings of loneliness and decrease the probability of future self-disclosures.

FUTURE DIRECTIONS

This chapter is intended to stimulate thinking and research on the relation of loneliness and self-disclosure. Both conceptual writing and empirical research suggest the relations among self-disclosure, intimacy, and loneliness are important. Researchers need to understand more about the role of self-disclosure in developing the intimate relationships that can alleviate loneliness. I have suggested that future research focus on the degree to which self-disclosure and loneliness can be considered traitlike personality variables. Perhaps both openness and loneliness are rather stable characterological traits that tend to covary inversely. An underlying personality construct like level of social risk taking and/or sensitivity to rejection may produce both low levels of openness and feelings of loneliness. On the other hand, self-disclosing behavior, as opposed to openness as a personality trait, might be important in relation to loneliness. If this is true, researchers might be able to decrease loneliness by manipulating self-disclosure, either in the laboratory with interviews or in naturalistic settings by teaching self-disclosure skills and encouraging their application. Such experimental manipulations of self-disclosure could also shed light on any causal relation between self-disclosing behavior and loneliness.

The role of existential feelings of loneliness and of norms regarding self-disclosure should also be considered in future research. Feeling that one is inherently separate and apart from other people might influence both self-disclosing behavior and feelings of loneliness. One's normative ideas about the appropriateness of self-disclosure might cause one to withhold communication and to feel deprived and lonely.

The heuristic model presented here may prove useful to researchers studying the relation of self-disclosure and loneliness. Research focusing on the role of early relationships in determining subsequent tendencies to self-disclose and to feel lonely would be especially interesting. Developmental factors may be important determinants of both openness and feelings of loneliness and thereby may account for observed correlations between self-disclosure and loneliness. The influence of the response of the recipient of self-disclosures in mediating the link between loneliness and self-disclosure also warrants further investigation. Finally, research needs to test the hypothesis that the relation of loneliness and self-disclosure, as measured in most research, reflects the fact that people with at least one satisfying intimate relationship report both relatively high levels of past self-disclosure and low levels of loneliness.

REFERENCES

Altman, I., & Taylor, D. A. (1973). *Social penetration: The development of interpersonal relationships*. New York: Holt, Rinehart, & Winston.

Anchor, K. N., Vojtisek, J. E., & Berger (1972). Social desirability as a predictor of self-disclosure in groups. *Psychotherapy: Theory, research, and practice, 9,* 262–264.

Archer, R. L. (1979). Role of personality and the social situation. In G. J. Chelune (Ed.), *Self-disclosure: Origins, patterns, and implications for openness in interpersonal relations* (pp. 28–58). San Francisco: Jossey-Bass.

Bell, R. R. (1981). *Worlds of friendship*. Beverly Hills, CA: Sage.

Berg, J. H., & Peplau, L. A. (1982). Loneliness: The relationship of self-disclosure and androgyny. *Personality and Social Psychology Bulletin, 8,* 624–630.

Bowlby, J. (1973). *Attachment and loss. Vol. II: Separation. Anxiety and anger*. New York: Basic Books.

Bragg, M. E. (1979). A comparative study of loneliness and depression. *Dissertation Abstracts International, 39,* 6109-B.

Brennan, T. (1982). Loneliness at adolescence. In L. A. Peplau & D. Perlman (Eds.), *Loneliness: A sourcebook of current theory, research and therapy* (pp. 269–290). New York: Wiley.

Brennan, T., & Auslander, N. (1979). *Adolescent loneliness: An exploratory study of social and psychological pre-dispositions and theory* (Vol. 1). Boulder, CO: Behavioral Institute.

Brundage, L. E., Derlega, V. J., & Cash, T. F. (1977). The effects of physical attractiveness and need for approval on self-disclosure. *Personality and Social Psychology Bulletin, 3*, 63–66.

Burhenne, D., & Mirels, H. L. (1970). Self-disclosure in self-descriptive essays. *Journal of Consulting and Clinical Psychology, 35*, 409–413.

Chaikin, A. L., & Derlega, V. J. (1974). *Self-Disclosure*. Morristown, NJ: General Learning Press.

Chelune, G. J. (1976). The self-disclosure situations survey: A new approach to measuring self-disclosure. *JSAS Catalog of Selected Documents in Psychology* (ms. No. 1367), *6*, 111–112.

Chelune, G. J., Sultan, F. E., & Williams, C. L. (1980). Loneliness, self-disclosure, and interpersonal effectiveness. *Journal of Counseling Psychology, 27*, 462–468.

Cozby, P. C. (1973). Self-disclosure: A literature review. *Psychological Bulletin, 79*, 73–91.

Crowne, D. P., & Marlowe, D. (1960). A new scale of social desirability independent of psychopathology. *Journal of Counseling Psychology, 24*, 349–354.

Cutrona, C. E. (1982). Transition to college: Loneliness and the process of social adjustment. In L. A. Peplau & D. Perlman (Eds.), *Loneliness: A sourcebook of current theory, research and therapy* (pp. 291–309). New York: Wiley.

Davis, J. D. (1976). Self-disclosure in an acquaintance exercise: Responsibility for level of intimacy. *Journal of Personality and Social Psychology, 33*, 787–792.

Davis, M. H., & Franzoi, S. L. (1985). *Private self-consciousness, self-disclosure, and loneliness among adolescents: A longitudinal analysis*. Unpublished manuscript.

Derlega, V. J. (1984). Self-disclosure and intimate relationships. In V. J. Derlega (Ed.), *Communication, intimacy, and close relationships*. New York: Academic Press.

Diogenes Laertius (1972). *Lives of eminent philosophers* (R. D. Hicks, Trans.). Cambridge MA: Harvard University Press. (Originally written in third century A.D.)

Erickson, E. H. (1963). *Childhood and society* (2nd ed.). New York: W. W. Norton & Co.

Franzoi, S. L., & Davis, M. H. (1985). Adolescent self-disclosure and loneliness: Private self-consciousness and parental influences. *Journal of Personality and Social Psychology, 48*, 768–780.

Ginter, E. J. (1982). Self-disclosure as a function of the intensity of four affective states associated with loneliness (Doctoral dissertation, University of Georgia, 1982). *Dissertation Abstracts International, 44*, 1338-A.

Goodstein, L. D., & Reinecker, J. M. (1974). Factors affecting self-disclosure: A review of the literature. In B. A. Maher (Ed.), *Progress in experimental personality research* (Vol. 7, pp. 49–77). New York: Academic Press.

Goswick, R. A., & Jones, W. H. (1981). Loneliness, self-concept, and adjustment. *The Journal of Psychology, 107*, 237–240.

Henry, J. (1980). Loneliness and vulnerability. In J. Hartog, J. R. Audy, & Y. A. Cohen (Eds.), *The anatomy of loneliness* (pp. 95–110). New York: International Universities Press.

Hojat, M. (1982). Loneliness as a function of selected personality variables. *Journal of Clinical Psychology*, 38, 137–141.

Horowitz, L. M., French, R., & Anderson, C. A. (1982). The prototype of a lonely person. In L. A. Peplau & D. Perlman (Eds.), *Loneliness: A sourcebook of current theory, research and therapy* (pp. 183–205). New York: Wiley.

Jones, W. H. (1981). Loneliness and social contact. *Journal of Social Psychology, 113*, 295–296.

Jones, W. H. (1982). Loneliness and social behavior. In L. A. Peplau & D. Perlman (Eds.), *Loneliness: A sourcebook of current theory, research and therapy* (pp. 238–252). New York: Wiley.

Jones, W. H., Freemon, J. E., & Goswick, R. A. (1981). The persistence of loneliness: Self and other determinants. *Journal of Personality, 49,* 27–48.
Jourard, S. M. (1968). *Disclosing man to himself.* Princeton, NJ: D. Van Nostrand.
Jourard, S. M. (1971). *Self-disclosure: An experimental analysis of the transparent self.* New York: Wiley.
Kiefer, C. W. (1980). Loneliness and the Japanese. In J. Hartog, J. R. Audy, & Y. A. Cohen (Eds.), *The anatomy of loneliness* (pp. 425–450). New York: International Universities Press.
Komarovsky, M. (1974). Patterns of self-disclosure of male undergraduates. *Journal of Marriage and the Family, 36,* 677–686.
Levin, I. (1985). *The relation of individual differences and social network structure to loneliness.* Unpublished master's thesis, University of Illinois at Chicago, Chicago.
Mahon, N. E. (1982). The relationship of self-disclosure, interpersonal dependency, and life changes to loneliness in young adults. *Nursing Research, 31,* 343–347.
McKirnan, D. J. (1980). The identification of deviance: A conceptualization and initial test of a model of social norms. *European Journal of Social Psychology, 10,* 75–93.
Miller, L. C., Berg, J. H., & Archer, R. L. (1983). Openers: Individuals who elicit intimate self-disclosure. *Journal of Personality and Social Psychology, 44,* 1234–1244.
Moustakas, C. E. (1961). *Loneliness.* Englewood Cliffs, NJ: Prentice-Hall.
Paloutzian, R. F., & Ellison, C. W. (1982). Loneliness, spiritual well-being, and the quality of life. In L. A. Peplau and D. Perlman (Eds.), *Loneliness: A sourcebook of current theory, research and therapy* (pp. 224–237). New York: Wiley.
Pedersen, D. M., & Higbee, K. L. (1969). Personality correlates of self-disclosure. *The Journal of Social Psychology, 78,* 81–89.
Peplau, L. A., & Perlman, D. (1982). Perspectives on loneliness. In L. A. Peplau & D. Perlman (Eds.), *Loneliness: A sourcebook of current theory, research and therapy* (pp. 1–18). New York: Wiley.
Peplau, L. A., Miceli, M., & Morasch, B. (1982). Loneliness and self-evaluation. In L. A. Peplau and D. Perlman (Eds.), *Loneliness: A sourcebook of current theory, research and therapy* (pp. 135–151). New York: Wiley.
Perlman, D., & Peplau, L. A. (1981). Toward a social psychology of loneliness. In S. Dick and R. Gilmour (Eds.), *Personal relationships 3: Personal relationships in disorder* (pp. 31–56). London: Academic Press.
Rogers, C. R. (1970). *Carl Rogers on encounter groups.* New York: Harper & Row.
Rook, K. S., & Peplau, L. A. (1982). Perspectives on helping the lonely. In L. A. Peplau & D. Perlman (Eds.), *Loneliness: A sourcebook of current theory, research, and therapy* (pp. 351–378). New York: Wiley.
Rubenstein, C., & Shaver, P. (1980). Loneliness in two northeastern cities. In J. Hartog, J. R. Audy, & Y. A. Cohen (Eds.), *The anatomy of loneliness* (pp. 319–337). New York: International Universities Press.
Rubenstein, C., & Shaver, P. (1982). The experience of loneliness. In L. A. Peplau & D. Perlman (Eds.), *Loneliness: A sourcebook of current theory, research and therapy* (pp. 206–223). New York: Wiley.
Russell, D., Peplau, L. A., & Ferguson, M. L. (1978). Developing a measure of loneliness. *Journal of Personality Assessment, 42,* 290–294.
Russell, D., Peplau, L. A., & Cutrona, C. E. (1980). The revised UCLA Loneliness Scale: Concurrent and discriminant validy evidence. *Journal of Personality and Social Psychology, 39,* 472–480.
Sermat, V. (1980). Some situational and personality correlates of loneliness. In J. Hartog, J. R. Audy, & Y. A. Cohen (Eds.), *The anatomy of loneliness* (pp. 305–318). New York: International Universities Press.

Sermat, V., & Smyth, M. (1973). Content analysis of verbal communications in the development of a relationship: Conditions influencing self-disclosure. *Journal of Personality and Social Psychology, 3*, 332–346.

Solano, C. H., Batten, P. G., & Parish, E. A. (1982). Loneliness and patterns of self-disclosure. *Journal of Personality and Social Psychology, 43*, 524–531.

Stokes, J. P. (1985a). The relation of social network and individual difference variables to loneliness. *Journal of Personality and Social Psychology, 48*, 981–990.

Stokes, J. P. (1985b). [Close relationships as mediators in the relation of self-disclosure and loneliness]. Unpublished raw data.

Stokes, J. P., & Levin, I. (1985, August). *Gender differences in predicting loneliness from social network variables.* Paper presented at the meeting of the American Psychological Association, Los Angeles.

Sullivan, H. S. (1953). *The interpersonal theory of psychiatry* (H. S. Perry & M. L. Gawel, Eds.). New York: Norton.

Waring, E. M., Tillmann, M. P., Frelick, L., Russell, L., & Weiss, G. (1980). Concepts of intimacy in the general population. *Journal of Nervous and Mental Disease, 168*, 471–474.

Watson, D., & Clark, L. A. (1984). Negative affectivity: The disposition to experience aversive emotional states. *Psychological Bulletin, 3*, 465–490.

Watts, Alan (1972). *The book.* New York: Vintage Books.

Weiss, R. S. (1973). *Loneliness: The experience of emotional and social isolation.* Cambridge, MA: M.I.T. Press.

Weiss, R. S. (1982). Issues in the study of loneliness. In L. A. Peplau & D. Perlman (Eds.), *Loneliness: A sourcebook of current theory, research and therapy* (pp. 71–80). New York: Wiley.

Young, J. E. (1982). Loneliness, depression, and cognitive therapy: Theory and application. In L. A. Peplau and D. Perlman (Eds.), *Loneliness: A sourcebook of current theory, research and therapy* (pp. 379–405). New York: Wiley.

10

The Relationship between Psychopathology and Self-Disclosure

An Interference/Competence Model

BRUCE N. CARPENTER

This chapter explores a fundamental question in the self-disclosure field: How is self-disclosure related to psychopathology? This can lead us to at least four underlying questions. Does the disclosure of individuals with psychopathology differ from that of individuals without such pathology? What is the nature of any difference? Why would such a difference exist? Finally, what are the implications of such a difference for helping us understand either psychopathology or the phenomenon of self-disclosure?

It is curious that the relationship between self-disclosure and psychopathology has not been systematically studied, even though mental health and disclosure have been widely linked in theory. Some theories even suggest that disclosure plays a significant etiological role in the development of mental disorders. It has also been argued that the disclosure of clients in psychotherapy is an important, if not an essential, feature for positive outcomes. This has encouraged an assumption that the problems that lead one to seek therapy may be caused by deficient

BRUCE N. CARPENTER • Department of Psychology, University of Tulsa, Tulsa, Oklahoma 74104.

self-disclosure. In contrast, the view held in this chapter is that considering problems in self-disclosure to be of primary etiological significance in psychopathology is not supported by research and ignores the nature and diversity of factors already established as causal in mental disorders. This is perhaps one reason why research on psychopathology has not focused closely on disclosure. Believing disclosure deviance is not a primary cause of psychological disorder still allows for an important therapeutic contribution for disclosure, as its therapeutic effects might be quite separate from its contribution to the development of disorders.

To evaluate these ideas and propose direction for the field, this chapter will first propose a model for relating self-disclosure and psychopathology. It will then explore special issues relevant to understanding disclosure in populations experiencing psychopathology. Finally, earlier theories and available evidence will be discussed in light of the model, and some population distinctions that require different application of principles will provide relevant examples.

BASIC FRAMEWORK

Not all self-disclosures are alike; they can be distinguished on many dimensions. However, in order to group and evaluate existing theories and to place in perspective the model to be proposed, we need a framework for understanding when self-disclosure occurs. I propose that a person self-discloses when three basic conditions exist: motivation is present to disclose, the opportunity to disclose exists, and the discloser has the skill necessary to take advantage of the opportunity. Further, these conditions, especially the environmental conditions and the discloser skill, determine the likelihood that the goals of disclosure behavior will be achieved.

Motivation

The motivation to self-disclose may evolve, for example, from anticipation of reward, maintenance or enhancement of relationships, anxiety reduction, and acting out of habits. Motivation sufficient to initiate or sustain behavior may not be present either because it has not developed or been maintained or because it has been inhibited by some conflicting motivation or state.

Opportunity

This is the existence of conditions for which the person perceives, either consciously or unconsciously, that a particular level or type of disclosure is at least possible and maybe even needed or expected. This implies that the discloser perceives the environmental conditions to be right for achieving disclosure goals. It is not completely independent of motivation or skill, as either may affect one's perception of when disclosure can occur. Of course, one can disclose any time others are present, but research reveals differences in disclosure across situations (e.g., in response to high versus low disclosure by others), some of which might be better considered as due to oppportunity than to motivation. Thus, for example, just after moving to a new city, opportunity is reduced because fewer target persons are known for disclosure.

Relational Competence

The term *relational competence* is preferred to *skill* because it better defines the domain of relevant skills. Relational competence comprises those characteristics of the individual that facilitate the acquisition, development, and maintenance of mutually satisfying relationships (Carpenter, Hansson, Rountree, & Jones, 1983; Hansson, Jones, & Carpenter, 1984). The concept incorporates, for example, such characteristics as assertiveness, lack of social anxiety, need achievement, and lack of shyness (Jones, Carpenter, & Quintana, 1985). Because self-disclosure is an important element in intimate relationships, the skill to use disclosure to promote and utilize relationships would also be considered part of relational competence. But further, because disclosure is best achieved when a relationship is optimal and when intimacy and mutual relational goals are achieved, the broader competence in developing and maintaining relationships should be more predictive of disclosure behavior. Clearly, those who may have the ability to disclose but lack other skills that help provide the relationships most important for disclosure will disclose differently than if they had such relationships.

A PROPOSED INTERFERENCE/COMPETENCE MODEL

I propose a model without substantial evidence, primarily because past research is insufficient and inconsistent. However, the model fits past research and the general attitude of psychopathologists toward social variables. It includes three primary mechanisms by which self-disclosure and psychopathology can be related. In disordered populations, all three mechanisms can and usually do operate, as well as affect one another. Further, for many individuals and within some diagnostic categories, we might specify which mechanism is most important for determining the relationship between self-disclosure and psychopathology.

Mechanism 1—Interference

The principle of interference is that psychopathology, by its very nature, disrupts functioning of all kinds, including interpersonal behavior. Thus, whatever an individual's earlier level of disclosure skill, opportunity for disclosure, or motivation to disclose, the introduction of psychopathology can interfere so as to alter disclosure behavior. The psychopathology does this by affecting motivation, opportunity, and/or relational competence. The direction of action is specifically that the psychopathology itself as well as the attendant conditions and related symptomatology of the psychopathology negatively influence self-disclosure. Further, the precursors of the actual disordered state can similarly encourage disclosure deviance. The resulting changes in disclosure behavior can be conscious or strategic, although this is not necessary and probably is less likely as pathology is greater; rather, as pathology increases, a dominant response pattern tends to emerge that is itself interfering.

Three general explanations are proposed for how psychopathology can affect disclosure motivation, disclosure opportunity, and relational competence. When any of these are operating, the interference mechanism is likely to affect disclosure.

1. *Atypical goals and perceptions.* Psychopathology can affect the emotional reactions and cognitive integration of interpersonal experiences such that the goals served by and the normative perception of self-disclosure and other intimate behavior is different from that of normals. An obvious example would be the paranoid, for whom disclosure would be viewed as increasing vulnerability rather than intimacy. Further, psychopathology can contribute over time to a total experience and personality pattern that also differs from normals, leading to the development of conflicting motivations and differing content of potential disclosure experiences. A schizophrenic may disclose in an attempt to establish relationships but will defeat that attempt if revelations focus on delusional thoughts and unusual perceptions. Thus, both the experience and content of disclosure can be affected such that the functions served by disclosure differ from those of normals. Disclosure behavior that appears appropriate to normal persons either may not serve the same purposes or may be believed to be under control of different causal laws (regardless of the accuracy of the belief) for disordered persons.

Because disclosure operates in an interpersonal environment, a feedback loop is important for monitoring the efficacy of disclosure behavior. Emotional and cognitive abnormalities can disrupt or alter such a loop so that the perception of normative-social functions served is out of harmony with the perceptions of others. Important abnormalities of this type might include, among others, poor self-esteem, hostility, depression, and delusional thinking. For example, the individual with extremely low self-esteem may assume others react negatively and interpret their behavior from such a perspective; or a very depressed person may have trouble even attending to social cues.

2. *Poor disclosure climate.* Aberrant behaviors (including emotions and cognitions) that are central, symptomatic, or secondary to a disorder contribute to a climate, both internal and interpersonal, that is not conducive to self-disclosure *per se* and/or to achieving the functions normally served by appropriate disclosure. For example, the high level of anxiety present in many disordered individuals can result in preoccupation, lack of spontaneity, and a halting, tense style that hinders the development of warm and comfortable interactions. In addition, the aberrant behaviors may be particularly obvious under situations normally calling for disclosure because the act of giving or receiving self-disclosure as well as other intimacy-producing behaviors may serve as triggers for pathological reactions. For example, for one with low self-esteem and a history of poor performance, the perception that disclosure is expected might cause the person to focus attention on inadequacy and to increase worry; consequently, self-disclosure behavior might instead get worse because of the greater cognitive and emotional disruption.

3. *Others' negative reactions to deviance.* Because self-disclosure occurs in an interpersonal environment, the reactions of the disclosure recipient will affect the interaction. Psychopathology of one or both parties can contribute to a general inadequacy in the relationship and to unusual feedback to disclosure behavior. For example, studies point to the abrupt and nonpersonal way mental patients are often treated by some professional staff (e.g., Rosenhan, 1973). It is recognized that the typical public reaction to those with apparent psychological disturbance shows even greater avoidance. Thus consistent negative feedback for even appropriate disclosure attempts may be common for some disordered persons.

Mechanism 2—Competence

The competence deficiencies of disordered individuals are well documented, including those relevant to interpersonal behavior. Based on this mechanism, it is proposed that persons with psychological disturbance are less competent in interpersonal situations as a consequence of their pathology and that this lack of competence results in deviant self-disclosure. (I do not include here the temporary loss of competence that can result from pathology interference.) Previous writings suggest that such incompetence can include problems in appropriateness (Derlega & Grzelak, 1979), in flexibility of disclosure pattern (Chelune, 1975), and in relational competence (Hansson *et al.*, 1984). Thus pathological populations may lack the skills to initiate or inhibit self-disclosure, to disclose so as to utilize the usual functions of disclosure, to disclose according to the expectations of others, and to develop relationships so as to make disclosure possible and appropriate. By this mechanism, competence may ultimately affect disclosure motivation and disclosure opportunity, but it is relational competence itself that is inadequate and is the primary focus.

Two general explanations are offered to suggest how deficiencies in this competence can develop. When either occurs, the competence mechanism is operative and likely to affect disclosure unless remedial action occurs.

1. *Incompetence as a symptom.* The same environmental or internal conditions that contribute to the development of the disorder result in the learning of inappropriate social behaviors. In this case, the disclosure incompetence would be a symptom or characteristic of the disorder. This could be evident, for example, in the hypochrondriac who seeks to tell anyone who will listen about the minute details of aches and pains. The individual has learned an inappropriate way of garnering attention and establishing relationships. However, it is pathological not because the disclosure is excessive or focuses on a particular content but rather because it reflects manipulativeness, a failure to develop more appropriate interactions, and the presence of a neurotic paradox (behavior that might yield immediate gains at the expense of enduring, more important, and more global goals).

2. *Incompetence as a result.* The psychopathology itself results in a reinforcement schedule or environmental circumstances that limit opportunities to develop appropriate relational skill or that encourage the learning of inappropriate social behaviors. Under this result, incompetence is secondary to the disorder. The results with many psychopathic youths who are incarcerated might be an example of this principle. The environment, given that such facilities for delinquents are frequently criticized as training grounds for increased psychopathy, likely includes reinforcement for manipulative and false disclosure.

Mechanism 3—Adjustment

Although the view of this chapter is that self-disclosure is not usually a primary cause of psychopathology, it does appear that disclosure behavior can have a causal effect on the intensity and duration of pathology and on the individual's reaction to potentially relevant stressors. Whereas the competence mechanism describes how a psychological disorder can affect the development of skills, the adjustment mechanism describes how competence in self-disclosure specifically can help the individual with psychopathology adjust to the disorder and deal effectively with stressors that arise either as a result of the disorder or from other causes. Thus a relationship between disclosure and psychopathology might be found in research in part because more severe or long-lasting cases will be evident in persons who have poor disclosure for whatever reason. Under this mechanism, disclosure deficit is seen as a contributing factor, rather than as either a necessary or sufficient cause of psychopathology. Any of the three factors affecting disclosure—motivation, opportunity, and skill—can be relevant here.

Two general explanations are offered to suggest how appropriate self-disclosure aids adjustment necessary to minimize and/or overcome psychological disorders.

1. *Utilizing resources.* Self-disclosure is an important element for seeking help from others and for effective use of most current forms of therapy. The act of requesting assistance for mental or behavioral difficulties is itself a form of disclosure, and this likely prevents many persons from seeking therapy. Further, most forms of psychotherapy require large amounts of rather intense and accurate disclosure. The reasons why such disclosure is considered necessary vary with different therapies. (For a more complete discussion of these issues, see the relevant chapters in this volume, such as those of Stiles [12] and Hendrick [14].) The motivational component of disclosure is perhaps most important for initially seeking help, whereas once in therapy high opportunity would be assumed, and the importance of client relational skill would increase somewhat. Even when we focus on nonprofessional forms of assistance, the aforementioned likely holds, except that the conditions of opportunity and relational competence may be even more important.

2. *Coping with stressors.* Perhaps the most widely held general model of psychopathology is the diathesis-stressor model, for which predisposed individuals develop pathology or manifest the greatest disorder when experiencing significant, relevant stressors. Although disclosure deficits do not usually cause a diathesis, appropriate disclosure may help one adjust more readily to stressors so that negative repercussions are minimized. Again, disclosure is not seen as a cause of the disorder, even though it can be relevant to the important precursor of stress; this is because appropriate disclosure is viewed as only one of several skills for alleviating stressors and because disclosure deficits are not usually considered important stressors themselves. Thus, a depression-prone individual, for whom depression seems to worsen with family difficulties, would likely have fewer family problems, and hence less depression, if he or she had good self-disclosure and if disclosure was important for dealing with potential family concerns.

Supplementary Mechanisms

In addition to the three primary mechanisms, additional mechanisms are operative in explaining the relationship between psychopathology and self-disclosure.

1. *Interaction of mechanisms.* The three primary mechanisms interact with one another. Psychopathology can interfere with the development of general social competencies and the specific competencies of disclosure skill, just as incompetence (including poor disclosure skill) contributes to greater pathology via stress and failure to utilize supportive and remedial opportunities.

2. *Disclosure deficits as a primary cause of psychopathology.* Deficient self-disclosure can play a primary etiological role for the development of psychopathology in some individuals, although our knowledge of most disorders would suggest that this is unusual, especially for more severe and more pervasive disorders. For example, although it is unlikely that most paranoid states develop this way, an occasional case of paranoia might result from extreme lack of disclosure and the isolation that could ensue. Problems resulting primarily from disclosure deficits would be mostly limited to interpersonal difficulties and failure to optimally achieve life goals in a world requiring social proficiency (e.g., loneliness and some marital problems).

3. *Relative importance of mechanisms.* Interference will be high when a disorder significantly affects mental functioning, as in schizophrenia, or is excessively arousing, as in anxiety disorders. Further, interference will be greatest at times when cognitive and emotional functioning are most impaired or negative arousal is greatest. In contrast, incompetence and poor adjustment will be high, depending primarily upon learning history. Such skill deficits tend not to fluctuate with variability in an individual's symptom severity. And although the skills underlying competence and adjustment are similar and probably are moderately correlated, they can be quite different. Thus we might be able to predict which of the primary mechanisms are operative or most important.

STUDYING ABNORMAL GROUPS

Because many persons interested in self-disclosure have only a modest background in abnormal psychology, several ideas relevant to the study of psychopathology are quickly reviewed here, with suggestions on how the issues are related to disclosure. Inattention to such issues is perhaps an important reason why the disclosure literature has not had greater impact on the study of psychopathology.

Disordered People or Disordered Behavior

The populations of interest may be viewed from either a "state" or a "trait" perspective. That is, we may compare disclosure behavior during periods of pathology at the time, to such behavior in the same persons when pathological behavior or feelings are not present. Or, we may compare disclosure in persons we believe to be deviant (even though abnormal behavior may fluctuate or come in episodes) to others without such deviance. Future research might examine the validity of either approach for self-disclosure.

Adjustment versus Disorder

As we search for differences in disclosure behavior, it should be remembered that psychopathology and adjustment need not be considered opposites. Most views of mental health and of abnormal behavior acknowledge that a person free of significant psychopathology need not be considered optimally functioning and that one who is not self-actualized may not have any mental disorder, in the usual sense. This is an important distinction because the mechanisms by which self-disclosure may be related to or promote positive adjustment (as in psychotherapy) might well be different from those by which self-disclosure may be related to negative outcomes, including pathology.

Diagnostic Distinctions

It is common to view a psychological disorder and the social processes as interacting. Therefore, the processes may not always operate in a particular abnormal group in the same way as with normals or as with other deviant groups. This limit in generalizability may inhibit the formulation of a general theory of self-disclosure and psychopathology because abnormal behavior is so diverse, although a few sensible distinctions can yield a manageable number of populations within which general principles would tend to remain similar. Perhaps the most important distinction is between those disorders for which a clear biological predisposition appears to exist and those for which no, or only a minor, predisposition exists. Although it remains unclear where to place some diagnostic categories, we could, for example, confidently separate out as predisposed those with organic brain syndromes, schizophrenia, manic-depressive psychosis, and some forms of depression. A primary reason for this distinction is that self-disclosure is less likely to play a prominent etiological and/or therapeutic role in such disorders. Rather, the focus would be more on how the disorder affects disclosure, although disclosure behavior may still be important for determining the nature and severity of specific symptoms.

Motivations

Persons with psychological difficulties are typically viewed as having special needs and motivations. Social behaviors related to disclosure may result from purposes related to one's psychopathology that are themselves important, not present in normals, and perhaps even nonpathological. These may often compete with or augment self-disclosure. For example, a schizophrenic person may discover that discussion of inner thoughts with even close family causes the family to become nervous and seek institutional care; thus the schizophrenic may strive to achieve greater family closeness and autonomy by not disclosing such thoughts. An example of an opposite effect would be the fact that some troubled individuals are far more disclosing and introspective during psychotherapy than are even many well-adjusted individuals, and this in spite of the nonreciprocal nature of disclosure in most therapies (see the chapter by Stiles [12] in this volume).

Role Expectations

Effects from labeling and from the special situations in which disordered individuals often find themselves, such as mental hospitals, create certain role expectations that affect the costs and benefits of disclosure. For example, the price may be too high for trying to act in some way not expected, or some persons may find acceptance and meaning in the patient role that is not available to them elsewhere because of their pathology. Whereas Jourard (1971) would stress that role conformity cannot replace "being," the significant differences between normals and many persons with psychological difficulties may cause existential strivings to diminish in importance. This could occur in part because of limited personal resources for meeting one's many needs and in part because more basic needs may conflict (e.g., attempts to not be noticed by others may minimize negative reactions). We may criticize society for allowing such conditions to exist, but as long as they do exist, it is unreasonable to expect troubled persons to resist such social pressures in an effort to achieve "fulfillment" or some other high-order need. It might be unfair and counterproductive to suggest that they would be better off with greater or different disclosure, when their level of disclosure may already be optimal because of their different circumstances, and hence, different goals.

Skills and Resources

Many persons with psychopathology have a variety of skill deficits relevant to self-disclosure. For example, the amount of self-disclosure could be affected because one may not know how to disclose fluently, perhaps due to lack of self-awareness or poor communication skills, or know how to talk about things other than self. Appropriateness could be affected by an improper reading of social cues and norms or misunderstanding of how disclosure may be tied to desired goals. Such skill deficits can result from faulty learning, interference, or other features that are part of, a consequence of, or contribute to the development of a disorder.

Similarly, the resources available to mentally troubled individuals are often deficient in ways that could interfere with learning self-disclosure skills or implementing skills already learned. In particular, appropriate others with whom it would be beneficial to disclose may be lacking. For inpatient populations, the primary social contacts will frequently be those who are themselves experiencing major difficulties or who are not able to provide appropriate rewards for self-disclosure. Another type of resource not discussed in the self-disclosure research is the content of the personal material available for communicating to others. Cognitive experiences may be such that they would be appropriate to disclose in only very few, infrequently occurring situations, and personal experiences may be predominately negative or unusual, such that the benefits of disclosure are not the same as for normals with more common or positive experiences. (An extended discussion of the relationship of disclosure to goals, strategies, and resources can be found in the chapter by Miller and Read [3] in this volume.)

Self-Disclosure and the Measurement of Psychopathology

The very nature of disclosure affects the evaluation of psychopathology. That is, because psychopathology is viewed as socially undesirable and because many of the characteristics we rely on for diagnosis are phenomenological in nature, willingness to disclose will likely affect measurement of psychopathology. My own awareness of this came as a result of an extensive interview study in which college students scoring deviantly on measures of psychosis proneness were interviewed for psychiatric symptomatology (Chapman *et al.*, 1984). I discovered that many of the students responded positively to questions about even extreme psychotic symptoms, although further inquiry often revealed that the basis for their answer was not very unusual at all. For example, students might admit to hearing voices that were not really there, but when describing the experience they would typically tell about thinking to themselves. Thus many of these subjects, who were functioning well, self-disclosed excessively both on the questionnaire and in the interview. In contrast, subjects with low scores on the questionnaire did not admit to such deviances, even though their experiences were perhaps the same. In this context, self-disclosure can be distinguished from social desirability, as desirability refers to the content, whereas disclosure here refers to admission regardless of content.

Thus past studies with pathological groups defined by self-report measures may have selected groups who differed not only in amount of the deviant characteristic of interest but also on self-disclosure. It would be invalid to examine difference in disclosure for such groups, as we have already selected them partially on the basis of disclosure differences. The concern may even be something of a problem for clinical populations, as the act of going to a clinic probably represents a form of self-disclosure. Similarly, defining groups on the basis of nonpathological characteristics might also introduce this confound if differences in disclosure are likely to affect scores on the grouping variable in a systematic way.

PAST THEORETICAL FORMULATIONS

Humanistic and Existential Approaches

Theorists on self-disclosure and related concepts have frequently asserted its positive role in mental health. In particular, Jourard (1964, 1971) proposed that optimal levels of disclosure are necessary for intimacy and self-understanding. His approach was essentially to examine disclosure from a stable, individual differences perspective and consider how this "trait" is related to other, positive, enduring characteristics of the individual that reflect adjustment and interpersonal success. Jourard's writings emphasize high disclosure as the important ingredient for positive mental health. Although his real focus was on the role of disclosure in mental health, Jourard also likened such health to the absence of neurosis. Thus, he argued that the relationship between disclosure and health is one in which a lack of disclosure underlies neurotic states.

Humanistic and existential theorists (e.g., Maslow, 1968; Mowrer, 1964; Rogers, 1961) have also frequently focused on concepts related to self-disclosure, such as genuineness, openness, and honesty. Such relational patterns were viewed as important for achieving self-knowledge, fulfillment, and belongingness. Their conceptualization of how such behaviors relate to psychopathology was similar to that of Jourard. Basically, such theories hold that these interpersonal behaviors that are similar to self-disclosure are prerequisites to adjustment, and in their absence some sort of pathology is likely to result. Such an approach tends to equate pathology with lack of striving and fulfillment (e.g., Maslow, 1971).

Behavioral and Skill Approaches

Chelune (1975, 1979a) gave greater attention to situational variables. His overview of past developments encouraged researchers to attend more to the variability of disclosure across situations, and, depending upon the situation, the appropriateness of disclosure. Chelune (1975) proposed parameters of disclosure that he saw as relevant to mental health. The first is one's affective manner of presentation, which, if incongruent with disclosing content, can serve as a distancing device in much the same way as Jourard hypothesized a lack of disclosure in neurotic individuals. The second parameter is flexibility of disclosure pattern, which focuses on an individual's ability to change disclosure level according to the situation or interaction partner.

Derlega and Grzelak (1979) focused on self-disclosure appropriateness. Their model specified that disclosure must serve certain personal and interpersonal functions, as well as match normative expectations, to be considered appropriate. Disclosure not meeting these conditions can be problematic, rather than beneficial. Therefore, as we examine the disclosure of disordered individuals, we might find it to be inappropriate, perhaps in amount, as suggested by Jourard, but also in functions served and/or adherence to social norms. From the traditional perspective in which poor disclosure behavior contributes to pathology, Derlega and Grzelak's model simply provides additional features of disclosure behavior to examine. Perhaps what is more important, however, the model specifies or implies several points relevant to how pathology can affect disclosure: (a) goals of disclosure behavior are personal and therefore may be atypical; (b) the discloser makes judgments about the utility of disclosure behavior for achieving goals; (c) disclosure behavior itself may not match intent; and (d) accurate knowledge or use of disclosure norms may be deficient. Each of these allows for individual differences to which pathology may contribute. Therefore, unlike most other theories, that proposed by Derlega and Grzelak allows us to hypothesize about not only how unusual disclosure may lead to poor adjustment but also how psychopathology might contribute to inappropriate self-disclosure (also see the chapter by Miller and Read [3] in this volume). Specifically, general deficits in skill (which are common in psychopathology) may result in failure to meet disclosure goals or to match disclosure norms, or atypical goals may result in disclosure behavior at odds with norms.

Therapy Approaches

Most of the interest in disclosure among troubled populations has focused on psychotherapy effects. Although psychotherapy and self-disclosure are discussed elsewhere in this book (see chapters by Stiles [12], Waring [13], and Hendrick [14]), because such therapy often involves individuals with severe psychological problems, a brief overview of theories is relevant here. Doster and Nesbitt (1979) have grouped various theories under four models: (a) The fulfillment model is closest to Jourard's, emphasizing that disclosure is important for growth and that difficulties occur because disclosure is not optimally occurring. Therefore, the disclosure that occurs in psychotherapy allows growth that did not occur before, presumably because such disclosure was not possible before for some reason. (b) The ambiguity-reduction model posits that success in therapy depends on the client's having a good grasp of psychotherapy goals, status, and process so as to properly play the client role. This understanding is achieved in part through self-disclosure. This model appears to make no assumptions regarding the relationship to pathology, seeing disclosure primarily from a practical perspective of trying to make other therapy processes clearer. (c) The interactional model focuses on how disclosure regulates and defines the relational aspects of therapy in an ongoing fashion. An assumption of this model is that the therapy relationship itself is paramount for positive change. This assumption implies that the client's other relationships are nonoptimal, perhaps due to inappropriate disclosure. (d) The social learning model posits that social skill, of which appropriate self-disclosure is a part, is necessary for good functioning. In this model, the goal of therapy is to train the client in relevant interpersonal skills.

Motivational Approaches

The only theory that specifically focuses on how self-disclosure operates with a particular disordered population is that of Shimkunas (1972). His is a motivational model of interpersonal behavior in schizophrenia, suggesting that intimacy is aversive to this group. Hence, when self-disclosure from such individuals is called for by the situation, they respond with increased overt pathology as a way of creating distance in the interaction. Winters and Neale (1983) have called this a "relief-from-aversion" theory.

Summary of Theories

In terms of the framework proposed earlier, the humanistic/existential theories, including that of Jourard, appear to be motivational, in that motivation is the condition for disclosure that is not met. They emphasize that nonoptimal (too little, or perhaps too much) self-disclosure exists because the individual lacks the proper motivation; and this lack occurs because priority is given to other, competing motivations. Further, these other motivations are seen as illegitimate because the goals are not those considered important from the humanistic perspective. Shimkunas's theory is also motivational, although he emphasizes more the relief benefit of increased interpersonal distance and seems to make no evaluative judgment about whether this benefit is appropriate or more important than those obtained by disclosure.

Chelune's theory allows for disruption of all three conditions for disclosure, that is, motivation, opportunity, and relational competence, depending upon the dimension to which one attends. However, he emphasized most strongly a situational perspective, for which lack of opportunity would be the most important condition affecting the disclosure of pathological groups. In contrast, Derlega and Grzelak's theory of appropriateness suggests that difficulties in skill, in particular those of relational competence, are most important for understanding deviance in disclosure. Finally, theories of self-disclosure in therapy imply deviations primarily in either opportunity or relational competence.

These theories then confirm that disclosure has been widely believed to be somehow related to adjustment. However, they differ considerably in their explanations of why this occurs. We see that most either emphasize or imply that disclosure problems cause psychopathology, which is contrary to the interference/competence model proposed here; however, they might be considered to be an expansion of the adjustment mechanism in which disclosure affects pathology. The clearest exceptions to this view of disclosure causing pathology are Shimkunas's model, which does not propose a direction of action, and Derlega and Grzelak's model, which specifically allows for pathology to negatively affect disclosure through a competence mechanism. In fact, the present interference/competence model offers a mechanism, that of competence, that is consistent with the suggestions of Derlega and Grzelak's that appropriate disclosure requires various skills, all of which might be adversely affected by psychopathology.

RESEARCH ON DISCLOSURE WITHIN DISORDERED POPULATIONS

Research on the disclosure of psychologically troubled individuals is rather scant, especially if we wish to get beyond a descriptive level. Further, some findings are inconsistent across studies, and controls are not sufficient to explain why different results occurred. A sizable proportion of the research uses analog groups, the results of which cannot be automatically generalized to actual clinical populations but that add some to our understanding. The findings of most of the relevent studies are briefly mentioned here.

Normal versus Abnormal Groups

Only three studies were found that compared normal with abnormal groups. In an unpublished study, Jourard (results mentioned in 1964, 1971) compared college counseling-center applicants with matched controls, finding a nonsignificant trend for counseling applicants to report less disclosure than the controls. However, he suggested that a significant result was obscured in his data by several applicants whose reports indicated much higher disclosure than even the controls. Mayo (1968) compared neurotic inpatients and normal controls on perceptions of self- and other disclosure. The neurotics were not only found to disclose less than the controls but also were less reciprocal in their pattern of disclosure. Chelune, Sultan, Vosk, Ogden, and Waring (1984) compared disclosure of couples seeking marital therapy with that of nonclinical couples. Whereas the couples did not differ on several disclosure variables, clinical couples were seen as speaking less and having less congruence between verbal content and affective manner (e.g., may appear to be angry but say feelings are happy).

Thus studies comparing the self-disclosure of normals with that of persons from clinical populations is scant. And whereas all of these subjects may have been experiencing distress sufficient to seek treatment, only Mayo's sample would be considered as having significant personal psychopathology. The studies do suggest deficient amounts of disclosure, as well as hint at other differences. However, because of limited data, the widely held view that pathological populations are deficient, or at least deviant, in self-disclosure has yet to be established. Further, the studies tell us nothing about why differences exist.

Analog Studies

The conclusion that neurotic individuals differ from normals on self-disclosure relies primarily on studies of student populations for which neurotics were defined by scores on some paper-and-pencil measure. Some studies use other populations or different means of assessing neuroticism, but this entire group of studies has the drawback of relying on nonclinical populations. In addition, the results of these studies are highly contradictory. For example, Hamilton (1971), Pederson and Higbee (males only; 1969), Pederson and Breglio (females only; 1968), Truax and Wittmer (1971), and Persons and Marks (1970) found neutotics defined by personality measures to be more disclosing than normals. Cozby (1972) obtained similar results when determining neuroticism from subjects' ratings of interpersonal situations.

In a study of college students, for which neuroticism was defined by elevated scores on the Minnesota Multiphasic Personality Inventory (MMPI), Cunningham and Strassberg (1981) found normals to spend more time disclosing intimate, personal information, but they were not different on total disclosure time or percentage of time in intimate disclosure. However, they did find an interaction between group membership and reciprocity of confederate disclosure, such that normals gave much more intimate disclosure under high, as opposed to low, confederate disclosure, whereas neurotics were moderate in disclosure under both conditions. Chaikin, Derlega, Bayma, and Shaw (1975) found that neurotics defined by the Maudsley Personality Inventory (MPI) did not differ from normals on intimacy disclosure, but an interaction with level of confederate disclosure was found that was essentially the same as that found by Cunningham and Strassberg (1981). Pederson and Higbee (females only; 1969) and Taylor, Altman, and Frankfurt (1965) also found greater disclosure with normal subjects, as opposed to those scoring high on measures of neuroticism. Other studies, each of which defined neuroticism using personality-based measures, found no disclosure differences between neurotics and normals (Hekmat, 1971; Pederson & Breglio [males only], 1968; Stanley & Bownes, 1966).

Several studies have also examined the relationship of self-disclosure to pathological characteristics that are more specific than neuroticism. For example, Post, Wittmaier, and Radin (1978) found that subjects experiencing "state anxiety" disclosed less than others, but "trait anxiety" was unrelated to disclosure. Berg and Peplau (1982) found that loneliness correlated negatively for women but not for men with reports of past disclosure, willingness to disclose, and social responsiveness.

It is clear that no consistent pattern emerges from these studies, and of those studies that found relationships between disclosure and neuroticism, the correlations or differences tend to be small. Cozby (1973) has suggested that this may be due to a curvilinear relationship, as first hinted at by Jourard (1964, 1971). Chaikin *et al.* (1975) suggested two other possibilities—that differences are due to assessment (because neuroticism or mental health is measured in such diverse ways) and that any relationship between the two is mediated by some other variable (they propose appropriateness of reciprocity). Also, Nelson-Jones and Coxhead (1980) allude to the concern that student "neurotic" groups may not be the same as clinical groups seeking treatment. In sum, the studies primarily examine whether the groups differ in amount of disclosure, although various definitions of disclosure are employed, with conflicting results and little attention to mechanisms. Together, they imply that the theories that specify only that pathological groups will have less (or more) disclosure than normals are inadequate for understanding the evidence.

Psychiatric Populations

Strassberg and Kangas (1977) found that for psychiatric inpatients greater disclosure on a sentence-completion test was related to greater elevation on several MMPI scales. McDaniel, Stiles, and McGaughey (1981) found more-distressed college psychology clinic clients to be more disclosing than less-distressed clients. Disclosure was not related to improvement, however.

The psychiatric disorder for which disclosure has been most studied is schizophrenia. All of the studies that compare schizophrenics to other groups (all the studies reviewed used psychiatric controls) found that schizophrenics have a lower rate of meaningful disclosure than controls. Shimkunas (1972) found that schizophrenics, in contrast to nonpsychotic psychiatric inpatients, did not respond with greater disclosure under experimenter demands for such. But further, the high demand condition, as compared to the low demand condition, elicited greater suspicion, delusional thinking, and autism for schizophrenics only. Shimkunas argued that this is a schizophrenic mechanism for avoiding intense interpersonal interactions. Cogan (1975) similarly found more autistic and delusional disclosures and less personal disclosures for schizophrenics than psychiatric controls under a condition of experimenter presence versus experimenter absence. Levy (1976) attempted to determine if conveying an expectation of high disclosure or if the emotional content of such a demand was responsible for the increased overt pathology of schizophrenics under Shimkunas's paradigm. Her results suggested that both greater emotionality of content and higher incongruence between the interviewer's own disclosure and the demand for disclosure (i.e., a discrepancy between the intimacy of the experimenter's own disclosure versus the intimacy requested of the subject) contributed to deviant responding.

In contrast to these studies, Strassberg, Roback, Anchor, and Abramowitz (1975) found that schizophrenic patients' perceptions of the therapist as more caring and more promoting of interaction were related to higher self-disclosure in group therapy. However, those with higher disclosure made less therapeutic progress. Similarly, Citkowitz and Lapidus (1980) found that disclosure of schizophrenic inpatients could be increased with interviewer modeling. Finally, Anchor, Vojtisek, and Patterson (1973) compared high and low trait-anxious schizophrenics on rated disclosure in a group setting. They found that trait anxiety and requests to disclose did not affect the number of verbalizations, but a greater proportion of verbalizations were personal for high-anxious subjects under the request to disclose condition. Thus several subgroups of schizophrenics appear to differ in disclosure behavior, and requests for disclosure do appear to result in greater disclosure under some conditions.

Summary of Findings

Several conclusions can be drawn concerning the results of these studies.

1. The assumed difference in self-disclosure between normal and psychologically disordered populations is not established. However, this seems to be because of a lack of research, rather than because of negative findings. Evidence for similar psychosocial variables, as well as collective clinical experience, suggests that atypical self-disclosure is common in psychiatric populations.

2. A single type of disclosure deviance for psychiatric groups or analog groups probably does not exist. Rather, there are probably some group distinctions in self-disclosure, but even within groups, a variety of deviances occur, often so as to cancel out findings for aggregate data. It may be more important to look for a variety of disclosure deviances and not use methodologies that assume the population is homogeneous.

3. Conflicting results when comparing groups are primarily due to inattention to curvilinear relationships and variability across or lack of homogeneity within psychopathological groups. Perhaps we should first determine if deviances of any kind are more common in psychiatric groups. Also, we might examine groups defined by some specific disclosure deviance, rather than examine disclosure within groups defined by some diagnostic criteria.

4. The most important differences between normal and abnormal groups are probably in type, rather than amount, of self-disclosure. In particular, attention to disclosure appropriateness seems promising. Thus we might examine adherence to disclosure norms, intimate versus nonintimate disclosure, responsiveness to feedback and social cues, and the like.

5. Essentially no research has been done to substantiate speculations about the etiological significance of self-disclosure deviance or about the mechanisms underlying the differences between pathological and normal individuals. However, studies with schizophrenics do suggest an aversive role for disclosure demand and/or for the emotionality of intimate disclosure.

APPLICATION OF THE INTERFERENCE/COMPETENCE MODEL

I have hinted throughout this chapter what relevant questions might come from the interference/competence model. Although the model is general and allows for a variety of explanations for some phenomena, reflecting our limited understanding of this area, specific hypotheses can be generated. Several examples are presented here in slightly greater detail for illustration.

Motivation versus Interference within Schizophrenia

Shimkunas (1972) has proposed that the increased pathology of schizophrenics under demand for intimate self-disclosure is their technique for reducing the anxiety associated with intimacy. Thus, it is motivational in nature and seems to imply intent. Theorists have proposed interpersonal aversiveness as a core characteristic of schizophrenia (e.g., Meehl, 1962), thus suggesting a basis for schizophrenic motivation to avoid intimacy. However, Shimkunas's interpretation has several potential problems. It does not incorporate findings of increased pathology under other emotionally arousing conditions not requiring disclosure. The sharing of most delusional thinking and much other bizarre behavior is often personal and highly revealing (although untrue, such thinking seems to be believed by the discloser at the time), suggesting that disclosure *per se* can still be high, even though inappropriate. There are probably much easier ways to minimize intimacy that also tend to be freer of negative repercussions, such as not responding or changing the subject. Finally, such purposeful behavior, whether conscious or nonconscious, seems incongruent with the severe decompensation of cognitive processes that is apparently occurring simultaneously.

The interference/competence model suggests several interpretations of the findings with schizophrenics: (1) The well-documented deviances in learning history and social skill suggest relational competence deficits such that schizophrenics do not know how to respond more appropriately (such deficits may suggest a primary reason for the development of interpersonal aversiveness, in that social interaction will frequently be problematic for them); (2) differing emotional and cognitive functioning may alter the experience of disclosure such that schizophrenic motivations and goals are in fact different from normals, with unusual disclosure intended to meet those idiosyncratic goals; and (3) the stress resulting from intimacy in one prone to experience interpersonal aversiveness heightens pathological behavior so that normal social behavior is impossible. The model allows all three of these mechanisms to operate simultaneously, and in fact, similar explanations of other deviant social behaviors of schizophrenics have been given for all three. However, the model further suggests that because of the severe nature of schizophrenia, interference will be high. Further, the interference mechanism suggests why other, inappropriate social behaviors (avoidance and delusional or autistic talk) increases simultaneously with presentation of an aversive condition and why disclosure behavior decreases in normative appropriateness as thought disorder increases. In contrast, relational incompetence, being a more stable attribute, may be used to explain some of the overall deficiency but not the changes across conditions.

Neurotic Disorders

Although previous studies have primarily examined nonspecific neurotic groups, for the purpose of exemplifying the model I will focus on two nonpsychotic disorders, compulsive personality disorder and dysthymic disorder. Both include significant disturbance of social behavior.

Compulsive personality disorder is characterized by difficulty in expressing warm emotions, perfectionism, overattention to detail, insistence on following a rigid plan, excessive devotion to work, and indecisiveness for fear of making a mistake. The dynamics of this disorder typically suggest that abnormal behavior results from a fear of vulnerability or loss of control. Self-esteem is typically poor, especially concerning social behavior, and compulsives often feel that attempts at social interaction will lead to failure, rejection, and embarrassment. Although they are often not cognizant of their rigid behavior, insight into what they are doing typically has little effect on behavior. Thus, their (hypothesized) poor self-disclosure seems to have little to do with fear of knowing self; instead, they find intimacy unpleasant because they have found themselves to be unsuccessful at it. The primary mechanism explaining the relationship between disclosure and abnormality for such persons would be that of competence. Social skill is deficient, adding to poor self-esteem and discomfort in interpersonal situations. Other behaviors develop in an effort to prove self-worth and to protect oneself from intimacy. The interference mechanism might be relevant for compulsives when placed in a situation demanding social skill, at which time we ought to see a decrement in social and other functioning. In fact, the interference mechanism makes it difficult to improve the social skills of such persons because they find social involvement so aversive. Finally, if disclosure diminishes, the adjustment mechanism could be operative so that, for example, reciprocal intimacy from others might be reduced, real needs would not be expressed, and problems generally could increase.

Dysthymic disorder is characterized by depressive symptomatology of a moderate degree that persists over time. Symptoms include somatic disturbance, such as insomnia and tiredness, feelings of inadequacy and self-deprecation, decreased effectiveness, difficulty in concentration, social withdrawal, loss of interest, irritability, pessimistic attitude, and the like. Thus significant interpersonal difficulties may be present along with other characteristics. A variety of dynamics have been offered to explain such problems, and individual reasons for the mood disturbance are probably quite heterogeneous. The nature of the pathology would suggest that both competence and interference could be relevant for understanding disclosure deviances. First, competence deficits contribute to interpersonal failures and deficiencies, which encourage poor self-esteem and depressive attitudes. Similarly, the excessive focus on self in depressives makes it difficult to adequately attend to proper social cues and receive benefit from intimate social interaction. Second, fatigue, loss of pleasure, reduced concentration, and related characteristics interfere with effective interpersonal behavior. Finally, a chronic negative mood state contributes to differing interpersonal goals and anormative reactions to disclosure, resulting in disclosure behavior that is deficient by normal standards but may be adequate for the dysthymic individual.

SUMMARY

We see, then, that studies have not systematically examined self-disclosure differences in pathological groups. Those interested in self-disclosure may be overstating the role of disclosure in the development and maintenance of psychiatric disorders. In contrast, psychopathologists probably have not shown much specific attention to disclosure behavior because they have viewed it as only one of several relevant social behaviors. Self-disclosure deviances are very likely related to psychopathology, although that is yet to be clearly demonstrated, and potential mechanisms are unexplored. But given the severe nature of most mental disorders and the multitude of potentially relevant factors, it is probably too simple to expect this one type of social behavior to play a major causal role. Rather, psychopathology is probably more often the causal component, disrupting disclosure just as it disrupts other important behaviors. Thus the beneficial effects of high disclosure in therapy probably reflect more the special interpersonal characteristics of this setting and facilitation of other processes, rather than the removal of a primary causal factor. Such a perspective encourages mental health practitioners to use disclosure as a valuable tool for stress reduction, garnering of support, improved information exchange, and so forth, rather than increasing disclosure as a primary goal in itself.

This chapter has described self-disclosure behavior as occurring when motivation, opportunity, and skill are present. Two main ways were proposed by which pathology alters disclosure behavior—interference and incompetence; and one main way by which disclosure influences pathology—failure to use disclosure for adjustment. Thus the abnormal circumstances under which a disorder develops and exists prevent (a) learning of optimally effective disclosure skills and/or (b) use of those skills because of cognitive and emotional disruption. The primary contributions that disclosure deficits have in the development of pathology are (a) the failure to use disclosure as a technique for dealing with problems and (b) as one of many sources of stress. In addition, disclosure deficits may play a prominent role in problems that are considered nonpathological, such as loneliness. What is needed to adequately evaluate these and other ideas relevant to disclosure of disordered populations is the study of actual clinical groups, designs that allow for detection of nonlinear effects and of a variety of disclosure deviances, and greater attention to the special issues relevant to study of abnormal groups.

REFERENCES

Anchor, K. N., Vojtisek, J. E., & Patterson, R. L. (1973). Trait anxiety, initial structuring and self-disclosure in groups of schizophrenic patients. *Psychotherapy: Theory, Research and Practice, 10,* 155–158.

Berg, J. H., & Peplau, L. A. (1982). Loneliness: The relationship of self-disclosure and androgyny. *Personality and Social Psychology Bulletin, 8,* 624–630.

Carpenter, B. N., Hansson, R. O., Rountree, R., & Jones, W. H. (1983). Relational competence and adjustment in diabetic patients. *Journal of Social and Clinical Psychology, 1,* 359–369.

Chaikin, A. L., Derlega, V. J., Bayma, B., & Shaw, J. (1975). Neuroticism and disclosure reciprocity. *Journal of Consulting and Clinical Psychology, 43,* 13–19.

Chapman, L. J., Chapman, J. P., Numbers, J. S., Edell, W. S., Carpenter, B. N., & Beckfield, D. (1984). Impulsive nonconformity as a trait contributing to the prediction of psychotic-like and schizotypal symptoms. *Journal of Nervous and Mental Disease, 172,* 681–691.

Chelune, G. J. (1975). Self-disclosure: An elaboration of its basic dimensions. *Psychological Reports, 36,* 79–85.

Chelune, G. J. (1979a). Measuring openness in interpersonal communication. In G. J. Chelune (Ed.). *Self-disclosure: Origins, patterns, and implications of openness in interpersonal relationships* (pp. 1–27). San Francisco: Jossey-Bass.

Chelune, G. J. (1979b). Summary, implications, and future perspectives. In G. J. Chelune (Ed.). *Self-disclosure: Origins, patterns, and implications of openness in interpersonal relationships* (pp. 243–260). San Francisco: Jossey-Bass.

Chelune, G. J., Sultan, F. E., Vosk, B. N., Ogden, J. K., & Waring, E. M. (1984). Self-disclosure patterns in clinical and nonclinical couples. *Journal of Clinical Psychology, 40,* 213–215.

Citkowitz, R. D., & Lapidus, L. B. (1980). Effects of paraphrasing, modeling, and cues in facilitating self-referent affective statements by chronic schizophrenics. *Psychological Reports, 47,* 523–536.

Cogan, J. M. (1975). The effect of the presence or absence of another person on the verbalizations of schizophrenics under a demand for intimate self-disclosure. *Dissertation Abstracts International, 36,* 3594B. (University Microfilms No. 76-1001)

Cozby, P. C. (1972). Self-disclosure, reciprocity, and liking. *Sociometry, 35,* 151–160.

Cozby, P. C. (1973). Self-disclosure: A literature review. *Psychological Bulletin, 79,* 73–91.

Cunningham, J. A., & Strassberg, D. S. (1981). Neuroticism and disclosure reciprocity. *Journal of Counseling Psychology, 28,* 455–458.

Derlega, V. J., & Grzelak, J. (1979). Appropriateness of self-disclosure. In C. J. Chelune (Ed.). *Self-disclosure: Origins, patterns, and implications of openness in interpersonal relationships* (pp. 151–176). San Francisco: Jossey-Bass.

Doster, J. A., & Nesbitt, J. G. (1979). Psychotherapy and self-disclosure. In G. J. Chelune (Ed.). *Self-disclosure: Origins, patterns, and implications of openness in interpersonal relationships* (pp. 177–224). San Francisco: Jossey-Bass.

Hamilton, L. K. (1971). The relationship between self-disclosure and neuroticism. *Dissertation Abstracts International, 32,* 3635B. (University Microfilms No. 71-30, 819)

Hansson, R. O., Jones, W. H., & Carpenter, B. N. (1984). Relational competence and social support. In P. Shaver (Ed.). *Review of personality and social psychology* (Vol. 5, pp. 265–284). Beverly Hills: Sage Publications.

Hekmat, H. (1971). Extraversion, neuroticism, and verbal conditioning of affective self-disclosures. *Journal of Counseling Psychology, 18,* 64–69.

Jones, W. H., Carpenter, B. N., & Quintana, D. (1985). Personality and interpersonal predictors of loneliness in two cultures. *Journal of Personality and Social Psychology, 48,* 1503–1511.

Jourard, S. M. (1964). *The transparent self.* New York: Van Nostrand Reinhold.

Jourard, S. M. (1971). *The transparent self* (rev. ed.). New York: Van Nostrand Reinhold.

Levy, S. M. (1976). Schizophrenic symptomatology: Reaction or strategy? A study of contextual antecedents. *Journal of Abnormal Psychology, 85,* 435–445.

Maslow, A. H. (1968). *Toward a psychology of being.* New York: Van Nostrand Reinhold.

Maslow, A. H. (1971). *The farther reaches of human nature.* New York: The Viking Press.

Mayo, P. R. (1968). Self-disclosure and neurosis. *British Journal of Social and Clinical Psychology, 7,* 140–148.

McDaniel, S. H., Stiles, W. B., & McGaughey, K. J. (1981). Correlations of male college students' verbal response mode use in psychotherapy with measures of psychological disturbance and psychotherapy outcome. *Journal of Consulting and Clinical Psychology, 49,* 571–582.

Meehl, P. E. (1962). Schizotaxia, schizotypy, schizophrenia. *American Psychologist, 17,* 827–838.

Mowrer, O. H. (1964). *The new group therapy.* New York: Van Nostrand.

Nelson-Jones, R., & Coxhead, P. (1980). Neuroticism, social desirability and anticipations and attributions affecting self-disclosure. *British Journal of Medical Psychology, 53,* 169–180.

Pederson, D. M., & Breglio, V. J. (1968). Personality correlates of actual self-disclosure. *Psychological Reports, 22,* 492–501.

Pederson, D. M., & Higbee, K. L. (1969). Personality correlates of self-disclosure. *Journal of Social Psychology, 78,* 81–89.

Persons, R. W., & Marks, P. A. (1970). Self-disclosure and recidivists: Optimum interviewer-interviewee matching. *Journal of Abnormal Psychology, 76*, 387–391.

Post, A. L., Wittmaier, B. C., & Radin, M. E. (1978). Self-disclosure as a function of state and trait anxiety. *Journal of Consulting and Clinical Psychology, 46*, 12–19.

Rogers, C. R. (1961). *On becoming a person*. Boston: Houghton Mifflin.

Rosenhan, D. L. (1973). On being sane in insane places. *Science, 179*, 250–258.

Shimkunas, A. M. (1972). Demand for intimate self-disclosure and pathological verbalizations in schizophrenia. *Journal of Abnormal Psychology, 80*, 197–205.

Stanley, G., & Bownes, A. F. (1966). Self-disclosure and neuroticism. *Psychological Reports, 18*, 350.

Strassberg, D. S., & Kangas, J. (1977). MMPI correlates of self-disclosure. *Journal of Clinical Psychology, 33*, 739–740.

Strassberg, D. S., Roback, H. B., Anchor, K. N., & Abramowitz, S. I. (1975). Self-disclosure in group therapy with schizophrenics. *Archives of General Psychiatry, 32*, 1259–1261.

Taylor, D. A., Altman, I., & Frankfurt, L. P. (1965). *Personality correlates of self-disclosure*. Unpublished manuscript.

Truax, C. B., & Wittmer, J. (1971). Self-disclosure and personality adjustment. *Journal of Clinical Psychology, 27*, 535–537.

Winters, K. C., & Neale, J. M. (1983). Delusions and delusional thinking in psychotics: A review of the literature. In *Clinical Psychology Review* (Vol. 3, pp. 227–253). New York: Pergamon Press.

11

The Dilemma of Distress Disclosure

DAN COATES and TINA WINSTON

Many observers agree that when we feel upset and unhappy, we will cope more successfully if we discuss our problems and negative feelings rather than keeping them to ourselves. Scholars of the human condition have long argued that an inability or unwillingness to openly express intense, negative emotions underlies many of the psychological and physical disorders that people develop (Creighton, 1886; Falconer, 1796; Freud, 1935). Many modern therapists have likewise maintained that the open expression of unpleasant feelings, what we call "distress disclosure," is necessary in order to overcome those feelings and maximize our psychological well-being (Jourard, 1971; Perls, 1969; Schutz, 1971). Nonprofessionals also tend to view the disclosure of problems and negative feelings as a good strategy for alleviating their troubles. In several studies where people have been asked what they do when they are feeling depressed, "talking it over with a friend" is always among the most frequently mentioned responses (Funabiki, Bologna, Pepping, & Fitzgerald, 1980; Parker & Brown, 1982; Rippere, 1977). Further, all of this faith in distress disclosure does not seem misplaced because there is evidence that people who are unable or unwilling to reveal their troubles are more likely to develop serious physical and psychological

---

DAN COATES • Department of Psychology, University of Missouri-St. Louis, St. Louis, Missouri 63121. **TINA WINSTON** • Department of Psychology, University of Wisconsin, Madison, Wisconsin, 53706. Preparation of this chapter and the original research reported here was supported by NIMH Grant RO1 MH39529-01 to Dan Coates.

problems (see Cooper, 1984; Locke & Colligan, 1986; Silver & Wortman, 1980, for reviews).

However, although there is little doubt that discussing our difficulties with others can serve a variety of positive functions, doing so may also carry certain costs. There is quite a bit of evidence that people do not like others who are suffering and unhappy (Lerner & Simmons, 1966; Strack & Coyne, 1983; Winer, Bonner, Blaney & Murray, 1981) and even some indication that distress disclosure in particular prompts rejection from others (Coates, Wortman, & Abbey, 1979; Coyne, 1976a, Peters-Golden, 1982). If others find distress disclosure unpleasant and unattractive, engaging in such disclosure could well result in the loss of at least some of our social support. Because social support is an important ingredient in the process of successfully coping (see Cohen & Wills, 1985; Schradle & Dougher, 1985; Wortman, 1984; for reviews), losing such support could ultimately have very detrimental effects on our adjustment and well-being. In surveys of various populations, it is often the people who say they spend the most time discussing their difficulties who also report being least helped by others (McFarlane, Norman, Streiner, & Roy, 1984). Indeed, people who keep their negative feelings "bottled up" and who turn out to be more sick in some studies (see Cooper, 1984, for a review) may have begun as individuals who talked about their troubles but painfully learned that no one wanted to hear about them.

Together, the two lines of research we have outlined here form the parameters for the dilemma of distress disclosure. Keeping our troubles to ourselves appears to carry negative consequences for our health and well-being, but openly and readily revealing those troubles could well be detrimental to our social acceptance. This dilemma represents a practical and perhaps quite difficult problem for distressed people—how to disclose enough of one's misery to gain the benefits such revelations can provide, without disclosing in such a way or to such an extent that it will drive others away. For theorists and researchers interested in the process of coping with stress, the disclosure dilemma represents an interesting puzzle. How is it that people who say they do share their negative feelings with others often end up being healthier and happier, despite the fact that such sharing may frequently minimize the extent and quality of available social support?

A possible solution to both the researcher's puzzle and the distressed person's problem may lie with certain individual differences. Observers have frequently proposed that individual variation in social skills may explain why some people have both less social support and more physical and psychological disorders, although attempts to identify just what these critical social skills are have so far not been very successful (Sarason, Sarason, Hacker, & Basham, 1985). Nonetheless, there is considerable intuitive appeal in the idea that people vary in their distress disclosure styles. Some may reveal their problems in a more restrained, tactful, or sensitive way that enables them to resolve the dilemma of distress disclosure. They know how to bring up and discuss difficulties without alienating the people around them and so are able to obtain the benefits of distress disclosure while still maintaining their social support. Others, though, may be less adept at striking the delicate balance that effective distress disclosure seems to require. They reveal their problems with an intensity, a persistence, or an inappropriateness that members of their social environments find unappealing and unattractive. These less-skilled disclosers could therefore be the ones who end up being sicker and more poorly adjusted. Either they continue to disclose their distress, and so drive away their social support, or, they try to maintain their relationships by keeping their problems to themselves, thereby forfeiting the benefits of distress disclosure. Obviously, if we could identify those people who are more adept at distress disclosure, we might be able to learn from them the social surival skills that could solve the distress disclosure dilemma for the less adept.

In the remainder of this chapter, we will begin by discussing the distress disclosure dilemma in more detail. How does it help to discuss our negative feelings with others, and how might it hurt? We will then consider the extent to which the individual difference variable of self-monitoring (Snyder, 1979) may distinguish between those who are more and less adept at distress disclosure. Finally, we present a study testing the idea that high self-monitors may point the way to successfully resolving the distress disclosure dilemma.

DISTRESS DISCLOSURE AND SOCIAL SUPPORT

Keeping our problems and negative feelings to ourselves can be dangerous to our health, both physical and psychological. For example, since at least ancient Roman times, physicians and other medical observers have been speculating that a certain cancer-prone personality type exists (see Cooper, 1984; Holden, 1978, for reviews). This personality type is characterized by a tendency to conceal or suppress negative emotions, so that someone with such a precancerous personality theoretically "puts on a happy face and denies any sense of loss, anger, distress, disappointment or despair" (Scarf, 1980, p. 37). In several studies where people with malignant tumors are compared to various control groups of noncancer patients, the people with cancer show a stronger tendency to hold in feelings of anger (Greer & Morris, 1975; Watson, Pettingale, & Greer, 1984) and to suppress any expression of depression (Dattore, Shontz, & Coyne, 1980; Thomas & Greenstreet, 1973; see also Cooper, 1984; Holden, 1978; for reviews). Further, there is evidence that once people have developed cancer, patients who readily express their anger and depression are more likely to survive than those who keep their troubles to themselves (Derogatis, Abeloff, & Melisaratos, 1979; see also Locke & Colligan, 1986, for a review). One important function distress disclosure may serve, then, is to help us avoid serious physical illness, especially the frightening disease of cancer.

Given its apparent beneficial impact on physical health, it is not surprising to find that distress disclosure also has been empirically associated with better mental health. For instance, in several survey or interview studies, various victimized groups have been asked whether they have a friendly confidant, or someone with whom they comfortably and openly talk over their troubles. Among highly stressed housewives (Brown & Harris, 1978), widows (Vachon *et al.*, 1982), rape victims (Atkeson, Calhoun, Resick, & Ellis, 1982; Meyer & Taylor, 1986), the recently divorced (Berman & Turk, 1979), breast cancer patients (Maguire, 1982), the unemployed (Pearlin, Lieberman, Menaghan, & Mullen, 1981) and other distressed groups (see Cohen & Wills, 1985, for a review of research on the buffering effects of having a confidant), those who report that they can and do discuss problems and aversive feelings with friends and family members are much less likely to show symptoms of serious depression. There is also evidence that interventions aimed at increasing distress disclosures by victims help to ease their emotional anguish (see Silver & Wortman, 1980, for a review). For example, Raphael (1977) found that when widows were encouraged to openly and fully express their grief, they were less likely to report symptoms of depression or physical illness a year after their husbands' deaths than were widows in a matched control group who did not receive such disclosure encouragement. Indeed, some theorists have proposed that it is through the promotion of serious depression that inhibited distress disclosure has its deleterious impact on physical health. When people try to cope with negative feelings in dysfunctional ways, such as by concealing or suppressing them, the resulting intense depression may directly impair the functioning of the immune system or other important physiological processes (see Cooper, 1984; Locke & Colligan, 1986, for reviews). Severe depression also may undermine physical health through indirect mechanisms because people who are depressed are less likely to maintain nutritious diets, get sufficient sleep, or generally take very good care of their bodies (Okun, Stock, Haring, & Witter, 1984).

So it appears that we are likely to be healthier and happier if we talk over our problems with others. But, how does distress disclosure have such beneficial effects? It is possible that expressing our problems and negative feelings helps to reduce our misery in ways that are completely personal, private, and asocial. For example, some theorists have suggested that the disclosure of distress directly reduces such negative affect through a catharsis effect (e.g., Freud, 1935). Theoretically, when we openly and readily express negative emotions, we use them up more quickly rather than letting them fester and grow into overwhelming proportions. However, research evidence indicates that the expression of negative feelings often leads to at least a temporary increase in those feelings rather than a catharsis or release of such feelings. People usually feel more angry and hostile, rather than less so, after they have acted in some aggressive way (Konecni, 1975). Similarly, athough such findings could admittedly be the result of demand characteristics, in studies where subjects are encouraged to think or talk about depressing things (e.g., Alloy, Abramson, & Viscusi, 1981; Schare & Lisman, 1984) or to act out nonverbal expressions of depression (see Buck, 1980, for a review), they typically report an immediate increase rather than decrease in their depression level. Therefore, it seems that the mere expression of negative feelings in no way assures a reduction in those feelings, and instead, may intensify such feelings.

What benefits distress disclosure provides, then, may accrue more directly through the interpersonal consequences of such disclosure rather than the intrapersonal ones. Although there is no certainty that revealing our problems and negative feelings to others will prompt the help we need or want from them, keeping our troubles to ourselves does virtually guarantee that we will not get sufficient comfort or aid. For example, several theorists have proposed that when people experience serious distress, they will also be inclined to doubt that such feelings are normal or appropriate (Coates & Peterson, 1982; Coates & Winston, 1983; Kopel, 1982; Nisbett, Borgida, Crandall, & Reed, 1976; Schachter, 1959). These doubts can lead to shame and guilt for not coping as well as others seem to (Nisbett *et al.*, 1976) or even to anxieties and fears over the possibility of being "crazy" (Marris, 1958; see also Silver & Wortman, 1980; Coates & Peterson, 1982, for reviews). If people talk over their negative feelings with others, many of these secondary doubts and fears can be alleviated through "normalizing" information from the social environment (Coates & Peterson, 1982; Coates & Winston, 1983). But when people try to conceal their troubles, such doubts and anxieties will likely only fester and further exacerbate the original, primary distress (Kopel, 1982). In addition, both professionals and laypeople recognize that at times of stress, being involved in intimate and caring relationships and having the knowledge that we are liked and appreciated by others can be basic sources of comfort and distress reduction (see also Barrera & Ainlay, 1983; Schradle & Dougher, 1985; Silver & Wortman, 1980, for reviews). However, disclosing ourselves, our fears and failures as well as our satisfaction and success, is essential to the development and maintenance of intimate relationships (Altman & Taylor, 1973; Derlega, 1984; Jourard, 1971). When we keep our troubles a secret, even if others do express liking and affection for us, we are more likely to feel that their approval is only for our "happy" act and not for the unhappy actor portraying it (Coates & Wortman, 1980; Jones & Wortman, 1973). People do sometimes feel lonely and unloved even when they are involved in close relationships (Margulis, Derlega, & Winstead, 1984; Rook, 1984). Such feelings that one is not fully known or accepted by significant others could readily result from an inability or unwillingess to disclose negative emotions and other unpleasant aspects of oneself in relationships (Chelune, Sultan, & Williams, 1980; Solano, Batten, & Parish, 1983). Finally, failure to disclose our distress is likely to minimize the instrumental aid others offer us, as well as the helpfulness of any advice or services they do provide. In some cases, others will not be able to know that anything is wrong unless we tell them and so will not help at all unless we disclose our distress. Research shows, for instance, that people with problems are much more likely to get advice and assistance from co-workers if they discuss their problems (Burke, 1982; Burke, Weir, & Duncan, 1976). Research on helping more generally shows that even if people can discern that something's amiss, they are not likely to take any action in ambiguous situations where it is not clear what kind of help would be appropriate (Darley & Latane, 1968). So, by disclosing our distress, we establish that we need help and clarify the nature of our problem, thereby increasing our chances of getting some assistance. With distress disclosure, we also increase the chances that any aid we do receive will better suit our needs. For example, as Maguire (1984) points out in his literature review, cancer patients often find it difficult to discuss their feelings of depression with their physicians, yet such feelings can provide important clues to the course of the disease, the effects of therapeutic drugs, and the patients' suitability for alternative treatments. So, if patients reveal their distress, their physicians will be better able to give them the treatment that will do the most good. Keeping our problems to ourselves, then, increases the likelihood that our negative feelings will become more complicated and intense, undermines the value of any expressions of caring or intimacy that others provide, and reduces both the extent and effectiveness of advice and instrumental assistance from the social environment.

If distress disclosure promotes health and well-being primarily by improving the quality of social support, it is all the more unfortunate and ironic that distress disclosure can also diminish social support. Yet there is considerable evidence to show that others will often find distress disclosure quite unattractive. When we disclose our distress, we let others know that we are hurt and suffering, which is apparently not a very good way to win friends. When subjects witness others being hurt in laboratory studies, for example, by being made to endure electric shocks, they typically dislike such victims more the more intensely they appear to suffer (Lerner & Simmons, 1966). Subjects also are uncomfortable when they interact with others who appear to be physically disabled and usually rate such interaction partners as less attractive than healthy, ablebodied people (e.g., Kleck, Ono, & Hastorf, 1966). People suffering from psychological rather than physical pain, such as individuals who are or appear to be depressed, also tend to be rather harshly rejected by strangers (e.g., Coyne, 1976b; Howes & Hokanson, 1979; Strack & Coyne, 1983; Winer *et al.*, 1981). Further, there is evidence that this tendency for strangers to dislike depressed others can be triggered specifically by distress disclosure. For example, Coates, Wortman, and Abbey (1979) found that subjects rated a rape victim as significantly less attractive when she admitted to feeling upset about the rape rather than remaining silent about her feelings. Coyne (1976a) has proposed that strangers often reject depressed people because they find the depressed's disclosure of their problems and unhappiness to be inappropriately intimate. Making a new friend can be a particularly ameliorative form of social support. For instance, Monroe, Bellack, Hersen, and Himmelhoch (1983) found that seriously clinically depressed women were more likely to recover from their condition if they reported that they had recently made a new friend. But, based on available research evidence, we are most unlikely to turn strangers into friends if we disclose our distress to them.

Of course, for most of us most of the time, intimates are more important sources of social support than strangers are. And we might expect that intimate others, such as family and friends, would react more favorably to distress disclosures than strangers do. However, although there has not been much research on intimates' reactions to expressions of distress (Coyne, 1985; Doerfler & Chaplin, 1985), what evidence is available indicates that friends and family members also find distress disclosures to be disturbing and unappealing. First of all, it seems that intimates often discourage distress disclosure. Peters-Golden (1982) interviewed 100 breast cancer patients and found that 56% felt avoided and 72% felt misunderstood by friends and family members once they disclosed the fact of their disease to them. Peters-Golden points out that others viewed the cancer patients' attempts to talk about their disease and related fears and anxieties as evidence of poor psychological adjustment. Intimates tended to avoid any conversations on these subjects, on the grounds that such talk could only make the patients feel worse. The cancer patients, though, "are both disturbed by this ban on communication, and confused by the assumption that avoiding the subject could actually be good for them" (Peters-Golden, 1982, p. 489).

If distressed people persist with their disclosures despite such discouragement from intimates, those intimates may react by becoming less supportive and helpful. Subjects in a study conducted by Sacco, Milana, and Dunn (1985) indicated that they would rather spend time with a nondepressed person they had known for 2 weeks than a depressed person they had known for a full year. McFarlane *et al.* (1984) found that among a random community sample, those who reported doing the most distress disclosing also reported receiving the least satisfying help and support. Pearlin and Schooler (1978) turned up very similar results in their community study (see also Wortman, 1984, for a review and discussion on this issue). So, people who readily, openly, and frequently engage in distress disclosure may often lose social support and become more hopeless and unhappy as a result. In several studies, a group of depressed people and control groups of nondepressed individuals have been asked how they deal with ordinary problems and day-to-day upsets (Billings, Cronkite, & Moos, 1983; Billings & Moos, 1984; Coyne, Aldwin, & Lazarus, 1981). Compared to the nondepressed, depressed people are much more likely to report using the coping strategy of information seeking, which consists primarily of discussing problems with friends and family to obtain their advice and counsel. Although intimates may not respond to distress disclosures with the total rejection that strangers do, it does appear that they also tend to find such disclosures very disturbing and react to persistent distress disclosure with discouragement and diminished support.

So, we now have a fairly complete picture of the distress disclosure dilemma. If we do not disclose our distress, others do not know how upset we are or what is bothering us and so cannot help us very much. But if we disclose our distress too much or too intensely, others find it annoying and disturbing and will not help us very much. Consistent with such a dilemma, some studies, at least, have found that both people who report never disclosing negative feelings and people who report extremely high levels of such disclosures are more likely to suffer from diseases such as cancer (Greer & Morris, 1975). Although most of the studies on disclosure and cancer indicate that nondisclosure is a greater risk than too much disclosure (see Cooper, 1984, for a review), it is obviously possible that some nondisclosers develop that tack as a result of the disapproval they receive for their attempts to disclose. There is evidence from one prospective study (Hagnell, 1966) and one retrospective study (Coppen & Metcalfe, 1963) that cancer patients are actually more open and outgoing than noncancer patients before they develop the disease. The fact that cancer patients so often turn out to be more repressed and reclusive after they develop a malignancy (see Locke & Colligan, 1986, for a review) could well reflect the patients' adaptation to the social rejection they get when they try to discuss their disease (see also Schwarz & Geyer, 1984). Indeed, people who feel they are forced by others to keep their problems to themselves could be the ones who are at the greatest risk of becoming ill and staying that way. Ogden and Von Sturmer (1984) found that individuals who say they regularly express their negative feelings and people who say they repress them but do not continue to experience them were equally likely to report good psychological and physical health. It was only people who say they hold in their negative feelings but continue to experience them anyway who reported high levels of dissatisfaction and unhealthy symptoms. The people who hold in their distress despite the fact that they continue to feel it may well be the ones who have learned that both strangers and intimates just do not want to hear about it.

The distress disclosure dilemma is apparently not without a good solution, though. Obviously, in all the research we have reviewed on the consequences of nondisclosure and excessive disclosure, there is always that group of people who say they do express and discuss their negative feelings, at least to some moderate extent, and who also report being relatively happy and healthy. Somehow, it seems, these people are able to disclose enough to get effective support but not so much that they alienate their supporters. Obviously, if we could identify who these successful disclosers are, we might be able to learn much more about what is required to resolve the distress disclosure dilemma. In the following section, we consider the possiblity that people who score high on the individual difference variable of self-monitoring (Snyder, 1974, 1979) may have the special social skills that are needed for sucessful distress diclosure.

SELF-MONITORING AND THE DISTRESS DISCLOSURE DILEMMA

The individual difference variable of self-monitoring has received considerable research attention from social psychologists (see. e.g., Mill, 1984; Synder, 1979, for reviews), and the results of this work indicate that people who score high on this dimension are likely to be more adept at distress disclosure for a number of reasons. First, and perhaps most importantly, high self-monitors are more concerned with, and more skilled at, impression management (Synder, 1979). High self-monitors are more sensitive than low self-monitors to cues that others provide. For instance, compared to low self-monitors, high self-monitors make more accurate interpretations of others' nonverbal communications (Mill, 1984). People often seem to be uncomfortable with someone else's distress disclosures (e.g., Coates *et al.*, 1979), but high self-monitors would be more likely to notice such discomfort, even if people expressed it only nonverbally. And, when high self-monitors believe that others may disapprove of what they are doing, unlike low self-monitors they tend to adjust and modify their behavior to make it more acceptable. For instance, high self-monitors are more likely to conceal their true feelings and attitudes when they think such expressions would not be appreciated by these around them (McCann & Hancock, 1983; Synder & Monson, 1975). Further, high self-monitors tend to have better social skills in general (Furnham & Capon, 1983; Riggio & Friedman, 1982) and to worker harder to insure smooth and pleasant interactions with others (Ickes & Barnes, 1977).

Taken together, this evidence suggests that when high self-monitors do reveal their problems to others, they will do it in a careful, sensitive, and tactful way. When high self-monitors notice that their expressions of unhappiness are beginning to make those around them uneasy, they are likely to tone down their presentation to make the interaction as enjoyable as possible for all involved. Low self-monitors, on the other hand, may not even notice others' discomfort and are more likely to persist in letting others know just how they feel, even if those around them are disturbed by such revelations. Although no study has specifically investigated how high and low self-monitors differ in making distress disclosures, there is some evidence that high self-monitors are more restrained in their expressions of negative feelings. Lippa (1978) videotaped high and low self-monitors as they role-played a high-school math teacher and then showed the tapes to judges. High and low self-monitors described themselves as equally worried and nervous while portraying the teachers, but judges rated the high self-monitors as significantly less anxious. Although the high self-monitors apparently felt just as upset as low self-monitors, they were able to appear to be calmer. If high self-monitors more generally present their negative feelings in such a low-keyed way, others are more likely to find their distress disclosures less disturbing than those of low self-monitors. As a result, high self-monitors may be able to discuss their woes while still retaining social support and the benefits such support can provide to health and well-being.

High self-monitors may benefit more from distress disclosure than low self-monitors do not only because they are more careful and skilled at impression management but also because they are more careful in selecting the partners with whom they discuss their problems. Studies by Snyder, Gangestad, and Simpson (1983) indicate that high and low self-monitors have different types of relationships with their friends. Low self-monitors generally choose to be with the friend they like best, no matter what activity they are going to do together. High self-monitors, on the other hand, tend to pick the friend who is best at the planned activity. For instance, high self-monitors choose the best tennis player they know when playing tennis is what they intend to do, even if this person is not the friend they like best. So, when the task at hand is dealing with distress, high self-monitors may be more inclined to seek out the friends who do the best job of discussing such issues, whereas low self-monitors may be more likely to go to those they like best, whether or not such individuals are very tolerant of others' misery or very skilled at distress management. There is evidence for rather wide-ranging individual differences in the ability to elicit disclosures from others (Miller, Berg, & Archer, 1983) and the tendency to respond to unhappy disclosures with comforting reassurance (Samter & Burleson, 1984). So, it is quite likely that not all our friends will be very receptive or helpful in response to our distress disclosures, but high self-monitors would probably do a better job of seeking out the ones who would be.

Of course, the high self-monitors' advantages in terms of impression management and social selection skills might also backfire on them. If they are too careful about whom they let in on their troubles, they may fail to get much in the way of help or counsel from most members of their social networks. When they do reveal their troubles to others, they may go too far in making sure that those others are not bothered by such relevations. Especially if anti-disclosure pressures from the socialenvironment are as strong as some studies suggest (e.g., Peters-Golden, 1982), sensitive high self-monitors may tone down both the frequency and intensity of their disclosure to the point of nondisclosure. As a result, high self-monitors could be very well liked by those around them but still often fail to get the help they need when they are hurt or suffering and so end up more sick and depressed. Sparacino, Ronchi, Bigley, Flesch, and Kuhn (1983) conducted a series of studies investigating the relationship between high self-monitoring and hypertension. They found that in some jobs and demographic categories, high self-monitors had lower blood pressure, but more often, they had higher blood pressure. These authors indicated that this could result from high self-monitors' tendency to control and inhibit their expressive behavior. So, it could turn out that high self-monitors tend to be nondisclosers, with the consequence that they are more likely to be unhappy and unhealthy than low self-monitors.

We conducted a study to investigate the hypothesis that high self-monitors are more successful at resolving the dilemma of distress disclosure. We administered measures of self-monitoring, distress disclosure, social support, and psychological distress to a large sample of college students. If high self-monitors tend to be nondisclosures, concealing their problems and negative feelings in order to maintain a good impression with others, then we would expect them to indicate that they generally reveal unpleasant emotions to a smaller extent than low self-monitors do. On the other hand, if high self-monitors engage in more than minimal distress disclosure, the question becomes whether they benefit more from such disclosures. If high self-monitors are more adept at revealing their problems and negative feelings, we should find, first, that they have more social support than low self-monitors do—especially when both high and low self-monitors are very distressed and their disclosures have the greatest potential for disturbing members of their social environments. Second, we should find that high self-monitors are less distressed than low self-monitors—especially among those high and low self-monitors who are at least moderate distress disclosers and so most likely to benefit or suffer from their skills at this social task. The details of our study, and its results, are presented next.

Method

Subjects. We distributed a questionnaire containing a consent form and instructions plus measures of self-monitoring, distress disclosure, social support, and psychological distress to 338 introductory psychology students. The questionnaires were returned by 318 of these students, 143 males and 175 females.

Measures. Given the research we have reviewed on the connection between distress disclosure and serious illness such as cancer or hypertension, it might seem appropriate to include a measure of such serious illness in our study. However, because our sample consisted of young and relatively healthy college students, the probable occurrence of such diseases was very small. Therefore, we concentrated on psychological distress because college students do experience depression and unhappiness at least at moderate rates, and such feelings could be the stepping stone between nondisclosure and physical maladies (cf. Okun *et al.*, 1984). We used two scales to measure psychological distress. One of these was the Beck Depression Inventory (Beck, Ward, Mendelson, Mock, & Erlbaugh, 1961). Although this scale was intended to measure clinical depression and is correlated with psychiatric diagnoses of depression (Bumberry, Oliver, & McClure, 1978), it is clearly a measure of rather severe psychological distress in general rather than clinical depression in particular (Gotlib, 1984). To fill out this scale, people indicate whether or not they agree with statements like "I am dissatisfied with everything," "I hate myself," and "I get tired from doing anything." Because it is correlated with psychiatric diagnoses of depression, this scale may be particularly sensitive to picking up dysphoric aspects of distress. The other scale we used was a psychological distress measure developed by Gurin, Veroff, and Field (1960). This scale primarily taps the extent to which people experience distress-related physical symptoms and asks people to answer "yes" or "no" to questions like "Do you feel you are bothered by all sorts of pain and ailments in different parts of your body?" and to indicate how often they experience headaches, upset stomach, dizziness, and similar unpleasant physical sensations. For our analyses, both scales were scored so that higher totals indicate greater distress.

To measure social support, we used three different scales. One was a measure of supportive behaviors developed specifically with college students by Barrera, Sandler, and Ramsay (1981). The scale asks students to indicate how often in the last month they have been the recipient of 40 different expressions from others representing instrumental support (e.g., "Gave you under $25"), informational support (e.g., "Told you what s/he did in a situation that was similar to yours") and emotional support (e.g., "Told you that you are OK just the way you are"). The other two support measures were developed by Procidano and Heller (1983) and measure satisfaction with support received from friends and satisfaction with support received from family members. The items on the two scales are the same, but the referent supporter is changed. These scales include items like "My friends give me the moral support I need" and "Members of my family are good at helping me solve problems," to which respondents reply, "Yes, no, or I don't know." Due to the fact that our sample was college students, most of them away from home, we expected that support from friends would be most important to them. But, because it is certainly not uncommon for college students to turn to family members for help, we decided to include a measure of support from this source as well. On all of these scales, higher scores indicated more perceived support.

We wanted to measure the extent to which people usually reveal their distress to others when they are upset, but we could not find a scale for this purpose. There are scales that measure the extent to which people generally express their feelings (see e.g., Cooley & Keesey, 1981) but not the extent to which they disclose negative feelings to others in particular. And there are scales that measure the range and intimacy of disclosure that people engage in (e.g., Chelune, 1976) but not the disclosure of negative feelings specifically. So, we formulated a scale of our own, consisting of the 20 items presented in Table 1. People responded to these items by circling a number on a 9 point scale anchored by *Always* and *Never*. This scale at least has good internal consistency. The Standardized Item Alpha for the study sample on this scale was .92. This scale was scored so that higher values indicate more reported distress disclosure.

To measure self-monitoring, we used the self-monitoring scale developed by Snyder (1974). On this scale, people answer "true" or "false" to questions like "In order to get along and be liked, I tend to be what people expect me to be rather than anything else" and "I'm not always the person I appear to be."

TABLE 1. Distress Disclosure Items

1. When I'm depressed, I tell a friend about my troubles.
2. I try to keep my troubles to myself, rather than sharing them with others.
3. When I'm feeling down and depressed, I feel better if I talk over my problems with someone.
4. I often talk to others about problems and difficulties that I am having.
5. Most of the time, I try not to let others know if I am feeling sad.
6. When I'm depressed, I tell a family member about my troubles.
7. When I'm having problems or difficulties, I prefer to deal with them myself rather than discussing them with others.
8. I usually find that talking over my problems with others is the best way to start solving them.
9. I don't like to talk to anyone when I'm sad or in a bad mood.
10. When I talk about things that have happened to me, I try to stick to positive or happy events rather than unpleasant or sad ones.
11. If I'm having problems or difficulties, I discuss them with somebody.
12. When I talk about myself with others, I try to focus on pleasant, positive, and happy topics.
13. When I'm sad, I let people know about it.
14. I usually keep my problems secret from others.
15. When I'm having difficulties, I find or call someone to talk about what is bothering me.
16. Even when something is bothering me, I try to stay positive and upbeat in my conversations with others.
17. If I feel unhappy, I usually talk to somebody about it.
18. I try to act cheerful and pleasant with others, even if I'm feeling down and depressed.
19. If I'm very unhappy, I usually find it quite difficult to talk to others about it.
20. When I'm depressed, I seek out others so that I can talk about what is bothering me.

RESULTS

Self-Monitoring and Distress Disclosure. We had anticipated, as one reasonable outcome, that high self-monitors would turn out to be nondistress-disclosers. However, this is apparently not the case. In our sample, there was no statistically significant relationship between the self-monitoring and distress disclosure scores ($r = .08$, $p < .07$). Of course, although high self-monitors may generally reveal their troubles to others as much as low self-monitors do, they could be particularly inclined to keep their problems a secret when they are very upset and more likely to upset others with their feelings. To check for this possibility, we entered our distress measures and the self-monitoring scores, along with appropriate interaction terms, as predictor variables in a multiple regression analysis with distress disclosure as the predicted variable. There were no statistically significant interactions, indicating that high and low self-monitors are equally likely to report disclosing distress no matter what their current level of distress is. So, it does appear that high self-monitors discuss their problems and negative feelings just as much as low self-monitors do. But, do high self-monitors benefit more from their distress disclosures?

Self-Monitoring, Distress Disclosure, and Social Support. Based on their acknowledged greater social skills, we might expect high self-monitors to generally have more social support than low self-monitors do. And, in our sample, that did turn out to be the case. Although there was no relationship between self-monitoring and support from family ($r = .02$, $p > .1$), high self-monitors did tend to report receiving more satisfying support from friends ($r = .15$, $p < .003$) and more supportive behaviors from others ($r = .21$, $p < .0001$). But, if along with their other social skills, high self-monitors are also more adept at distress disclosure, we would expect them not only to have more support most of the time but to have more support in particular when they are distressed and inclined to let others know about it.

To explore this issue, we conducted a series of multiple regression analyses, in which we entered the self-monitoring, distress, and disclosure measures as predictor variables, along with appropriate interaction terms and each of the support measures as a dependent variable. There were no significant interactions among the predictor variables on the support from family or supportive behavior measures. But there was a significant self-monitoring by depression-level interaction on reported satisfaction with support from friends (Beta $= .30$, $t = 1.95$, $p < .05$). This interaction is based on the continuous measures of these variables from the total sample, but as an aid to interpreting this finding, mean support scores for high and low self-monitors at different depression levels are presented in Table 2. As these means show, high and low self-monitors are about equally satisfied with support from friends at low depression levels. But at high depression levels, high self-monitors are more satisfied with such support than low self-monitors are. High self-monitors appear to be particularly adept at retaining more social support when they are very distressed.

There was some indication that it is, in particular, high self-monitors' skills at distress disclosure than help them to keep supportive relationships even when they are rather upset. Our analyses revealed a nearly significant, three-way interaction among depression, self-monitoring, and distress disclosure on reported satisfaction with support from friends (Beta = .28, t = 1.89, $p < .06$). Inspection of the relevant means indicated that at high depression levels, high self-monitors are particularly likely to have more satisfying support than low self-monitors when both report disclosing their distress at higher levels. Again, these results are consistent with the proposition that when they are depressed, high self-monitors are more careful about how they disclose their distress and are therefore more likely to retain satisfying support when they do so. However, this interaction was only of borderline significance, and because of the three-way split, the number of subjects in some of these categories was very small.

It appears, then, that high self-monitors are better able than low self-monitors to reveal their troubles without alienating the people around them. But high self-monitors enjoy this advantage only when it comes to support from friends, rather than support from family or supportive behaviors from all sources. However, our sample consisted of college students, most of whom were away from home, and support from friends did seem to be the most important kind of social assistance for these people. The strongest relationship between any of the support and distress measures was the correlation between satisfaction with support from friends and the depression scores ($r = -.35$, $p < .0001$). The other social support measures were only weakly related to depression (support from family, $r = -.12$, $p < .02$; supportive behaviors, $r = -.10$, $p <$

TABLE 2. Self-Monitoring by Depression Interaction on Reported Satisfaction with Support from Friends[a]

	High depressed	Low depressed
High self-monitors	14.11 (55)	17.61 (82)
Low self-monitors	10.27 (22)	16.45 (55)

[a]Subjects who could not be clearly classified as depressed or nondepressed on the Beck Depression Inventory are not included here. The scores are the mean perceived support scores for all subjects in each category. The number of subjects in each category are provided in parentheses.

.05), and none of the support measures were very predictive of scores on the distress symptom checklist (support from friends, $r = -.04$, $p > .1$; support behaviors, $r = -.06$, $p > .1$; support from family, $r = -.16$, $p < .001$). So, if these students found any form of social support to be very helpful at all, it was satisfying support from friends that most eased their unhappiness.

Overall, then, this pattern of results is quite consistent with the hypothesis that high self-monitors are more successful than low self-monitors at solving the dilemma of distress disclosure. High self-monitors do reveal problems and negative feelings to others, at least as much as low self-monitors do. But when they are very upset and most likely to upset others with their distress disclosures, high self-monitors have more social support than low self-monitors do. And there is some indication that this is particularly true among high and low self-monitors who are most inclined to let others know they are troubled. Apparently, high self-monitors use the same sort of sensitive and tactful approach in their distress disclosures that they use in their other social interactions, with the result that they can hold on to more social support at the times when they really need it. Given these findings, we would further expect that high self-monitors who do engage in distress disclosure also would be less seriously distressed than similar low self-monitors. When high self-monitors are troubled and talk it over with others, they get more of the social support they need to solve their problems and ease their negative feelings before their difficulties become too complicated or intense. Low self-monitors get less help from others when they disclose their distress and so would be more likely to continue suffering from that distress. We discuss the psychological distress results next.

Self-Monitoring, Distress Disclosure, and Psychological Distress. There was no statistically significant relationship between the self-monitoring and depression scores ($r = .02$, $p < .1$), indicating that high self-monitors are just as likely to be depressed as low self-monitors are. However, it would be expected that high self-monitors' advantage in distress disclosure would emerge most strongly among people who engage in such disclosure to at least a moderate extent because special skills in this domain would obviously not be much help to people who usually avoid this activity. In the total sample, there was a significant negative relationship between reported distress disclosure and depression scores ($r = -.25$, $p < .0001$), showing that people who say they talk about their problems more are less distressed at the moment. Is this particularly true for the socially skillful, high self-monitors?

We conducted a multiple regression analysis in which depression scores were used as the dependent variable, and the self-monitoring and distress disclosure measures, along with the appropriate interaction term, were entered as predictor variables. This analysis revealed a significant self-monitoring by distress disclosure interaction on depression scores (Beta = .50, t = 2.02, $p < .05$). Again, this interaction is based on continuous scores from the total sample, but pertinent means are presented in Table 3, to facilitate interpretation. As these means show, at low disclosure levels, high and low self-monitors report equivalent and relatively high levels of depression. At moderate and high levels of disclosure, though, high self-monitors are more depressed than low self-monitors. This was not an expected finding, because we had anticipated that among those who regularly discuss troubles with others, high self-monitors would be less distressed rather than more so. However, it is possible that these results still reflect the greater disclosure skills of high self-monitors. As we have already seen, when they are very distressed, high self-monitors have more social support than low self-monitors do. So, our findings here could simply show that when they are very upset, high self-monitors engage in more distress disclosure than low self-monitors do because they have more opportunities to discuss their troubles with others. But working against such an explanation is another earlier finding. There was no significant interaction between self-monitoring and the distress measures on reported distress disclosure and no significant relationship between self-monitoring and distress disclosure overall. So there is no evidence that low self-monitors discuss their problems less when they are very upset than high self-monitors do.

Rather, the most reasonable interpretation of these results is that they are contradictory to the hypothesis that high self-monitors are more successful at distress disclosure. High self-monitors apparently benefit less, on an emotional level, than low self-monitors do from their distress disclosures. Perhaps high self-monitors do go to far too please others when they discuss their problems and negative feelings. Although they do reveal their troubles, they do so in such a low-key way or with so few people that most members of their social environments remain unaware of the full range or exact nature of their difficulties. Consequently,

TABLE 3. Self-Monitoring by Distress Disclosure Interaction on Depression Scores[a]

	Low disclosure	Moderate disclosure	High disclosure
High self-monitors	8.66 (61)	7.41 (59)	5.57 (70)
Low self-monitors	8.50 (36)	4.76 (37)	3.80 (25)

[a]The number of subjects in each category is provided in parentheses. The values given are mean depression scores for all subjects in each category.

others maintain a positive impression of high self-monitors but are largely unable to provide the specific type or extent of help that high self-monitors need to ease their depression. So, rather than resolving the dilemma of distress disclosure, high self-monitors may get trapped in it, maximizing social adjustment at the price of emotional adjustment with their toned-down, carefully conducted distress revelations.

High self-monitors also tend to experience more headaches, upset stomachs, dizziness, and the like than low self-monitors do. There was a weak but positive relationship between self-monitoring scores and reported stress-related physical symptoms ($r = .15, p < .004$). However, this higher symptom rate does not appear to be related to high self-monitors' distress disclosure style. We conducted a multiple regression analysis with the symptom scores as the dependent variable and the self-monitoring scale, distress disclosure scale, and their interaction term as predictor variables. These was no overall relationship between distress disclosure and reported symptoms ($r = -.04, p > .1$) and no significant interaction between self-monitoring and distress disclosure. In our sample, then, problems like headaches and nightmares were largely unaffected by extent or style of distress disclosure. It will be recalled that this distress symptom measure was also poorly related to the social support index. So, although it is not clear why high self-monitors report more of these symptoms, it does not appear to be in any way the result of what happens when they talk over their troubles with others.

When all of our findings are considered together, they indicate that high self-monitors have not resolved the dilemma of distress disclosure very successfully. Their social skills do get them more satisfying social support, especially when they are more depressed. But this social support does not seem to do them much good because when they talk over problems with others, they are more depressed than similarly disclosing low self-monitors. So, rather than solving the dilemma, high self-monitors seem to seek others' approval at the price of more limited and less helpful distress disclosure. We consider the implications of these findings in the next section of this chapter.

Discussion

Previous research indicates that people who keep their problems to themselves are more likely to be unhappy and unhealthy (see Cooper, 1984; Silver & Wortman, 1980; Wortman, 1984, for reviews). But past studies also indicate that when people openly and readily reveal their distress to others, they are likely to experience diminished social support (Coates *et al.*, 1979; McFarlane *et al.*, 1984; Pearlin & Schooler, 1978; Peters-Golden, 1982) and may eventually become more sick and depressed as a result (Billings *et al.*, 1983; Billings & Moos, 1984; Coyne *et al.*, 1981). Based on earlier work demonstrating their impressive social skills, we thought that high self-monitors could resolve this distress disclosure dilemma. We expected that they could reveal their difficulties in a way and to an extent that would enable them to get the help they need from others, without disturbing and alienating those others. However, as it turns out, neither high nor low self-monitors appear to be completely successful at distress disclosure.

High self-monitors do have more perceived social support than low self-monitors, especially when they are more upset. But high self-monitors do not seem to benefit much from their social support because they are more depressed when they talk problems over with others than low self-monitors are. This is certainly not the first study to suggest that higher levels of social support are not always beneficial, but it does point out another reason for why this occurs. For example, Kobasa (Kobasa, 1984; Kobasa & Pucetti, 1983) found that certain distressed executives were more likely to be sick when they reported more social support from their spouses. Kobasa explains that support from spouses may have helped the executives feel too comfrotable and at ease. Consequently, they were less worried about, and less motivated to solve, their problems on the job, which were the basic sources of their stress and disease. Revenson, Wollman, and Felton (1983) found that cancer patients who reported having more social support also reported having a reduced sense of personal mastery. Apparently, as others did more for the cancer patients, they felt less capable of doing things for themselves. This is quite consistent with other research showing that help from others can sometimes lower self-esteem (see Fisher, Nadler, & Whitcher-Alagna, 1982, for a review) and decrease persistence at important tasks (see Coates, Renzaglia, & Embree, 1983, for a review). However, the present study indicates that social support could also be less than helpful because distressed people may often have to conceal much of the extent and range of their difficulties, as high self-monitors seem to do, in order to retain very much or any help from others. But because any help others do provide in these circumstances will be rather poorly informed, it could frequently turn out to be not very helpful at all, as was apparently the case for the high self-monitors in our study.

High self-monitors were also more likely to report physical symptoms of distress than low self-monitors were, but there was no evidence that this was due to the way they disclosed distress or the social consequences of such disclosures. However, there could be other reasons why the high self-monitors in our study reported more headaches, upset stomachs, and the like. In their research on hypertension and self-monitoring, Sparacino *et al.* (1983) conclude that high self-monitors are less likely to have high blood pressure when they are in occupations where their social skills are useful and likely to pay off but more inclined to suffer from high blood pressure in occupations where their impression management skills do them less good. All of the participants in this study were introductory psychology students, which was one of several very large classes that most of them were taking at a very large university. Students' opportunities to influence the outcome of such courses with social skills are extremely limited because no single student could ordinarily expect or get much direct interaction with the professor. As a result, high self-monitors in large introductory classes, just like those in routinized, inflexible jobs (Sparacino *et al.*, 1983), may experience more frustration and more somatic problems than low self-monitors.

Not only was there little relationship between distress disclosure, social support, and distress symptoms among high self-monitors, reported symptoms were also poorly related to these other variables in the total sample as well. It is somewhat surprising that disclosure and support were not very strongly related to problems like headaches and nausea, given earlier research indicates that these variables are related to serious illness like cancer (Cooper, 1984; Wortman, 1984). We did find that disclosure and support were at least moderately related to the depression measure, but any emotional distress associated with these variables apparently had not been translated into somatic symptoms. Although emotional distress may be an intervening variable between factors like disclosure and support and the development of disease (Okun *et al.*, 1984), other variables, like age and general state of health, may intervene between emotional turmoil and the occurrence of physical symptoms. Because our sample was young and generally healthy, their negative affective states may not yet be having much somatic influence. With an older or more illness-prone sample, stronger connections between support, disclosure, and physical symptoms could well have emerged.

Although high self-monitors are not very successfull at solving the distress disclosure dilemma, neither are low self-monitors. High self-monitors sacrifice their own well-being in order to make their distress disclosure as rewarding as possible for their partners. Low self-monitors appear to sacrifice their partner's well-being in order to make their distress disclosures as rewarding as possible for themselves. Compared to high self-monitors, low self-monitors are less depressed when they regularly talk over problems with others, but they have less social support, especially when they are more upset and inclined to let others know about it. It is somewhat puzzling how low self-monitors manage to benefit emotionally from their distress disclosures despite the evidence that they also decrease their social support with their unhappy revelations. Although there is not very strong support for such a process from past research, perhaps distress disclosure does serve some important intrapersonal functions, like the cathartic reduction of negative feelings (Freud, 1935; also see Stiles's chapter in this volume [12]). If so, distress disclosure could obviously have psychological advantages despite its social disadvantages. It could also be, though, that the complete, intense, and perhaps demanding distress disclosures of low self-monitors are effective in getting immediate help, if not much liking, from others. Just as behaviors are often inconsistent with pertinent attitudes (Wicker, 1969), we will often help others we find rather unlikable (e.g., Lerner & Matthews, 1967). Of course, help offered under such circumstances may well be rather begrudgingly given and quite short-lived (Brickman *et al.*, 1982; Coates & Wortman, 1980), but none the less effective in easing short-term crises and upsets. In a sample of young, healthy, and capable college students, most problems are probably fairly mild and transient, at least when compared to the potential extremes of human misery. In college samples, the vast majority of people who score in the depressed range of the Beck scale fall to nondepressed scores within 2 months' time (Hammen, 1980; Hatzenbuehler, Parpal, & Matthews, 1983). So, even though they may be less satisfied than high self-monitors with the treatment they get when they are depressed, the open and complete distress disclosures of low self-monitors in our study could still be getting them what they need, at least temporarily, from those around them. Nonetheless, when low self-monitors have more serious, chronic, or persistent problems and engage in more frequent distress disclosure as a result, they may well find others increasingly unwilling to help at all (Coates & Wortman, 1980; Coyne *et al.*, 1981; McFarlane *et al.*, 1984).

Neither high nor low self-monitors appear to be very good examples of the successful distress discloser. Clearly, there are people who manage to reveal their troubles and problems to others, while maintaining their social support and enhancing their health and well-being in the process—for example, victims who have confidants and lower depression rates (see Cohen & Wills, 1985, for a review). But our attempt to identify such individuals by their self-monitoring scores did not prove very successful. Perhaps that is because we were looking in the wrong place. Maybe the effectiveness of distress disclosure depends more upon the tolerance and patience of the social environment than the social skills and disclosure style of the distressed individual. Indeed, if others are generally inclined to find distress disclosure unattractive (e.g., Coates *et al.*, 1979), it could well be impossible for distressed people to resolve the dilemma on their own. If they are sensitive and accomodating, like high self-monitors, they will have to conceal much of their woe. If they are blunt and direct, like low self-monitors they will eventually erode others' willingness to help them. The only way out of the distress disclosure dilemma may be to have others around us who do not find such disclosures unappealing, who continue to be supportive while allowing us to fully reveal our troubles. Maybe future research on the distress disclosure dilemma, then, could be more fruitful if it focused on donors rather than recipients of support, investigating individual differences that might be related to tolerance of others' expressed distress (Samter & Burleson, 1984) and interventions aimed at improving comforting skills.

REFERENCES

Alloy, L. B., Abramson, L. Y., & Viscusi, D. (1981). Induced mood and the illusion of control. *Journal of Personality and Social Psychology, 41*, 1129–1140.

Altman, I., & Taylor, D. A. (1973). *Social penetration: The development of interpersonal relationships*. New York: Holt, Rinehart & Winston.

Atkeson, B. M., Calhoun, K. S., Resick, P. A., & Ellis, E. M. (1982). Victims of rape: Repeated assessment of depressive symptoms. *Journal of Consulting and Clinical Psychology, 50*, 96–102.

Barrera, M. & Ainlay, S. L. (1983). The structure of social support: An empirical and conceptual analysis. *Journal of Community Psychology, 11*, 133–143.

Barrera, M., Sandler, I. N., & Ramsay, T. B. (1981). Preliminary development of a scale of social support: Studies on college students. *American Journal of Community Psychology, 9*, 435–447.

Beck, A. T., Ward, C. H., Mendelson, M., Mock, J., & Erlbaugh, J. (1961). An inventory for measuring depression. *Archives of General Psychiatry, 4*, 53–63.

Berman, W. H., & Turk, D. C. (1981). Adaptation to divorce: Problems and coping strategies. *Journal of Marriage and the Family, 18*, 179–189.

Billings, A. G., & Moos, R. H. (1984). Coping, stress, and social resources among adults with unipolar depression. *Journal of Personality and Social Psychology, 46*, 877–891.

Billings, A. G., Cronkite, R. C., & Moos, R. H. (1983). Social-environmental factors in unipolar depression: Comparisons of depressed patients and nondepressed controls. *Journal of Abnormal Psychology, 92*, 119–133.

Brickman, P., Rabinowitz, V. C., Karuza, J., Coates D., Cohn, E., & Kidder, L. (1982). Models of helping and coping. *American Psychologist, 37*, 368–384.

Brown, G. W., & Harris, T. (1978). *Social origins of depression*. London: Tavistock Publications.

Buck, R. (1980). Nonverbal behavior and the theory of emotion: The facial feedback hypothesis. *Journal of Personality and Social Psychology, 38*, 811–824.

Bumberry, W., Oliver, J. M., & McClure, J. (1978). Validation of the Beck Depression Inventory in a university population using psychiatric estimate as a criterion. *Journal of Consulting and Clinical Psychology, 46*, 150–155.

Burke, R. J. (1982). Disclosure of problems and informal helping in work settings. *Psychological Reports, 50*, 811–817.

Burke, R. J., Weir, T., & Duncan, G. (1976). Informal helping processes in work settings. *Academy of Management Journal, 19*, 370–377.

Chelune, G. J. (1976). The Self-Disclosure Situations Survey: A new approach to measuring self-disclosure. *JSAS Catalog of Selected Documents in Psychology, 6*, 111–112.

Chelune, G. J., Sultan, F. E., & Williams, C. L. (1980). Loneliness, self-disclosure, and interpersonal effectiveness. *Journal of Counseling Psychology, 27*, 462–468.

Coates, D., & Peterson, B. A. (1982). Depression and deviance. In G. Weary & H. L. Mirels (Eds.), *Integrations of clinical and social psychology* (pp. 154–170). New York: Oxford University Press.

Coates, D., & Winston, T. (1983). Counteracting the deviance of depression: Peer support groups for victims. *Journal of Social Issues, 39*(2), 169–194.

Coates, D., Renzaglia, G. J., & Embree, M. C. (1983). When helping backfires: Help and helplessness. In J. D. Fisher, A. Nadler, & B. DePaulo (Eds.), *New directions in helping: Recipient reactions to aid* (pp. 251–279). New York: Academic Press.

Coates, D., & Wortman, C. B. (1980). Depression maintenance and interpersonal control. In A. Baum & J. E. Singer (Eds.), *Advances in environmental psychology: Applications of personal control* (Vol. 2, pp. 149–181). Hillsdale, NJ: Lawrence Erlbaum.

Coates, D., Wortman, C. B., & Abbey, A. (1979). Reactions to victim. In I. H. Frieze, D. Bar-Tal, & J. S. Carroll (Eds.), *New approaches to social problems* (pp. 21–52). San Francisco, CA: Jossey-Bass.

Cohen, S., & Wills, T. A. (1985). Stress, social support and the buffering hypothesis. *Psychological Bulletin, 98*, 310–357.

Cooper, C. L. (1984). The social-psychological precursors to cancer. *Journal of Human Stress, 2*, 4–11.

Coppen, A. J., & Metcalfe, M. (1963). Cancer and extraversion. *British Journal of Medicine, 20*, 18–19.

Cooley, E. J., & Keesey, J. C. (1981). Relationship between life change and illness in coping versus sensitive persons. *Psychological Reports, 48*, 711–714.

Coyne, J. C. (1976a). Toward an interactional description of depression. *Psychiatry, 39*, 28–40.

Coyne, J. C. (1976b). Depression and the response of others. *Journal of Abnormal Psychology, 853*, 186–193.

Coyne, J. C. (1985). Studying depressed persons' interactions with strangers and spouses. *Journal of Abnormal Psychology, 90*, 439–447.

Coyne, J. C., Aldwin, C., & Lazarus, R. S. (1981). Depression and coping in stressful episodes. *Journal of Abnormal Psychology, 90*, 439–447.

Creighton, C. (1886). *Illustrations of unconscious memory in disease, including a theory of alternatives*. London: H. K. Lewis.

Darley, J. M., & Latane, B. (1968). Bystander intervention in emergencies: Diffusion of responsibility. *Journal of Personality and Social Psychology, 8*, 377–383.

Dattore, P. J., Shontz, F. C., & Coyne, L. (1980). Premorbid personality differentiation of cancer and noncancer groups: A test of the hypothesis of cancer proneness. *Journal of Consulting and Clinical Psychology, 48*, 388–394.

Derlega, V. J. (1984). Self-disclosure and intimate relationships. In. V. J. Derlega (Ed.), *Communication, intimacy, and close relationships* (pp. 1–9). Orlando, FL: Academic Press.

Derogatis, L. R., Abeloff, M. D., & Melisaratos, N. (1979). Psychological coping mechanisms and survival time in metastatic breast cancer. *Journal of the American Medical Association, 242*, 1504–1508.

Doerfler, L. A., & Chaplin, W. F. (1985). Type III error in research on interpersonal modes of depression. *Journal of Abnormal Psychology, 94*, 227–230.

Falconer, W. (1796). *A dissertation on the influence of the passions upon disorders of the body*. London: C. Dilly.

Fisher, J. D., Nadler, A., & Whitcher-Alagna, S. (1982). Recipient reactions to aid. *Psychological Bulletin, 91*, 27–54.

Freud, S. (1935). *A general introduction to psychoanalysis*. New York: Washington Square Press.
Funabiki, D., Bologna, N. C., Pepping, M., & FitzGerald, K. C. (1980). Revisiting sex differences in the expression of depression. *Journal of Abnormal Psychology, 89,* 194–202.
Furnham, A., & Capon, M. (1983). Social skills and self-monitoring processes. *Personality and Individual Differences, 4,* 171–178.
Gotlib, I. H. (1984). Depression and general psychopathology in university students. *Journal of Abnormal Psychology, 93,* 19–30.
Greer, S., & Morris, T. (1975). Psychological attributes of women who develop breast cancer: A controlled study. *Journal of Psychosomatic Research, 19,* 147–153.
Gurin, G., Veroff, J., & Field, S. (1960). *Americans view their mental health*. New York: Basic Books.
Hammen, C. L. (1980). Depression in college students: Beyond the Beck Depression Inventory. *Journal of Consulting and Clinical Psychology, 48,* 126–128.
Hagnell, O. (1966). The premorbid personality of persons who develop cancer in a total population investigated in 1947 and 1957. In *Psycho-Physiological Aspects of Cancer, Annals of the New York Academy of Sciences, 19,* 846.
Hatzenbuehler, L. C., Parpel, M. C., & Matthews, L. (1983). Classifying students as depressed or nondepressed using the Beck Depression Inventory: An empirical analysis. *Journal of Consulting and Clinical Psychology, 51,* 360–366.
Holden, C. (1978). Cancer and the mind: How are they connected? *Science, 200,* 1363–1369.
Howes, M. J., & Hokanson, J. E. (1979). Conversational and social responses to depressive interpersonal behavior. *Journal of Abnormal Psychology, 88,* 625–634.
Ickes, W., & Barnes, R. D. (1977). The role of sex and self-monitoring in unstructured dyadic interactions. *Journal of Personality and Social Psychology, 35,* 315–330.
Jones, E. E., & Wortman, C. B. (1973). *Ingratiation: An attributional approach*. Morristown, NJ: General Learning Press.
Jourard, S. M. (1971). *The transparent self*. Princeton, NJ: Van Nostrand.
Kleck, R., Ono, H., & Hastorf, A. H. (1966). The effects of physical deviance upon face-to-face interactions. *Human Relations, 19,* 425–436.
Kobasa, S. C. (1984). How much stress can you survive? The answer depends on your personality. *American Health Magazine,* 3(8), 64–77.
Kobasa, S. C., & Pucetti, M. C. (1983). Personality, social resources and stress resistance. *Journal of Personality and Social Psychology, 45,* 839–850.
Konecni, V. J. (1975). The mediation of aggressive behavior: Arousal level vs. anger and cognitive labeling. *Journal of Personality and Social Psychology, 32,* 706–712.
Kopel, S. A. (1982). Commentary: Social psychological processes in the development of maladaptive behaviors. In G. Weary & H. L. Mirels (Eds.), *Integrations of clinical and social psychology* (pp. 171–178). New York: Oxford University Press.
Lerner, M. J., & Matthews, G. (1967). Reactions to the suffering of others under conditions of indirect responsibility. *Journal of Personality and Social Psychology, 5,* 319–327.
Lerner, M. J., & Simmons, C. H. (1966). Observers' reactions to the 'innocent victim': Compassion or rejection? *Journal of Personality and Social Psychology, 4,* 203–210.
Lippa, R. (1978). Expressive control, expressive consistency, and the correspondence between expressive behavior and personality. *Journal of Personality, 46,* 438–461.
Locke, S., & Colligan, D. (1986). *The new medicine of mind and body*. New York: Dutton.
Maguire, C. P. (1982). Psychiatric morbidity associated with mastectomy. In M. Baum (Ed.), *Clinical trials in early breast cancer*. Basel: Birkhausser Verlag.
Maguire, P. (1984). The recognition and treatment of affective disorder in cancer patients. *International Review of Applied Psychology, 33,* 479–491.

Margulis, S. T., Derlega, V. J., & Winstead, B. A. (1984). Implications of social psychological concepts for a theory of loneliness. In V. J. Derlega (Eds.), *Communication, intimacy, and close relationships* (pp. 133–160). Orlando, FL: Academic Press.

Marris, R. (1958). *Widows and their families.* London: Routledge & Kegan Paul.

McCann, C. D., & Hancock, R. D. (1983). Self-monitoring in communicative interactions: Social-cognition consequences of goal-directed message modification. *Journal of Experimental Social Psychology, 19,* 109–121.

McFarlane, A. H., Norman, G. R., Streiner, D. L., & Roy, R. G. (1984). Characteristics and correlates of effective and ineffective social support. *Journal of Psychosomatic Research, 28,* 501–510.

Meyer, C. F., & Taylor, S. E. (1986). Adjustment to rape. *Journal of Personality and Social Psychology, 50,* 1226–1234.

Mill, J. (1984). High and low self-monitoring individuals: Their decoding skills and empathic expression. *Journal of Personality, 52,* 372–388.

Miller, L. C., Berg, J. H., & Archer, R. L. (1983). Openers: Individuals who elicit intimate self-disclosure. *Journal of Personality and Social Psychology, 44,* 1234–1244.

Monroe, S. M., Bellack, A. S., Hersen, M., & Himmelhoch, J. M. (1983). Life events, symptom course, and treatment outcome in unipolar depressed women. *Journal of Consulting and Clinical Psychology, 51,* 604–615.

Nisbett, R. E., Borgida, E., Crandall, R., & Reed, H. (1976). Popular induction: Information is not necessarily informative. In J. S. Carroll & J. W. Payne, (Eds.), *Cognition and social behavior* (pp. 89–111). Hillsdale, NJ: Erlbaum.

Ogden, J. A., & Von Sturmer, G. (1984). Emotional strategies and their relationship to complaints of psychosomatic and neurotic symptoms. *Journal of Clinical Psychology, 40,* 772–779.

Okun, M. A., Stock, W. A., Haring, M. J., & Witter, R. A. (1984). Health and subjective well-being: A meta-analysis. *International Journal of Aging and Human Development, 19,* 111–132.

Parker, G. B., & Brown, L. B. (1982). Coping behaviors that mediate between life events and depression. *Archives of General Psychiatry, 39,* 1386–1391.

Pearlin, L. I., Lieberman, M. A., Menaghan, E. G., & Mullen, J. T. (1981). The stress process. *Journal of Health and Social Behavior, 22,* 337–356.

Pearlin, L. I., & Schooler, C. (1978). The structure of coping. *Journal of Health and Social Behavior, 19,* 2–21.

Perls, F. S. (1969). *Gestalt therapy verbatim.* La Fayette, CA: Real People Press.

Peters-Golden, H. (1982). Breast cancer: Varied perceptions of social support in the illness experience. *Social Science and Medicine, 16,* 483–491.

Procidano, M. E., & Heller, K. (1983). Measures of perceived social support from friends and from family: Three validation studies. *American Journal of Community Psychology, 11,* 1–24.

Raphael, B. (1977). Prevention intervention with the recently bereaved. *Archives of General Psychiatry, 34,* 1450–1454.

Revenson, T. A., Wollman, C. A., & Felton, B. J. (1982). Social supports as stress buffers for adult cancer patients. *Psychosomatic Medicine, 45,* 321–331.

Riggio, R. E., & Friedman, H. S. (1982). The interrelationships of self-monitoring factors, personality traits, and nonverbal social skills. *Journal of Nonverbal Behavior, 7,* 33–45.

Rippere, V. (1977). "What's the thing to do when you're feeling depressed?" —A pilot study. *Behaviour Research and Therapy, 15,* 185–191.

Rook, K. S. (1984). Promoting social bonding: Strategies for helping the lonely and socially isolated. *American Psychologist, 39,* 1389–1407.

Sacco, W., Milana, S., & Dunn, V. (1985). Effect of depression level and length of acquaintance on reactions of others to a request for help. *Journal of Personality and Social Psychology, 49,* 1728–1737.

Samter, W., & Burleson, B. R. (1984). Cognitive and motivational influences on spontaneous comforting behavior. *Human Communication Research, 11,* 231–260.

Sarason, B. R., Sarason, I. G., Hacker, T. A., & Basham, R. B. (1985). Concomitants of social support: Social skills, physical attractiveness and gender. *Journal of Personality and Social Psychology, 49,* 469–480.

Scarf, M. (1980). Images that heal: A doubtful idea whose time has come. *Psychology Today, 14,* 32–46.

Schachter, S. (1959). *The Psychology of Affiliation.* Stanford, California: Stanford University Press.

Schradle, S. B., & Dougher, M. J. (1985). Social support as a mediator of stress: Theoretical and empirical issues Clinical Psychology Review, *5,* 641–661.

Schutz, W. C. (1971). *Here comes everybody.* New York: Harper & Row.

Schwarz, R., & Geyer, S. (1984). Social and psychological differences between cancer and noncancer patients: Causes or consequences of the disease? *Psychotherapy and Psychosomatics, 41,* 195–199.

Schare, M. L., & Lisman, S. A. (1984). Self-statement induction of mood: Some variations and cautions on the Velten procedure. *Journal of Clinical Psychology, 40,* 97–99.

Silver, R. L., & Wortman, C. B. (1980). Coping with undesirable life events. In J. Garber & M. E. P. Seligman (Eds.), *Human helplessness* (pp. 279–340). New York: Academic Press.

Snyder, M. (1974). The self-monitoring of expressive behavior. *Journal of Personality and Social Psychology, 30,* 526–537.

Snyder, M. (1979). Self-monitoring processes. In L. Berkowitz (Ed.), *Advances in experimental social psychology* (Vol. 12, pp. 25–86). New York: Academic Press.

Snyder, M., & Monson, T. C. (1975). Persons, situations, and the control of social behavior. *Journal of Personality and Social Psychology, 32,* 637–644.

Snyder, M., Gangestad, S., & Simpson, J. A. (1983). Choosing friends as activity partners: The role of self-monitoring. *Journal of Personality and Social Psychology, 45,* 1061–1072.

Solano, C. H., Batten, P. G., & Parish, E. A. (1982). Loneliness and patterns of self-disclosure. *Journal of Personality and Social Psychology, 43,* 524–531.

Sparacino, J., Ronchi, D., Bigley, T. K., Flesch, A. L., & Kuhn, J. W. (1983). Self-monitoring and blood pressure. *Journal of Personality and Social Psychology, 44,* 365–375.

Strack, S., & Coyne, J. C. (1983). Social confirmation of dysphoria: Shared and private reactions to depression. *Journal of Personality and Social Psychology, 44,* 798–806.

Thomas, C. B., & Greenstreet, R. L. (1973). Psychobiological characteristics in youth as predictors of five disease states: Suicide, mental illness, hypertension, coronary heart disease and tumor. *Johns Hopkins Medical Journal, 132,* 16–43.

Vachon, M. L. S., Rogers, J., Lyall, W. A., Lancee, W. J., Sheldon, A. R., & Freeman, S. J. J. (1982). Predictors and correlates of adaptation to conjugal bereavement. *American Journal of Psychiatry, 139,* 998–1002.

Watson, M., Pettingale, K. W., & Greer, S. (1984). Emotional control and autonomic arousal in breast cancer patients. *Journal of Psychosomatic Research, 28,* 467–474.

Wicker, A. W. (1969). Attitudes versus actions: The relationship of verbal and overt behavioral responses to attitude objects. *Journal of Social Issues, 25*(4), 41–78.

Winer, D. L., Bonner, T. O., Blaney, P. H., & Murray, E. J. (1981). Depression and social attraction. *Motivation and Emotion, 5,* 153–166.

Wortman, C. B. (1984). Social support and the cancer patient: Conceptual and methodological issues. *Cancer, 53,* 2339–2362.

12

"I Have to Talk to Somebody"

A Fever Model of Disclosure

WILLIAM B. STILES

In this chapter, I consider some consequences of the propositions (a) that people tend to disclose when they are distressed and (b) that they obtain some benefit from doing so. To put it more strongly, I propose that the amount of disclosure tends to increase with the intensity of a person's distress and that this disclosure tends to help to relieve the distress. I call this a *fever model* because it suggests that disclosure's relation to psychological distress is analogous to a fever's relation to physical infection: both are a sign of disturbance and part of a restorative process.

This chapter first offers a definition of disclosure. Then it reviews disclosure's association with psychological distress and with relief from distress, offering a theoretical understanding of each. Next it considers the central importance of client disclosure in psychotherapy and discusses how the fever model can help resolve three seeming paradoxes in the psychotherapy research literature: first, that high disclosure is associated both with sickness and with restoration of health, that is, with neurosis, anxiety, and depression and with psychotherapeutic "good process," as judged by experts; second, that despite demonstrations that client disclosure represents good psychotherapeutic process, greater disclosure is not consistently associated empirically with better psychotherapeutic outcomes; and third, that although therapists' verbal techniques

WILLIAM B. STILES • Department of Psychology, Miami University, Oxford, Ohio 45056.

vary greatly depending on their theoretical approach, reviews of psychotherapy outcome research show little or no differential effectiveness of different psychotherapies—that is, outcomes appear equivalent even though contents appear nonequivalent (Stiles, Shapiro, & Elliott, 1986).

Then this chapter focuses on the social meanings of disclosure. Although the fever model takes an intrapsychic starting point, it has implications for target selection (who will be disclosed to when a person is distressed), for the intimacy and relative status of the discloser in his or her social relationships, and for the strategic use of disclosure. Finally, this chapter suggests some questions and directions for further research.

DEFINITION OF DISCLOSURE

For the fever model, disclosure is defined as an utterance (e.g., a sentence or an independent clause) that concerns the speaker's experience and uses the speaker's internal (subjective) frame of reference (Stiles, 1978, 1981). Thus disclosures are distinguished from attentive utterances, which concern the other person's experience (e.g., questions, acknowledgements, reflections, judgments, or interpretations of the other), and from informative utterances that use an external, objective frame of reference (statements of fact, descriptions of observable events). This definition also specifies that in the fever model, disclosure (a) refers to observable behavior rather than questionnaire responses, (b) is a discrete category rather than a continuously measured dimension, and (c) concerns the intersubjective, relational aspect of speech rather than its content.

To elaborate, disclosure here refers to the disclosing behavior itself, not to self-report measures, such as Jourard's (1971a) Self-Disclosure Questionnaire or Miller, Berg, and Archer's (1983) Self-Disclosure Index. As reviewed elsewhere in this volume, evidence of behavioral prediction from such questionnaires is mixed, though it seems to be better if the target as well as the content is specified (Miller *et al.*, 1983).

Disclosure here is measured by coding rather than rating. Rating measures are continuous scales, and they can be applied to a discourse segment of any length. They assess the degree to which disclosure has taken place, or in some cases the revealingness, intimacy, or some other quality of the disclosure. A particularly well-developed rating scale for disclosure in psychotherapy is the Experiencing Scale (Klein, Mathieu, Gendlin, & Kiesler, 1969; Klein, Mathieu-Coughlin, & Kiesler, 1986), which "attempts to assess the degree to which the patient communicates his personal, phenomenological perspective and employs it productively in the therapy session" (Klein *et al.*, 1969, p. 1). Coding measures are categories to which discrete segments of speech (e.g., speech turns, sentences, or utterances) are assigned.

Most coding categories used to classify psychotherapeutic discourse (or other social discourse) can themselves be classified as content categories, intersubjective categories, or paralinguistic categories (Russell & Stiles, 1979). Content categories concern the denotative or connotative meaning of what is said, for example, "references to family members" or "positive feelings." Categories based on standard tables of revealing or embarrassing topics are content categories. Intersubjective categories concern the (illocutionary) speech acts that are performed (cf. Searle, 1969; Stiles, 1981)—what is *done* by the speaker, for example, "question," "command," "blame," rather than what is *said*. Intersubjective categories are implicitly relational—they imply an other as well as a speaker (one asks another person a question, blames another person, etc.). Paralinguistic categories concern the nonverbal accompaniments to language—the style or manner in which things are said, for example, the "focused" voice tone that Rice (Rice & Koke, 1981; Rice & Wagstaff, 1967) has found to signal productive psychotherapeutic process.

Psychotherapy research on disclosure has most often used intersubjective definitions (Elliott *et al.*, 1982; Goodman & Dooley, 1976). (However, social psychological research has more often used content definitions.) I have used an intersubjective definition in my own psychotherapy research (McDaniel, Stiles, & McGaughey, 1981; Stiles, 1979, 1984; Stiles, McDaniel & McGaughey, 1979; Stiles & Sultan, 1979), and I use this definition for the fever model: Disclosure *form* is defined syntactically, as a first-person declarative utterance. Disclosure *intent* is defined as expressing the speaker's experience from the speaker's own internal frame of reference, that is, as revealing subjective information. "Pure disclosures" are thus first-person statements that reveal subjective information. Subjective information is distinguished from objective information by asking whether access to the speaker's private awareness is necessary for determining the truth or sincerity of the utterance. Thus the criterion for judging a statement's intent as disclosure is its epistemological status (private versus public criterion of truth) rather than its social meaning. To illustrate, "I've been very lonely" is a pure disclosure—a first-person statement, the truth of which depends on the speaker's private experience. "It has been difficult for me" is disclosure in intent but not in form because it is third person. "I seldom go out of the house at night" is disclosure in form but not in intent, insofar as access to the speaker's private experience is not necessary, in principle, for determining the utterance's truth. Disclosure defined in this way can be coded in tapes and transcripts of psychotherapeutic and other discourse with high reliability (e.g., Cansler & Stiles, 1981; Stiles, 1984). By adhering to this intersubjective definition (particularly the frame of reference criterion) even when it conflicts with content definitions, the fever model can be more precisely meshed with other theoretical accounts of psychopathology and psychotherapeutic change (e.g., see discussion of Rogers, 1951, 1958, later).

It is easy to manufacture examples that make the fever model definition seem at odds with an intuitive notion of disclosure. For example, the bland statement, "I feel fine today," is coded as disclosure (first person, reveals subjective information), whereas "My father had incestuous relations with me when I was a child" is not (the information is objective, even though feelings about it are likely to be intense). On the other hand, revelations of such affectively charged facts seem likely to be surrounded by expressions of feeling. Empirical comparisons of intersubjective measures of disclosure with content measures (Morton, 1978) and with rating-based indexes of psychotherapeutic "good process" (Klein *et al.*, 1986; McDaniel *et al.*, 1981; Stiles *et al.*, 1979) show substantial convergence. Thus for aggregated measures (i.e., measures of degree of disclosure across a substantial sample of discourse), alternative definitions appear likely to give similar results.

Within the intersubjective definition of disclosure, it is possible to make many further distinctions—deep versus shallow, sincere versus insincere, feelings versus thoughts, here and now versus there and then, and so on. Each disclosure subtype presumably serves different functions, and the fever model is not intended to deny the importance of these differences. However, the fever model focuses on the common property that all reveal epistemologically private information.

A distinction that is important for the fever model is between *expressive* and *strategic* functions of disclosure (see Davis & Franzoi, Chapter 4, this volume; Derlega & Grzelak, 1979). Expressive functions are intrinsic—purposes or benefits of disclosing that come from the act itself, particularly catharsis and self-understanding. Strategic functions are extrinsic or instrumental—purposes or benefits that come from the external consequences of disclosure, principally effects on the intimacy, status, or other aspects of relationships with other people. Probably every disclosure serves some mixture of expressive and strategic functions; however, it is useful to use the term *expressive disclosure* or *strategic disclosure* depending on which function is predominant.

The fever model is concerned primarily with expressive disclosure. Later I will argue that the fever model suggests ways in which the strategic functions are derived from, and in that sense are secondary to, the expressive functions.

A FEVER MODEL OF EXPRESSIVE DISCLOSURE

Disclosure and Psychological Distress

Why do people disclose? People who are distressed are preoccupied with their problems. They may be described as trapped in their own frame of reference. That is, the subjective meaning of events—including the feelings that are engendered—become so salient and so persistent that they overwhelm other thinking. A person in psychological distress finds it difficult to view events objectively or from others' perspectives; instead, he or she is preoccupied with internal states and meanings. This preoccupation tends to be represented in speech: distressed people talk about their distress (Carpenter, Chapter 10, this volume; Coates & Winston, Chapter 11, this volume; Coyne, 1976a,b; Funabiki, Bologna, Pepping, & Fitzgerald, 1980; Lorentz & Cobb, 1953; McDaniel *et al.*, 1981; Parker & Brown, 1982; Persons & Marks, 1970; Rippere, 1977; Silver & Wortman, 1980; Weintraub, 1981; Wortman & Dunkell-Schetter, 1980). Such talk is rich in disclosure.

As represented in this chapter's title, "I have to talk to somebody," upsetting or stressful events generate a subjective sense of pressure, of something being bottled up. Often the pressure incorporates emotion—usually anger, despair, fear, remorse, or some other negative feeling, though great joy and happiness can also impell people to disclose. Although the pressure is probably greatest immediately or shortly afterward, powerful or psychologically important events can leave a need to talk that lasts for months or years (e.g., bereavement, war experiences). The distress may result from an isolated traumatic event, from enduring social or environmental stressors, or from the individual's internal psychological makeup (or any combination); regardless of its source, according to the model, it must be expressed (e.g., via disclosure) or actively inhibited (cf. Pennebaker & Hoover, 1985). If the distress arises from the interplay of the person's personality with his or her social situation, the pressure to disclose can become a more or less permanent feature of his or her social relationships.

The mechanism by which distress leads to disclosure may be construed as an increase in private self-consciousness, as discussed by Davis and Franzoi (Chapter 4, this volume). Powerful emotion forces attention to internal, subjective matters, and hence away from external, objective matters. As Davis and Franzoi point out, there are several possible paths by which an intensified private self-consciousness might lead to high disclosure, including greater availability of subjective material to awareness because of accumulated subjective knowledge or because of greater salience, or functional motivation for catharsis and self-understanding.

The fever model suggests that disclosure varies with psychological distress both across time (for individuals) and across people (see reviews by Coates & Winston, Chapter 11, this volume, Silver & Wortman, 1980). Across time, in a study of psychotherapeutic interaction (Stiles, 1984), the level of client disclosure was higher in sessions rated by the client, therapist, and external rater as relatively rough on the Session Evaluation Questionnaire's Smoothness Index, which reflects perceived client comfort versus distress (Stiles, 1980). People who have experienced trauma, bereavement, or other great stress report that they confide more in others (Coates & Winston, Chapter 11, this volume; Pennebaker & Hoover, 1985; Silver & Wortman, 1980). Oddly, although distressed people's tendency to disclose their distress is well known, there appears to be no systematic documentation that life stress leads to higher levels of observable disclosing behavior in discourse samples of nonpsychotherapeutic interaction.

The association across people of high levels of disclosure with psychological dysfunction—neurosis, anxiety, depression, and other psychological disturbance—is well documented (Coyne, 1976a,b; Lorentz & Cobb, 1953; McDaniel *et al.*, 1981; Persons & Marks, 1970; Weintraub, 1981; Wortman & Dunkell-Schetter, 1980). For example, Weintraub (1981) asked psychiatric inpatients representing several diagnostic groups to speak into a tape recorder for 10 minutes and coded their productions into several speech categories. In comparison to normal (nondistressed) controls, the patient (distressed) groups used a substantially larger proportion of disclosures. McDaniel *et al.* (1981) coded all client utterances in three of their psychotherapy sessions and found substantial correlations of clients' percentage of disclosure with pretherapy measures of disturbance, including the Minnesota Multiphasic Personality Inventory (MMPI) Depression scale and ratings of psychological distress made by the therapist and by an independent interviewer, as well as by the clients themselves.

Disclosure and neuroticism may be uncorrelated or negatively correlated when disclosure is measured by the Jourard Self-Disclosure Questionnaire (Johnson, 1981; Mayo, 1968; Stanley & Bownes, 1966). Perhaps the questionnaire measures felt freedom to disclose or the sense of being known to another, rather than frequency of disclosing utterances. It is possible that relatively neurotic individuals *feel* as though they are unable to disclose their concerns, even though their talk actually contains relatively many subjective statements. (They may be preoccupied with their feelings but unable to reveal the roots of their difficulties, in effect, feeling an even greater self-preoccupation than they show.) This point urgently requires research.

It should be noted that the evidence associating distress and disclosure is correlational. The fever model, as well as other models offered in this volume (e.g., Coates and Winston's, Chapter 11, and Davis and Franzoi's, Chapter 4), implies a causal direction: distress *produces* disclosure. However, the evidence permits other possibilities, for example, that excessive disclosure is in itself distressing or that some other factor leads to both distress and disclosure (see Carpenter, Chapter 10 this volume, for a discussion).

Sometimes—because of the nature of the distress, the distressed person's personality or role, the audience, or the social context—preoccupation with self is displaced or expressed in some indirect way. For some people, preoccupation with bodily states, symptoms, or illnesses can serve (almost metaphorically) as a substitute for thinking about underlying sources of psychological distress. For others, a particular subject, such as politics or morality, can provide a symbolic substitute. In such cases, the resulting talk is only barely recognizable as disclosure, though it shares a compulsive, inattentive quality with more obvious disclosures of distress.

Intrapsychic Benefits of Disclosure: Catharsis and Self-Understanding

The fever model holds that distressed people benefit from their expressive disclosing. Among these benefits are catharsis and self-understanding (cf. Davis & Franzoi, Chapter 4, this volume; Derlega & Grzelak, 1979).

Catharsis. There is a primitive sense of relief that arises from successfully explaining a personal difficulty to another person. This cathartic effect, described as "getting it off my chest," "getting it out in the open," and so on, seems to require (or at least seems much facilitated by) some indication of receipt or understanding from the other. But the benefit seems more related to the depth and extent of the disclosure itself and especially to the intensity of accompanying affect than to any specific quality of the other's response, at least so long as the response is an accepting one (see Berg, Chapter 6, this volume; Hendrick, Chapter 14, this volume).

Catharsis is an old concept in psychotherapy theory and has long been recognized as important in bereavement (Glick, Weiss, & Parkes, 1974; Lindemann, 1944). Freud (1935; Freud & Breuer, 1893–1895/1966) considered it as the fundamental active ingredient in the early versions of the "talking cure," though he later rejected it because its beneficial effects on his patients seemed transitory. Presumably, his patients' difficulties arose from an interaction of events with underlying neurotic conflicts; catharsis might be sufficient when no personality problems are implicated, for example, for victims of trauma or bereavement (but see Coates & Winston, 1983, Chapter 11, this volume, for a less sanguine view of catharsis).

Victims of stress, trauma, or bereavement are less likely to become depressed or to develop physical symptoms if they confide their feelings in trusted others (Atkeson, Calhoun, Resnick, & Ellis, 1982; Berman & Turk, 1981; Brown & Harris, 1978; Burgess & Holmstrom, 1974; Pennebaker & O'Heeron, 1984; Vachon *et al.*, 1982; see reviews by Pennebaker & Hoover, 1985; Silver & Wortman, 1980). Pennebaker and his associates (Pennebaker & Hoover, 1985; Pennebaker & O'Heeron, 1984) have argued (consistent with the fever model) that the inhibition of disclosure following a traumatic event (i.e., the lack of catharsis) produces a chronic physiological arousal that ultimately results in physical symptoms.

Self-Understanding. Another, perhaps more lasting intrinsic benefit of disclosure is the growth of self-awareness, self-acceptance, and self-understanding, or insight. This process has been extensively discussed by psychotherapy theorists, and it appears to lie at the core of many psychotherapies. Rogers's client-centered theory expresses this in a way that is directly consistent with the fever model.

As conceptualized by Rogers (1951, 1958), psychotherapy involves an alteration of the client's "self" through recognizing, facing, and reevaluating its inconsistencies. Because the client is the only person who can fully know his or her own field of experience, the best vantage point for facilitating change is from the client's internal frame of reference—the constellation of associated experiences, perceptions, ideas, feelings, memories, and so forth, from which an experience gets its meaning. In therapeutic discourse, a client can place an experience either in an external, objective frame of reference or in an internal, subjective frame of reference. That is, a client can either give objective descriptions of events or reveal the events' personal meanings, feelings, and values.

The self, according to Rogers, is a differentiated portion of the organism's perceptual field; hence it consists of experiences:

> an organized, fluid, but consistent conceptual pattern of characteristics and relations of the *I* or the *me* together with the values attached to these concepts. (Rogers, 1951, p. 498)

Thus, at least in part, the self *is* the client's internal frame of reference. When a person reveals the personal meaning of an experience, that meaning consists of the experience's relation to the self. Talk that uses the client's internal frame of reference (i.e., disclosure) should thus be therapeutic because it brings distorted or misvalued experiences and inconsistent feelings to awareness, where they can be reevaluated, reconciled with the self, and accepted. Talk that uses an external frame of reference (i.e, reciting of objective information) does not serve psychotherapeutic purposes because it fails to expose the relation of events to the self (see Hendrick, Chapter 14, this volume).

To the extent that distorted or misvalued experiences are remnants of earlier distress, the growth of self-understanding may itself involve stress. Psychotherapy may lead to reexperiencing elements of old or chronic stresses, disclosing about them, and obtaining relief. Thus psychotherapy may actually create distress in the short term, while providing a setting in which it can be freely disclosed.

Disclosure and Psychological Homeostasis

Taken together, the propositions that distress leads to disclosure and that disclosure leads to relief imply that disclosure helps automatically to maintain psychological adjustment, analogous to the way body temperature or blood leukocyte levels help to maintain physiological homeostasis. The fever model holds that disclosure is an element in a natural, internally regulated process of maintaining psychological well-being. It suggests that an individual's level of disclosure normally rises and falls to express (and thus come to terms with) the emotional meaning of day-to-day life experiences.

It follows that under normal circumstances (e.g., social availability of suitable recipients), the level of an individual's disclosing will approximate an optimum level, analogous to the homeostatically regulated variables that constitute the "wisdom of the body."

Disorders of Disclosure Regulation. This automatic mechanism may not work perfectly for all individuals. Some people may be blocked in their ability to disclose, for external (social) or internal (psychological) reasons. For example, some people may have no relationships that are suitable for free disclosure (Stokes, Chapter 9, this volume), analogous to hypothermia brought on by exposure. For others, psychological defensiveness may inhibit disclosure (cf. discussion of self-defense motive by Davis & Franzoi, Chapter 4, this volume). Other reasons include lack of social skills (Jones, Hobbs, & Hockenbury, 1982; Solano, Batten, & Parish, 1982) or socialization for stoicism or for otherwise nondisclosing roles (cf. Derlega & Grzelak, 1979; Hill & Stokes, Chapter 5, this volume), analogous to an acquired immune deficiency, that is, an inability to react restoratively to psychological disturbance.

On the other hand, some people may disclose excessively or counterproductively, analogous to autoimmune fevers, as in rheumatoid arthritis. Scherwitz and his colleagues (Scherwitz, Graham, & Ornish, 1985; Sherwitz, McKelvain, Laman *et al.*, 1983) have presented persuasive evidence that high levels of self-involvement, measured by the incidence of self-references (use of "I," "me," "my," "mine") in a standard interview, are significantly predictive of risk of coronary heart disease. Following a logic similar to Davis and Franzoi's (Chapter 4, this volume), Scherwitz argues that self-references reflect higher internal attention to self and, following a logic similar to Pennebaker and Hoover's (1985), that such self-involvement is physiologically arousing and stressful to the cardiovascular system. It seems possible that excessive self-involvement may be understood, in part, as a disorder of disclosure regulation.

Although an inability to disclose appropriately need not imply other psychological disorders, it is likely (according to the fever model) to lead to difficulties in dealing with life's stresses (cf. Gendlin, 1978; Gendlin, Beebe, Cassens, Klein, & Oberlander, 1968).

The suggestion that some people inhibit disclosure, whereas others disclose excessively recalls Jourard's (1971a,b) theory that disclosure levels bear a curvilinear relation to adjustment. However, as just reviewed, the fever model distinguishes high disclosure attributable to distress (a normal restorative response) from high disclosure attributable to specific disclosure-related personality problems (e.g., excessive self-involvement). In the same way, the fever model distinguishes low disclosure attributable to low distress (healthy concern for other people and events) from low disclosure attributable to social impediments (e.g., roles that inhibit disclosure) or psychological blocks (e.g., defensiveness about troubling experiences).

CLIENT DISCLOSURE IN PSYCHOTHERAPY

Psychotherapy offers a setting, a role, and even a vocabulary through which the benefits of expressive disclosure (i.e., catharsis and self-understanding) can be realized. Coding studies show that client disclosure is a central and characteristic feature of psychotherapy. On average, one half to two thirds of client utterances in therapy have disclosure intent, that is, reveal subjective experience (McDaniel *et al.*, 1981; Stiles, 1984; Stiles & Sultan, 1979). This preponderance of disclosure distinguishes psychotherapy clients' speech from that of people in other expository roles, such as general medical patients giving a medical history (Stiles, Putnam, & Jacob, 1982) or people in social conversation (Premo & Stiles, 1983).

Client Disclosure and the Fever Model

The fever model explains clients' unusually high levels of disclosure as follows: Clients come to therapy precisely because they are distressed, so that they can discuss their troubles. In therapy, clients can experience the cathartic relief of disclosure ("I've never told anyone this before") and can come to terms with the upsetting forces in their lives by examining their own subjective responses to them. The setting allows clients to disclose freely without fear of damaging social relationships. The client role is systematically designed to encourage disclosure, even by individuals who have no external intimate relationships or who lack the social skills to form them. In the absence of social constraints, the distress-produced pressure to disclose can be released.

A high level of client disclosure is consonant with the purposes of counseling and psychotherapy as viewed from a variety of theoretical perspectives (e.g., Gendlin, 1978; Greenson, 1967; Jourard, 1971a,b; Perls, 1969; Rogers's, 1951, 1958, client-centered theory, as mentioned before; Schutz, 1971; see also Hendrick, Chapter 14, this volume). It is through disclosing to the therapist that clients can come to know and accept their own experience, to learn of their unconscious impulses, or to form and express an authentic (or transference) relationship with the therapist.

In addition to being trustworthy and receptive listeners, psychotherapists may provide a vocabulary in which clients can express their feelings. For example, the reflections that client-centered therapists use to help the client "symbolize" (i.e., put into words) his or her internal experience may also help clarify terms and thus make disclosure more efficient (cf. Berg, Chapter 6, this volume). Even behaviorally oriented treatments routinely provide a vocabulary by which clients can express themselves (Kornblith, Rhem, O'Hara, & Lamparski, 1983).

Disclosure and Psychotherapeutic Good Process

Implicitly or explicitly, depending on their theory, knowledgeable observers recognize disclosure's contribution to beneficial counseling and psychotherapeutic process. It is so much a part of the concept of good process that many studies have used clients' disclosure, or willingness to disclose, as a measure or even an implicit criterion of good process (e.g., Bundza & Simonson, 1973; Chesner & Baumeister, 1985; DeForest & Stone, 1980; Derlega, Lovell, & Chaikin, 1976; Halpern, 1977; Riley, Cozby, White, & Kjos, 1983; Simonson, 1976; see review by Hendrick, Chapter 14, this volume). Empirically, observers such as professional psychotherapists or clinical psychology graduate students give better ratings to segments of therapeutic discourse that contain higher levels of client disclosure (see review by Klein *et al.*, 1986). In one study (Stiles *et al.*, 1979), the percentage of client utterances coded as disclosure in brief segments of interviews was correlated .58 with those segments' ratings on the Experiencing Scale, a fully anchored 7-point rating scale designed to measure the primary client process variable in client-centered therapy (Gendlin *et al.*, 1968; Gendlin & Tomlinson, 1967; Kiesler, 1971; Klein *et al.*, 1969, 1986; Rogers, 1958). In another study (McDaniel *et al.*, 1981), clients' percentage of disclosure was correlated .66 with Patient Exploration and .65 with Therapist Exploration, as measured by the Vanderbilt Psychotherapy Process Scale (Gomes-Schwartz, 1978; O'Malley, Suh, & Strupp, 1983), a more psychodynamically oriented measure. These correlations confirm empirically the conceptual convergence of utterance-level coding measures of disclosure with more impressionistic good process ratings.

Three Paradoxes and Possible Resolutions

The fever model offers resolutions to three seeming paradoxes in the psychotherapy research literature. The first paradox is the seeming association of disclosure with both sickness and with restoration health: as reviewed before, disclosure increases with psychological distress and dysfunction (depression, neurosis, trauma, bereavement), but high disclosure is also judged to represent good psychotherapeutic process and thus health. The fever model shows that there need be no contradiction; like a fever, disclosure can be both an index of dysfunction and part of a "homeostatic" corrective response. By disclosing, a person both signals distress and relieves distress. Thus the fever model's resolution is that the association with sickness takes a cross-sectional perspective, comparing disclosure rates with distress at a point in people's lives, whereas the association with restoration of health takes a longitudinal perspective, comparing disclosure rates with *movement toward* health.

The second paradox concerns the failure of disclosure levels to accurately predict psychotherapy outcome. Despite the strong theoretical and empirical reasons why high levels of client disclosure, experiencing, or exploration are desirable, empirical tests have failed to demonstrate clear positive correlations between these "good process" measures and psychotherapy outcome. Results are inconsistent across studies (Gendlin *et al.*, 1968; Gomes-Schwartz, 1978; Kiesler, 1971; Klein *et al.*, 1986; McDaniel *et al.*, 1981; Strassberg, Anchor, Gabel, & Cohen, 1978). The fever model suggests that clients normally disclose at optimum levels; those who are more distressed tend to disclose more and therefore are (appropriately) judged by experts as making good use of the setting. However, the more distressed clients do not necessarily have better outcomes. Indeed, one might expect clients who are initially more dysfunctional to have worse outcomes. Moreover, as clients improve, they presumably feel less distressed, and their rate of disclosure should decrease; so their average level (across many sessions) may be lower than the level for clients who fail to improve. (Disclosure does not solve all problems.) For these reasons, process-outcome correlations get muddled. More generally, the fever model's resolution is a statistical one: variation in disclosure (across clients) will not predict variation in outcome because disclosure is normally at an optimum level. Outcomes would not be better if clients disclosed more. Disclosure-outcome correlations would be high only if many clients had substantial deficiencies in their ability to disclose (i.e., if many people were unable to make use of the opportunity psychotherapy provided). Expressed as an analogy, one would not expect measures of recovery from physical infection to be positively correlated with the degree of elevation in body temperature or leukocyte level, even though these indexes directly reflect the process of recovery.

The third paradox is that despite the plethora of purportedly distinct psychotherapeutic treatments (Abt & Stuart, 1982; Goldfried, 1980; Parloff, 1976), influential reviews of comparative outcome research (Luborsky, Singer, & Luborsky, 1975; Smith & Glass, 1977; Smith, Glass, & Miller, 1980), together with frequently cited studies (e.g., Sloane, Staples, Cristol, Yorkston, & Whipple, 1975), have reported no differential effectiveness.

> Despite volumes devoted to the theoretical differences among different schools of psychotherapy, the results of research demonstrate negligible differences in the effects produced by different therapy types. (Smith & Glass, 1977, p. 760)

In contrast to this apparent equivalence of outcome, psychotherapists' verbal interventions vary greatly and systematically depending on their theoretical orientations (Brunink & Schroeder, 1979; DeRubeis, Hollon, Evans, & Bemis, 1982; Hill, Thames, & Rardin, 1979; Luborsky, Woody, McClellan, O'Brien, & Rosenzweig, 1982; Stiles, 1979; Strupp, 1955). There really are different ingredients in the different psychotherapies, although which of these are active and which are flavors and fillers remain undetermined. This paradox has been very troubling because it suggests that it does not matter what the therapist does, an unpalatable conclusion for professional psychotherapists. An impressive variety of resolutions of this paradox have been offered, and an enormous amount of research has been generated (Stiles *et al.*, 1986).

The fever model's resolution is that client disclosure represents a major restorative process that is common across psychotherapies, regardless of the therapist's techniques. The outcome equivalence may, *in part,* reflect this common core process. This resolution rests on the observation that, despite the great variation in therapists' behaviors, clients' verbal behaviors are strikingly consistent across therapeutic styles, and, as noted before, they consist largely of disclosure (McDaniel *et al.*, 1981; Stiles, 1984; Stiles & Sultan, 1979). Thus client disclosure is a prominent common ingredient of different psychotherapies; the fever model suggests that it is an active ingredient. (Of course, this is not to say that disclosure is the *only* active ingredient.)

Is More Disclosure Better?

The fever model's suggestion that disclosure is a common active ingredient of many different psychotherapies does not imply that more disclosure is necessarily better or that everyone would benefit from high levels of disclosure (cf. Jourard, 1971b). By analogy, a fever would not benefit someone who had no physical infection. Similarly, manipulating or forcing distressed people to disclose more than they do may not be helpful, just as artificially increasing the fever of someone who is ill is unlikely to promote faster recovery.

The fever model implies that expressive disclosure is a homeostatic restorative mechanism—part of the "wisdom of the body," perhaps a component of an "actualizing tendency." It should normally be most beneficial to allow it free reign rather than to artificially increase or decrease it.

Of course, as noted before, some distressed people who show up in therapy may be blocked in their ability to disclose, perhaps because of defensiveness (Davis & Franzoi, Chapter 4, this volume), early training for stoicism, or constricting social norms (e.g., see the discussion of sex roles and disclosure by Hill & Stull, Chapter 5, this volume; Derlega & Grzelak, 1979). For such people, training in intensive disclosure, such as that offered by Gendlin (1978), could enhance their ability to make use of psychotherapy or of their friends.

Disclosure and Social Support. The fever model suggests that it is normally not necessary to actively intervene to alter disclosure levels, as these are self-regulating. A more constructive intervention might be to provide a setting in which high levels of disclosure can take place, for example, professional counseling or psychotherapy, peer counseling, self-help groups, or arrangements with family or friends.

The model offers a mechanism for the hypothesized buffering effect of social support on stress (Caplan, 1974; Cobb, 1976; but see Billings & Moos, 1984). People with strong interpersonal relationships, in which they can disclose freely, use these relationships when stress arises.

However, not everyone has adequately supportive, trusting relationships, in some cases because they lack the social skills required to establish or maintain intimacy (Jones *et al.*, 1982; Solano *et al.*, 1982, Stokes, Chapter 9, this volume). Counseling or psychotherapy may be particularly useful for people who currently have no intimate relationships.

SOCIAL MEANINGS OF DISCLOSURE

The fever model takes an intrapsychic starting point. It describes disclosure as a response to internally felt distress, independent of its interpersonal functions (i.e., it concerns expressive disclosure). However, as emphasized in many of this volume's other chapters, disclosure is replete with social meaning and may be undertaken in pursuit of external social goals (see, for example, the executive model proposed by Miller and Read, Chapter 3, this volume). It makes much difference to whom and under what conditions one discloses. Insofar as social meanings constrain disclosure, they delimit the fever model.

Intimacy and Status Effects

Disclosure figures prominently on two of the principal dimensions of social relations—intimacy and status (Derlega, 1984; Derlega & Chaikin, 1977; Derlega & Grzelak, 1979; McAdams, 1984). Between equals, disclosure promotes intimacy, partly by the revelation of private knowledge and feelings to another and partly by demanding reciprocity. Widening and deepening of mutual disclosure is characteristic of the growth of intimacy, and a feeling of knowing and being known to another is a central feature of intimate relationships (Altman, 1973; Altman & Taylor, 1973; Baxter, Chapter 8, this volume; Derlega, 1984; Worthy, Gary, & Kahn, 1969).

With respect to status and power, disclosure appears to demote the speaker relative to the other or at least to confirm the speaker's relative inferiority. For example, Slobin, Miller, and Porter (1968) showed that employees in a large business tended to disclose to their immediate superiors and to receive disclosures from their immediate subordinates much more than the reverse. In laboratory tasks, with instructions merely to discuss a topic or a problem (i.e., without explicitly assigned roles), freshmen disclosed more to seniors than vice-versa and seniors disclosed more to professors than vice-versa (Cansler & Stiles, 1981), and children disclosed more to parents than vice versa (Stiles & White, 1981). Some family therapists (e.g., Minuchin, 1974) enjoin parents not to confide too much in their children, in order to preserve intergenerational boundaries (status as well as intimacy). By contrast, children are permitted to disclose to parents, although they may choose not to do so in adolescence, when they begin to compete for adult status.

The mechanism of disclosure's contribution to deference is not so well understood as the role of reciprocity in disclosure's contribution to intimacy (see Derlega & Grezelak, 1979, for a discussion of norms affecting disclosure). Perhaps the deference function, like the intimacy function, depends on making the speaker vulnerable (cf. Derlega & Chaikin, 1977)—analogous to wolves exposing their throats to higher-ranking members of the pack to display deference (as well as trust!), communicating an intention not to challenge the superior's position. Presumably, the discloser gains from such behavior by deflecting aggressive assertions of dominance by the superior. That is, by making himself or herself vulnerable, the discloser acknowledges the superior's power and thereby gains trust and sympathy. Feeling secure in his or her status, the superior need not exercise the potentially destructive power over the discloser.

Like throat exposing, expressive disclosure can make the speaker truly vulnerable (Hatfield, 1984) and hence can demonstrate real trust and real submission to the other. However, disclosure may also be used symbolically—to deepen acquaintance or to express deference even though the disclosure's content is not particularly sensitive or potentially embarrassing. Furthermore, selective disclosure may not really express intimacy or deference. (See later discussion of strategic disclosure.)

Outlets for Expressive Disclosure

Theoretically, because of the social implications of disclosure (greater intimacy, lower status), the benefits of expressive disclosure can be realized only in a relationship that is *safe* in two senses. First, the recipient and the situation must be perceived as trustworthy. Disclosure can arouse fears of exposure, abandonment, angry attacks, loss of control, impulsive destructive acts, or engulfment and loss of individuality (Hatfield, 1984). Whether or not these fears are realistic, they must be overcome before disclosure can take place. The discloser must be able to count on the recipient not to take advantage of his or her vulnerability or to misuse confidences either within the relationship or outside of it (Derlega & Chaikin, 1977). Second, the speaker's status relative to the other must be secure. Because disclosure tends to demote the speaker, it tends to be avoided (except for strategic purposes) in tenuous relationships or relationships where relative status is even potentially in question.

Social meanings thus restrict extensive expressive disclosure to (a) equal-status intimate relationships in which the partners disclose more or less mutually, in relationships in which the discloser is (b) satisfied with being inferior, or (c) unassailably superior, or in (d) relationships that have very sharply delimited boundaries that prevent any extension into other parts of the discloser's life. In all except (a), disclosing entails little risk of losing status, so one can (relatively) safely take advantage of the relationship for self-expression.

Equal-status intimate relationships have, deservedly, received the most attention, insofar as spouses and close friends are probably the most common outlet when people "have to talk to somebody." Other authors in this volume have reviewed this extensive literature. People to whom the speaker is unconflictedly inferior constitute another large class of potential expressive disclosure recipients: teachers, supervisors, parents, and other senior relatives are examples. The formulation excludes those with whom one is actively competing for status—including some close superiors as well as equals (but disclosure may be used strategically in these cases, e.g., to deflect attack; cf. Slobin *et al.*, 1968), and it excludes inferiors with whom competition is socially conceivable (a much larger class than those in current active competition). The formulation permits disclosure to inferiors if the status gulf is so wide and secure that a breach is not socially conceivable, for example, by aristocrats to servants. (Occasionally, pets may stand as surrogates in this function.) Among adults, such secure relationships of superiors to inferiors are rare in modern competitive meritocracies.

This formulation also accounts for the seemingly paradoxical stranger-on-the-train phenomenon as a logical consequence. One can disclose intimate details to a stranger if the relationship will terminate before he or she has any chance to make destructive use of the information or to challenge the one's social position.

For individuals whose distress is severe or prolonged, the burden on their primary relationships may become intolerable. Theoretically, when disclosure exceeds reasonable expectations of reciprocity, the essential long-term mutuality of intimate relationships is lost. Additional disclosure serves to demote the speaker in the other's eyes, making him or her a less desirable partner. Continual expressive disclosure appears to lead to ambivalence, manipulation, and rejection by strangers and by intimates (Coyne, 1976a,b; Coates & Winston, Chapter 11, this volume).

For people whose disclosure credit with their spouses and intimate friends is exhausted, as well as for people who have no secure intimate relationships, social provision is made in the form of such institutions as confessors, counselors, and psychotherapists. (Perhaps prayer serves this purpose for some people.) Within such special relationships, unlimited disclosure is possible, and its explicit purpose is the discloser's personal benefit, rather than the advancement of the discloser–recipient relationship. Unlike natural relationships, these are sharply circumscribed in time, place, and purpose. It is in these relationships, which are relatively undistorted by disclosure's social functions, that the analogy of disclosure to fever is most evident.

Strategic Disclosure

Of course, as many of this volume's other chapters make clear, disclosure is a crucial part of strategic self-presentation, quite apart from its psychological value for catharsis or self-understanding. Indeed, much of the social psychological literature (intimacy literature excepted), make disclosure appear primarily a tool for impression management (Baumeister, 1982; Derlega & Grzelak, 1979; Goffman, 1959; Schlenker, 1980, 1984).

I speculate that these strategic functions may be mainly derivative; that is, disclosure's ability to promote intimacy or convey deference may derive from the usual social consequences of expressive disclosure. Because expressive disclosure between equals requires a secure and reciprocal relationship, disclosure is a sign of trust; consequently, strategic disclosure can be used intentionally to promote deeper acquaintance. Because expressive disclosure to a superior makes the discloser vulnerable and requires acceptance of an inferior status, strategic disclosure can express deference even when submission is not felt and no real vulnerability is exposed. Thus the effectiveness of strategic disclosure may derive from common social knowledge of the psychological meaning of expressive disclosure.

Of course, strategic disclosures may not always be sincere. One can "disclose" information that is untrue or, more subtly, selectively reveal subjective information that is misleading or calculated to produce particular impressions (Baumeister, 1982; Goffman, 1959; Schlenker, 1980, 1984). Obvious examples include bragging and verbal politeness ("I had a lovely time"; cf. Brown & Levinson, 1978).

Is Intimacy-Building Disclosure Expressive or Strategic?

Taken to one extreme, the fever model could suggest that disclosure in the absence of psychological distress must be strategic. However, such a position is challenged by the extensive mutual disclosure between people who are intimate or who are becoming intimate (Altman, 1973; Altman & Taylor, 1973; Derlega, 1984). Forming an intimate relationship involves high levels of disclosure in the absence of psychological distress. Yet intuitively, truly intimate disclosure contrasts sharply with strategic pseudointimate disclosure.

This comparison raises the following important theoretical question: Is the disclosure that occurs in the formation of truly intimate relationships best considered as expressive or strategic—or as serving some third type of function? (See Derlega & Grzelak's, 1979, analysis of relationship development functions of disclosure.) It would be consistent with the fever model to consider such disclosure as expressive: the powerful emotions of attraction and love, like distress, may create a need to talk to somebody. Perhaps the sense of fulfillment—even joy—that can come from being known to another through disclosure is the upper end of a continuum whose lower end is cathartic relief from distress. That is, perhaps the joy and the relief, both powerful positive emotions, are attributable to the same psychological mechanisms. Although they occur in different circumstances, intimacy-building disclosure resembles distress disclosure. In both cases, revealing one's subjective state in an atmosphere of trust yields a feeling of relative elation. This hypothesis requires research.

Alternatively, perhaps forming a new intimate relationship merely opens a new forum for expressive disclosure. This alternative suggests that the content of intimate disclosures should center on problems and distress, contrary to the stereotype of intimates sharing (positive) dreams and plans. Nevertheless, the possibility emphasizes the need for empirical studies of the content of intimacy-building disclosure.

RESEARCH DIRECTIONS

First research priority must be given to assessing the model's two main propositions. Given a clear definition of disclosure, both are testable, although both require multiple studies because of the broad and potentially imprecise meanings of the core concepts, "distress" and "psychological benefit."

The first proposition, that people tend to disclose when they are distressed, is the easier to test. It can be assessed correlationally by comparing self-reported levels of distress with amount of disclosure under standard (facilitative) conditions. It could be tested experimentally by assessing verbal behavior before and after subjecting people to stress (or, more naturalistically, finding comparable groups who have or have not been subjected to stress and then assessing their verbal behavior). Studies cited previously seem to support this proposition, but other studies seem contradictory (see Carpenter, Chapter 10, this volume).

Because "distress" is such a broad concept, much further work is needed to ascertain the generality or limits of the phenemonon. Obviously, such research demands careful attention to ethical and humanitarian considerations.

The second proposition, that distressed people obtain some benefit from disclosing, is harder to test, first because expressive disclosure is neither randomly distributed nor easily manipulated but internally regulated, and second because of difficulties in measuring benefit.

Statistically, variation in disclosure cannot be correlated with measures of improvement if disclosure levels are always at optimum, insofar as "optimum" implies that any potential outcome effects attributable to disclosure have already been extracted (in fact, maximized). Experimentally increasing disclosure (e.g., by instructions, coaching, or modeling) is unlikely to effect improvements, except in individuals who are initially inhibited. Forcibly preventing disclosure by distressed people as an experimental manipulation is scientifically more promising, but this would raise severe ethical problems.

The fever model thus implies that research on disclosure's psychotherapeutic benefits must be more subtle than simply correlating disclosure levels with degree of improvement or experimentally manipulating disclosure levels and assessing gains. I will not attempt to propose alternative strategies here, but see Rice and Greenberg (1984) for a promising approach.

Linguistic studies of psychotherapy and social conversation (Elliott, 1983; Goodwin, 1979, 1981) and studies of role behaviors (Stiles, Orth, Scherwitz, Hennrikus, & Vallbona, 1984) convincingly demonstrate that disclosure (like all verbal behavior) is powerfully constrained by relationship, role, and the specific conversational context of particular utterances. Emphatically, disclosure levels are not random or haphazard but are intricately bound up in ongoing interaction and social expectations, so that manipulation aimed at increasing or decreasing disclosures in naturalistic settings may have extensive and unpredictable effects. By the same token (and despite this chapter's and this book's narrow focus), disclosure cannot be fully understood in isolation from other sorts of verbal behaviors or other aspects of social context.

The complexities and difficulties of measuring psychological "benefit" are witnessed by a large and vexed literature (e.g., Lambert, Christiansen, & DeJulio, 1983; Lambert, Shapiro, & Bergin, 1986; Stiles, 1983; Strupp & Hadley, 1977). Nevertheless, it should be possible to assess, for example, changes in distressed people's affective state before and after disclosing, as compared with controls who are not given an opportunity to disclose. Again, ethical considerations must be paramount. Human distress is ubiquitous, and opportunities for measuring it and seeing how it is relieved are available for researchers willing to build sensitivity and compassion into their experimental designs.

Acknowledgments

I thank Robert Elliott, Bill Henricks, Bill Sloan, and Larry Scherwitz for their comments and suggestions on drafts of this chapter.

REFERENCES

Abt, L. E., & Stuart, I. R. (Eds.). (1982). *The newer therapies: A sourcebook*. New York: Van Nostrand Reinhold.

Altman, I. (1973). Reciprocity of interpersonal exchange. *Journal for the Theory of Social Behavior, 3*, 249–261.

Altman, I., & Taylor, D. A. (1973). *Social penetration: The development of interpersonal relationships*. New York: Holt, Rinehart & Winston.

Atkeson, B. M., Calhoun, K. S., Resick, P. A., & Ellis, E. M. (1982). Victims of rape: Repeated assessment of depressive symptoms. *Journal of Consulting and Clinical Psychology, 50*, 96–102.

Baumeister, R. F. (1982). A self presentational view of social phenomena. *Psychological Bulletin, 91*, 3–26.

Berman, W. H., & Turk, D.C. (1981). Adaptation to divorce: Problems and coping strategies. *Journal of Marriage and the Family, 43*, 179–189.

Billings, A. G., & Moos, R. H. (1984). Coping, stress, and social resources among adults with unipolar depression. *Journal of Personality and Social Psychology, 46*, 877–891.

Brown, G. W., & Harris, T. (1978). *Social origins of depression*. London: Tavistock.

Brown, P., & Levinson, S. (1978). Universals in language usage: Politeness phenomena. In E. Goody (Ed.), *Questions and politeness: Strategies in social interaction* (pp. 56–324). Cambridge, England: Cambridge University Press.

Brunink, S. A., & Schroeder, H. E. (1979). Verbal therapeutic behavior of expert psychoanalytically-oriented, Gestalt, and Behavior therapists. *Journal of Consulting and Clinical Psychology, 47*, 567–574.

Bundza, K. A., & Simonson, N. R. (1973). Therapist self-disclosure: Its effect on impressions of therapist and willingness to disclose. *Psychotherapy: Theory, Research, and Practice, 10*, 215–217.

Burgess, A. W., & Holmstrom, L. (1974). *Rape: Victims of crisis*. Bowie, MD: Brady.

Cansler, D. C., & Stiles, W. B. (1981). Relative status and interpersonal presumptuousness. *Journal of Experimental Social Psychology, 17*, 459–471.

Caplan, G. (Ed.). (1974). *Support systems and community mental health*. New York: Basic Books.

Chesner, S. P., & Baumeister, R. F. (1985). Effect of therapist's disclosure of religious beliefs on the intimacy of client self-disclosure. *Journal of Social and Clinical Psychology, 3*, 97–105.

Coates, D., & Winston, T. (1983). Counteracting the deviance of depression: Peer support groups for victims. *Journal of Social Issues, 39*, 169–194.

Cobb, S. (1976). Social support as a moderator of life stress. *Psychosomatic Medicine, 38*, 300–314.

Coyne, J. C. (1976a). Depression and the response of others. *Journal of Abnormal Psychology, 85*, 186–193.

Coyne, J. C. (1976b). Toward an interactional description of depression. *Psychiatry, 39,* 28–40.

DeForest, C., & Stone, G. L. (1980). Effects of sex and intimacy level on self-disclosure. *Journal of Counseling Psychology, 27,* 93–96.

Derlega, V.J. (1984). Self-disclosure and intimate relationships. In V. J. Derlega (Eds.), *Communication, intimacy, and close relationships* (pp. 1–9). Orlando, FL: Academic Press.

Derlega, V. J., & Chaikin, A. L. (1977). Privacy and self-disclosure in social relationships. *Journal of Social Issues, 33,* 102–115.

Derlega, V. J., & Grzelak, J. (1979). Appropriateness of self-disclosure. In G. Chelune (Ed.), *Self-disclosure* (pp. 151–176). San Francisco: Jossey-Bass.

Derlega, V. J., Lovell, R., & Chaikin, A. L. (1976). Effects of therapist disclosure and its perceived appropriateness on client self-disclosure. *Journal of Consulting and Clinical Psychology, 44,* 866.

DeRubeis, R., Hollon, S., Evans, M., & Bemis, K. (1982). Can psychotherapies for depression be discriminated? A systematic investigation of cognitive therapy and interpersonal therapy. *Journal of Consulting and Clinical Psychology, 50,* 744–756.

Elliott, R. (1983). "That in your hands . . .": A comprehensive process analysis of a significant event in psychotherapy. *Psychiatry, 46,* 113–129.

Elliott, R., Stiles, W. B., Shiffman, S., Barker, C. B., Burstein, B., & Goodman, G. (1982). The empirical analysis of help-intended communications: Conceptual framework and recent research. In T. A. Wills (Ed.), *Basic processes in helping relationships* (pp. 333–356). New York: Academic Press.

Freud, S. (1935). *A general introduction to psychoanalysis.* New York: Washington Square Press.

Freud, S. & Breuer, J. (1966). *Studies on hysteria* (J. Strachey, Trans.). New York: Avon Books. (Original works published 1893–1895).

Funabiki, D., Bologna, N. C., Pepping, M., & FitzGerald, K. C. (1980). Revisiting sex differences in the expression of depression. *Journal of Abnormal Psychology, 89,* 194–202.

Gendlin, E. T. (1978). *Focusing.* New York: Bantam.

Gendlin, E. T., & Tomlinson, T. M. (1967). The process conceptualization and its measurement. In C. R. Rogers, E. T. Gendlin, D. J. Kiesler, & C. B. Truax (Eds.), *The therapeutic relationship and its impact: A study of psychotherapy with schizophrenics* (pp. 109–131). Madison: University of Wisconsin Press.

Gendlin, E. T., Beebe, J., III, Cassens, J., Klein, M., & Oberlander, M. (1968). Focusing ability in psychotherapy, personality, and creativity. In J. M. Shlein (Ed.), *Research in psychotherapy* (Vol. 3), pp. 217–238). Washington, DC: American Psychological Association.

Glick, I. O., Weiss, R. S., & Parkes, C. M. (1974). *The first years of bereavement.* New York: Wiley.

Goffman, E. (1959). *Presentation of self in everyday life.* New York: Doubleday.

Goldfried, M. R. (1980). Toward the delineation of therapeutic change principles. *American Psychologist, 35,* 991–999.

Gomes-Scharwtz, B. (1978). Effective ingredients in psychotherapy: Prediction of outcome from process variables. *Journal of Consulting and Clinical Psychology, 46,* 1023–1035.

Goodman, G., & Dooley, D. (1976). A framework for help-intended communication. *Psychotherapy: Theory, Research, and Practice, 13,* 106–117.

Goodwin, C. (1979). The interactive construction of a sentence in natural conversation. In G. Psathas (Ed.), *Everyday language: Studies in ethnomethodology.* New York: Irvington.

Goodwin, C. (1981). *Conversational organization: Interaction between speakers and hearers*. New York: Academic Press.
Greenson, R. R. (1967). *The technique and practice of psychoanalysis* (Vol. 1). New York: International Universities Press.
Halpern, T. P. (1977). Degree of client disclosure as a function of past disclosure, counselor disclosure, and counselor facilitativeness. *Journal of Counseling Psychology, 24*, 41–47.
Hatfield, E. (1984). The dangers of intimacy. In V. J. Derlega (Ed.), *Communication, intimacy, and close relationships* (pp. 207–220). Orlando, FL: Academic Press.
Hill, C. E., Thames, T. B., & Rardin, D. K. (1979). Comparison of Rogers, Perls, and Ellis on the Hill Counselor Verbal Response Category System. *Journal of Counseling Psychology, 26*, 198–208.
Johnson, M. N. (1981). Anxiety/stress and the effects on disclosure between nurses and patients. In D. C. Sutterly & G. F. Donnelly (Eds.), *Coping with stress*. Rockville, MD: Aspen.
Jones, W. H., Hobbs, S. A., & Hockenbury, D. (1982). Loneliness and social skill deficits. *Journal of Personality and Social Psychology, 42*, 682–689.
Jourard, S. M. (1971a). *Self-disclosure: An experimental analysis of the transparent self*. New York: Wiley.
Jourard, S. M. (1971b). *The transparent self* (rev. ed.). New York: Van Nostrand.
Kiesler, D. J. (1971). Patient experiencing and successful outcome in individual psychotherapy of schizophrenics and psychoneurotics. *Journal of Consulting and Clinical Psychology, 37*, 370–385.
Klein, M. H., Mathieu, P. L., Gendlin, E. T., & Kiesler, D. J. (1969). *The experiencing scale: A research and training manual* (Vol. 1). Madison: Wisconsin Psychiatric Institute.
Klein, M. H., Mathieu-Coughlan, P., & Kiesler, D. J. (1986). The experiencing scales. In L. Greenberg & W. Pinsof (Eds.), *The psychotherapeutic process: A research handbook* (pp. 21–71). New York: Guilford Press.
Kornblith, S. H., Rehm, L. P., O'Hara, M. W., & Lamparski, D. M. (1983). The contribution of self-reinforcement training and behavioral assignments to the efficacy of self-control therapy for depression. *Cognitive Therapy and Research, 7*, 499–528.
Lambert, M. J., Christiansen, E. R., & DeJulio, S. S. (Eds.). (1983). *The assessment of psychotherapy outcome*. New York: Wiley.
Lambert, M. J., Shapiro, D. A., & Bergin, A. E. (1986). Evaluation of therapeutic outcomes. In S. L. Garfield & A. E. Bergin (Eds.), *Handbook of psychotherapy and behavior change* (3rd ed., pp. 157–211). New York: Wiley.
Lindemann, E. (1944). Symptomatology and management of acute grief. *American Journal of Psychiatry, 101*, 141–148.
Lorentz, M., & Cobbs, S. (1953). Language behavior in psychoneurotic patients. *A. M. A. Archives of Neurology & Psychiatry, 69*, 684–694.
Luborsky, L., Singer, B., & Luborsky, L. (1975). Comparative studies of psychotherapies: Is it true that "Everyone has won and all must have prizes"? *Archives of General Psychiatry, 32*, 995–1008.
Luborsky, L., Woody, G. E., McLellan, A. T., O'Brien, C. P., & Rosenzweig, J. (1982). Can independent judges recognize different psychotherapies? An experience with manual-guided therapies. *Journal of Consulting and Clinical Psychology, 30*, 49–62.
Mayo, P. R. (1968). Self-disclosure and neurosis. *British Journal of Social and Clinical Psychology, 7*, 140–148.
McAdams, D. P. (1984). Human motives and personal relationships. In V. J. Derlega (Ed.), *Communication, intimacy, and close relationships* (pp. 41–70). Orlando, FL: Academic Press.

McDaniel, S. H., Stiles, W. B., & McGaughey, K. J. (1981). Correlations of male college students' verbal response mode use in psychotherapy with measures of psychological disturbance and psychotherapy outcome. *Journal of Consulting and Clinical Psychotherapy, 49,* 571–582.

Miller, L. C., Berg, J. H., & Archer, R. L. (1983). Openers: Individuals who elicit intimate self-disclosure. *Journal of Personality and Social Psychology, 44,* 1234–1244.

Minuchin, S. (1974). *Families and family therapy.* Cambridge: Harvard University Press.

Morton, T. L. (1978). Intimacy and reciprocity of exchange: A comparison of spouses and strangers. *Journal of Personality and Social Psychology, 37,* 72–81.

O'Malley, S. S., Suh, C. S., & Strupp, H. H. (1983). The Vanderbilt Psychotherapy Process Scale: A report of the scale development and a process-outcome study. *Journal of Consulting and Clinical Psychology, 51,* 581–586.

Parker, G. B., & Brown, L. B. (1982). Coping behaviors that mediate between life events and depression. *Archives of General Psychiatry, 39,* 1386–1391.

Parloff, M. B. (1976, February 21). Shopping for the right therapy. *Saturday Review,* pp. 14–16.

Pennebaker, J. W., & Hoover, C. W. (1985). Inhibition and cognition: Toward an understanding of trauma and disease. In R. J. Davidson, G. E. Schwartz, & D. Shapiro (Eds.), *Consciousness and self-regulation* (Vol. 4). New York: Plenum Press.

Pennebaker, J. W., & O'Heeron, R. C. (1984). Confiding in others and illness rates among spouses of suicide and accidental death. *Journal of Abnormal Psychology, 93,* 473–476.

Perls, F. S. (1969). *Gestalt therapy verbatim.* La Fayette, CA: Real People Press.

Persons, R. W., & Marks, P. A. (1970). Self-disclosure with recidivists: Optimum interviewer-interviewee matching. *Journal of Abnormal Psychology, 76,* 387–391.

Premo, B. E., & Stiles, W. B. (1983). Familiarity in verbal interactions of married couples versus strangers. *Journal of Social and Clinical Psychology, 1,* 209–230.

Rice, L. N., & Greenberg, L. (Eds.). (1984). *Patterns of change.* New York: Guilford Press.

Rice, L. N., & Koke, C. J. (1981). Vocal style and the process of psychotherapy. In J. K. Darby (Ed.), *Speech evaluation in psychiatry.* New York: Grune & Stratton.

Rice, L. N., & Wagstaff, A. K. (1967). Client voice quality and expressive style as indexes of productive psychotherapy. *Journal of Consulting Psychology, 31,* 557–563.

Riley, G. D., Cozby, P. C., White, G. D., & Kjos, G. L. (1983). Effect of therapist expectations and need for approval on self-disclosure. *Journal of Clinical Psychology, 39,* 221–226.

Rippere, V. (1977). "What's the thing to do when you're feeling depressed?"—A pilot study. *Behaviour Research and Therapy, 15,* 185–191.

Rogers, C. R. (1951). *Client-centered therapy.* Boston: Houghton-Mifflin.

Rogers, C. R. (1958). A process conception of psychotherapy. *American Psychologist, 13,* 142–149.

Russell, R. L., & Stiles, W. B. (1979). Categories for classifying language in psychotherapy. *Psychological Bulletin, 86,* 404–419.

Scherwitz, L., Graham, L. E., II, & Ornish, D. (1985). Self-involvement and the risk factors for coronary heart disease. *Advances,* 2(2), 6–8.

Scherwitz, L., McKelvain, R., Laman, C., Patterson, J., Dutton, L., Yusim, S., Lester, J., Kraft, I., Rochelle, D., & Leachman, R. (1983). Type A behavior, self-involvement, and coronary atherosclerosis. *Psychosomatic Medicine, 45,* 47–57.

Schlenker, B. R. (1980). *Impression management: The self concept, social identity, and interpersonal relations.* Belmont, CA: Brooks/Cole.

Schlenker, B. R. (1984). Identities, identifications, and relationships. In V. J. Derlega (Ed.), *Communication, intimacy, and close relationships* (pp. 71–104). Orlando, FL: Academic Press.

Schutz, W. C. (1971). *Here comes everybody*. New York: Harper & Row.
Searle, J. R. (1969). *Speech acts: An essay in the philosophy of language*. Cambridge, England: Cambridge University Press.
Silver, R. L., & Wortman, C. B. (1980). Coping with undesirable life events. In J. Garber & M. E. P. Seligman (Eds.), *Human helplessness* (pp.). New York: Academic Press.
Simonson, N. R. (1976). The impact of therapist disclosure on patient disclosure. *Journal of Consulting Psychology, 23*, 3–6.
Sloane, R. B., Staples, F. R., Cristol, A. H., Yorkston, N. J., & Whipple, K. (1975). *Psychotherapy versus behavior therapy*. Cambridge: Harvard University Press.
Slobin, D. I., Miller, S. H., & Porter, L. W. (1968). Forms of address an social relations in a business organization. *Journal of Personality and Social Psychology, 8*, 289–293.
Smith, M. L., & Glass, G. V. (1977). Meta-analysis of psychotherapy outcome studies. *American Psychologist, 32*, 752–760.
Smith, M. L., Glass, G. V., & Miller, T. I. (1980). *The benefits of psychotherapy*. Baltimore: Johns Hopkins University Press.
Solano, C. H., Batten, P. G., & Parish, E. A. (1982). Lonliness and patterns of self-disclosure. *Journal of Personality and Social Psychology, 43*, 524–531.
Stanley, G., & Bownes, A. F. (1966). Self-disclosure and neuroticism. *Psychological Reports, 18*, 350.
Stiles, W. B. (1978). Verbal response modes and dimensions of interpersonal roles: A method of discourse analysis. *Journal of Personality and Social Psychology, 36*, 693–703.
Stiles, W. B. (1979). Verbal response modes and psychotherapeutic technique. *Psychiatry, 42*, 49–62.
Stiles, W. B. (1980). Measurement of the impact of psychotherapy sessions. *Journal of Consulting and Clinical Psychology, 48*, 176–185.
Stiles, W. B. (1981). Classification of intersubjective illocutionary acts. *Language in Society, 10*, 227–249.
Stiles, W. B. (1983). Normality, diversity, and psychotherpay. *Psychotherapy: Theory, Research, and Practice, 20*, 183–189.
Stiles, W. B. (1984). Client disclosure and psychotherapy session evaluations. *British Journal of Clnical Psychology, 23*, 311–312.
Stiles, W. B., & Sultan, F. E. (1979). Verbal response mode use by clients in psychotherapy. *Journal of Consulting and Clinical Psychology, 47*, 611–613.
Stiles, W. B., & White, M. L. (1981). Parent-child interaction in the laboratory: Effects of role, task, and child behavior pathology on verbal response mode use. *Journal of Abnormal Child Psychology, 9*, 229–241.
Stiles, W. B., McDaniel, S. H., & McGaughey, K. (1979). Verbal response mode correlates of experiencing. *Journal of Consulting and Clinical Pathology, 47*, 795–797.
Stiles, W. B., Putnam, S. M., & Jacob, M. C. (1982). Verbal exchange structure of initial medical interviews. *Health Psychology, 1*, 315–336.
Stiles, W. B., Orth, J. E., Scherwitz, L., Hennrikus, D., & Vallbona, C. (1984). Role behaviors in routine interviews with hypertensive patients: A repertoire of verbal exchanges. *Social Psychology Quarterly, 47*, 244–254.
Stiles, W. B., Shapiro, D. A., & Elliot, R. (1986). "Are all psychotherapies equivalent?" *American Psychologist, 41*, 165–180.
Strassberg, D. S., Anchor, K. N., Gabel, H., & Cohen, B. (1978). Self-disclosure in individual psychotherpay. *Psychotherapy: Theory, Research, and Practice, 15*, 153–157.
Strupp, H. H. (1955). An objective comparison of Rogerian and psychoanalytic techniques. *Journal of Consulting Psychology, 19*, 1–7.

Strupp, H. H., & Hadley, S. W. (1977). A tripartite model of mental health and therapeutic outcomes: With special reference to negative effects in psychotherapy. *American Psychologist, 32,* 196–197.

Vachon, M. L. S., Rogers, J., Lyall, W. A., Lancee, W. J., Sheldon, A. R., & Freeman, S. J. J. (1982). Predictors and correlates of adaptation to conjugal bereavement. *American Journal of Psychiatry, 139,* 998–1002.

Weitraub, W. (1981). *Verbal behavior: Adaptation and psychopathology.* New York: Springer-Verlag.

Worthy, M., Gary, A. L., & Kahn, G. M. (1969). Self-disclosure as an exchange process. *Journal of Personality and Social Psychology, 13,* 59–63.

Wortman, C. B., & Dunkell-Schetter, C. (1980, September). *Social interaction and depression.* Paper presented at the American Psychological Association Convention, Montreal, Quebec, Canada.

13

Self-Disclosure in Cognitive Marital Therapy

EDWARD M. WARING

Problems with intimacy form the most frequent basis for couples with marital discord seeking therapy (Horowitz, 1979). Self-disclosure is one specific type of communication that has been demonstrated to be positively associated with intimacy in marriage (Waring & Chelune, 1983).

This chapter will explore the therapeutic use of self-disclosure between spouses in marital therapy, especially *cognitive* self-disclosure that involves sharing personal attitudes, beliefs, and ideas about one's own marriage as well as one's parents' marriage. The approach is called cognitive marital therapy, and I hope to show how it can facilitate self-disclosure and marital intimacy among couples who have had troubled marriages.

CLINICAL EXAMPLE

I will describe a case of marital discord and illustrate the relevance of intimacy and self-disclosure to clinical work in couples.

This couple was referred because they were drifting apart and having increasingly bitter and frequent arguments. They had been

---

EDWARD M. WARING • Department of Psychiatry, University Hospital, London, Ontario N6A 5A5 Canada.

married for 8 years and had two daughters who were 7 and 4 years old. The husband was a professional man who traveled extensively, and the wife was at home with the two girls.

When the couple was asked about their theories of why the drifting apart and arguments began, the wife identified her bitterness toward her husband after the birth of the second child. He spent little time at home and his temper became more evident; he stopped being a companion, leaving her feeling lonely. The husband stated that after the birth of both children, he found his wife boring and preoccupied with the children and domestic life.

The couple next disclosed that they met through her work as a secretary/receptionist. He was one of many businessmen who reported through her office. She said that she found him physically attractive, mature, and assertive, whereas her previous boyfriends had been passive. She thought he was married at the time they first dated. He corrected his wife and said his previous wife and he had already separated. The husband said that he found his current wife physically attractive and pleasant. He revealed that her parents had not been pleased with their courtship. The couples both agreed that they found they had some mutual interests in music and enjoyed dining and entertainment related to professional interests. When asked about his previous marriage, the husband revealed that his first wife and he were both ambitious, career-oriented people whose business resulted in frequent separations. A business opportunity for his first wife led to her moving and his decision not to accompany her. He acknowledged that he and his first wife had had difficulties in resolving differences of opinion but separated on good terms with no children. The wife revealed that she had not thought about why his previous marriage had failed and that her decision to date a married man was motivated in part by rebellion.

The couple spontaneously disclosed that they had separated after 6 months of courtship when she learned he was seeing someone else at a time when arguments in their relationship about commitment were leading them to reconsider their relationship. They both had romances during this 3 month hiatus and spontaneously got back together when he called her. They both denied jealousy or bitterness about these transient romances.

He described his parents' marriage as quite poor. He attributed this to his father who was intimidating and bad tempered. Verbal and physical abuse of his mother and siblings had occurred, and there had been two brief separations in his parents' marriage. He was not close to his family and avoided visits or contacts. She described her parents' marriage as good but said that her mother had been overly involved with her as she was an only child. She described her mother as placating and always trying to please everyone including her father who was a private man. There was a suggestion that the father had an affair.

They described their first few years of marriage as being quite happy. Frequently weekly separations for both were not upsetting, but he said he was quite bored and lonely at times on the road. They enjoyed an active social life when together, and when she was alone, she spent considerable time with her family.

The birth of the children was planned, and they were both pleased. She left work and devoted her time to the children. He, as mentioned, was not as comfortable with his role as a father. There had been no affairs or external distressing relationships. She found his family difficult to deal with, and he found his mother-in-law to be somewhat intrusive.

They indicated clearly that they were both committed to the relationship and wanted to see it improve. They both agreed that expression of affection had been worse since the arguments and that she tended to be more expressive. They both agreed that attempts to resolve differences of opinion frequently led to arguments and that his temper flared more frequently. He suggested that he generally preferred to keep his thoughts to himself and was not a good listener at home because he felt tired from his work that involved listening to clients. She disclosed that she enjoyed conversation and was a bit of a mind reader. They both agreed their sexual relationship was good. They felt their relationship to friends and extended family was positive except for continued turmoil with his parents. They felt good about themselves as a couple. They still had mutual goals, values, and activities.

I suggested that their lack of intimacy was probably related to an inability to resolve differences of opinion that had been present during courtship. They both had observed and experienced power conflicts in their families of origin with the husband's parents arguing and her mother dominating the marriage. They both accepted that 10 sessions to facilitate self-disclosure might be helpful. He wanted to know what my success rate was. So I gave him an article to read. She was a bit disappointed that I was not going to tell them something to do to improve things in the next week.

The first therapy session with this couple with a presenting problem of drifting apart will be used to illustrate the process of self-disclosure as it occurs early in the course of a typical therapy session.

THERAPIST: What's your theory of why you have drifted apart as a couple?
WIFE: George refuses to accept my point of view about anything!

THERAPIST: Your theory is that your drifting apart was due to your husband not respecting your opinions?
WIFE: Yes.
THERAPIST: Why did you select a man who doesn't respect your opinions?
WIFE: He wasn't that way when we met.
THERAPIST: What is your idea about why he has changed?
WIFE: He changed after the children were born. I don't know why.
THERAPIST: George, what were you thinking when you wife was talking?
HUSBAND: I was thinking that Alice wants me to agree with all her decisions.
THERAPIST: What's your theory about why your wife wants total consensus?
HUSBAND: She wants to control the kids' behavior.
THERAPIST: Why did you marry someone who appears to want control of decisions?
HUSBAND: She always knew what she wanted and I liked that at first because I didn't.

One can observe the process of self-disclosure commencing as the wife begins to think about her reasons for marrying a passive man and the husband begins to think about why he did not know what he wanted. Both spouses will now be exploring their own motives for spouse selection and hopefully with an objectivity provided by the passage of time. Each spouse can become a resource regarding observations and explanations of their own and their mate's earlier motives.

THERAPIST (*to wife*): What were you thinking while your spouse was talking?
WIFE: I was thinking that I didn't know what I wanted as clearly as George thinks. I was pretty confused.
THERAPIST: What's your theory of what was causing your confusion?
WIFE: Because of my father's affair and I was confused about who I could trust.
THERAPIST: What's your theory of why your father had an affair?
WIFE: I don't know. He was spending a lot of time with his secretary who was a young woman. I don't know.
THERAPIST (*to husband*): What were you thinking while your wife was talking?
HUSBAND: I think he was tired of being taken for granted at home; at least that's what he told me once.
THERAPIST: What's your theory about why spouses are taken for granted?

We are now a long way from the original focus of drifting apart in the present. We are now exploring reasons for an affair that occurred in the wife's parents' marriage. We are now attempting to encourage the husband to disclose his understanding of men being taken for granted in marriage. Perhaps we will discover this occurred in his parents' marriage.

COGNITIVE SELF-DISCLOSURE

The structured experience illustrates how self-disclosure between spouses can be facilitated in marital therapy. It is a technique that I will suggest, decreases marital discord and promotes intimacy. Now I will present the theoretical and clinical reasons why *cognitive* self-disclosure (which focuses on sharing attitudes, beliefs, and ideas about one's marriage and one's parents' marriage) is a specific tool of this technique.

A cognitive view of psychotherapy is exerting a major influence on therapeutic practice. Examples include Beck's (1967) use of cognitive restructuring to alter negative self-concept in depression and Meichenbaum's (1977) cognitive-behavior therapy. Greenberg and Safran (1984) suggest that cognition and affect operate as two interdependent systems in human experience. Rachman (1984) suggests that if the problem lies in the cognitive system, the therapeutic interventions should focus upon cognitions, although the feeling domain may vary accordingly. It may be that the failure to develop, maintain, or sustain intimacy in the marital interpersonal system resides in the cognitive domain.

Kelly (1955) developed a theory of personality in the context of interpersonal relationships based on the concept of "personal constructs." This theory suggests that our relationships are like experiments in which we pigeonhole significant others and look for evidence to support our theories. A man may have developed the personal construct that women cannot be trusted. He will look for evidence in his wife's behavior to confirm his belief system. He will ignore behaviors that are discrepant from his idea and may even behave in a way that might facilitate untrustworthy behavior. Kelly (1955) suggested that a therapist should help both spouses experience one another as discrepant from their "cognitive schema" or idea that determines the spouse's expectation. One way of accomplishing this is to help spouses disclose these cognitive "personal constructs" and explore how they were developed in observation and experience of personal relationships in the family of origin.

Segraves (1982) outlines a theoretical integration of differing approaches to the treatment of marital discord that suggests a cognitive approach. Segraves develops Kelly's theory and suggests that one's level of intimacy is a partial function of the cognitive perception of the spouse.

This personal construct is determined by cognitions based on observation and experience of one's parents' intimacy. Segraves's model suggests that (1) faculty cognitive interpersonal schemata of intimate members of the opposite sex are of primary importance in the genesis and maintenance of marital discord; (2) spouses tend to behave toward spouses in such a way as to invite behaviors that are congruent with cognitive schemata; and (3) maladaptive interactional patterns maintain individual psychopathology in spouses.

Cognitive schemata or personal constructs develop through observing and experiencing one's parents' level of intimacy. Couples with discord tend to say that unhappiness in their parents' marriage caused them emotional suffering as children. However, rather than perceiving this discord as a problem of their parents as a "couple," they invariably report that one of their parents was responsible for the discord. For instance, a father's drinking, or a mother's infidelity, or one parent's domination or selfishness may be said to have caused the discord. When asked why the father drank or why the mother married or stayed with an alcoholic, the offspring will say he or she has never thought about it. But the couple will then say they looked for a spouse who did not drink or thought you could rescue a man who did drink.

Spouses will ignore the interaction between a father's drinking and a mother's lack of affection. They will behave toward their own spouse in a way that will invite behaviors congruent with their cognitive schema. The failure of the wife to understand why her husband selected an unaffectionate woman may serve to maintain individual maladaptive problems. In summary, a person may attribute to a spouse a characteristic of a parent. The person believes that this characteristic was responsible for the parents' marital discord that caused them psychological suffering in childhood.

COGNITIVE SELF-DISCLOSURE—CLINICAL ASPECTS

I will now describe clinical experience that suggests that cognitive self-disclosure, defined as statements beginning with "I think" and "I am," is preferable to the disclosure of feelings and needs. I will then describe the technical aspects of cognitive self-disclosure.

Couples with interpersonal problems come to the therapist feeling frustrated, angry at their spouse, and hopeless about resolving their discord. Is there a place for self-disclosure of hostile feelings? Should a therapist encourage spouses to verbalize hatred, bitterness, or other forms of anger?

In interviews with married couples selected at random from the City of London, Ontario, directory and free of marital discord, we have found that most couples believe arguments, criticism, and anger produce distance and not intimacy (Waring, Tillmann, Frelick, Russell, & Weisz, 1980). Levinger and Senn (1967) have suggested that disturbed couples demonstrate more disclosure of hostile feelings than satisfied couples.

Common sense suggests therapy should attempt to decrease such negative interactions. Many couples confide that they have discontinued therapy with counselors who encourage early and open expression of anger because the couple can fight on their own at home.

Facilitating self-disclosure of negative feelings may prevent the spouse from listening. Harrel and Guerney, Jr. (1976) have demonstrated that training spouses in listening skills is an effective form of marital counseling. Bowen (1975), however, suggests that spouses and therapists need to respond with empathy rather than to react emotionally to what is disclosed. People do not easily "respond" to disclosure of anger. They usually react with self-justified anger. Noller (1984) suggests that spouses become defensive and generally become involved in a circle of negativity. Finally, in almost all forms of psychotherapy after someone discloses their anger, the therapist attempts to understand why they are angry. Because all spouses are angry or hurt and an expression of rage produces distance, why not explore the cognitive attribute while suppressing the expression of anger? In summary, there is growing clinical support for the notion of suppressing self-disclosure of negative feelings in marital therapy.

Why not train the couple to disclose positive feelings? First, most couples do not genuinely feel very positive about their spouses when they come for therapy. Second, we have learned that disclosures that are not affectively congruent produce distance and not closeness (Chelune, Rosenfeld, & Waring, 1986; Chelune, Sultan, Vosk, Ogden, & Waring, 1984; Chelune, Waring, Vosk, Sultan & Ogden, 1984). Nonverbal communication, including the hostile expression of self-disclosure, may negate a positive message and produce confusion and not clarification (Noller, 1984). Learning to express one's true feelings may be much less constructive than mental health professionals have suggested.

Why not focus on the self-disclosure of needs? Rokeach (1973) has argued that needs are an instrumental expression of values that again are complex cognitive schemata. Cognitive self-disclosure will help elucidate the conflicting values and beliefs that are behind the emotional demand component of expecting a spouse to meet one's needs. For example, a spouse may disclose that he or she needs more affection. The spouse may have reasons for withholding affection or may not be an affectionate person. The cognitive question is why the spouse needs the affection, or why he or she selected an unaffectionate spouse.

Finally, it must be noted that most couples find the self-disclosure of their thinking about interpersonal relationships in general, especially about their families of origin and in their own marriage, to be quite interesting. Simulating this type of interpersonal curiosity is described by many couples as akin to exploring their own roots.

COGNITIVE MARITAL THERAPY: THE TECHNIQUE

Cognitive marital therapy begins with an evaluation interview with the couple or with all family members present (Waring & Russell, 1980). The focus of the evaluation is to elicit each spouse's "theory" of why the presenting problem or symptom has appeared. The children's cognitive explanation of why the family is not functioning optimally and the couple's theories regarding their parents' relationship is elicited. A developmental history of the couple's courtship, marriage, and family is obtained as well as about their parents' marriage.

The interviewer asks only "why" or "theory" questions and avoids and suppresses emotional interchange and/or behavioral interpretation or confrontation. The interviewer evaluates the couple's relationship based on the eight dimensions of marital intimacy from the Waring Intimacy Questionnaire:

Conflict Resolution—the ease with which differences of opinion are resolved.
Affection—the degree to which feelings of emotional closeness are expressed by the couple.
Cohesion—a feeling of commitment to the marriage.
Sexuality—the degree to which sexual needs are communicated and fulfilled by the marriage.
Identity—the couple's level of self-confidence and self-esteem.
Compatibility—the degree to which the couple is able to work and play together comfortably.
Autonomy—the success with which the couple gains independence from their families of origin.
Expressiveness—the degree to which thoughts, beliefs, attitudes, and feelings are shared within the marriage.

This questionnaire identifies strengths in the couple's relationship as well as deficiencies that are contributing to their lack of intimacy (Waring, E. M., McElrath, D., Lefroe, D., & Weisz, G., 1981).

The interviewer then explains to the couple or the entire family how using cognitive self-disclosure to increase marital intimacy will decrease discord. The couple is offered ten 1-hour sessions to increase their intimacy or to improve one of the specific 8 areas of intimate relationships. The goal is to improve family functioning or to reduce the symptomatology of the presenting patient who may be a depressed spouse, a delinquent child, or an anxious patient. The specific rules and behaviors of the cognitive family therapy sessions are outlined, and then a negotiation and discussion follows until a specific treatment contract is made.

Only the couple is involved in the sessions of structured cognitive self-disclosure; their children are excluded. The session begins with the therapist stating, "We are here to understand why you are not close." As the therapy proceeds, the session begins with the major "why" questions that was left unanswered from the previous session. The couple may talk only to the therapist in an alternate pattern during the sessions. No feeling or behavior is identified, confronted, or interpreted. The spouses alternate in talking about any biographical material they think is relevant to answering the "why" question. The therapist, in a standardized manner, asks the other spouse, "What were you thinking while your spouse was talking?", thus facilitating cognitive self-disclosure. The therapist may also ask a spouse his or her theory on the question the other cannot answer. The therapist may share his or her cognitive theories. The therapist does not use interpretation or cognitive restructuring to relate material disclosed to current conflict. When the couple understands a particular "why" question, a more sophisticated "why" question becomes apparent.

Although the preceding description sounds tedious for the therapist in this stereotyped format, the material and revelations are surprisingly fascinating, and clinical understanding is enhanced through the perceptiveness of the therapist's "why" questions. Case examples and descriptions are available in previously referenced publications. Videotapes demonstrating cognitive marital therapy are available from the author (Waring, 1981).

HOW DOES SELF-DISCLOSURE FACILITATE INTIMACY?

The majority of couples who seek counseling because of persistent arguments, poor communication, affairs, or lack of closeness are able to accept the notion that improving the quality and quantity of their interpersonal intimacy may reduce their presenting problem. Several empirical studies support the assumption that deficiences in the quality and quantity of intimacy are associated with poor marital adjustment (Waring, 1984b). Self-disclosure is *one* aspect of how close a couple feels toward one another and thus a factor that could increase the couple's intimacy.

Gordon Chelune and I (Waring & Chelune, 1983) have previously reported research that suggests that self-disclosing behavior is a major determinant of various aspects of marital intimacy. The 20 couples in this study were comprised of 10 couples with clinical problems and 10 couples from the general population. All couples participated in a standardized, structured interview that allowed us to obtain behavioral ratings of the 8 dimensions of marital intimacy (Waring, E. M., McElrath, D., Mitchell, P., & Derry, M. N., 1981) previously described. The videotapes of these interviews were then blindly rated, using the Modified Self-Disclosure Coding System that measures the amount of self-disclosure, self-reference, and whether it is positive, negative, or neutral, the depth of content, the affective congruence, the education, and the rate.

The results of this study indicate that the linear combination of the quantitative aspects of self-disclosing behavior accounted for almost half of the variance in the qualitative ratings of a couple's general level of intimacy. Thus, although self-disclosure and intimacy cannot be considered synonymous, this study suggests that self-disclosure is a major determinant of the level of intimacy among married couples.

The self-disclosure measures were most closely related to two dimensions of marital intimacy—expressiveness and compatibility. Compatibility and expressiveness were two aspects of intimacy that related significantly to self-disclosure in the Waring and Chelune (1983) study. Expressiveness and self-disclosure, almost by definition, would be expected to go together. Individuals who are able to disclose themselves to their spouses in terms of "I feel," "I think," or "I am" should have the ability to express clear unambiguous messages about themselves and their relationship. A factor in spouse selection may be self-disclosure of values that allows a conscious choice about whether or not a couple is compatible. Failure to self-disclose attitudes about religion, child rearing, or sexuality may produce incompatibility. The self-disclosure of unexpressed values, attitudes, and beliefs between spouses with marital discord may facilitate a greater understanding of behaviors that have been a source of conflict.

In addition to being a major determinant of expressiveness and compatibility, self-disclosure also appears to play a major part in two other qualitative aspects of intimacy: identity and intimate behaviors. Erikson's (1950) psychosocial theory of development suggests that to develop intimacy, one must first develop a sense of identity. Self-disclosure is thought to be instrumental in achieving a sense of identity because two major functions it serves are clarifying one's values and evaluating whether these values are acceptable to one's peer group (Derlega & Grzelak, 1979). Similarly, on a concrete level, the disclosure of positive self-statements in an affectively congruent manner on ego-relevant topics forms a major part of what we qualitatively label intimate behavior (Chelune, Sultan, Vosk, Ogden, & Waring, 1984; Chelune, Waring, Vosk, Sultan, & Ogden, 1984). Thus a structured technique of spouse disclosure may be modeling what we define as intimate behavior. Although other behaviors (e.g., eye contact, touching, etc.) undoubtedly contribute to the dimension of intimate behaviors, self-disclosure appears to account for approximately half of the variance in the ratings of this dimension.

I will now describe the specific ways in which this theory promotes intimacy through (1) amount of self-disclosure, (2) the reciprocity of self-disclosure, (3) the ego relevance of disclosures, and (4) the ability of spouses to respond rather than react to self-disclosure.

INCREASING THE AMOUNT OF SELF-DISCLOSURE BETWEEN SPOUSES

Increasing the amount of self-disclosure by each spouse in a marriage would be expected to increase the amount of intimacy, because, as noted previously, the process of self-disclosure is a major determinant of a couple's perception of intimacy. A relationship between the amount of self-disclosure and marital adjustment has been demonstrated empirically (Davidson, Blaswick, & Halverson, 1983).

Some cautionary comments about increasing the amount of self-disclosure between spouses should be noted. A spouse revealing that he or she is having an affair is, in my view, not self-disclosing but self-exposing, and this behavior will usually produce distance and not closeness (Cozby, 1973). Self-disclosure would involve revealing the motivations for the dissatisfactions that might lead to an affair. A spouse who uses the opportunity of an assessment interview to say that he or she has never really loved his or her spouse is not engaging in self-disclosure. This behavior is simply dishonest. If the spouse were willing to disclose the motivations for the dishonesty or why he or she would marry someone they did not care for in the first place, self-disclosure would occur.

Does too much self-disclosure harm a relationship (Gilbert, 1980)? I believe self-exposure and dishonesty are common in couples with marital problems and prevent intimacy. For example, if a couple marries because the woman is pregnant, but after the wedding she reveals that she lied about the pregnancy, this can hardly be considered honest self-disclosure.

There are several implications of self-disclosure in cognitive marital therapy that should be clarified. Usually, when a spouse is more involved in self-disclosure, the disclosures become more personal and private, and the degree of exploration of the psychological motivations for spouse selection becomes more sophisticated. The disclosures must also be affectively congruent for therapy to work effectively. This calls for psychological and interpersonal honesty. If a spouse says that he or she supports the mate's growing independence, the spouse should both act supportive and not speak in a sarcastic tone. Often spouses may not be able to disclose motivations or needs because the reasons are beyond their awareness (i.e., unconscious) or they have not asked themselves or thought about the reasons for a behavior. Finally, not all disclosures may be constructive. Our results clearly indicate that negative self-statements are related inversely to intimacy (Chelune *et al.*, 1986). Spouses who repeatedly state that they feel worthless may produce distance. Marital therapists may be well advised not to encourage couples to merely "let it all hang out." Self- disclosure of negative self-concepts and negative feelings such as criticism will not increase intimacy. In summary, increasing the amount of self-disclosure between spouses can be expected to increase intimacy if the disclosures are positive or neutral in both feeling and content and are honest.

The process of self-disclosure occurs from the first time a couple meets, through courtship and throughout marriage. Attraction to the opposite-sex person is usually related to issues of physical attraction, reputation, and situational factors. But as the individuals get to know one another, they reveal attitudes and values about children, sexuality, power, and religion that facilitate closeness if similar. Couples with marital problems often deny the importance of disclosing these values and attitudes, believing that love and/or marriage will somehow almost magically prevent conflicts about these issues. However, when children need to go to church or decisions about contraception are pressing, these issues become the focus for dispute. Self-disclosure must explore why these incompatibilities were minimized during courtship and may facilitate closeness by allowing couples to recognize incompatibilities.

Examples may help the reader understand what increasing the amount of self-disclosure really means. A spouse may seek counseling because she believes her husband is selfish. Self-disclosure would involve her attempts to explain why she selected or stays married to a selfish person. A husband may want help with his frustration that his wife is not interested in sex. His self-disclosure might involve exploring why sexual refusal makes him so angry or why he selected an asexual person or what he is doing to sexually turn off his wife. A couple who says they cannot communicate may use self-disclosure to explore why they are giving a clear message that they have nothing to talk about.

RECIPROCITY OF SELF-DISCLOSURE

Studies on interpersonal relationships in marriage have emphasized that marital adjustment is related to a factor referred to variously as "compatibility," "homogamy," "reciprocity," "equity," or "collusion"

(Hatfield & Walster, 1981; Lidz, 1968; Murstein, 1974; Willi, 1982). It appears that similarity of unconscious motivation, personality, attitudes, values, social factors, and even physical appearance and size predict marital adjustment. If similarity is an important aspect of marital adjustment, one suspects that similarity in the amount, type, and depth of self-disclosure may enhance intimacy.

Social exchange theory suggests that a balance in the amount of self-disclosure between partners will predict greater intimacy (Burgess, 1981). According to social exchange theory, we consciously review the costs and the rewards of our relationships, and if the rewards outweigh the costs, the relationship will continue. A spouse may believe that the mate is selfish and demanding but also attractive and a good companion and as a result tolerate the costs to maintain the rewards.

Psychodynamic therapists believe social exchange theory is simplistic and denies the importance of unconscious motivation in spouse selection and sustaining marital discord (Martin, 1976; Willi, 1982). As evidence, they point to the type of relationships in which costs obviously outweigh rewards but in which the couple wish to continue the relationship for unconscious neurotic reasons. This observation may be an example of reciprocity or equity operating at the unconscious level (Martin, 1976; Willi, 1982).

Willi (1982) suggests unconscious equity may operate in cases of marital discord in that many couples collude at an unconscious level to remain at the same level of emotional immaturity. Dominion (1979) has reviewed data that suggests that couples are compatible for neuroticism. It is possible that couples with good adjustment show "conscious" equity, whereas couples with poor adjustment show "unconscious" equity. Neurotic individuals may avoid self-disclosure because of a fear that they may reveal incompatibilities or inequities. Facilitating self-disclosure may facilitate intimacy in these marriages by revealing equity or compatibility for specific insecurities.

In summary, theories from psychodynamic psychology, developmental psychology, social psychology, and interpersonal psychology suggest that reciprocity or equity is a characteristic that promotes compatibility and homogamy. Self-disclosure between spouses should be reciprocal in amount, depth, time, and content to maximize the therapeutic potential of this technique.

EGO RELEVANCE OF DISCLOSURES

Couples with marital discord could disclose their attitudes about nuclear war, politics, or religion. This disclosure might increase their intimacy, but most couples would consider these topics irrelevant to their discord. Fortunately, most couples who perceive deficiencies in their level of closeness seem to accept that the quality of the interpersonal relationships between their grandparents, parents, siblings, and peers prior to their marriage may be relevant to their current discord. For example, a couple who seek therapy for persistent arguments will often reveal that their parents also had problems resolving conflicts. Often they will blame one parent for these arguments initially, but self-disclosure may help them identify behaviors in the other parents that sustained the arguments and also operate in their own marriage. There are, of course, a few couples who do not accept the relevance of these relationships, and this type of therapy is not indicated for these couples.

Psychodynamic theories suggest that the quality of attachment between an infant and his or her mother lays the groundwork for the development of intimacy in adulthood (Bowlby, 1958). Although there is considerable psychological truth to this hypothesis, couples are unable to disclose verbally the quality of these relationships before the age of 3. They may, however, be able to report what they have been told about the relationships by others.

What appears to be more relevant to the development of intimacy in adulthood is the child's observation and experience of the parent's marriage between the ages of about 4 to 15 (Waring, 1981). The child observes how his or her parents express affection, how they resolve differences of opinion, how they relate to in-laws and other couples, how they spend their leisure time, and how they communicate with one another. The child also experiences feelings of insecurity regarding the marriage when there is tension between the parents regarding commitment, sexuality, or difficulties with alcoholism, affairs, or physical or verbal abuse. Spouses in therapy with marital problems often report that their own insecurity in their childhood is due to one of the parents who they believed caused their parents' marital discord or disruption. They often report that they have made conscious decisions not to repeat patterns they observed in their parents' marriages. Couples also believe that relationships with grandparents, siblings, and peers have also influenced their attitudes and beliefs about relationships with the opposite sex. Experience with self-disclosure to siblings, best friends, and relatives of thoughts that they believe they cannot reveal to parents is also important.

Finally, exploration of the motives that attracted individuals to their spouse and led to the decision to marry are also relevant to understanding their problems with intimacy. In summary, couples' observations of their parents' relationships and the couples' own motives ensures the relevance of the content and often provides illuminating insights.

RESPONDING VERSUS REACTING TO SELF-DISCLOSURE

Bowen (1975) has suggested that couples who cannot resolve interpersonal conflict will involve a third-party (including a therapist) to reduce tension but will also avoid resolving the issue. Spouses often respond emotionally (usually with tears or anger) to disclosures that they do not wish to hear. Empathic listening must be used in responding to self-disclosure in order to promote intimacy. Couples often have personal constructs or beliefs that they are reluctant to give up. The therapist must ensure that the spouse appears to be listening. A fundamental rule of self-disclosure therapy is that a spouse may not interrupt while the other spouse is disclosing. The therapist must be aware that when a spouse attempts to break this rule, the couple are reacting to a primary conflict that is always an impasse for developing intimacy. When a therapist feels that therapy is *not* progressing because of characteristics of *one* spouse, that therapist is also reacting and not responding to the other spouse's contribution to the difficulty with intimacy.

EFFECTIVENESS OF SELF-DISCLOSURE APPROACH

I have suggested that developing a specific technique that facilitates self-disclosure between spouses can be an effective method of marital therapy, especially for couples who have deficiencies of intimacy.

Does the therapy work? The tentative answer is a qualified "yes." Is appears to be as effective as other brief marital therapies. Does it work because the process of cognitive self-disclosure enhances marital intimacy? This question has not been answered.

Our first study was an uncontrolled clinical trial that suggested that both the couples and the therapists perceived improvement in symptoms of nonpsychotic emotional illness and marital adjustment (Russell, Russell, & Waring, 1980). This pilot study demonstrated a remarkable compliance with all couples who commenced therapy, completing the 10 sessions. The couples were quite satisfied and to our surprise seldom requested further sessions. They reported improved closeness and greater understanding of themselves and their spouses.

Next, we employed objective assessment instruments that measured symptoms, marital quality, and family function before and after therapy and at 6 month follow-up (Waring & Russell, 1980). Summary evaluations involving questionnaires, therapist reports, couples' reports, and blind evaluations suggested that two thirds of the couples demonstrated clinical improvement. There was a significant reduction in symptoms of nonpsychotic emotional illness and improvement of family functioning. Again treatment adherence was excellent, and if the technique was not going to be helpful, it was obvious after two or three sessions.

A more recent preliminary study was based on a consecutive series of 24 couples who showed significant improvement in symptoms of nonpsychotic emotional illness as well as improved marital intimacy and marital adjustment (Waring, 1984a).

We have also completed a study evaluating the combination of antidepressants and cognitive marital therapy in women with major affective disorders (Waring, 1985). In this clinical sample, self-disclosure was not as effective as more supportive psychotherapy. A similar study of women with less severe depression is currently underway. Also, we are about to begin a study that compares cognitive self-disclosure in moderately distressed couples with low intimacy in comparison to waiting-list controls.

The details of these studies are available in previous publications. Although their preliminary nature does not allow definitive conclusions from these studies on the effectiveness of marital therapy based on facilitating self-disclosure, clinical experience suggests that the approach is efficient and human, although further research on effectiveness is indicated. In future research, it will be feasible to measure specific components of self-disclosure in therapy sessions, before and after therapy, and correlate these measures with changes in marital intimacy (Waring, 1984a; Waring & Reddon, 1983).

CONCLUSIONS

Assuming that future research demonstrates that the technique of cognitive marital therapy is effective, what does the therapy tell us about self-disclosure in marriage? Does the process of self-disclosure facilitate intimacy independent of type or content of disclosures? Does the couple learn through modeling, a type of communication that has been lacking in their relationship? Does cognitive restructuring of undisclosed schemata facilitate change? Does preventing the couple from speaking directly for ten 1 hour sessions produce a paradoxical increase in conversation outside the sessions? Are nonspecific psychotherapy factors such as restoration of morale by preventing arguments or encouraging interpersonal curiosity operating? These questions must remain unanswered until studies that vary technique, type of disclosure, content of disclosure, and other therapy and therapist components and correlate these with specific outcome measures are completed.

Clinical experience from couples who have participated and therapists who have been trained to use the technique have generated some hypotheses. The majority of couples say that they have never communicated in both the style and about the content of self-disclosure employed in the therapy in the time that they have been married. Obviously, they are learning a novel way of communicating about relationships.

Couples rarely report learning or revealing some specific cognitive schema that has changed their feelings or attitudes. Perhaps more than 10 sessions would be necessary for this type of cognitive restructuring to occur. However, they report a greater understanding of their spouse and often, to their surprise, their relationship has improved without their doing anything specific. Couples report that greater understanding and improved communication makes them feel closer. In support of the hypothesis that is the process of cognitive self-disclosure rather than content, couples also tell me that I have not done very much but the relationship has improved anyway.

Some preliminary comments about clinical experience with facilitating cognitive self-disclosure and its effect on intimacy are possible. Couples who both objectively and subjectively derive the greatest benefit spend more time disclosing about the past than the present and about their parents' marriage rather than about their own. The greater the understanding of their own responsibility for mate selection of a spouse with certain qualities or traits (which decreases the amount of projection onto the spouse), the greater the improvement in measures of marital quality. The greater the other spouse can facilitate cognitive restructuring with objective data about his or her own parents' relationship, the greater the improvement in marital intimacy.

The couples articulate that understanding their spouse, learning to be better listeners without reacting defensively or emotionally, and learning about their parents play a role in improving their closeness. The ability to enjoy listening to their parents describe their own marriage is a good clinical predictor of positive outcome.

Finally, the technique has impressed on this observer that the experience and observation of one's parents' level of intimacy has a more obvious influence on developing a parallel repetitive pattern in the current marital relationship than the quality of the affectionate bond between the child and either parent (Waring *et al.*, 1980). In fact, the spouse in a maladjusted marriage would appear to be acting as "a misguided marital counselor," emotionally reacting and attempting to change behaviors of their spouses, which on examination turn out to be the behaviors of the parent who was perceived to be the cause of the parents' lack of intimacy.

In summary, I have described a specific technique designed to facilitate cognitive self-disclosure. The technique appears effective in reducing symptoms of nonpsychotic emotional illness. Whether this change is produced by improving specific deficiencies of marital intimacy as theoretically postulated remains to be determined by specific prospective intervention studies. Other specific treatment techniques can be designed empirically to facilitate marital intimacy as operationally defined.

I have attempted to describe one specific use of self-disclosure in one specific type of therapy—enhancing intimacy in marital relationships. Hopefully, this chapter will encourage both therapists and researchers to examine the many questions raised and perhaps stimulate other innovative uses of self-disclosure as a therapeutic intervention.

REFERENCES

Beck, A. T. (1967). *Depression: Clinical, experimental, and therapeutic aspects.* New York: Harper & Row.

Bowen, M. (1975). Family therapy after twenty years. In S. Arieti (Ed.), *American handbook of psychiatry* (Vol. 5), pp. 367–392. New York: Basic Books.

Bowlby, J. (1958). The nature of the child's tie to his mother. *International Journal of Psychoanalysis, 39,* 350–372.

Burgess, R. L. (1981). Relationships in marriage and the family. In S. Duck & R. Gilmour (Eds.), *Personal relationships* (Vol. 1), pp. 000–000). New York: Academic Press.

Chelune, G. J., Sultan, F. E., Vosk, B. N., Ogden, J. K., & Waring, E. M. (1984). Self-disclosure patterns in clinical and nonclinical couples. *Journal of Clinical Psychology, 40,* 213–215.

Chelune, G. J., Waring, E. M., Vosk, B. N., Sultan, F. E., and Ogden, J. K. (1984). Self-disclosure and its relationship to marital intimacy. *Journal of Clinical Psychology, 40,* 216–219.

Chelune, G. J., Rosenfeld, L. B., & Waring, E. M. (1985). Spouse disclosure patterns in distressed and non-distressed couples. *American Journal of Family Therapy, 13,* 24–32.

Cozby, P. C. (1973). Self-disclosure: A literature review. *Psychological Bulletin, 79,* 73–91.

Davidson, B., Blaswick, J., & Halverson, C. (1983). Affective self-disclosure and marital adjustment: A test of equity theory. *Journal of Marriage and the Family, 45,* 93–102.

Derlega, V. J., & Grzelak, J. (1979). Appropriateness of self-disclosure. In G. J. Chelune (Ed.), *Self-disclosure: Origins, patterns, and implications of openness in interpersonal relationships* (pp. 151–176). San Francisco: Jossey-Bass.

Dominion, J. (1979). Definition and extent of marital pathology. *British Medical Journal, 2,* 478–479.

Erikson, E. (1950). *Childhood and society.* New York: Norton Press.

Gilbert, S. P. (1980). *Measured neuroticism, instructions and levels of intimacy input as determinants of self-disclosure in nursing students.* Unpublished doctoral dissertation, University of Pennsylvania.

Greenberg, L. S., & Safran, J. D. (1984). Hot cognition—Emotion coming in from the cold: A reply to Rachman and Mahoney. *Cognitive Therapy and Research, 8,* 591–598.

Harrell, J., & Guerney, Jr., B. G. (1976). Training married couples in conflict negotiation skills. In D. H. L. Olson (Ed.), *Treating relationships* (pp. 151–166). Lake Mills, IO: Graphic.

Hatfield, E., & Walster, G. W. (1981). *A new look at love*. Reading, MA: Addison-Wesley.

Horowtiz, L. M. (1979).Cognitive structure of interpersonal problems treated in psychotherapy. *Journal of Consulting and Clinical Psychology, 47*, 5–15.

Kelly, G. A. (1955). *The psychology of personal constructs*. New York: W. W. Norton.

Levinger, G., & Senn, D. J. (1967). Disclosure of feelings of marriage. *Merrill Palmer Quarterly, 13*, 237–249.

Lidz, T. K. (1968). *The person: His development through the life cycle.*. New York: Basic Books.

Martin, P. (1976). *A marital therapy manual*. New York: Brunner/Mazel.

Meichenbaum, D. (1977). *Cognitive-behavior modification: An integrative approach*. New York: Plenum Press.

Murstein, B. I. (1974). *Love, sex, and marriage through the ages*. New York: Springer.

Noller, P. (1984). *Nonverbal communication and marital interaction*. Oxford: Pergamon.

Rachman, S. (1984). A reassessment of the "primacy of affect." *Cognitive Therapy and Research, 8*, 579–584.

Rokeach, M. (1973). *The nature of human values*. New York: Free Press.

Russell, A., Russell, L., & Waring, E. M. (1980). Cognitive family therapy: A preliminary report. *Canadian Psychiatric Association Journal, 25*, 64–67.

Segraves, R. T. (1982). *Marital therapy*. New York: Plenum Press.

Waring, E. M. (1981). Facilitating marital intimacy through self-disclosure. *American Journal of Family Therapy, 9*, 33–42.

Waring, E. M. (1984a). *An outcome study on the effectiveness of cognitive family therapy*. Paper presented at the Ontario Psychiatric Association Convention Convention, Toronto, Canada.

Waring, E. M. (1984b). The measurement of marital intimacy. *Journal of Marital and Family Therapy, 10*, 185–192.

Waring, E. M. (1985). *Effectiveness of combined antidepressants and marital therapy in depressed females*. Paper presented at the Ontario Psychiatric Association Convention, Toronto, Canada.

Waring, E. M., & Chelune, G. J. (1983). Marital intimacy and self-disclosure. *Journal of Clinical Psychology, 39*, 183–190.

Waring, E. M., & Reddon, J. R. (1983). The measurement of intimacy in marriage: The Waring Intimacy Questionnaire. *Journal of Clinical Psychology, 39*, 53–57.

Waring, E. M., & Russell, L. (1980). Cognitive family therapy: An outcome study. *Journal of Sex and Marital Therapy, 6*, 258–273.

Waring, E. M., Tillman, M. P., Frelick, L., Russell, L., & Weisz, G. (1980). Concepts of intimacy in the general population. *Journal of Nervous and Mental Disease, 168*, 471–474.

Waring, E. M., McElrath, D., Lefcoe, D., & Weisz, G. (1981). Dimensions of intimacy in marriage. *Psychiatry, 44*, 169–175.

Waring, E. M., McElrath, D., Mitchell, P., & Derry, M. E. (1981). Intimacy and emotional illness in the general population. *Canadian Journal of Psychiatry, 26*, 167–172.

Willi, J. (1982). *Couples in collusion*. New York: J. Aronson.

14

Counseling and Self-Disclosure

SUSAN S. HENDRICK

Why the title "Counseling and Self-Disclosure?" One may well question the need to have chapters on counseling and self-disclosure as well as on psychotherapy and self-disclosure; after all, are they not the same thing? Has not all the information contained in this chapter already been presented in preceding chapters? To provide the raison d'être for the chapter, it is useful to understand something about counseling psychology and the working assumptions it brings to the counseling relationship.

This chapter gives an overview of Counseling Psychology and presents some of the similarities and differences between counseling and psychotherapy. Then a brief presentation of the variety of research on self-disclosure precedes a more detailed focus on research on self-disclosure and counseling, with particular emphasis on studies published in counseling journals such as *The Journal of Counseling Psychology*, the primary outlet journal for counseling psychologists. The problems and gaps in the existing literature are explored, and finally, areas of interest for future research are presented along with several models for looking at self-disclosure as a multidimensional phenomenon within the counselor–client relationship.

SUSAN S. HENDRICK • Department of Psychology, Texas Tech University, Lubbock, Texas 79409.

COUNSELING PSYCHOLOGY

Counseling psychology emerged from several different but distinct traditions: (1) vocational guidance, (2) psychometric developments, and (3) the general psychotherapy movement (Watkins, 1983; Whiteley, 1984).

The vocational guidance tradition began with the 1909 publication of Frank Parson's book, *Choosing a Vocation,* and with the opening of the Vocation Bureau in Boston. The ensuing vocational guidance movement had as its goals the improvement of educational/vocational decision making by young adults through establishing appropriate guidance services in public schools and community agencies. This approach stimulated a flourishing literature in both the instrumentation (e.g., Kuder, 1977; Strong, 1943) and the theoretical base (e.g., Ginzberg, 1952; Holland, 1959; Roe, 1956; Super, 1953) of career development.

The psychometric trend influenced counseling psychology primarily in the development of instruments related to interest, aptitudes, and abilities, insofar as they affected vocational decision making. There was a related interest in general intellectual assessment and a secondary concern with assessment of personality, with the latter subsequently linked to the third tradition influencing counseling psychology—the psychotherapy movement. The development of counseling and psychotherapy from a nonmedical, nonpsychoanalytic model occurred in large measure as a result of Carl Rogers's *Counseling and Psychotherapy,* published in 1942. Rogers's belief that psychotherapeutic activities could be performed by a wider range of professionals (not just physicians) and to a wider range of persons (not so well functioning *and* well functioning) expanded the role of counseling. Although Division 17 did not come into being as a charter division of the American Psychological Association until 1946 and then under the name of Counseling and Guidance (officially changed to Counseling Psychology in 1953) (Whiteley, 1984), the early trends formed the foundation of the later professional specialty area.

Counseling psychology has modified some of its original emphasis on vocational choice and educationally based counseling to include counseling/therapy with mild to moderately disturbed persons (Tipton, 1983) in agency and independent practice settings. However, it still has its roots largely in education and vocational guidance, emphasizing working with "normal" people (e.g., college students) who are experiencing situational questions and problems, and for the most part it endorses a developmental model. Other professionals practicing counseling/therapy, however (e.g., clinical psychologists, psychiatrists, psychiatric social workers), tend to work out of a mental health orientation, employ their skills with persons exhibiting more severe pathology, and often endorse a medical model. Thus the counseling psychologist has a uniquely developmental orientation to bring to the counseling process.

DIFFERENTIATING COUNSELING AND PSYCHOTHERAPY

When asked about the differences between counseling and psychotherapy, a psychology graduate student responded that "counseling is what counseling psychologists do, and therapy is what clinical psychologists do." Although this might appear to some to be a reasonable definition, it makes no move toward clarifying the work of psychiatrists, social workers, marriage and family counselors, pastoral counselors, and so on. In fact, Meador and Rogers (1979) point out that the choice of the word *counseling* for Rogers's seminal book, *Counseling and Psychotherapy,* was chosen more for political than descriptive reasons.

> Originally the term "counseling" was chosen because it was a modest term, and because the word "therapy" immediately aroused a fight whenever it was used. Psychiatrists felt that therapy was their field. (p. 139)

Although many writers have associated *non directive* with the word *counseling* because of Rogers's influence, nondirective really refers to the stylistic aspects of how a professional might conduct either counseling or therapy. Janis (1983) notes that counseling may involve asking more questions and giving more directions than therapy, though his rationale does not appear to take into account the popular and rather directive cognitive-behavioral therapies. Still others (e.g., Corsini, 1968) assert that counseling and psychotherapy differ both in objectives and techniques, with counseling operating from an educational-developmental stance and psychotherapy from a more remediative position. A not infrequent consultant, Webster (1963) states that counseling is "the use of psychological methods in testing the interests of and giving professional guidance to individuals" (p. 190), whereas therapy is "remedial treatment" of a biological or psychological disorder (p. 916).

There has been some tendency to consider counseling and psychotherapy on a continuum, with counseling a sort of advice-giving, directive behavior at one end and psychotherapy an in-depth, largely passive except for—occasional—brilliant—neo—analytic—interpretations at the other. However, Rogers's original nondirective counseling was certainly at the passive end of the continuum, and the advent of the cognitive-behavioral therapies has carried a certain amount of directiveness into the psychotherapy realm. A more accurate representation of the directiveness dimension in relation to counseling and psychotherapy might well involve a simple 2 × 2 design, with counseling and psychotherapy as columns and directive/nondirective as rows. That representation, however, assumes counseling and therapy as dichotomous rather than continuous variables, and continuous they surely are. Length of treatment could be proposed as a variable differentiating counseling and therapy, but "long-term" counseling and "brief psychotherapy" exist to dispel that proposition. We noted before the importance of describing the populations with whom counseling or therapy is conducted. Tipton (1983) has discussed the fact that counseling psychologists describe themselves as working with "a relatively normal and a mild to moderately disturbed population of adults" (p. 842), whereas clinical psychologists are more inclined to view "a severely disturbed population as well as a mild to moderately disturbed population" (p. 843) as central to their professional role. Is counseling appropriate for the "normal" or near normal and therapy for the more severely disturbed? Not according to Tipton, who throughout his article uses "counseling/therapy" as the designation for the professional-client process. Baruth and Huber (1985) use the two terms interchangeably also, even while noting that others (e.g., Belkin, 1980; Hansen, Stevic, & Warner, 1982) have viewed the two as related but qualitatively different, with counseling emphasizing "mobilization" of the personality to deal with specific problems and therapy emphasizing "reorganization" of the personality to deal with life in general as well as with specific problems.

Thus no one scholar appears to provide "the" definitive statement regarding counseling and therapy. I preceive the two as highly related, frequently overlapping processes that are often, but not always, implemented with similar populations in relatively similar settings. No single feature differentiates the two, yet each has a somewhat different emphasis and ambience.

SELF-DISCLOSURE IN GENERAL

As defined by Sidney Jourard (1964), self-disclosure refers to the process of telling another person about oneself, honestly sharing thoughts and feelings that may be very personal and private. Jourard was one of the first psychologists to develop the area of self-disclosure for extended research and discussion, and his name is still strongly associated with the area. He believed that the physical and psychological health of individuals and the success of relationships requires adequate self-disclosure to strip away restrictive social masks.

A wide variety of research has been conducted that employs self-disclosure as a relevant variable. Social penetration theory (Altman & Taylor, 1973), a theory of both personality and relationship development, includes self-disclosure as the primary vehicle for relationship progress. Although breadth of disclosure is typically greater in the initial stage of a relationship, intimacy (or depth) increases as the relationship continues. Considerable research on self-disclosure has been based on tenets of exchange theory, such as the concept of reciprocity. The basic tenet that "disclosure begets disclosure" has been confirmed in various studies (e.g., Ehrlich & Graeven, 1971; Jourard, 1971); however, self-disclosure appears to be less strictly reciprocal and more flexible in well-established relationships (Derlega, Wilson, & Chaikin, 1976). Such flexibility has important implications for married couples, although research findings have been inconsistent. Morton (1978) found spouses to be less reciprocally self-disclosing than were strangers, whereas other research has shown spouses to be highly reciprocal (e.g., Hendrick, 1981; Komarovsky, 1967). Variable self-disclosure is not surprising in intimate relationships, and Gilbert (1976) has suggested that there is an apparent dichotomy between intimacy and security needs in marriage, whereby intimacy is fostered by self-disclosure and security is threatened by it. This intimacy/security dichotomy has implications for the counselor–client relationship and will be discussed more fully later.

Self-disclosure has also been examined in relation to the process of interpersonal liking (another area of relevance to counseling). The relationship between self-disclosure and liking is not always a direct, positive one because liking can be influenced by the timing (Wortman, Adesman, Herman, & Greenberg, 1976), the intimacy (Worthy, Gary, & Kahn, 1969), and the context (e.g., Hoffman-Graff, 1977) of the disclosure. Direct links between disclosure and personality have not been effectively substantiated, though some research suggests that highly disclosing persons are better adjusted than persons who disclose less (Jourard, 1971; Strassberg, Anchor, Gabel, & Cohen, 1978). In an extensive review of the disclosure literature, Cozby (1973) hypothesized that "mentally healthy" persons are characterized by high disclosure to those close to them and moderate disclosure to others in their social environment.

Interesting but contradictory research has examined gender differences in self-disclosure. Some studies have shown women to disclose more than men (e.g., Chelune, 1977; DeForest & Stone, 1980; Hendrick, 1981), whereas other research has revealed no major gender differences in disclosure (e.g., Feigenbaum, 1977; Komarovsky, 1974). Still other research indicates that men will disclose more under certain circumstances (e.g., Derlega, Winstead, Wong, & Hunter, 1985). A related issue that appears to be extremely relevant to the counseling relationship is the fact that men and women do appear to differ in self-disclosure, depending on who the target person is to whom they disclose (Jourard,

1971; Komarovsky, 1974). Indeed, Miller, Berg, and Archer (1983) state that the use of a "general" construct of self-disclosure is not useful; the target person of the self-disclosure must be specified. These authors have in fact developed a target-specific self-disclosure measure that correlates highly with the longer and frequently used Jourard Self-Disclosure Questionnaire (Jourard & Resnick, 1970).

The literature on self-disclosure is interesting, varied, and often contradictory. Research that relates self-disclosure to relationship progress, liking, gender, and so on has natural implications for the counseling process, and research specifically addressing these and other issues within the counseling setting will be presented in detail later.

SELF-DISCLOSURE IN COUNSELING

Self-disclosure has become a familiar concept in counseling psychology. Though professionals differ in the ways they employ, endorse, and research self-disclosure, at least the term and the concept it describes, virtually unknown two decades ago, are now consistently studied in relation to the counseling process. Research on self-disclosure in the counseling relationship is extensive and focuses considerable energy on the issue of counselor disclosure, as it influences both (1) the client's perceptions and evaluations of the counselor and (2) the client's attitudinal and behavioral willingness to disclose.

Clients' Perceptions of Counselors

The nature of the counseling/therapeutic *relationship* is widely recognized as a critical component of successful counseling. As psychology has moved in the direction of more elaborate and sophisticated theory and techniques, it has become apparent that "technology" is not enough. Like John Naisbitt, who in his bestseller, *Megatrends* (1984), discusses the phenomenon of "high tech-high touch" (e.g., the need for intimate interaction to accompany society's technological advances), scholars have realized that it is often the counseling relationship that makes or breaks the therapeutic outcome (Gelso & Carter, 1985). Successful therapists of every orientation probably pay considerable conscious (or unconscious) attention to relationship aspects. Indeed "there appears to be no effective way of separating techniques from relationship factors via research; the two are inseparably intertwined" (Strupp, 1984, p. 22). A number of studies have attempted to examine the implications of counselor disclosure. In an early study, Graff (1970) examined counselor self-disclosure as a dimension of counseling effectiveness, relating graduate student counselors' scores on a self-disclosure measure to client and supervisor ratings of the counselor. Substantial correlations were found between disclosure and the criterion measures of counseling effectiveness (e.g., counseling climate, client satisfaction, overall competence, effective counselor responses). Although the study has numerous methodological flaws, it helped establish self-disclosure as a potent variable in counseling.

Self-disclosure can be either positive or negative, with positive disclosure revealing positive counselor qualities or experiences, and negative disclosure revealing personal weaknesses, disruptive experiences, and the like. Hoffman-Graff (1977) studied counselor use of positive or negative self-disclosure and its effects (along with those of interviewer–subject gender pairing) on subjects' perceptions. After meeting with interviewers who offered either positive or negative self-disclosure, subjects completed several questionnaires relevant to the interview. Results revealed that negative disclosers were seen as more empathic and warm than were positive disclosers. A number of explanations were given for the findings, but the contribution of the study was largely its demonstration that "self-disclosure" is not a unitary construct and cannot be treated as one. A similar study (Hoffman & Spencer, 1977) yielded comparable results, with negatively disclosing interviewers perceived as more credible and unconditionally regarding than positive interviewers.

Self-disclosure has been found to interact with a number of relevant variables. A counseling analog study (Merluzzi, Banikiotes, & Missbach, 1978) varied counselors' gender, experience, and self-disclosure level, with perceived counselor expertness, attractiveness, and trustworthiness serving as dependent measures, in a test of Strong's (1968) social influence model in counseling. Results for self-disclosure indicated that low-disclosing counselors were rated as more expert and more trustworthy than high-disclosing counselors, though the latter were perceived as more attractive. One interesting finding was that experienced high-disclosing counselors obtained the highest attractiveness rating. Gender-relevant findings were not of major importance. Another analog study (Nilsson, Strassberg, & Bannon, 1979) studied subjects' ratings of videotaped counseling vignettes with experimental conditions of "no disclosure, intrapersonal disclosure, and *inter*personal disclosure" (the last is similar to the concept of "self-involving" disclosure that will be discussed more fully in the next section). Both types of disclosures yielded more favorable evaluations than the no-disclosure condition on all the personal evaluation items, but the authors note that "those items designed to tap subjects' evaluations of the Counselor as a professional did not by themselves distinguish the disclosing from the nondisclosing Counselors" (p. 402). A study with somewhat different outcomes was conducted by Curtis (1981), using an analog format with mental health agency clients as subjects. Results indicated that the written patient–counselor dialogues containing high self-disclosure elicited lower ratings on perceived empathy, competence, and trust. In a recent study (Lee, Uhlemann, & Haase, 1985), counselors' verbal and nonverbal responses in a 20-minute interview were evaluated separately by clients and outside judges as well as by the counselors themselves. Although counselor self-disclosure, along with other behaviors, accounted for a modest percentage of the variance for attractiveness, the key finding of this study is that clients and external judges perceived counselor behavior differently. Indeed,

> judge-determined counselor verbal and nonverbal response categories were inefficient predictors of the client-perceived expertness, trustworthiness, and attractiveness levels of the counselor. (p. 183)

Thus we must be specific not only about self-disclosure itself (e.g., positive/negative, interpersonal/intrapersonal, high/medium/low) but also about those who evaluate it (e.g., experimental subjects, actual clients, counselor supervisors). Indeed, Cash and Salzbach (1978) point out that self-disclosure may mitigate the effects of counselor variables such as physical attractiveness.

Although the literature on client perceptions of counselor disclosure is somewhat mixed, self-disclosing counselors are generally evaluated more positively. However, the variety of designs employed and the heavy reliance on analog research necessitate caution when drawing overall conclusions. The variety of instruments used for counselor/interviewer rating is also a problem.

In addition to employing counselor self-disclosure as an independent variable and client evaluation of the counselor as the dependent measure, numerous studies have used actual counselee self-disclosure as a dependent variable.

Counselor and Counselee Self-Disclosure

Early research in counselor and client self-disclosure was largely designed to test Jourard's (1964) belief that "self-disclosure begets self-disclosure." In a much-cited study, Bundza and Simonson (1973) provided subjects with one of three transcripts of simulated counseling sessions. The three conditions represented in the transcripts were "no self-disclosure," "warm support," and "warm support plus self-disclosure." Subjects rated the counselor portrayed in their transcript and also indicated their own willingness to disclose personal information to the counselor. Results revealed that the counselor who was both supportive (warm) and disclosing was rated the most nurturant and elicited greatest subject willingness to disclose.

Client expectations have been found to be important in counseling and were the basis of the Derlega, Lovell, and Chaikin (1976) study in which subjects' expectancies about the appropriateness of counselor self-disclosure affected their subsequent reactions to a disclosing counselor. Subjects who were told that personal counselor disclosure was appropriate talked more intimately to a high- than low-disclosing counselor. However, differential (high, low) counselor self-disclosure did not affect subjects' responses when they had been told that counselor self-disclosure was inappropriate or where no expectancy had been induced. Thus expectancy had an effect in one condition. In another exploration of client expectancy, Simonson (1976) manipulated counselor disclosure and warmth in an analog study. Results indicated that subjects who had heard an audiotape of a "warm" and *moderately* disclosing counselor subsequently disclosed more when being interviewed by that counselor than did subjects exposed to a warm nondisclosing or a highly (e.g., personally) disclosing counselor. "Cold" counselors, at every level of self-disclosure, elicited less communication from subjects. An additional finding of interest was a .82 correlation between the administered Jourard Self-Disclosure Questionnaire and actual interview disclosure. Consistent with several previous studies, the author suggested that accurate knowledge of a counselor's communication style (e.g., expectations congruent with subsequent reality) promotes increased client disclosure. The interplay of client expectations and tendency to reciprocate was shown in an adaptation of a social psychology role-play paradigm used by DeForest and Stone (1980), who ascertained intimacy of subjects' willingness to disclose after the subjects had been given a written indication of a counselor's general disclosure style. The reciprocity hypothesis was strongly supported, with participant disclosures increasing in linear fashion from low to medium to high in correspondence with counselor disclosure conditions. However, client "expectations" of counselor style may well have influenced reciprocity. Also focusing on client expectations as an influence on the counseling situation, Riley, Cozby, White, and Kjos (1983) exposed subjects identified as high or low in need for approval to experimental conditions reflecting either clear expectation of high counselor self-disclosure or ambiguous expectations. As predicted, subjects who were high in need for approval expressed greater willingness to disclose in the clear expectation rather than in the ambiguous expectation condition. Such findings are similar to those of Shaffer, Smith, and Tomarelli (1982) in their non-counseling-related study of self-monitoring and self-disclosure. Here, high self-monitors were more likely to reciprocate the emotionality, intimacy, and descriptive content of a confederate's self-disclosure in a dyadic situation than were low self-monitors, a reminder that "client" variables are powerful influences on self-disclosure.

Broadening the research focus, Halpern (1977) examined disclosure and specific related situational variables in a study involving college students receiving individual counseling services. Her results did not offer total support for any *single* theory of self-disclosure in counseling. A client's past tendency to disclose was significantly related to the present tendency to disclose in counseling; however, client perception of the counselor as self-disclosing and facilitative also had a positive, significant relationship to clients' perceptions of their own disclosure. Once again, it is the client's behavioral tendencies, client perceptions (and expectations) of the counselor, and other variables that interact to influence self-disclosure. Attempting to go beyond the familiar, college-setting study, Kiyak, Kelley, and Blak (1979) administered a self-disclosure questionnaire to court-referred youths and their volunteer counselors several times over a period of weeks. Results showed self-disclosure to vary in a nonlinear fashion for both counselors and counselees. This study's primary importance is its attempt to assess self-disclosure in a real-world counseling setting.

Not only amount but also flexibility of counselor self-disclosure has been assessed. Neimeyer and Fong (1983) assessed disclosure flexibility of counselors in training at the beginning of a 3-month training period. Ratings were also done of these counselors' effectiveness, based on three audiotaped counseling sessions conducted over the training period. More flexible counselors offered more effective responses to clients but only during the first of the three sessions. In another examination of self-disclosure flexibility, this time from the client perspective, Neimeyer, Banikiotes, and Winum (1979) investigated differences between high, middle, and low-flexibility disclosure subjects in their ability to accurately perceive facilitative counselor responses. In fact, high flexibility disclosers exhibited more affective sensitivity and were more accurate in perceiving facilitative counselor responses than were middle or low flexibility subjects. Thus various disclosure characteristics influence the communication process.

In an examination of the effects of a model's race and sex as well as length of model disclosure on subjects' self-disclosure, Casciani (1978) found that only gender had a significant effect, with subjects disclosing at more depth and for longer periods after observing same-sex models. That particular types of counselor self-disclosure can have a deleterious effect on client self-disclosure was shown by Chesner and Baumeister (1985), who assessed the effects of counselor religious affiliations on the intimacy of client disclosure. Christian subjects disclosed less intimately to a counselor identified as either a devout Christian or a devout Jew than a counselor who did not disclose religious affiliation. Jewish clients, on the other hand, only disclosed less to the devout Christian counselor;

disclosure to the devout Jew and to the control counselor did not differ significantly. The authors note that disclosure of religious affiliation did *not help* client self-disclosures in any situations but actively *hurt* disclosure in several instances. Counselors who did not disclose any religious information received the best client disclosure throughout.

Problems with the literature on counselor disclosure as it affects client disclosure are similar to those discussed in the previous section. Use of undergraduate populations, analog studies, and a variety of designs, measures, and related variables has resulted in findings that may appear interesting in and of themselves but that are for the most part unrelated to each other.

Self-Disclosure and Related Counselor and Client Characteristics

Because the topic of client disclosure has been thoroughly addressed in another chapter, we will only briefly discuss a few studies that have explored the impact of various counselor characteristics (other than self-disclosure) on client self-disclosure. The issue of counselor personality characteristics and client disclosure was explored by Barnes and Berzins (1978) in a study of the Type A-Type B counselor dimension. (Type A counselors have been shown to be more reserved and less risk taking, whereas Type B's appear more open and willing to take risks). Type A and Type B undergraduate volunteers were evaluated as they conducted interviews with schizophrenic and neurotic male state hospital inpatients. Although B interviewers looked forward to conducting the interviews more than did the A's, A-type interviewers obtained greater self-disclosure from the schizophrenic patients. B-type interviewers performed better with the neurotic patients, however. The authors propose interviewer effectiveness to be "a joint function of interviewer personality characteristics and the stiuational context" (p. 1368). Using male undergraduates in an analog study to test an A-B hypothesis involving complementarity of counselor and client, Lynch, Kogut, and Smith (1976) found that A-type counselors were generally more successful than B-type counselors, though B interviewers covered more topics than did A interviewers. Again, the issue seems not to be "who is the best counselor?" but "who is the best counselor for a given client with a given problem at a given time in a given context?"

A number of other variables such as counselor dogmatism (Wright, 1975) and spatial-environmental conditions of counseling (Lecomte, Bernstein, & Dumont, 1981) have been shown to have differential effects on client self-disclosure, but no consistent pattern of results has emerged. Simonson and Bahr (1974) investigated possible interactive effects of counselor self-disclosure (no disclosure, demographic disclosure, personal disclosure) and counselor status (professional, paraprofessional) on subject disclosure and attraction to the counselor. They found that moderately (demographic) disclosing professional and paraprofessional counselors were liked and disclosed to equally well but that highly (personally) disclosing paraprofessionals were liked and disclosed to much more than were personally disclosing professionals. These findings substantiated the authors' hypothesis that the psychological distance between the client and the professional counselor is too great to permit intense, personal counselor disclosure; the "expectations" of the client regarding appropriate professional distance are violated. Expectations and "distances" are different for the paraprofessional.

Giannandrea and Murphy (1973) took a somewhat different angle as they assessed the impact of a number of interviewer similarity self-disclosures on subject/client willingness to return for a second counseling interview. Although no treatment effects were found on the counselor evaluation scale completed by the clients, client return behavior was significantly higher when disclosure level was moderate. In assessing the relationships between the cognitive styles of field-dependent/field-independent clients and their self-disclosure in counseling, Sousa-Poza and Rohrberg (1976) examined detailed transcripts of counseling sessions. Although field-dependent clients directly disclosed significantly more than did field-independent clients, the authors note that many factors other than amount of direct self-disclosure influence the communication and indeed the total context of the counselor–client relationship.

Although these research findings substantiate the general importance of counselor and client-relevant variables to client self-disclosure, again we find no common threads linking one study to another. However, one emerging area in self-disclosure research appears to offer some much-needed continuity.

Self-Disclosing versus Self-Involving Counselor Communication

Self-disclosing counselor communication refers to personal experiences or qualities of the counselor that do not directly involve the client, whereas self-involving counselor communication refers to the counselor's immediate feelings and reactions within the counseling context. A self-disclosing counselor might say, "I was depressed for several months after my divorce," whereas the self-involving counselor would more likely say, "As you talk about your divorce, I'm aware of feeling very sad." McCarthy and Betz (1978) initially explored the differential effects of these two types of counselor communication in an analog format and found that the self-involving counselor was rated as more expert, more trustworthy, and somewhat more attractive than the self-disclosing counselor. The former also elicited client disclosure with fewer counselor referents, more self-referents, and more present-tense (as opposed to past- or future-tense) phrases. In what was essentially a replication of this study, McCarthy (1979) found that self-involving counselors were evaluated as significantly more expert, attractive, and trustworthy than disclosing counselors and were able to elicit more self-referent, present-tense phrases from clients. Attempting to extend this line of research while bridging the gap between analog and real-world research, Dowd and Boroto (1982) assessed the differential effects of counselors ending a taped counseling session by (1) giving past disclosure, (2) giving present disclosure, (3) making self-involving statements, (4) summarizing, or (5) offering interpretations on subjects' ratings of counselor expertness, attractiveness, and trustworthiness, as well as their willingness to see the counselor for a session. Results showed no significant differences between conditions for expertness and trustworthiness, but the first three conditions elicited a higher attractiveness rating than did the last two conditions. Subjects were most willing to see the counselor who ended the session with interpretations and least willing to see the summarizing counselor. The authors explain the differences between their findings and those of McCarthy and Betz (1978) on the basis of methodological differences and the possibility that structuring statements (such as interpretations) are more appealing to clients. McCarthy (1982) countered, however, finding that high self-disclosing *and* high self-involving counselors (in an analog study) were perceived as more expert and trustworthy than low-disclosing counselors and were more able to elicit client self-referents and present-tense statements. The highly disclosing counselor also elicited more affective words. (A related finding of interest was that paraprofessional counselors were rated as more trustworthy and attractive than professional counselors [see Simonson & Bahr, 1974]).

Combining the issues of disclosing versus involving and positive versus negative communication, Remer, Roffey, and Buckholtz (1983) asked subjects to read counseling typescripts and both (1) rate the counselor on expertness, attractiveness, and trustworthiness and (2) write client responses to the counselor. Results were mixed, with positive self-involvement yielding higher attractiveness ratings and more client-affective words, and negative self-involvement yielding fewer client past-tense verbs. The authors note that this study helps to "fill in a gap in counselor response effectiveness research" (p. 125).

Continued building of the literature can be seen in a study by

Reynolds and Fischer (1983), who varied self-involving and self-disclosing counselor statements along a positivity–negativity dimension in an analog study. After listening to counseling tapes, subjects rated the involving counselor as more professional than the disclosing counselor and more able to keep the counseling focus on the client rather than the counselor. The positivity–negativity dimension produced no significant differences. The authors propose support for the McCarthy and Betz (1978) and McCarthy (1979) studies, although noting that future research must take into account such issues as improved instruments for assessing clients' feelings about counselors, use of both genders as clients and counselors (this study used only females), more employment of real-world settings and less reliance on analog studies, assessment of related variables such as disclosure content, and so on. Although it is clear that much work remains, research in the area of self-disclosure versus self-involvement by counselors has made a promising start.

PROBLEMS IN EXISTING LITERATURE

Self-disclosure as a variable in the counseling process is alive and well. Although there does not yet exist a comprehensive model for the employment of self-disclosure, the counseling psychologist's question does not appear to be *if* but *when*. No counseling researchers in the area (except perhaps Jourard) have viewed self-disclosure as a panacea, but the deep mistrust of disclosure as violator of the transference relationship has been much less representative of counseling psychologists than of other professionals such as psychiatrists and clinical psychologists. Research reviewed in this chapter has not typically asked whether opacity should characterize a counselor. Rather, the questions have concerned positive and negative self-disclosure (e.g., Hoffman-Graff, 1977; Hoffman & Spencer, 1977), perceived counselor expertness, attractiveness, trustworthiness, and self-disclosure (e.g., Lee *et al.*, 1985; Merluzzi *et al.*, 1978), the reciprocity effect in self-disclosure (e.g., Bundza & Simonson, 1973; Halpern, 1977), the differential effects of self-involving versus self-disclosing counselor communication (e.g., McCarthy & Betz, 1978; Reynolds & Fischer, 1983), similarity of self-disclosure (e.g., Murphy & Strong, 1972), and a number of other counseling-related issues. Thus the fundamental question is not *if* the counselor should disclose but *when*—under what circumstances? Given that this basic premise seems to underlie most counseling research in the area (see Gelso & Carter, 1985, for another counseling approach to transference issues), what implications does that premise have for research as it now exists and research as it should exist in the future?

First, if self-disclosure research is to grow and prosper, it must develop more coherence than it has had thus far. Although each research study we have discussed could be individually criticized, problems in the area are thematic and go beyond any one study.

Designs

Numerous designs have been used, most of them based on an analog model that involves undergraduate subjects reading transcripts, hearing audiotapes, or viewing videotapes of counselors. The "counselors" may be either actual counselors, students training to be counselors, or confederates. Although analog studies are often disparaged in comparison to the real thing, such studies will inevitably form the basis of self-disclosure research. Actual behavioral observation of counselors and clients in session (or of any such close relationship) is laborious (e.g., Gottman, 1979) and presents issues of confidentiality, demand characteristics, and the like. Such behavioral research could more fruitfully be undertaken when some of the underlying questions have been explored in baseline analog studies. And in these baseline studies, use of transcripts *or* audiotapes *or* videotapes would offer useful continuity within the exploration of a particular research question. I am not suggesting that only one type of design or stimulus material be used throughout but rather that consistent methods be used in exploring a given issue (e.g., positive versus negative counselor self-disclosure to clients).

Measures

Some of the same problems that exist with methods also exist with measures. The Jourard Self-Disclosure Questionnaire (JSDQ; Jourard & Resnick, 1970), the Self-Disclosure Inventory (SDI; Jourard, 1964), the Self-Disclosure Situations Survey (SDSS; Chelune, 1975, 1976), and various behavioral measures of self-disclosure (e.g., intimacy of client responses, tense of client responses, focus [self or other] of client responses) have all been employed in counseling research. In addition, a new social psychological disclosure measure, the Self-Disclosure Index (Miller, Berg, & Archer, 1983) shows considerable promise.

Measures for evaluating counselors have also varied from subjective client or supervisor ratings to the Barrett-Lennard Relationship Inventory (Barrett-Lennard, 1962), the Counselor Rating Form (LaCrosse & Barak, 1976), and others. Again, the critical issue is not so much which measure is used (although the Jourard measures are problematic; see Cozby, 1973) but that measures be used consistently in a given line of research. Although along with a discussion of dependent measures comes the critical questions of measuring willingness to disclose versus actual disclosure and measuring via paper-and-pencil questionnaires versus behavioral assessment, such questions recall the methodological issue discussed earlier. Again, it is likely that initial exploratory research will use paper-and-pencil measures in an analog format, with later extension of the paradigm into behavioral assessments in real-world settings.

Other Research Issues

One of the most exciting and frustrating aspects of counseling research on self-disclosure is the vast array of independent variables that have been explored. These include (but are not limited to) positive and negative self-disclosure, counselor race, A or B style, status, flexibility, level of counselor disclosure, self-disclosure versus self-involvement, and so on. Most of these findings have been provocative, and most (with the exception of studies on involvement/disclosure) have been disconnected. No areas have been systematically explored in the same way that social psychologists explore such phenomena as similarity-attraction, self-monitoring, or attribution. Such systematic exploration is sorely needed.

Thus the overarching critique of this whole area of research is that there has not yet been the systematic building of lines of research that can give us satisfactory answers to our questions regarding self-disclosure in the counseling relationship and process. There has been some fine research—but it has not been enough. Since it is apparent that the topic of self-disclosure will continue to be researched, we must do more. Yet unlike ". . . the American tourist in a foreign country who, when he cannot be understood by the local citizen, resorts to speaking louder and louder—in English!" (Hendrick & Hendrick, 1983, p. 196), it is critically important that we *not* just do "more of the same." We need to develop our own megatrends for this research.

NEW DIRECTIONS FOR RESEARCH IN COUNSELING AND SELF-DISCLOSURE

An important point to be kept in mind is that this chapter addresses issues involving self-disclosure and counseling psychologists (and closely related professionals) who operate within the developmental-educational framework outlined at the beginning of this chapter. There are many counseling situations in which counselor self-disclosure could be unproductive at best or damaging to the client at worst (for alternative approaches to self-disclosure see Glazer, 1981; Weiner, 1972), but these are usually situations where client problems are severe and/or are enmeshed within the counselor/client relationship. However, these situations are not typically a major concern in the counseling settings with which this chapter is concerned. Again, our question is not "if" but "when"?

Reprise on Designs

We noted earlier that analogue designs might usefully provide the basis for extended research into specific questions regarding self-disclosure. For instance, Study I on a research question such as the use of high, moderate, or low counselor self-disclosure might involve a typescript or tape of counselor disclosure and a research subject's (1) written evaluation of specific counselor characteristics and (2) written statement of the client's willingness to disclose to such a counselor (e.g., Nilsson *et al.*, 1979). Study II in the series might replicate Study I and add an interview in which a subject's actual disclosure to the "counselor" could be measured (e.g., Bundza & Simonson, 1973). Study III might provide an experimental interview session as the stimulus material (replacing the typescript or tape) in which differential "counselor" disclosure would be offered. Then the subject's actual disclosure and written evaluations of the counselor could be measured as they were in Study II (e.g., DeForest & Stone, 1980). A fourth study might move several of the previously used measures into a real counseling situation. Such development of study building on study presupposes results in early studies that are significant enough both statistically and conceptually to warrant further exploration. Although we do not propose that this type of research approach would offer a miraculous answer to the problems in self-disclosure research, it is an approach that has been successful in other areas of psychology (e.g., Byrne, 1971).

Reprise on Measures

A number of self-disclosure instruments favored by counseling researchers were mentioned earlier and will probably continue to be used. A new measure, the Self-Disclosure Index (Miller *et al.*, 1983), was employed successfully by its developers in several studies and is currently being used by the present author in ongoing research. Miller and her colleagues underscored the importance of designing a self-disclosure measure that could be target-specific because disclosure can vary, depending on the identity of the person to whom one is disclosing. They thus designed an instrument with 10 items or stems (e.g., "my deepest feelings") for which the target person could be varied. Research by this author (Hendrick & Hendrick, 1985) employed the Self-Disclosure Index as part of a larger questionnaire measure of attitudes toward love and sex that was administered to 218 undergraduate subjects at Texas Tech University in the spring of 1985. The index was included twice, first for "partner" as the target person and second for "same-sex friend" as the target person. Exploratory correlational analyses revealed significant and theoretically meaningful correlations between both versions of the index and the love attitude and sexual attitude scales developed by Hendrick, Hendrick, Foote, and Slapion-Foote (1984) and Hendrick, Hendrick, Slapion-Foote, & Foote (1985). For example, there was a significant positive correlation ($r = .34$) between disclosure to a love partner and a scale measuring passionate love, and a significant negative correlation ($r = -.25$) between such disclosure and another scale measuring game-playing love. Internal reliability analyses for both versions of the index provided a standardized item Alpha of .88 for disclosure to a love partner and one of .91 for disclosure to a same-sex friend. Although the measure is brief (10 items) and therefore quite limited in content, it offers ease of administration, target specificity, and validity and reliability that are promising (Miller *et al.*, 1983).

Another measure developed by the same authors is the Opener Scale, a 10-item measure of an individual's self-perceived ability to *elicit* disclosure from others. This scale was used in the same spring, 1985, Texas Tech research study and produced numerous significant correlations as well as a standardized item Alpha of .90. This scale could be emphasized in counselor–client self-disclosure research in a number of ways. It could be used to (1) assess a counselor's perception of his or her ability to elicit disclosure from clients (or a specific client), (2) assess a client's perception of a counselor's ability to elicit disclosure, and (3) provide a difference score between 1 and 2. Scores could then be related to numerous other variables such as actual client disclosure, client satisfaction, and so on. The Self-Disclosure Index and the Opener Scale appear to be ideal instruments for future research on counselor and client self-disclosure.

Potential Paradigms

A basic issue in the study of self-disclosure in counseling has been Jourard's (1964) reciprocity norm about counselor self-disclosure eliciting client self-disclosure. Although variants of this norm undoubtedly do operate, it seems essential that we not take the word *reciprocity* too literally. Reciprocity refers to a mutual giving and taking, an alternate moving forward and moving back (Webster, 1963, p. 715); however, it does not mean *equality*. Although our disclosure as counselors may sometimes foster disclosure from our clients, we cannot expect the disclosures to be necessarily equal in terms of duration, depth, or any other dimension. In fact, they probably should *not* be equal. By its very nature, the counseling process is unequal—in power, in knowledge, in self-confidence, and so on. If the counselor does not (at least at the beginning of the counseling process) possess "more" of a good number of these relevant positive characteristics than the client, the client is probably wasting his or her time and money in counseling! If, on the other hand, at the end of the counseling process, the client has not appreciably grown in a number of these relevant ways, the process has probably not been successful. Part of the counselor's responsibility to the client is role modeling (see Hendrick & Hendrick, 1984) that by its very nature is unequal (e.g., one "models" and the other "learns"). Thus continuing research on self-disclosure must not confuse *reciprocal* with *equal*. Indeed, Martin Buber (1958) states that, although counseling is best done in the context of an "I-Thou" relationship, full mutality is not possible or even desirable (p. 133). In addition, clients may experience the intimacy/security needs dichotomy proposed by Gilbert (1976) in relation to marriage. Thus counselor disclosure that is too intimate may threaten a client's security within the counseling relationship.

Some research in counseling and self-disclosure already models the direction needed for the future, most clearly that exploring self-disclosing versus self-involving counselor communication (e.g., McCarthy, 1979; McCarthy & Betz, 1978; Reynolds & Fischer, 1983). This research area appears to be continuing, and further research will be welcome. In addition, a number of the variables discussed in this chapter will continue to be explored, hopefully systematically.

Another potential direction for counseling self-disclosure research would take us in the direction of social psycohlogy. One social psychology experiment that appears to make up for in intuitive appeal what it lacks in methodological rigor is the Aronson, Willerman, and Floyd (1966) study that evolved out of the John F. Kennedy Bay of Pigs fiasco in the early 1960s. Although this event appeared to be a major political blunder, Kennedy's personal popularity increased greatly after the incident. In exploring possible reasons why this occurred, Aronson and his colleagues performed an experiment in which subjects evaluated confederates who appeared either extremely superior intellectually or extremely average. In addition, the confederates either showed themselves to be clumsy or not. Results showed that the most-liked confederate was the one who was brilliant—but clumsy! It appeared that human fallibility, added to very desirable characteristics, produced higher attractiveness. There is some conceptual similarity in the Merluzzi *et al.* (1978) study in which high-disclosing counselors who were perceived as "experienced" obtained the highest attractiveness ratings from subjects. To the extent that a counselor's self-disclosure reflects his or her fallibility and willingness to be vulnerable to the client, such disclosure may facilitate the counselor–client relationship *as long as* the counselor is also perceived as a knowledgeable expert. Using the Aronson et al. paradigm to explore the possible relationships between counselor expertness and vulnerability (as shown through disclosure) could be an interesting research direction.

In some sense, much of the research on self-disclosure in counseling is concerned with a relative "balance" of therapeutic factors (e.g., expertness and vulnerability). Argyle and Dean's (1965) "affiliative-conflict" or "equilibrium" model of visual interaction behavior states that intimacy in dyadic interaction is influenced by eye contact and related factors. Because there are forces in the interaction moving the dyad partners toward greater intimacy, whereas other factors move them away from intimacy, persons will seek to find a comfortable *equilibrium point* where the factors are in balance. However, if one factor such as eye contact increases, other factors must either increase or decrease in some way to maintain the equilibrium. Perhaps the therapy dyad functions the same way in regard to relationship factors that influence intimacy. Thus the exemplar of counselor expertness versus counselor vulnerability could be explored within the equilibrium paradigm to see if changes in one result in changes in the other. On the other hand, perhaps in congruence with Patterson's (1976) arousal model of intimacy, if there is an extremely positive counselor–client relationship, increased disclosure by the counselor will result in increased perception of expertness by the client. If there is some negativity or ambivalence in the relationship, however, increased disclosure may induce perceptions of decreased expertness. Whatever the answers to these particular questions, it is clear that a number of social psychological models could be used by counselors in their self-disclosure research.

CONCLUSIONS

Beyond our use of designs, measures, and paradigms is our willingness to explore the subject of self-disclosure in counseling in new (or old) ways. Mahrer, Fellers, Durak, Gervaize, and Brown (1981) have pointed to the need to do "more systematic study of the antecedents and consequences of self-disclosure as used by counselors in both actual and analogue counseling sessions" (p. 175). We need to study what kinds of counselor and client statements elicit counselor self-disclosure and what kinds of counselor and client statements are elicited by it. We could also profit perhaps by "returning to the drawing board" in a sense and asking research subjects as well as actual clients what kinds of characteristics (including type and amount of self-disclosure) they would find most helpful in/from a counselor. This is descriptive research, without the advantages of current methodological sophistication, yet one viable way of finding an answer is to directly ask a question. Although cries of "transference," "countertransference," "demand characteristics," "social desirability," and so on can be heard, such open-ended descriptive research is one of the *several* research methods that needs to be used with self-disclosure.

Counseling outcome research is not just useful; it is mandatory. Not only can self-disclosure be assessed as part of an outcome study, but clients with successful outcomes can be asked retrospectively about the process and content aspects of counselor self-disclosure that have been influential during the therapy process. We may find that although disclosure of the therapist's parenting strategies is helpful in family counseling, disclosure of the therapist's sexual practices may be harmful in sex counseling.

What we are most likely to find is that counselor self-disclosure is sometimes helpful and sometimes not, both across and within counseling relationships. Some content areas of disclosure are probably nearly always appropriate, some never appropriate, and most sometimes appropriate. Disclosure will interact with relevant counselor and client characteristics (e.g., status of counselor, dependency of client) to differentially affect such variables as perceived therapist attractiveness and trustworthiness, client disclosure, and so on. The valences (positive or negative) and flexibility of disclosure will also be influential. The complexity seems overwhelming, but what we can hope to find is some common threads, common themes, that will point us in the right research, and then counseling, directions.

Self-disclosure is a multifaceted process that must be explored multimodally. A number of the research approaches suggested by Harvey, Christensen, and McClintock (1983) for the study of close relationships can be directly applied to the counselor–client relationship (also a "close relationship"). We can no more expect simple answers in the counseling context than we can in the marital context. What is desirable is a variety of approaches to self-disclosure in counseling with *consistency* of research development within a given approach.

REFERENCES

Altman, I., & Taylor, D. (1973). *Social penetration: The development of interpersonal relationships.* New York: Holt, Rinehart & Winston.

Argyle, M., & Dean, J. (1965). Eye contact, distance and affiliation. *Sociometry, 28,* 289–304.

Aronson, E., Willerman, B., & Floyd, J. (1966). The effect of a pratfall on increasing interpersonal attractiveness. *Psychonomic Science, 4,* 227–228.

Barnes, D. F., & Berzins, J. I. (1978). A and B undergraduate interviewers of schizophrenic and neurotic inpatients: A test of the interaction hypothesis. *Journal of Consulting and Clinical Psychology, 46,* 1368–1373.

Barrett-Lennard, G. T. (1962). Dimensions of therapist response as causal factors in therapeutic change. *Psychological Monographs, 76*(43, Whole No. 562).

Baruth, L. G., & Huber, C. H. (1985). *Counseling and psychotherapy: Theoretical analyses and skills applications.* Columbus, OH: Charles E. Merrill.

Belkin, G.S. (1980). *An introduction to counseling.* Dubuque, IA: William C. Brown.

Buber, M. (1958). *I and thou* (2nd ed.). New York: Charles Scribner's Sons.

Bundza, K. A., & Simonson, N. R. (1973). Therapist self-disclosure: Its effect on impressions of therapist and willingness to disclose. *Psychotherapy: Theory, Research, and Practice, 10,* 215–217.

Byrne, D. (1971). *The attaction paradigm.* New York: Academic Press.

Casciani, J. M. (1978). Influence of model's race and sex on interviewees' self-disclosure. *Journal of Counseling Psychology, 25,* 435–440.

Cash, T. F., & Salzbach, R. F. (1978). The beauty of counseling: Effects of counselor physical attractiveness and self-disclosures on perceptions of counselor behavior. *Journal of Counseling Psychology, 25,* 283–291.

Chelune, G. J. (1975). Self-disclosure: An elaboration of its basic dimensions. *Psychological Reports, 36,* 79–85.

Chelune, G. J. (1976). The self-disclosure situations survey: A new approach to measuring self-disclosure. *JSAS Catalog of Selected Documents in Psychology, 6*(1367) 111–112.

Chelune, G. J. (1977). Sex differences, repression-sensitization and self-disclosure: A behavioral look. *Psychological Reports, 40,* 667–670.

Chesner, S. P., & Baumeister, R. F. (1985). Effect of therapist's disclosure of religious beliefs on the intimacy of client self-disclosure. *Journal of Social and Clinical Psychology, 3,* 97–105.

Corsini, R. J. (1968). Counseling and psychotherapy. In E. F. Borgatta & W. W. Lambert (Eds.), *Handbook of personality theory and research* (pp. 1105–1129). Chicago: Rand McNally.

Cozby, P. C. (1973). Self-disclosure: A literature review. *Psychological Bulletin, 79,* 73–91.

Curtis, J. M. (1981). Effect of therapist's self-disclosure on patients' impressions of empathy, competence, and trust in an analogue of a psychotherapeutic interaction. *Psychological Reports, 48,* 127–136.

DeForest, C., & Stone, G. L. (1980). Effects of sex and intimacy level on self-disclosure. *Journal of Counseling Psychology, 27,* 93–96.

Derlega, V. J., Lovell, R., & Chaikin, A. L. (1976). Effects of therapist disclosure and its perceived appropriateness on client self-disclosure. *Journal of Consulting and Clinial Psychology, 44,* 866.

Derlega, V. J., Wilson, M., & Chaikin, A. L. (1976). Friendship and disclosure reciprocity. *Journal of Personality and Social Psychology, 34,* 578–582.

Derlega, V. J., Winstead, B. A., Wong, P. T. P., & Hunter, S. (1985). Gender effects in an initial encounter: A case where men exceed women in disclosure. *Journal of Social and Personal Relationships, 2,* 25–44.

Dowd, E. T., & Boroto, D. R. (1982). Differential effects of counselor self-disclosure, self-involving statements, and interpretation. *Journal of Counseling Psychology, 29*, 8–13.

Erlich, H. J., & Graeven, D. B. (1971). Reciprocal self-disclosure in a dyad. *Journal of Experimental Social Psychology, 7*, 389–400.

Feigenbaum, W. M. (1977). Reciprocity in self-disclosure within the psychological interview. *Psychological Reports, 40*, 15–26.

Gelso, C. J., & Carter, J. A. (1985). The relationship in counseling and psychotherapy: Components, consequences, and theoretical antecedents. *The Counseling Psychologist, 13*(2), 155–243.

Giannandrea, V., & Murphy, K. C. (1973). Similarity self-disclosure and return for a second interview. *Journal of Counseling Psychology, 20*, 545–548.

Gilbert, S. (1976). Self-disclosure, intimacy and communication in families. *The Family Coordinator, 25*, 221–231.

Ginzberg, E. (1952). Toward a theory of occupational choice. *Occupations, 30*, 491–494.

Glazer, M. (1981). Anonymity reconsidered. *Journal of Contemporary Psychotherpay, 12*, 146–153.

Gottman, J. M. (1979). *Marital interaction: Experimental investigations*. New York: Academic Press.

Graff, R. W. (1970). The relationship of counselor self-disclosure to counselor effectiveness. *The Journal of Experimental Education, 38*(3), 19–22.

Halpern, T. P. (1977). Degree of client disclosure as a function of past disclosure, counselor disclosure, and counselor facilitativeness. *Journal of Counseling Psychology, 24*, 41–47.

Hansen, J. C., Stevic, R. R., & Warner, R. W. (1982). *Counseling: Theory and Process* (3rd ed.). Boston: Allyn & Bacon.

Harvey, J. H., Christensen, A., & McClintock, E. (1983). Research methods. In H. H. Kelley *et al.* (Eds.), *Close relationship* (pp. 449–485). New York: W. H. Freeman.

Hendrick, C., & Hendrick, S. (1983). *Liking, loving, & relating*. Monterey, CA: Brooks/Cole.

Hendrick, C., & Hendrick, S. (1984). Toward a clinical social psychology of health and disease. *Journal of Social and Clinical Psychology, 2*, 182–192.

Hendrick, C., Hendrick, S., Foote, F. F., & Slapion-Foote, M. J. (1984). Do men and women love differently? *Journal of Social and Personal Realtionships, 1*, 177–195.

Hendrick, S., & Hendrick, C. (1985). [Relationships between love attitudes and relevant variables]. Unpublished raw data.

Hendrick, S., Hendrick, C., Slapion-Foote, M. J., & Foote, F. F. (1985). Gender differences in sexual attitudes. *Journal of Personality and Social Psychology, 48*, 1630–1642.

Hendrick, S. S. (1981). Self-disclosure and marital satisfaction. *Journal of Personality and Social Psychology, 40*, 1150–1159.

Hoffman, M. A., & Spencer, G. P. (1977). Effect of interviewer self-disclosure and interviewer-subject sex pairing on perceived and actual subject behavior. *Journal of Counseling Psychology, 24*, 383–390.

Hoffman-Graff, M. A. (1977). Interviewer use of positive and negative self-disclosure and interviewer-subject sex pairing. *Journal of Counseling Psychology, 24*, 184–190.

Holland, J. L. (1959). A theory of vocational choice. *Journal of Counseling Psychology, 6*, 35–45.

Janis, I. L. (1983). *Short-term counseling: Guidelines based on recent research*. New Haven: Yale University Press.

Jourard, S. M. (1964). *The transparent self*. Princeton, NJ: Van Nostrand Reinhold.

Jourard, S. M. (1971). *Self-disclosure: An experimental analysis of the transparent self*. New York: Wiley.

Jourard, S. M., & Resnick, J. L. (1970). The effect of high revealing subjects on the self-disclosure of low revealing subjects. *Journal of Humanistic Psychology, 10*, 84–93.

Kiyak, H. A., Kelley, T. M., & Blak, R. A. (1979). Effects of familiarity on self-disclosure in a client-counselor relationship. *Psychological Reports, 45,* 719–727.
Komarovsky, M. (1967). *Blue-collar marriage.* New York: Vintage Books.
Komarovsky, M. (1974). Patterns of self-disclosure of male undergraduates. *Journal of Marriage and the Family, 36,* 677–686.
Kuder, G. F. (1977). *Activity interests and occupational choice.* Chicago: Science Research Associates.
LaCross, M. B., & Barak, A. (1976). Differential perception of counselor behavior. *Journal of Counseling Psychology, 23,* 170–172.
Lecomte, C., Bernstein, B. L., & Dumont, F. (1981). Counseling interactions as a function of spatial-environmental conditions. *Journal of Counseling Psychology, 28,* 536–539.
Lee, D. Y., Uhlemann, M. R., & Haase, R. F. (1985). Counselor verbal and nonverbal responses and perceived expertness, trustworthiness, and attractiveness. *Journal of Counseling Psychology, 32,* 181–187.
Lynch, D. J., Kogut, D., & Smith, J. (1976). A test of the complementarity hypothesis in A-B research. *Journal of Consulting and Clinical Psychology, 44,* 865.
Mahrer, A. R., Fellers, G. L., Durak, G. M., Gervaize, P. A., & Brown, S. D. (1981). When does the counsellor self-disclose and what are the in-counselling consequences? *Canadian Counsellor, 15*(4), 175–179.
McCarthy, P. R. (1979). Differential effects of self-disclosing versus self-involving counselor statements across counselor-client gender pairings. *Journal of Counseling Psychology, 26,* 538–541.
McCarthy, P. R. (1982). Differential effects of counselor self-referent responses and counselor status. *Journal of Counseling Psychology, 29,* 125–131.
McCarthy, P. R., & Betz, N. E. (1978). Differential effects of self-disclosing versus self-involving counselor statements. *Journal of Counseling Psychology, 25,* 251–256.
Meador, B. D., & Rogers, C. R. (1979). Person-centered therapy. In R. J. Corsini (Ed.), *Current psychotherapies* (2nd ed.), pp. 131–184. Itasca, IL: W. E. Peacock.
Merluzzi, T. V., Banikiotes, P. G., & Missbach, J. W. (1978). Perceptions of counselor characteristics: Contributions of counselor sex, experience, and disclosure level. *Journal of Counseling Psychology, 25,* 479–482.
Miller, L. C., Berg, J. H., & Archer, R. L. (1983). Openers: Individuals who elicit intimate self-disclosure. *Journal of Personality and Social Psychology, 44,* 1234–1244.
Morton, T. L. (1978). Intimacy and reciprocity of exchange: A comparison of spouses and strangers. *Journal of Personality and Social Psychology, 36,* 72–81.
Murphy, K. C., & Strong, S. R. (1972). Some effects of similarity self-disclosure. *Journal of Counseling Psychology, 19,* 121–124.
Naisbitt, J. (1984). *Megatrends.* New York: Warner Books.
Neimeyer, G. J., & Fong, M. L. (1983). Self-disclosure flexibility and counselor effectiveness. *Journal of Counseling Psychology, 30,* 258–261.
Neimeyer, G. J., Banikiotes, P. G., & Winum, P. C. (1979). Self-disclosure flexibility and counseling-relevant perceptions. *Journal of Counseling Psychology, 26,* 546–548.
Nilsson, D. E., Strassberg, D. S., & Bannon, J. (1979). Perceptions of counselor self-disclosure: An analogue study. *Journal of Counseling Psychology, 26,* 399–404.
Patterson, M. L. (1976). An arousal model of interpersonal intimacy. *Psychological Review, 83,* 235–245.
Remer, P., Roffey, B. H., & Buckholtz, A. (1983). Differential effects of positive versus negative self-involving counselor responses. *Journal of Counseling Psychology, 30,* 121–125.
Reynolds, C. L., & Fischer, C. H. (1983). Personal versus professional evaluations of self-disclosing and self-involving counselors. *Journal of Counseling Psychology, 30,* 451–454.

Riley, G. D., Cozby, P. C., White, G. D., & Kjos, G. L. (1983). Effect of therapist expectations and need for approval on self-disclosure. *Journal of Clinical Psychology, 39,* 221–226.

Roe, A. (1956). *The psychology of occupations.* New York: Wiley.

Rogers, C. R. (1942). *Counseling and psychotherapy.* Boston: Houghton-Mifflin.

Shaffer, D. R., Smith, J. E., & Tomarelli, M. (1982). Self-monitoring as a determinant of self-disclosure reciprocity during the acquaintance process. *Journal of Personality and Social Psychology, 43,* 163–175.

Simonson, N. R. (1976). The impact of therapist disclosure on patient disclosure. *Journal of Counseling Psychology, 23,* 3–6.

Simonson, N. R. , & Bahr, S. (1974). Self-disclosure by the professional and paraprofessional therapist. *Journal of Consulting and Clinical Psychology, 42,* 359–363.

Sousa-Poza, J. F., & Rohrberg, R. (1976). Communicational and interactional aspects of self-disclosure in psychotherapy: Differences related to cognitive style. *Psychiatry, 39,* 81–91.

Strassberg, D. S., Anchor, K. N., Gable, H., & Cohen, B. (1978). Client self-disclosure in short-term psychotherapy. *Psychotherapy: Theory, Research and Practice, 15,* 153–157.

Strong, E. K., Jr. (1943). *Vocational interests of men and women.* Stanford, CA: Stanford University Press.

Strong, S. R. (1968). Counseling: An interpersonal influence process. *Journal of Counseling Psychology, 15,* 215–224.

Strupp, H. H. (1984). Psychotherapy research: Reflections on my career and the state of the art. *Journal of Social and Clinical Psychology, 2,* 3–24.

Super, D. E. (1953). A theory of vocational development. *American Psychologist, 8,* 185–190.

Tipton, R. M. (1983). Clinical and counseling psychology: A study of roles and functions. *Professional Psychology: Research and Practice, 14,* 837–846.

Watkins, C. E., Jr. (1983). Counseling psychology versus clinical psychology: Further explorations on a theme or once more around the "identity" maypole with gusto. *The Counseling Psychologist, 11*(4), 76–92.

Webster's seventh new collegiate dictionary. (1963). Springfield, MA: G. & C. Merriam Co.

Weiner, M. F. (1972). Self-exposure by the therapist as a therapeutic technique. *American Journal of Psychotherapy, 26,* 42–51.

Whiteley, J. M. (1984). Counseling psychology: A historical perspective. *The Counseling Psychologist, 12*(1), 3–109.

Wortman, C., Adesman, P., Herman, E., & Greenberg, R. (1976). Self-disclosure: An attributional perspective. *Journal of Personality and Social Psychology, 33,* 184–191.

Worthy, M., Gary, A. L., & Kahn, G. M. (1969). Self-disclosure as an exchange process. *Journal of Personality and Social Psychology, 13,* 59–63.

Wright, W. (1975). Counselor dogmatism, willingness to disclose and clients' empathy ratings. *Journal of Counseling Psychology, 22,* 390–394.

15

Commentary

Self-Disclosure, A Very Useful Behavior

RICHARD L. ARCHER

I have been invited to close this volume on self-disclosure with a commentary. My comments begin with a quick wide-angle view of the entire undertaking and how it relates to past work on self-disclosure. From this point, I will proceed to focus on particular features of the individual chapter offerings as the main body of my commentary. The uses of self-disclosure, a functional approach, will be introduced as the method for inventorying the ways in which disclosure is employed by the various authors. Finally, in one last look, I will conduct a kind of roll call of the chapters by way of summary.

A WIDE-ANGLE VIEW

Self-disclosure has frequently struck personality and social psychologists as an odd rock upon which to build an area of research. When I was in my first years as an assistant professor, one of my most valued colleagues would periodically engage me in a discussion about it, beginning with, "You say you study self-disclosure, but that's a *behavior*. Is there a *theory* of self-disclosure?" (Wicklund, personal communication, 1976). At the time I thought this was an odd question. In trying to provide

RICHARD L. ARCHER • Department of Psychology, Southwest Texas State University, San Marcos, Texas 78666–4616.

a good-faith answer, though, I quickly conceded that with the exception of Jourard's (1964, 1971) personality work on the transparent self and Altman and Taylor's (1973) account of social penetration in relationship development, there were no systematic attempts to explain what moves people to disclose self-information. Instead, I explained that the interests of self-styled self-disclosure researchers like myself were riveted on phenomena such as disclosure reciprocity and disclosure-induced liking.

Since then, there has been a lot of water under the bridge. Although the sheer number of published studies has increased dramatically, so has the number of critics from within the ranks proposing changes in the methods and focus of disclosure research (see Archer & Earle, 1983). I believe that a common concern behind these appeals was the growing awareness that the area was *isolated*: ironically, self-disclosure research, which investigates intimate communication, was failing to communicate itself to personality and social psychology or social science at large.

The first and foremost comment I have to offer is that if the entries comprising this volume are any indicator, the prognosis for self-disclosure research is beginning to improve. Interestingly enough, my optimism does not stem from any remarkable upsurge of interest to be seen here in the general theories of disclosure motivation my colleague asked for—although some of the chapters, notably Stiles's (Chapter 12) fever model and Berg's (Chapter 6) analysis of responsiveness, come close. Neither is it the product of any widespread adoption of the critics' many proscriptions for rehabilitating disclosure research (although all the contributors duly consider shortcomings in the literature and offer suggestions of their own for circumventing them).

Although we are considering what the contributors do *not* do, please note that along with Berg and Derlega in their introductory Chapter 1, these authors are not in the least preoccupied with preserving and defining an independent area of research labeled self-disclosure. Previous volumes, for example, Chelune (1979), have already done so. What is more important, despite the value of these earlier reviews in gaining visibility and providing entry to the literature, further reviews at this juncture may actually be counterproductive. Continuing to circumscribe self-disclosure may further isolate it!

What this volume *has* done is to bring together a number of active investigators and practitioners who are *using* the concepts and methods of self-disclosure as a means (and not the only means) to understand some other wider issue in personality, relationships, or therapy. Perhaps my preceding observation that they are trying to circumvent past shortcomings is particularly appropriate. It is almost as if, in an effort to overcome the isolation of self-disclosure research, its investigators stopped trying to draw in other social scientists from the outside and decided to "bring the mountain to Mohammed."

In reality, however, this tour de force of the uses of self-disclosure reflects no conscious strategy, much less a conspirational one. In fact, many of the contributors would be unwilling to cast even themselves as "self-disclosure investigators." But, because self-disclosure furnishes them with a useful (i.e., practical and generative) perspective and set of methods with which to pursue their own chosen issues, it looks to me like self-disclosure has finally arrived. It is at last entering the mainstream just as the critics always hoped.

FOCUSING ON FEATURES

Orientations and Functions

Having argued that the common thread loosely woven through these chapters is the uses of self-disclosure, I am committed to a functional look at the particulars. The chief advantage to approaching the chapters in this way is that it provides a basis for an inventory. It allows us to see which among disclosure's multiple uses is receiving its fair share of attention and which is not. For example, Archer and Earle (1983) imposed a set of functionally based categories on studies of self-disclosure and of intimate communication in groups. The flood of research on some functions and the trickle of research on others led them to argue that the field of self-disclosure

> finds itself unwittingly marooned in social exchange and self-presentation and neither fish (the study of developing self-conceptions through communication) nor fowl (the study of developing relationships through communication). (Archer & Earle, 1983, p. 307)

Similarly, a functionally based inspection of the contributions that comprise this volume could be used again to gauge the depth and breadth of current activity in disclosure theory, research, and therapy. Happily, two servicable conceptions of disclosure's uses are available for this task, Archer and Earle's (1983) interpersonal orientations of disclosure mentioned before and Derlega and Grzelak's (1979) functional approach to self-disclosure appropriateness cited in several chapters in this volume.

At first blush, the obvious contrasts between these schemes stand out. Archer and Earle's intent was to unify disclosure and group process research, whereas Derlega and Grzelak's was to explore the reasons that underlie self-disclosure appropriateness/effectiveness. Consequently, Archer and Earle's orientations form a hierarchy from least to most

TABLE 1. Orientations and Functions of Disclosure Compared

	Archer and Earle (1983)	Derlega and Grzelak (1979)
Orientation	Use	Function
1. Self	Expresses self's feelings	1. Expression
	Clarifies self-concept	2. Self-clarification
2. Self to other	Locates self in reference to others	3. Social validation
3. Other to self	Obtains benefits for self from others	5. Social control
4. Other	Elicits self-information from others	4. Relationship development
5. Self and other	Addresses the relationship between self and others	

interpersonal, whereas Derlega and Grzelak's functions are simply organized into classes.

Coming a bit closer to these two conceptions, the comparisons become more striking. Whether they are called "orientations" or "functions," Archer and Earle and Derlega and Grzelak agree that self-disclosure may be put to a limited number of uses.[1] In its most individual and direct form, disclosure is used to express strong and immediate feelings. (e.g., "I feel *great!*"). More cognition is involved in disclosing to *find* one's feelings and beliefs (e.g., "The more I listen to myself, the more I realize I *do* love her"). Alternatively, there is the option to use disclosure to find out where one stands with others (e.g., "You mean you think a guy who's made the choices I have deserves a woman like her?"). With a little more planning, disclosure has strategic uses, securing for us more than just evaluations from others (e.g., "Now that you know how much I really love you, you've just *got* to marry me"). A similar if more equitable use of disclosure is to trade it for information about others (e.g., "I've been married before, but we didn't have any children. What about yourself?"). Finally, disclosure is used in its most complex and social form to represent and negotiate the terms of relationships with others (e.g., "I've always thought of us as a two-career family. What will happen to us if you quit the firm?).

These "orientations" and "functions" appear side by side in Table 1. Archer and Earle's self orientation is obviously Derlega and Grzelak's self-clarification function. Derlega and Grzelak identify the even more basic (intrapersonal) expression function that should probably also fall within the self-orientation. The self-to-other orientation translates directly

[1]In this chapter, the various uses of disclosure are referred to as orientations, functions, classes, and categories interchangeably.

as the social validation function and the other-to-self just as directly to social control. At the more interpersonal level, it is Archer and Earle who further distinguish the other orientation, eliciting reciprocal self-disclosure, from the self-and-other orientation, disclosure about the nature of the relationship. Derlega and Grzelak combine both in their relationship development function.

To summarize, the two conceptions are alike in organizing disclosure into five similar categories. They differ primarily in that Derlega and Grzelak divide the intrapersonal uses more finely, whereas Archer and Earle more thinly slice the interpersonal ones.

Of course, any particular instances of disclosure, including my earlier examples from a love affair, may and undoubtedly do serve multiple functions. Similarly, each chapter in this book manages to mention most if not all of them. To sharpen my chapter descriptions (and avoid losing the readers' interest), I will try to associate each with the particular function or two that most typify it.

The Self-Orientation. Self-oriented or self-clarifying disclosures are concerned with exploring the nature and contents of oneself, *for* oneself. Although this function has a fundamental ring, Archer and Earle (1983) were surprisingly hard pressed to find studies that investigated (rather than assume) how it operated. Consequently, Davis and Franzoi's (Chapter 4) empirical link between private self-consciousness and self-disclosure and Stiles's (Chapter 12) fever model are particularly welcome.

Davis and Franzoi's self-report data demonstrate that, far from being the inevitable route to loneliness, the disposition to attend to emotions, motives, and memories is a precursor of the tendency to disclose and hence, to relationship development. But, does the link merely reflect differential accumulation or salience of self-information on the part of those who are high and low in self-consciousness, or do they actually have different complex needs for self-expression, knowledge, or defenses? The authors are stymied in the attempt to choose from among these nonmotivational and motivational explanations by a serious lack of direct and discriminating evidence about process. Davis and Franzoi have done a thorough job of framing these questions and even offer the necessary research designs to answer them. I certainly hope that this offer will be taken up and that the chapter will serve as a blueprint for their own and others' future studies on the self-consciousness–self-disclosure relationship.

Although Davis and Franzoi begin with empirical findings, Stiles's fever model of disclosure starts with theory. He might be said to be answering the question, "How could Jourard (1964, 1971) *and* his critics all be right about the role of self-disclosure in psychopathology and therapy?" This is easy: Disclosure is psychologically analogous to a fever.

Thus high disclosure can be *simultaneously* "a sign of disturbance and part of the restorative process" (Stiles, Chapter 12, this volume). Stiles pictures disclosure as the subjective expression of the speaker's experience distinguished by Derlega and Grzelak (1979). By carrying forward this fresh and instructive analogy to embrace exposure-induced hypothermia and autoimmune fevers, it can account for overly low disclosure due to an absence of relationships and overly high disclosure produced by excessive self-involvement. In addition to proposing an orderly, hopeful resolution to the perplexing psychotherapy outcome literature, the fever model also raises some researchable questions about the role of disclosure in relationships (expressive vs. strategic). It will be intriguing to see just how far Stiles will be able to push this analogy empirically and predictively.

The Self-to-Other Orientation. Self-to-other or self-validating disclosures are directed to locating oneself in relation to others by means of eliciting feedback. Despite the traditional interest of group process researchers (e.g., Latané, Ekman, & Joy, 1966) in this kind of communication (or perhaps because of it), it is not a primary focus for the chapter authors. Certainly Davis and Franzoi (Chapter 4) and, to a lesser extent, Stiles (Chapter 12) mention the supporting role of feedback in the self-consciousness-disclosure link and the fever model, respectively. Clearly, however, obtaining information from others takes a back seat to *self*-expression and clarification in both.

Other chapters dealing with psychological distress, including Coates and Winston's (Chapter 11), Stokes's (Chapter 9) on loneliness, and of course, Hendrick's (Chapter 14) on counseling, Waring's (Chapter 13) on marital therapy, and Carpenter's (Chapter 10) clinical contributions, must deal with self-to-other disclosure, too. Even so, it will be seen that neither feedback from friends and family nor from a psychotherapist is the central issue for them. So let me forge on.

The Other-to-Self Orientation. Other-to-self or social control disclosure is by nature strategic. It is a means to obtain benefits from others. Archer and Earle (1983) note that this kind of ingratiating, self-presentational disclosure has been a favored perspective of experimental social psychologists. Among this book's contributors, Coates and Winston (Chapter 11), Stokes (Chapter 9), and Hill and Stull (Chapter 5) still adopt this perspective. Their own research designs are correlational rather than experimental, however, and their issues are far away from the impression-formation literature.

Coates and Winston, like Stiles (Chapter 12), grapple with the problem of increased disclosure during psychological distress. Unlike Stiles, they decide that it *is* primarily a problem because, although it is informative for the hearer, it also generates his or her avoidance. So ironically, direct disclosure of distress is a very uncertain avenue to obtain social support to weather it. Coates and Winston wonder if high self-monitors, people who tend to monitor their own behavior in reference to the parameters of the social situation in which they find themselves, have found the way out of this dilemma to successful distress disclosure. Unfortunately, their data suggest that although high self-monitors are indeed more adept at securing social support, they are if anything *more* distressed than lows. Apparently for all their tact, high self-monitors also carry with them the baggage of an inflated concern over social approval that leads them to play down their distress. Coates and Winston then argue that a hunt for willing donors rather than successful solicitors may be a better way to attack the problem. Perhaps, and certainly it *is* a worthwhile route for investigators. Nevertheless, their self-monitoring results do not preclude other approaches based on teaching social skills or even a look at other skill-based traits such as the high (responsive) opener (see Berg, Chapter 6; Henrick, Chapter 14; and Miller & Read, Chapter 3).

It is intriguing (and reassuring) that Stokes's (Chapter 9) examination of the loneliness-disclosure relation comes up with a view of rejected distress disclosure so similar to that of Coates and Winston. The chief difference between these two accounts of correlational self-report studies is that the predictive trait for Coates and Winston is self-monitoring, whereas for Stokes it is loneliness. Both chapters see supportive relationships as the goal for the distressed discloser. But, where Coates and Winston's research tests a trait that might improve those relationships, Stokes's research straightforwardly demonstrates how important relationships are to loneliness. Like Davis and Franzoi (Chapter 4), Stokes is struck by the complexities of model building where disclosure and personality are concerned. In an effort to include predispositions for loneliness, he is led to the work of Bowlby (1973) and Rubenstein and Shaver (1980) on parent–child attachment as a promising basis for future study. I, too, suspect that Stokes and the many other personality, social, and developmental psychologists who have been excited by the recent attachment work will not be disappointed by where it leads.

Hill and Stull, on the other hand, take on the unevitable task of bringing order to Jourard's (1971) classic issue of gender and self-disclosure, which eventually leads them to the other-to-self orientation. In the process of scrutinizing the yield from five different research strategies, they run up against the inherent limitations of trait-based self-report designs like Davis and Franzoi's (Chapter 4), Coates and Winston's (Chapter 11), and their own, where gender differences are the focus. After a valiant but futile search for a general pattern, Hill and

Stull are forced to conclude that "the original prediction that traditional male role expectations inhibit men's disclosure is too simple because it does not take into account the many situational factors that affect disclosure" (Hill & Stull, Chapter 5, this volume). In addition to reciting the old woes of individual differences, traits, and their measures, these authors, too, invite us to consider the varying functions disclosure can serve. In particular, Hill and Stull point up the complex styles and differing amounts of disclosure that are bound to emerge between the sexes as males and females employ strategies to obtain benefits from one another. I share their hope that investigators will let go of the seemingly unanswerable and increasingly uninteresting question of whether, without reference to context, females or males disclose more.

The Other Orientation. Other-orientation disclosure is one way disclosure can function in relationship development. Like other-to-self disclosure, it is a means to obtain something, but that "thing" is reciprocal disclosure rather than some other benefit. Hopefully, what goes around comes around. Like no other orientation, other-oriented disclosure has enjoyed the attentions of investigators in and out of the lab (see Archer & Earle, 1983). The guiding light of social exchange theory (e.g., Altman & Taylor, 1973) can clearly be seen in this research tradition.

Unlike self-to-other disclosure, this well-tilled soil has not ceased to interest the contributors to this book. Berg's (Chapter 6) concept of conversational responsiveness, Hendrick's (Chapter 14) consideration of self-disclosure in counseling, Carpenter's (Chapter 10) view of disclosure and psychopathology, and yes, even Chelune's (Chapter 2) neuropsychological perspective, I think belong here.

In responsiveness, Berg has found a neat way to explain and tie together the findings on disclosure reciprocity, disclosure-induced liking, and even counselor disclosure. I classify it as other oriented because it focuses upon the efforts of the recipient of disclosure. As Berg attempts to subsume relational responsiveness within conversational responsiveness—"behaviors . . . through which the recipient indicates interest in and understanding of that communication" (Berg, Chapter 6, this volume)—he also seems to be moving away from the benefits perspective of social exchange (other-to-self disclosure) to the information perspective of communication theory (other disclosure). A look at Fitzpatrick's (Chapter 7) and Baxter's (Chapter 8) approaches (which I will discuss in the last orientation) confirms that Berg is not alone in this change of perspective. Berg presents a compelling case for responsiveness as a parsimonious, *descriptive* concept. Like Stiles's (Chapter 12) fever model, a lot depends on how it fares in the competitive market of *predictive* concepts. At times, responsiveness (at least relational responsiveness) skates perilously close to personalism in its meaning.

But then, I might be showing a sentimental bias (cf, Jones & Archer, 1976). I believe, along with Berg, that if new concepts generate new disclosure studies and especially if they improve prediction they are welcome.

Hendrick's and Carpenter's chapters explore the applied "helping" professions of psychology, counseling, and psychotherapy, in relation to self-disclosure. I am convinced by Hendrick's arguments that any attempt to distinguish between the two is bound to be unsatisfactory in some way. However, the notion that counseling mobilizes the personality whereas therapy reorganizes it is an appealing one. Counseling has developed its own journals and its own self-disclosure literature. Hendrick assesses these studies on how a counselor must behave and be perceived to secure the confidence and disclosure of the client. In viewing them, it occurred to me that investigators in counseling, more than any other group, have taken it upon themselves to evaluate Jourard's (1964, 1971) humanistic notions about two-way openness in the counselor/therapist–client relationship. It is also painfully obvious that they have been hindered in this undertaking by the frequent resort to analog designs in addition to all the other methodological problems that plague disclosure research. In the end, Hendrick appears to endorse the conceptual spirit of Jourard's approach rather than the concrete letter: Self-*involving* rather than self-*disclosing* counselor communication may be just the ticket to successful process. Like the parallel between Coates and Winston's (Chapter 11) and Stokes's (Chapter 9) views of distress disclosure, it is noteworthy and encouraging that her self-involving counselor has so much in common with Berg's responsive one.

In my opinion, Carpenter's task in describing the relationship between psychopathology and disclosure is every bit as daunting as Hill and Stull's (Chapter 5) was for gender and disclosure. The number of disclosure citations that mention psychopathology is just as vast as that exploring gender. Unfortunately, after examining them, Carpenter, too, finds himself facing a lack of evidence and in no better position to make a decisive statement. Here again, investigators have doggedly pursued the issue in simplistic terms without much attention to process: Is more or less disclosure than "normal" symptomatic or even causal in psychopathology? What qualifies this chapter as other oriented is Carpenter's well-founded skepticism about disclosure as a major cause of psychopathology. Instead, he makes the more plausible argument that disclosure may be symptomatic (i.e., informative) of the nature of the psychopathology. If self-disclosure investigators from the personality area have been overzealous in their claims, Carpenter conceeds that, "in contrast, psychopathologists probably have not shown much specific attention to disclosure behavior because they have viewed it as only one of several relevant social behaviors" (Carpenter, Chapter 10, this volume).

To direct this attention, an inference/competence model of the relationship between disclosure and psychotherapy is proposed. A useful if a little ironic aspect of this model's mechanisms is that they, too, are broadly applicable to any social behavior.

The last of the chapters I would include in the other orientation is Chelune's neuropsychological perspective on disclosure. This is easily the most unusual contribution to a volume on self-disclosure. It illustrates just how far afield of traditional disclosure issues one can go and still find disclosure a useful concept. Chelune's interest is in the hemispheric specialization of the cerebrum. As most people with an introductory exposure to neuropsychology know, the left hemisphere specializes in linguistic processing and the right in visual-spatial and paralinguistic processing. Because the degree of specialization differs between individuals, Chelune comes up with and confirms the hypothesis that these neurological differences will be associated with differing abilities to perceive incongruities in linguistic and paralinguistic modes of disclosure. We might expect Chelune to relate such fundamental individual differences primarily to the most basic and intrapersonal uses of disclosure—expression and self-clarification. Instead, he paints a vivid picture of a person with diffuse (low) hemispheric specialization who tragically appears unresponsive both when receiving and sending intimate communication. However, it is not an absence of concern but a neurological deficit that is to blame. So surprisingly, Chelune focuses on the implications of hemispheric specialization for responsive communication, thus earning a place in the other orientation. Along with Carpenter's chapter, his reminds us to search widely for predisposing factors of disclosure and their effects.

The Self-and-Other Orientation. Self-and-Other-oriented disclosure serves the highest relationship development function. This is so because it acknowledges the interdependence between participants in an interaction. In short, it deals with the relationship itself. Among disclosure investigators, it is probably the most discussed and the least investigated (see Archer & Earle, 1983). Virtually every contributor to this book has taken pains to relate his or her topic to questions of close relationships. I hope no offense will be taken, however, if I restrict coverage of this function to three chapters: Fitzpatrick's (Chapter 7) consideration of disclosure in marriage, Baxter's (Chapter 8) of relationship disengagement, and Waring's (Chapter 13) of cognitive marital therapy. To me, these three are bound most tightly to the central tenet of relationships—interdependence.

Fitzpatrick rightly observes that in our time the exchange of intimate disclosure has become part of the very definition of a close relationship. Little wonder then, that self-report studies of marital satisfaction typically find it correlated with verbal intimacy and that Altman and Taylor (1973) give disclosure the central role in relationship development. Fitzpatrick's premise is, however, that when stable marriage styles are examined more closely "enormous differences emerge in the degree to which couples engage in and value, self-disclosure" (Fitzpatrick, Chapter 7, this volume). She uses relational definition data to build a three-part typology of marriages that differ in interdependence. The surprise for devotees of Altman and Taylor is that the independents, who have the most flexible, equalitarian marriages and disclose the most, also have the most *conflict*. Traditionals, on the other hand, with their more restrictive conventional roles and beliefs; they disclose less but also experience less strife. Separates are just that: the most distant and least disclosing. Fitzpatrick's work demonstrates how valuable the distinction between disclosing feelings and facts is for marriages. More important, it redirects the research on disclosure and marital satisfaction away from the personalities of the individual spouses and back to the unique and complex reltionships their combination produces.

Baxter's description of relationship disengagement, like her fellow communication researcher, Fitzpatrick's treatment of marriages, argues against Altman and Taylor's (1973) social penetration as the only or even the most typical path relationships take. Altman and Taylor hypothesize that the way out of a close relationship is through fewer and less intimate disclosures, a simple reversal of the way partners came in. Rather than social exchange, Baxter's perspective on disengagement is a rhetorical/strategic one. The goal-directed strategic nature of communications across the last stages of the relationship are responsible for the changing uses disclosure serves: first to reduce uncertainty, then to negotiate the "unbonding," and finally to present the unbonded relationship to the outside world. A key distinction is made between personal self-disclosure, information about self, and relational disclosure, commenting on the relationship (called self and other by Archer & Earle, 1983). Although the reversal hypothesis may often be correct in predicting a decline in personal self-disclosure during disengagement, it appears that increased relational self-disclosure is also quite likely if the participants have been very close. So, for Baxter, just as for Hill and Stull (Chapter 5), Carpenter (Chapter 10), and Fitzpatrick (Chapter 7), the broadly framed question of more or less disclosure leads down a blind alley.

Waring's cognitive marital therapy describes a transition from Baxter's dissolving relationship to Fitzpatrick's stable marriage. Like those chapters, it also holds surprises for anyone steeped in the traditional role of disclosure in relationships. Presumably a marital therapy built on disclosure will involve spouses in expressing their underlying feelings, right? Wrong. Waring's cognitive self-disclosure deliberately minimizes the exchange of feelings and needs, maximizing instead "sharing attitudes, beliefs, and ideas about one's marriage and one's parents' marriage (Waring, Chapter 13, this volume). In a radical departure from other current relationship counseling techniques, spouses are not directed to talk to each other! They alternately answer the therapist's questions about why they do what they do and what they were thinking about when the other was talking. Nevertheless, Waring argues that this indirect approach promotes intimacy through an increased amount, reciprocity, and ego-relevance of disclosure and an increased ability to respond (rather than react) to the spouse's disclosure. So far the limited outcome research Waring presents suggests that it works as well as other brief marital therapies. I hope he continues and expands his program of outcome studies to test whether this "novel way of communicating about relationships" (Waring, Chapter 13, this volume) really does enhance intimacy, presumably through restructuring cognitive schemata. If so, then there are a number of old counselors and therapists who will be learning new tricks.

That completes my orientation-by-orientation tour of the uses of disclosure as they are widely represented in this book. Observant readers will realize that one chapter, Miller and Read's (Chapter 3), has been left out. Frankly, I believe that their analysis of self-disclosure in a goal-based model of personality resists any attempt to classify it primarily under a particular function as I have done with the other contributions. The reason is that they have come up with a more fine-grained, cognitive version of the functional approach *itself.* Instead of Archer and Earle's (1983) short, hierarchical list of orientations or Derlega and Grzelak's (1979) comparable set of functions, Miller and Read have gone a bit further and in the process, perhaps gone them one better. In this model, the single notion of function is elaborated into both the individual's goals and his or her plans for attaining them. In addition, the model considers the resources the individual requires to carry out the plans and his or her beliefs about the world that affect their execution. Miller and Read's goal-based model has the added advantage that it offers disclosure researchers in personality the chance to profit from the concepts and findings of social cognition. Finally, the model, like Carpenter's (Chapter 10) interference/competence model, is a broad one applicable to other issues than self-disclosure. I trust that these selling points will appeal to researchers trying to anchor their disclosure studies on something more fresh, systematic, and integrative than the old empirical questions, "who discloses" and "when they do so" (Archer, 1979), as Miller and Read wish. However, I would also allege that this cognitive approach is yet another example of the potential and influence of the functional approach is disclosure research.

ONE LAST LOOK

By now, the bases for my optimism about the current self-disclosure theory, research, and therapy collected here should be clearly in focus. With the possible exception of self-to-other (feedback eliciting) disclosure, a past favorite, the full range of disclosure's uses are receiving attention. It is especially heartening that the contributors to this volume are addressing the uses of disclosure in relationship development and in self-development. These were considered the areas of greatest weakness in the literature by Archer and Earle (1983). The contributors are to be commended for their efforts as are editors, Derlega and Berg, for their selections.

Of course, a number of the *old* interests are still there. Self-disclosure researchers are still interested in personality traits, but the chapters by Davis and Franzoi (Chapter 4), Hill and Stull (Chapter 5), Stokes (Chapter 9), and Coates and Winston (Chapter 11) show a new methodological sophistication *and* awareness of the approach's limits. They are still interested in counseling and therapy, but the chapters by Waring (Chapter 13), Carpenter (Chapter 10), and Hendrick (Chapter 14) indicate that their thinking has progressed beyond the insights of Jourard (1964, 1971). They are still interested in close relationships, but the chapters by Fitzpatrick (Chapter 7) and Baxter (Chapter 8) demonstrate that they are more concerned with interdependence than were Altman and Taylor (1973).

There is also something *new* and perhaps long overdue in the way of self-disclosure theory seen in the chapters of Berg (Chapter 6) and Stiles (Chapter 12). Even for those who thought they had seen everything in the way of self-disclosure applications, there is something new seen in the chapter by Chelune (Chapter 2).

Finally, the chapter by Miller and Read (Chapter 3) reveals how the disclosure area can benefit from *borrowing* and incorporating concepts from other areas of social and behavioral science. With something old, something new, and something borrowed, how could any commentary be blue about the future prospects for self-disclosure?

REFERENCES

Altman, I., & Taylor, D. A. (1973). *Social penetration: The development of interpersonal relationships*. New York: Holt, Rinehart, & Winston.

Archer, R. L. (1979). Role of personality and the social situation. In G. J. Chelune (Ed.), *Self-disclosure: Origins, patterns, and implications for openness in interpersonal relations* (pp. 28–58). San Francisco: Jossey-Bass.

Archer, R. L., & Earle, W. B. (1983). The interpersonal orientations of disclosure. In P. B. Paulus (Ed.), *Basic group processes* (pp. 289–314). New York: Springer-Verlag.

Bowlby, J. (1973). *Attachment and loss. Vol. II: Separation, anxiety, and anger.* New York: Basic Books.

Chelune, G. J. (Ed.). (1979). *Self-disclosure: Origins, patterns, and implications for openness in interpersonal relations.* San Francisco: Jossey-Bass.

Derlega, V. J., & Grzelak, J. (1979). Appropriateness of self-disclosure. In G. J. Chelune (Ed.), Self-disclosure: Origins, patterns, and implications for openness in interpersonal relations (pp. 151–176). San Francisco: Jossey-Bass.

Jones, E. E., & Archer, R. L. (1976). Are there special effects of personalistic self-disclosure? *Journal of Experimental Social Psychology, 12,* 180–193.

Jourard, S. M. (1964). *The transparent self.* New York: D. Van Nostrand.

Jourard, S. M. (1971). *Self-disclosure: An experimental analysis of the transparent self.* New York: Wiley.

Latané, B., Ekman, J., & Joy, V. (1966). Shared stress and interpersonal attraction. *Journal of Experimental Social Psychology* (Suppl. 1), 80–94.

Rubenstein, C., & Shaver, P. (1980). Loneliness in two Northeastern cities. In J. Hartog, J. R. Audy, & Y. A. Cohen (Eds.), *The anatomy of loneliness* (pp. 319–337). New York: International Universities Press.

Author Index

Subject Index

Batch number: 10761599

Printed by Printforce, the Netherlands